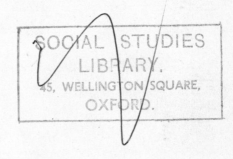

THE STRUCTURE OF
HUMAN PERSONALITY

THE STRUCTURE OF
HUMAN PERSONALITY

H. J. EYSENCK

Reader in Psychology, University of London;
Director, Psychological Dept., Institute of Psychiatry,
Maudsley and Bethlem Royal Hospitals

WITH 37 ILLUSTRATIONS

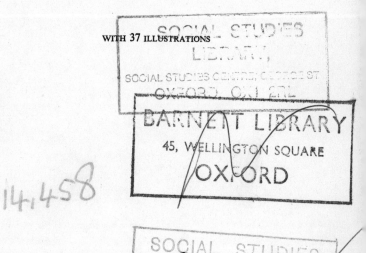
LONDON · METHUEN & CO. LTD.
NEW YORK · JOHN WILEY & SONS INC.

First Published in 1953

CATALOGUE NO. 5410/U [Methuen]

PRINTED AND BOUND IN ENGLAND BY
HAZELL WATSON AND VINEY LTD
AYLESBURY AND LONDON

To
L. L. THURSTONE
In Profound Admiration

If there are some subjects on which the results obtained have finally received the unanimous assent of all who have attended to the proof, and others on which mankind have not yet been equally successful; on which the most sagacious minds have occupied themselves from the earliest date, and have never succeeded in establishing any considerable body of truths, so as to be beyond denial or doubt; it is by generalizing the methods successfully followed in the former enquiries, and adapting them to the latter, that we may hope to remove this blot on the face of science.

J.S. MILL.

CONTENTS

ILLUSTRATIONS

ACKNOWLEDGEMENTS

Acknowledgement is due to the following authors and publishers for permission to reproduce tables and figures:

Fig. 1, R. Stagner (1948) and The McGraw-Hill Book Company; Figs. 11
and 26, W. H. Sheldon (1949) and Harper Brothers; Fig. 15, R. D. North (1949)
and *The Journal of Personality*; Fig. 17, D. W. Fiske (1949) and *The Journal of
Abnormal and Social Psychology*; Fig. 18, F. Goldman-Eisler (1951) and *The
Journal of Mental Science*; Figs. 27 and 28, A. B. Van der Merwe and P. A.
Theron (1948) and Paul B. Hoeber, Inc.; Fig. 29, G. L. Freeman (1948) and
The Cornell University Press; Fig. 33, R. B. Cattell (1946) and The World Book
Company; Fig. 34, A. L. Baldwin (1946) and *The Journal of Personality*; Fig. 36,
C. Buhler (1949); Table 9, C. W. Heath (1945) and The Harvard University
Press; Table 10, J. Lovett Doust (1952) and *The British Journal of Social Medi-
cine*; Table 11, T. W. Richards and M. P. Simons (1941) and *The Journal of
Genetic Psychology*; Table 12, M. Roff (1949) and *Child Development*; Table 15,
C. Lovell (1945) and *Educational and Psychological Measurement*; Table 16, T.
Husen (1951); Tables 20 and 21, H. Hartshorne and M. A. May (1929) and The
Macmillan Company; Table 23, W. Line and J. D. M. Griffin (1935) and *The
American Journal of Psychiatry*; Table 24, J. C. Brengelmann (1952) and *Psycho-
logische Rundschau*; Table 28, I. L. Child (1950) and *The Journal of Personality*;
Table 29, C. W. Darrow and L. L. Heath (1932) and The University of Chicago
Press; Table 30, R. P. Darling (1949) and *The Journal of Abnormal and Social
Psychology*; Table 31, M. A. Wenger (1941) and *The Journal of Experimental
Psychology*; Table 34, M. Sherman and H. Jost (1942) and *The Journal of
Psychology*; Table 35, Stanford University Press, publishers of *The Vocational
Interests of Men and Women*, by E. K. Strong (1943); Table 36, L. Thurstone
(1932) and *The Personnel Journal*; and Table 41, *Journal of Applied Psychology*,
publishers of an article by R. Crutcher (1934).

INTRODUCTION

IN SPITE OF the great interest that psychologists, psychiatrists, and psycho-analysts have shown in the subject, no detailed account appears to exist of those natural phenomena on which our views of the organization or structure of personality are based. There are, it is true, many professions of faith; thus we are assured that "personality is an emergent 'gestalt' phenomenon whose organization cannot be accounted for in terms of atomistic concepts", and that "the unique totality of personality determines the very nature and meaning of the individual sub-wholes or 'parts'; it is not determined by them". Proof of such far-reaching asseverations is hardly ever attempted; occasionally recourse is had to philosophical deduction (which is irrelevant) or analogy with perceptual phenomena (which is improper), but, by and large, reliance is placed more on intuitive agreement than on scientific demonstration. Such demonstration, including the demand for proof which it implies, is indeed often declared to be superfluous; clinical experience and phenomenological observation are believed to be able to take its place. This view is maintained, even although it would appear to make impossible any rational choice between opposing experiences and observations, by explicitly denying the very principles of scientific method on the basis of which one expert's views might be shown to be correct and another's to be faulty.

It consequently appeared worth-while to bring together in one volume some of the major theories of personality organization, and to comb the literature for empirical studies either undertaken with the aim of testing deductions from these hypotheses or at least having some direct bearing on them. The first chapter represents an attempt to set forth these theories in broad outline, and to discuss some of their implications; the remainder of the book is devoted to a critical presentation of the evidence, arranged according to the technique employed—rating, self-rating, objective testing, constitutional assessment, autonomic measurement, and so forth. Also discussed in the first chapter is the problem of a proper statistical model for the investigation of personality organization, and an attempt is made to show that at the present moment the method of factor analysis alone enables us to represent the known facts in terms of a strictly quantitative conceptual schema.

There are three main criticisms of such a conclusion which merit at least a brief answer. (Criticisms based essentially on a misunderstanding of factor analysis, either with respect to its aims or its methods, will not be dealt with here. They are deplorably prevalent in the literature, so much so that it might be wise to follow psychoanalytic practice and lay it down that criticism of factor analysis should be confined to those who had themselves been factor analysed!)

The first point often made is a denial of the importance of the problem which factor analysis attempts to tackle. Essentially, types, traits, syndromes, and the various other concepts which psychology and psychiatry have elaborated in their attempts to describe the organization of personality, all of which are in principle similar to factors by virtue of their derivation on the basis of consistencies of behaviour similarities, are said to be artefacts which are used to imprison the unique personality, a veritable bed of Procrustes which distorts the essence of the phenomena under observation. That these concepts are artefacts is of course undeniable, as by definition all concepts are artefacts; the concepts of extraversion, hysteria, or suggestibility are artefacts in precisely the same sense that an electron, magnetism, or an ohm are artefacts. Spearman's "g" (general intelligence) is in the same position as Newton's "g" (gravitational force). Science attempts to bring order into the multiplicity of phenomena; it does so by introducing concepts which have no counterpart in the world of reality. These concepts may be useful or worthless; their value must be decided on other grounds than that of their being "artefacts" (Eysenck, 1953).

Granted, then, that such concepts are unavoidable for the solution of our problem, is the problem itself worth-while? In all sciences we find a division between "statics" and "dynamics", between attempts to create taxonomies, classifications, or nosologies, and attempts to derive causal laws and developmental sequences. The table of the elements of chemistry, the dimensional analysis of physics, the taxonomic principles of flora and fauna in biology—these are all examples of the "static" type of analysis. To deny the importance of either type of approach is an admission of prejudice, because the history of science shows over and over again the essential dependence of these two types of approach on each other, and the fact that advances in one may lead to important advances in the other. Both are vital to the development of science, and there appears to be no reason why psychology should be a solitary exception to this general rule. We may conclude, therefore, that the "static" approach implied in the study of *organization* has its valid place beside the "dynamic" approach implied in the study of *development*.

It is here that the second objection comes in. How, it is maintained, can we study organization without detailed knowledge of development? Physical diseases are classified in terms of their causes, i.e. by reference to development; without such knowledge of causes we may be gravely mistaken in our principles of nosology. Must not the same apply in psychiatry, and with reference to mental disorders? Biological classification proceeds by way of evolutionary concepts, i.e. again in terms of development; should psychology be an exception?

There are two answers to this point. The short answer is that while principles of organization derived from firmly established principles of development are, of course, infinitely preferable to principles of organization established in any other way, psychology cannot be said to have a choice in the matter because these firmly established principles of development are completely missing. In the absence of any knowledge of the causes of mental disorders, we must needs fall back on some other method of classification; in the absence of any knowledge of the determinants of personality development in general, we clearly cannot base our system of organization on these non-existing principles. In other words, although no one would deny the advantages of being able to base one's principles of organization on principles of development, some other method is called for at the moment in view of the conspicuous lack of the latter. (There is, of course, no lack of theories; quite on the contrary, there is such a multiplicity of theories regarding development, none of them based on firm scientific ground of proof and verification, that any choice between them becomes a matter of temperament rather than of reason.)

A somewhat longer answer may be made in terms of historical considerations. If we take botany as our example, we find that taxonomy began with the Greeks; Theophrastus may be considered to have been the first to classify plants and to describe them accurately (300 B.C.). Like more recent attempts in psychology, "the writings of the Greeks embodied too few observations on what plants are and too much philosophizing as to how they might be expected to be" (Swingle, 1946), but, nevertheless, their attempts at classification were an indispensable preliminary to later work which superseded theirs. There is no need to trace the development of systems of taxonomy through the work of Bauhin, Ray, Linnæus, Jussieu,

Candolle, Endlicher, and others who preceded the publication of Darwin's *Origin of Species* in 1859; the important point to note is that the principle of evolution could not have been established, or even conceived, without these previous attempts at taxonomy, and that its establishment gave a new foundation to taxonomy but did not change its general outline as much as might have been anticipated. "After the first wave of excitement was over, systematists quite generally accepted the doctrine and began to revise their systems to fit the new principle of phylogenetic relationships. Fortunately, much that had already been done was usable, for all but the morphological systems had been pretty much eliminated from botanical taxonomy, and *morphology has proved the best single criterion of phylogeny*" (Swingle, 1946).

Thus, in botany, and in zoology as well, it has proved possible to work out natural groupings on the basis of morphology, i.e. on the basis of correlational clusters of surface characteristics, which adumbrated rather closely the "true" relationships as established on the basis of developmental (phylogenetic) principles. Morphology in botany corresponds to the study of behavioural acts in psychology, and the rather non-rigorous methods used by the earlier workers to establish "natural groupings" are based on precisely the same principle as is factor analysis. It is to be hoped that in due course principles of development will be found in psychology which correspond to that of evolution in biology; it seems reasonable to expect that here also such new discoveries may lead to an improvement in, but not a complete change of, the principles of organization already developed.

The third objection, which is often raised against factorial methods, refers to the subjectivity of choice between one system of factor axes and another, and to the apparent and often acrimonious disputes between factor analysts. Where practitioners of the same methodology arrive at contradictory findings, it is often said there must be some vital flaw in the method used. Let us consider these points in some detail. There is of course a certain subjectivity implied in all dimensional work; this is true in physics as much as in psychology. As the physicist Bridgman points out, "there is nothing absolute about dimensions . . . they may be anything consistent with a set of definitions which agree with the experimental facts". To object to such subjectivity is to misunderstand altogether the nature of science and its methodology. Where there are alternative solutions to the problem posed by a set of experimental facts, these solutions are mathematically convertible into one another, or else give rise to different deductions which can be experimentally checked. Thurstone's disproof of Spearman's original contention regarding the sufficiency of "*g*" and "*s*" as the only factors to account for the intercorrelations between cognitive tests may be quoted here as an example of such experimental check.

What, then, about the alleged disagreements? These occur in all sciences, and are often much more fundamental than those which have arisen in the brief history of factor analysis. The fundamental opposition in mathematics between Kronecker and Weierstrass; the continuing difficulties implied in reconciling the theories of light advanced by Newton and Huyghens in physics; the antagonism between Engler and Prantl on the one hand and Bessey and Hallier on the other in botany; the differences between Fisher and Pearson in statistics; the heated disputes between Glover and Klein in psychoanalysis—should these lead us to discard mathematics, statistics, physics, botany, and psycho-analysis as unworthy of our attention? Indeed, factor analysis, at the moment, appears to have reached a point in its development where there are hardly any fundamental issues on which agreement is not fairly complete; Thurstone's brilliant development of his system to embrace oblique and second-order factors has led to a reconciliation of opposing viewpoints which leaves room only for very minor disagreements.

The history of this book itself may illustrate the influence of these developments. A collection of references was undertaken first in connection with the preparation of *Dimensions of Personality*, and then again in connection with *The Scientific Study of Personality*; but in view of what appeared to be marked contradictions between results reported by different writers, no attempt was made to work these references up into some connected whole. The development of Thurstone's system in terms of second-order factors, and an opportunity for the writer to discuss some of the resulting problems with Thurstone personally, changed the somewhat pessimistic outlook, and a reassessment was begun which resulted in the present book. The reader will be able to judge for himself to what extent the results summarized may be said to give a congruent picture; to the writer himself the amount of agreement found was a revelation.

It is the writer's hope, as it presumably is that of all the students whose work is reported here, that from these studies there should arise a system of taxonomy, or classification, or nosology, which may be regarded as firmly based on biological reality, and which will find considerable support in principles of ontogenetic development when these are established, as well as aid in its turn in the discovery of these principles. Even if these hopes should be judged ill-conceived, however, and even if the reader be unwilling to admit the writer's contention regarding the importance and value of the factorial technique, nevertheless there is here a store of facts regarding human behaviour which any theory which attempts to cover the total human personality must account for. Most psychological theories only blossom in a climate of their author's devising, and die of inanition when exposed to the sharper winds of facts gathered outside the sanctified circle; here is a set of facts on which the theoretician may try out the inclusiveness of his hypotheses. The test is a very clear and simple one: does his theory help him predict the observed correlations? Is his picture of personality organization inclusive enough to permit of cross-checking with the data here recorded? If the answer be no, then the theory is clearly segmental only and does not cover the whole of personality. Nor would it be adequate to claim that the facts recorded are unimportant or uninteresting. In science we cannot pick and choose; the theory of gravitation must account for all the facts subsumed under it, and even such minor deviations as the slight eccentricity of Mercury's motion, or the minute bending of light rays when passing the sun, were sufficient to dethrone what used to be the most strongly established theory in the history of science.

One word regarding the method of presentation adopted. It appeared useless to present to the reader a simple summary of all relevant research, uncritical and undigested. Instead, the writer has adopted a highly critical attitude, and has not hesitated to point out flaws in experimental design, method of analysis, or even in calculation which reduce the value of a given paper. These are fairly objective matters, on which agreement would be reasonably high among competent judges. It is to be feared that other judgments are less objective; while the writer has made an attempt to keep the book clear of purely personal preferences, he has no illusions regarding the success of this undertaking, and can only hope that the reader will be a charitable judge of any deviations from this ideal. It is perhaps a matter of personality, but to the writer it appears better to err in the direction of excess of critical rigour than in the opposite direction of eclectic acceptance of good and bad indiscriminately—a tendency exemplified in so many of our text-books on personality.

While only primary sources were used for the preparation of this book, acknowledgment should be made to several authors whose writings have exerted some influence on the presentation. The most important of these are probably G. W. Allport, whose book on *Personality* has been more influential perhaps than any other in the development of this branch of study; A. A. Roback, whose *Psychology of Character* is the most learned historical introduction, as well as the most lucid; P. E. Vernon, whose *Assessment of Psychological Qualities by Verbal Methods* is a masterpiece of condensation and critical evaluation; C. Spearman, whose *Abilities of Man* has a place secure in the history of psychology; and L. L. Thurstone, whose *Multiple Factor Analysis* is the foundation-stone on which all later workers may securely build. As without his brilliant unification of apparently antagonistic elements this book could not have been written, it is most fittingly dedicated to him as a small token of indebtedness.

INSTITUTE OF PSYCHIATRY,
  Maudsley Hospital.
    30*th Dec.*, 1951.

CHAPTER I

THEORIES OF PERSONALITY ORGANIZATION

"EXPERIMENT WITHOUT theory is blind; theory without experiment is lame." There is perhaps no field in psychology where this saying of Kant's applies with greater force than in the study of the structure of personality. Observers have been struck again and again by the fact that what should be a unitary field of study is cleft in two; that instead of an harmonious co-operation between theory and experiment, we have, on the one hand, an experimental school which investigates in the minutest detail processes having only the most tangential relevance to personality or to any plausible theoretical orientation, and, on the other, theoretical schools of the "dynamic" type whose theorizing proceeds without any proper basis in ascertained fact and without any consciousness of the need for verification. Most psychologists would agree that this division of labour has been carried to such extremes that it is threatening the very conception of "personality" as a legitimate field of scientific study.

Corresponding to this division into "experimentalists" and "theoreticians", there are a number of other divisions among students of personality hardly less deep and hardly less acrimoniously debated. Yet to the onlooker it often appears that while both sides are right in their positive claims, they are wrong and one-sided in their condemnation of what other schools and other points of view have to contribute. Few would seriously argue that experiment could fruitfully be carried on without theory or theory lead to important advances without the check of experimentation. Similarly, most of the other disputes which appear so formidable in cold print seem amenable to compromise when each side's arguments are carried to their logical conclusion.

As an example, we may take the very definition of the term "personality" itself. Here we find immediately an apparently irreconcilable opposition between those who lay stress on *behavioural acts* and those who lay stress instead on *dynamic concepts*. As an example of the behavioural type of definition, we may quote Watson (1930), according to whom personality is "the sum of activities that can be discovered by actual observation over a long enough period of time to give reliable information". As an example of the dynamic type of definition we may quote Prince (1924), according to whom "personality is the sum-total of all the biological innate dispositions, impulses, tendencies, appetites, and instincts of the individual, and the acquired dispositions and tendencies".

It is obvious that the concepts which enter into one kind of definition—observable behavioural acts—play no part in the other, which deals entirely with dynamic concepts—impulses, dispositions, instincts, and the like. Yet the opposition clearly cannot be as complete as it appears. We have no direct knowledge of instincts, dispositions, and impulses; they are abstract conceptions created to unify and make intelligible the observable behavioural acts from which they are abstracted. Without these behavioural acts the concepts would have no assignable meaning: all we can know about human behaviour must ultimately derive from observations of behaviour. Yet such observation of behaviour by itself is not enough. We must have concepts which denote aspects of behaviour common to a number of situations; science cannot exist without abstractions based on common properties. Both definitions therefore are one-sided; a proper definition must stress both the empirical source of our data and the theoretical nature of our unifying concepts.

For the purposes of this book, we shall adopt the following definitions: Personality is the more or less stable and enduring organization of a person's character, temperament, intellect, and physique, which determines his unique adjustment to the environment. Character denotes a person's more or less stable and enduring system of conative behaviour ("will"); Temperament, his more or less stable and enduring system of affective behaviour ("emotion"); Intellect, his more or less stable and enduring system of cognitive behaviour ("intelligence"); Physique, his more or less stable and enduring system of bodily configuration and neuro-endocrine endowment. It will be noted that this definition, which owes a great deal to Roback (1927), Allport (1937), and McKinnon (1944), stresses very much the concept of *system*, *structure*, or *organization*; in this it goes counter to the doctrine of *specificity of behaviour*, which held almost complete sway in American research from the early nineteen-twenties until quite recently. A few words may therefore be said regarding this issue of specificity versus generality, particularly as from one point of view all the experimental work reviewed in this book is intimately related to this problem.

Common-sense psychology unhesitatingly describes and explains behaviour in terms of traits, such as persistence, suggestibility, courage, punctuality, absent-mindedness, stage-struckness, "being one for the girls", stuck-upness, and queerness, or posits the existence of types, such as the dandy, the intellectual, the quiet, the sporty, or the sociable type. For the greater part, orthodox psychology has taken over these concepts, and has presented us with traits such as ascendance-submission, perseveration, security-insecurity, and with types such as extraversion-introversion, schizothymia-cyclothymia, or Spranger's *Lebenstypen*. This easy acceptance of these concepts has been challenged, however, by a number of critics, who hold that "there are no broad, general traits of personality, no general and consistent forms of conduct which, if they existed, would make for consistency of behaviour and stability of personality, but only independent and specific stimulus-response bonds or habits".

This theory of specificity has its roots deep in the experimental tradition, and its *à priori* improbability should not prevent us from glancing at the main sources from which it draws its strength. The first of these sources is the Thorndikian type of learning theory prevalent around the first decades of this century. Learning is conceived in terms of S-R (stimulus-response) bonds after the manner of the reflex or the conditioned reflex, and these bonds are, of course, conceived to be entirely specific. If the organization of personality is largely a matter of learning—and here the great majority of writers have favoured an anti-hereditarian view, without however basing themselves on any convincing experimental evidence—then the specificity of the learning process should be mirrored in the final product of learning, i.e. the adult personality. And while S-R theories in the field of learning have been challenged by S-S (sign-significate) theories which maintain that learning is part of a larger problem of organization, particularly perceptual organization, these non-specific theories came into the field more recently, have been somewhat less influential historically, and have not carried over into the field of personality description to the same extent as the specificity theories.[1]

A second source, not unrelated to the first, has been the vast volume of work done on the problem of "transfer of training". It used to be assumed that certain specific acts (learning verses by

[1] For a review of experimental studies of these theoretical issues, see Hilgard (1948), Hilgard and Marquis (1940), and the appropriate chapters in S. S. Stevens (1951).

heart, or doing problems in arithmetic, or writing out French irregular verbs) would in the course of time lead to improvement in
general abilities or faculties (memory, will-power, logical ability,
and so on). James and Thorndike showed in a number of investigations that this easy assumption had little empirical foundation. When
two groups of subjects were equated for their ability in a given task,
such as learning poetry by heart, for instance, and one group subjected to a period of training in memorizing material which might
even be closely similar to that on which they had been tested, while
the other group was not given any training, then the predicted
superiority of the former group over the latter on a repetition of the
original task was not observed. Learning, apparently, is relatively
specific: there is no general effect on the hypothetical faculties
which such training was supposed to improve. Any transfer effects
which might be observed were considered to be due, not to the
action of broad mental "faculties", but to the fact that the original
and the practised activities had certain elements in common. This
theory is known as the "theory of identical elements"; in Thorndike's (1903) own words, "a change in one function alters any other
only in so far as the two functions have as factors common elements.
. . . To take a concrete example, improvement in addition will alter
one's ability in multiplication because addition is absolutely identical
with a part of multiplication, and because certain other processes—
e.g. eye movements and the inhibition of all save arithmetical impulses—are in part common to the two functions." Development of
personality, no less than of linguistic or numerical skills, is therefore
seen as specific training of individual association, never as generalized
improvement of larger mental units or "faculties".[1]

A third source of the specificity theory of personality organization,
equally influential as the other two, has been the direct experimental
attack on the problem by Hartshorne and May (1928, 1929, 1930).
These writers carried out a large-scale project, described in some
detail on a later page, in which many hundreds of children were
given the opportunity to behave in a dishonest, deceitful manner
under conditions which apparently made discovery impossible, but
which in reality were completely under experimental control. Other
types of behaviour (persistent, moral, charitable, impulsive, and self-
controlled behaviour, for instance) were also investigated by means
of ingenious and largely novel techniques. The statistical treatment

[1] A recent review of the voluminous literature on "transfer of training" is given
by Gagné, Foster and Crowley (1948).

of the data was beyond cavil, and in view of the brilliance of the design and the technical excellence of the execution, this study has rightly been regarded as crucial in respect to the theory of specificity. When therefore Hartshorne and May found very low intercorrelations between their tests, and discovered that children who were honest, or persistent, or co-operative, or charitable in one test-situation were not always honest, or persistent, or co-operative, or charitable in another, their conclusion that these alleged qualities were "groups of specific habits rather than general traits" was very widely accepted as finally settling the issue in favour of the theory of specificity.

This powerful and imposing theoretical structure was subject to a variety of damaging criticisms, however, and none of the three sources on which it bases itself has remained unscathed. We have already mentioned that S-R theories were opposed by writers whose outlook was formed or at least influenced by Gestalt notions; Köhler, Koffka, Tolman, Adams, Zener, and others have developed theories which account for the observed facts without invoking the specific connections posited by the followers of Thorndike, and, indeed, Thorndike himself has admitted concepts into his system which are incompatible with a completely specifist point of view. There is no sign of any decision in this battle of learning theories, but it is already clear that if one's theory of personality organization must be determined by one's learning theory, then there is still freedom of choice between a "specific" and a "general" type of learning theory. It would seem to follow that a direct attack on the problem of specificity in the field of personality itself would be more promising than a somewhat lengthy wait for a decision in the field of learning theory.

Much the same must be said about the conclusion to be drawn from investigations into the problem of "transfer of training" and of "identical elements". Allport's (1937) brilliant criticism of the specifist contention is probably too well known to need repetition. By showing that the very notion of an "element" is completely ambiguous in the writings of those who support the Thorndikian view, and that the alleged "identity" of these elements is merely an *a posteriori* justification of the observed phenomena, without any value in predicting and without any possibility of verification, he has succeeded in throwing great doubt on the tenability of this whole view. When his criticisms are seen in the light of experimental work, which fails to show the theoretically predicted correspondence between improvement after practice, and the similarity between original task and practised task, we can only conclude that regardless of the eventual outcome of the argument regarding "transfer of training" and the theory of identical elements, our decision with regard to the question of specificity in the field of personality must rest on direct evidence from that field, rather than in deductions from principles of such uncertain validity.

We are thus led to a re-examination of the results of the Hartshorne-May study. While the detailed results are presented in a later chapter, we may here note certain doubts regarding the interpretation of their perfectly valid results made by these two authors. Let us examine first of all their finding that a child who behaves in a dishonest manner in one situation does not necessarily behave in a dishonest manner in another situation; their conclusion is that honesty is not a general trait but specific to the two situations. But this would assume that the two situations made equal demands on the hypothetical honesty of the child, a view for which there is no evidence at all. A child may fail a difficult item in an intelligence test and pass an easy one; because he passes one and fails on another, we do not argue that he is not behaving in a consistent manner! A child may tell what he considers a white lie, but balk at cheating; or he may cheat, but balk at stealing. To imagine that an advocate of the view that a general trait of honesty existed would necessarily deny the existence of degrees of temptation, or of degrees of immorality as between one act and another, is quite unrealistic, and there is no such implication in the "generality" theory. Related to the first point is a second, made by Hartshorne and May, and by many other writers since, namely that while some children do show the postulated trait, i.e. are always honest or persistent, and while others are consistent in never showing it, i.e. being always dishonest or lacking in persistence, the majority sometimes show the trait and sometimes not. Thus the trait is supposedly applicable only to a few cases, i.e. those who demonstrate it consistently, and not to others. By a similar argument it might be maintained that the concept of intelligence is applicable only to those who never fail an item or to those who fail every item! If we conceive of honesty as constituting a continuum, then the most honest should indeed never cheat and the least honest always; intermediate grades of honesty should be reflected in action by cheating when temptation is strong or when the immorality involved is rather slight, and by not cheating when temptation is weak or the immorality involved strong. For a given degree of temptation and immorality of the act, we would then be able to predict with as much accuracy for the intermediate child as for the extreme, just as we can predict for the child of average intelligence as easily as for the genius or the dunce whether he will succeed or fail with any given problem.

As a third argument, Hartshorne and May advance the view that the very low intercorrelations between the different tests for each one of the various personality qualities measured—honesty, persistence, self-control, and so on—make the assumption of the existence of such qualities very unlikely. Yet on the specificity theory these correlations should be zero; in actual fact they are almost in every case positive. Thus it is reported that "the twenty-three tests used in securing our total character score, for example, intercorrelate $+ \cdot 30$ on the average". Such intercorrelations are admittedly lower than those found between intelligence tests, but we must be careful not to compare an intelligence test, composed of fifty to a hundred items, with a single test of honesty, or persistence, which in truth would correspond rather to an item in a much larger test battery for the measurement of honesty, or persistence, made up of fifty or a hundred such items. We shall see, in our discussion of the detailed results of this experiment, that reliabilities and validities approaching and sometimes even exceeding values of $\cdot 85$ and $\cdot 90$ are found in Hartshorne and May's own work for such batteries of "honesty" or "persistence" tests. Such results are inconceivable on any strict specifistic hypothesis, and must therefore be held to controvert that position.

In the fourth place, we must take into account the fact that Hartshorne and May used social and ethical concepts as the qualities whose specificity or generality was to be investigated. Now, even if the chosen qualities had been shown to be entirely specific, it would not follow that because certain socio-ethical qualities lacked generality, therefore more genuinely psychological qualities would also be found to be specific; as Watson (1933) points out, the experiment may beg the question by selecting the wrong type of quality to investigate. We may find consistency in the habits of frequenters of library by observing whether they choose books from the fiction, science, history, or poetry racks; our failure to observe such consistency when we direct our attention to the colour of the binding of the books selected does not prove the specificity of the choices!

In the fifth place, the preceding argument appears to apply with particular strength when children constitute the experimental population, as they did in these studies. Socio-ethical concepts are clearly not innate; they are acquired through social learning. The young child has only had insufficient time to integrate the teaching he has received from a variety of sources into some kind of general *set*, some standard which he or she can apply to a variety of different situations; integration should hypothetically be incomplete in the young child and progress as the child advances in age. Such is indeed the fact, as demonstrated in Hartshorne and May's own data, and McKinnon's (1933) later work with adult subjects. This latter writer found considerable consistency in the honest and dishonest behaviour of his subjects, and even succeeded in predicting their reactions to the test on the basis of a five minutes' interview. We may therefore with some confidence assert that in part at least the lowness of the correlations found by Hartshorne and May was due to the youth of their subjects; if the investigations were to be repeated with older subjects, higher coefficients could confidently be expected.

It may be asked whether Hartshorne and May were not aware of some at least of these criticisms. The answer must be that they were, and that they recognized the difficulties raised for their hypothesis of specificity by the observed correlations, low as they were. Their reply was not to deny the observed correlations, but to explain them in terms of "identical elements". As we have seen, they speak of "groups of specific habits rather than general traits". But in doing so they have given up what is most significant about the theory they hold, namely the complete specificity of conduct, and have admitted at least the partial generality of behaviour. Their explanation, it is true, is in terms of specific S-R bonds, but, as we have seen above, little faith can at the moment be placed in any explanation in terms of learning theory, in view of the lack of agreement between different investigators. We are left, therefore, with a very clear admission of the existence of generality in behaviour. A child who is honest, or persistent, or co-operative in one situation does tend to be honest, or persistent, or co-operative in another situation, although prediction is very far from perfect. Our task, then, must be to enquire into the *degree* of generality manifested in human conduct, and to construct a theoretical model which will faithfully represent the facts in so far as they have been established by experimental enquiry. In doing so we will do well to bear in mind that although Hartshorne and May have failed to show that human conduct is completely specific, they have shown conclusively that it is far less general than we tend to imagine, and far more strongly determined by the specific situation in which it occurs than used to be thought at one time. There is truth in the contentions of the adherent of the theory of specificity, as well as in those of the adherent of the theory of generality; the problem ceases to be a theoretical one, and becomes instead quantitative and empirical.

In looking for a model for our description of personality organization, we find two claimants in the field, two concepts which have for a long time been used by those who have theorized about the mechanics of consistent and congruent behaviour—the concepts, namely, of "trait" and "type". The former of these has found a particularly warm champion in Stern (1921), who writes: "We have the right and the obligation to develop a concept of trait as a definitive doctrine; for in all activity of the person, there is besides a variable portion, likewise a constant purposive portion, and this latter we isolate in the concept of trait." And how are these traits to be discovered? According to Allport (1937), who has done much to popularize this concept in the Anglo-Saxon countries, "traits . . . are discovered not by deductive reasoning, not by fiat, not by naming, and are themselves never directly observed. They are discovered in the individual life—the only place where they can be discovered—only through an inference (or interpretation) made necessary by the demonstrable consistency of the separate observable acts of behaviour". And again: "Traits are not directly observable; they are inferred (as any kind of determining tendency is inferred). Without such an inference the stability and consistency of personal behaviour could not possibly be explained. Any specific action is a product of innumerable determinants, not only of traits but of momentary pressures and specialized influences. But it is the repeated occurrence of actions having the *same significance* (equivalence of response) following upon a definable range of stimuli having the same personal significance (equivalence of stimuli) that makes necessary the postulation of traits as states of Being. Traits are not at all times active, but they are persistent even when latent, and are distinguished by low thresholds of arousal."

It will be clear from these quotations that the notion of *trait* is intimately connected with the notion of *correlation*. Stability, consistency, repeated occurrence of actions—all these terms, when translated into more rigorous and operationally definable language, refer to co-variation of a number of behavioural acts. Such co-variation, as we shall see, may refer to correlations between tests, correlations between persons, or even to correlations between different occasions of measurement within the same person. A trait may be defined as a co-variant set of behavioural acts; it appears thus as an organizing principle which is deduced from the observed generality of human behaviour.

The concept of *type* has fared very badly at the hands of psychologists in the Anglo-Saxon countries; they mostly seem to share Stagner's (1948) belief that "the shift from type to trait conceptions

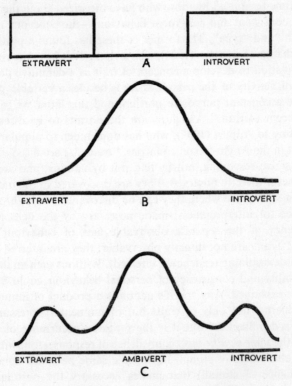

Fig. 1.—Three Conceptions of the Type Theory.

has generally paralleled the progress of psychology as science". As the same writer points out: "There are at least three different conceptions of psychological types, as they appear in the writings of various authors. These have been diagrammed in Fig. 1. Some writers still seem to think of types as pigeon-holes, mutually exclusive classifications with clear dividing lines, into which people can be segregated (Fig. 1, A). Others use the type concept as more or less equivalent to a trait, contrasting types defining the end of a continuum between which people are distributed according to the normal curve (Fig. 1, B). A third usage proposes that true types differ from traits, in that the distribution is multimodal, with people clustering at certain points which approximate a pure type (Fig. 1, C)."

Stagner's discussion leaves out of account two points which may be important in coming to a conclusion regarding the value of the "type" concept as a model for personality organization. In the first place, as will be seen from Fig. 1, B and C, these two different concepts of type are related to the hypothetical distribution of the population with respect to the alleged type, i.e. either unimodal or multimodal. But no knowledge of the form of distribution of any kind of mental quality is possible without the prior determination of a scientifically meaningful *metric*. We can plot raw scores on tests or questionnaires, but not even the veriest tyro in statistical analysis will assume that such scores give us any knowledge regarding the distribution of the hypothetical underlying trait—particularly when, as is usually the case, our measuring instrument measures more error than true variance! Until a proper metric is proposed, no argument from the form of distribution can be regarded as relevant; as no such metric has hitherto even been suggested in the field of personality measurement, it does not appear possible to argue the merits of the "type" concept on this basis.

In the second place, the distinction drawn between continuous and discontinuous distributions (Fig. 1, A, as opposed to B and C) is perfectly valid, but it does not in any way reflect the theories and hypotheses of those whose concepts have been most influential in creating modern typology, namely Jung and Kretschmer. They do reflect a widespread misconception of the views held by these writers, and by many others who have worked in the same tradition. These misconceptions have become so widely accepted that a brief outline of the correct position is imperative.

If we consider Jung's (1921) position first, we note that in his view "every individual possesses both the mechanism of introversion and that of extraversion, and it is only the relative strength of the one as compared with the other which creates the type. . . . A rhythmic alternation of these two psychic functions characterizes the normal course of life. . . . External circumstances and inner dispositions frequently favour one mechanism and impede or restrict the other. This quite naturally leads to the dominance of one of the mechanisms. If this dominance should, for whatever reason, become chronic, then we would be faced with a *type*, i.e. the habitual dominance of one mechanism. . . . Type never denotes more than the relative dominance of the one mechanism. . . . It follows that there can never be a pure type in the sense that the one mechanism is completely dominant to the exclusion of the other." These quotations could be multiplied many times, but they will suffice to show that Jung was very far from conceiving of all human beings as being either extraverted or introverted. Rather, he considered that most of them were characterized by a balance between the extravertive and the introvertive mechanisms; a relatively small number he considered to be unbalanced and characterized by the more or less marked dominance of one function or the other. Nothing is farther from his thoughts than the hypothesis of discontinuity; stress is laid again and again on the notion of complete continuity and balance. Admittedly his description is in terms of ideal types, i.e. of completely introverted or extraverted individuals, but he emphasises repeatedly that these are abstractions, in the same sense that Newton's laws of motion are idealized abstractions, not to be found in actual experiment.

What, then, is at the basis of his concept of type? We may answer this question by quoting a passage from Kretschmer (1948), who seems to hold a view of typology similar to that of Jung, and who has discussed this concept with admirable lucidity. According to him, "the concept of type is the most important fundamental concept of all biology. Nature . . . does not work with sharp contrasts and precise definitions, which derive from our own thought and our own need for comprehension. In nature, fluid transitions are the rule, but it would not be true to say that, in this infinite sea of fluid empirical forms, nothing clear and objective could be seen; quite on the contrary. In certain fields, groupings arise which we encounter again and again; when we study them objectively, we realize that we are dealing here with focal-points of frequently occurring groups of characteristics, concentrations of correlated traits. . . . What is essential in biology, as in clinical medicine, is not a single correlation but groups of correlations; only those lead to the innermost connections. It is daily experience in the field of typology, which can be deduced quite easily from the general theory, that in dealing with groups of characteristics one obtains higher correlations than with single characteristics. . . . What we call, mathematically, focal-points of statistical correlations, we call, in more descriptive prose, constitutional types. . . . A true type can be recognized by the fact that it leads to ever more connections of biological importance. Where there are many and ever-new correlations with fundamental biological factors . . . we are dealing with focal-points of the greatest importance."

A type is defined, then, as a group of correlated traits, just as a trait was defined as a group of correlated behavioural acts or action tendencies. According to this view, then, the difference between the concepts of *trait* and *type* lies not in the continuity or lack of continuity of the hypothesized variable, nor in its form of distribution, but in the greater inclusiveness of the type concept. The relationship between the two concepts is presented diagrammaticaly in Fig. 2,

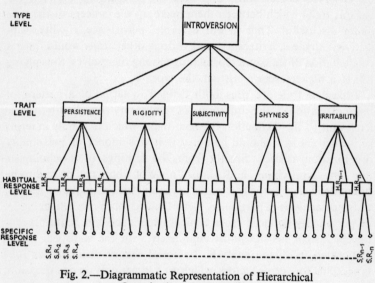

Fig. 2.—Diagrammatic Representation of Hierarchical
Organization of Personality.

taken, as is the explanatory text, from Eysenck (1947). "We are dealing with four levels of behaviour organization. At the lowest level, we have specific responses, $S.R._1$, $S.R._2$, $S.R._3$, . . . $S.R._n$. These are acts, such as responses to an experimental test or to experiences of everyday life, which are observed once, and may or may not be characteristic of the individual. At the second level, we have what are called habitual responses, $H.R._1$, $H.R._2$, $H.R._3$, . . . $H.R._n$. These are specific responses which tend to recur under similar circumstances; i.e. if the test is repeated, a similar response is given, or if the life-situation recurs, the individual reacts in a similar fashion. This is the lowest level of organization; roughly speaking, the amount of organization present here can be measured in terms of reliability coefficients, i.e. in terms of the probability that on repetition of a situation behaviour will be consistent.

"At the third level, we have organizations of habitual acts into traits T_1, T_2, T_3, ... T_n. These traits—irritability, persistence, rigidity, etc. —are theoretical constructs, based on observed intercorrelations of a number of different habitual responses; in the language of the factor analyst, they may be conceived of as group factors.

"At the fourth level, we have organization of traits into a general type; in our example, the *introvert*. This organization also is based on observed correlations, this time on correlations between the various traits which between them make up the concept of the type under discussion. Thus in our example, persistence, rigidity, subjectivity, shyness, irritability, and various other traits would form a constellation of traits intercorrelating among themselves, thus giving rise to a higher-order construct, the type."

Type and trait are thus both defined in terms of a pattern of intercorrelations; the question of continuity or distribution is irrelevant to the distinction between them, which is merely in terms of inclusiveness. It should be noted that this model of personality organization derives directly from the writings of psychologists like Jung, Kretschmer, and Allport, none of whom can be said to be orientated very positively towards psychometric techniques in general or factor analysis in particular. Nevertheless, this hypothetical model of personality deduced from clinical experience and acute psychological insight fits in almost completely with the statistical model elaborated by factor analysts. Factorial theory distinguishes four types of factor: error factors, which are present only on one occasion, but not on others; specific factors, which are peculiar to a single test or trait whenever it occurs; group or primary factors, common to certain of the tests or traits, but absent in others; and general or second-order factors, common to all the tests or traits used in an investigation. "It will be noted that the four levels of personality organization correspond closely to the four types of factor. . . . An 'habitual response' is merely a 'specific response' divested of its error component and made into a specific factor; a 'trait' is a system of 'specific responses' divested of its error and specific variance; a 'type' is a system of 'specific responses' which has lost its error, specific, and group-factor variance." (Eysenck, 1947.)

The remainder of this chapter will deal with the outstanding type theories suggested in the literature; the remainder of the book will deal with empirical attempts to verify theories regarding the existence and interrelationship of traits, and of the hypothesized types. But before dealing with these attempts to apply the methods of factor analysis to psychological theories of personality organization, it may be worth while to draw attention to a feature of the scheme illustrated in Fig. 2 which has caused a great deal of difficulty to many psychologists in their endeavours to follow the arguments presented by factor analysts. This difficulty results from the fact that we have two main alternative ways of approaching our problem, namely the ways identified respectively with the names of Spearman and Thurstone, and that superficially their two methods sometimes appear to give different or even contradictory results. This apparent contradiction has been most apparent in the field of intellectual ability, where the debate regarding the existence of Spearman's "g" has attracted a good deal of attention; it is equally noticeable, however, in the non-cognitive areas of personality research.

Let us assume that our main interest lies in the type-factor of introversion, and that we use Spearman's technique in order to test our hypothesis. We would choose one test of persistence, one test of rigidity, one test of subjectivity, one test of shyness, and one of irritability; we would then correlate these tests over our experimental population and discover the existence of a general factor ("introversion") which satisfied our statistical criteria, such as the vanishing of the tetrad differences. We might also be led to the (erroneous) conclusion that group factors, or traits, did not exist because they did not emerge in our analysis. If group factors did appear, we might be tempted to discount their existence on the plea that the tests which gave rise to them were "too similar" and consequently that these group factors were really only "overlapping specifics".

On the other hand, let us assume that our main interest was in the traits, or group factors, and that we used Thurstone's technique in order to test our hypotheses regarding these factors. We would choose a number of tests of persistence, of rigidity, of subjectivity, and so on, intercorrelate them over our experimental population and discover the existence of a number of group factors, identified in in terms of our traits, which satisfied our statistical criteria, such as simple structure. By forcing these factors to remain orthogonal and uncorrelated, we would make it impossible to discover from our analysis the existence of any higher-order concepts, such as introversion, based on these proscribed inter-trait correlations. Thus the results reached by adherents of one school might be entirely different from those of the other, and apparently quite irreconcilable.

Recent years have brought a solution of this conflict. It became clearer and clearer that Spearman-type hypotheses could no longer be maintained, either in the cognitive or in the orectic field, because the statistical criteria were hardly ever satisfied when the number of cases studied was large enough to make sampling errors relatively unimportant. Similarly, it became clear that Thurstone-type hypotheses could no longer be maintained because the demands of simple structure and those of orthogonality of factor structure were found to be irreconcilable. As is well known, Thurstone finally achieved a solution which enabled a reconciliation to be effected in terms of oblique factors and second-order factors. Such a solution still emphasizes interest in the trait-level type of hypotheses, and extracts primary factors from the matrix of intercorrelations first of all, to go on to the investigation of type-level hypotheses only as a second step, by extracting second-order factors from the intercorrelations of the primary factors. Followers of Spearman still retain a prime interest in "general factors", as they call Thurstone's second-order factors, and extract these first of all; they no longer deny, however, the existence of "group factors", as they call Thurstone's primary factors, and proceed to deal with them after the extraction of the general factor. It is debatable whether one procedure is preferable to the other (the present writer has a distinct preference for Thurstone's method), but it can hardly be doubted that the differences which have remained are of detail only, and in no way preclude complete agreement on the general outline of the model offered.

This agreement on matters so fundamental is of course welcomed by all those who felt somewhat disturbed by what seemed to be the eternal differences of opinion between different schools of factor analysis. However, in a survey of the experimental literature such as the present, we shall be dealing with many articles and books written before reconciliation was effected, and, indeed, the great majority of our sources will be seen to fall into that period. This has necessitated a somewhat detailed discussion of several researches, as well as the reinterpretation of others. On the whole, however, the writer was surprised and delighted to see what large measure of agreement there was between writers who saw themselves as protagonists of opposed doctrines, and who in their more argumentative moments would have left their opponents hardly an intellectual shred to cover their nakedness. Ultimately the facts asserted themselves, and demanded that factors at all levels of complexity of organization be taken into account. Our discussion will throughout proceed on the basis of such recognition of the hierarchical structure of personality, and will deal very fully with the experimental evidence in favour of this position.

So far we have discussed almost exclusively the *formal* properties of the hypotheses which are going to be discussed in these pages. We must now turn, at least briefly, to their *content*. In doing so, we shall not attempt to duplicate the admirable historical account of theories of personality and character given by Roback (1927), nor shall we follow Jung (1921) in tracing these concepts through the writings of poets and philosophers. We shall, instead, restrict ourselves to those theories which have influenced and in large measure determined the empirical studies described in the following chapter; without some brief acquaintance at least with the theories of Jordan, Gross, Heymans, Wiersma, Jung, Spearman, and Kretschmer no adequate understanding is possible of the factorial studies set up to test these theories.

Jordan (1890) may perhaps be considered with some justification the first of the modern theorists. He posits two antithetical types, without of course losing sight of the fact that intermediate gradations also exist. "There are numberless varieties of character . . . many divisions, conspicuous types, intervening gradations, equal or unequal developments, varying combinations. In domestic and social life, intermediate characters produce perhaps the most useful and the happiest results, but the progress of the world at large is mainly due to the combined efforts of the supremely impassioned and reflective, and the supremely active and unimpassioned temperaments." The main principle of division, then, according to Jordan, is one which opposes the *reflective* to the *active* type of person; he goes on to point out that the reflective type tends to be more emotional ("impassioned") than the active type. Jung identifies the "less impassioned and more active type" with his extravert, and the "more impassioned and less active type" with his introvert, although he is not altogether happy with many details of Jordan's descriptive hypothesis.[1]

[1] The implied opposition between visceral and motor outlet has been verified by Jones (1930), who showed that even in infants disturbing stimuli produced *either* striped-muscle behaviour *or* visceral (autonomic) responses, the one tending to preclude the other. MacFarlane (1939) has drawn attention to a similar opposition between "internalizing" and "externalizing" children. Cf. also Himmelweit's (1952) analysis of Ackerson's data on p. 89, and Freeman and Pathman (1942). Jordan's observation cannot therefore be dismissed too easily as "armchair theorizing".

A brief quotation may give the reader an idea of the flavour of Jordan's writing. "In the matter of character men and women may be put into three classes. One class (frequently called in these pages, because of its leading characteristics, the active and unimpassioned class) includes those who tend to be more or less ready, or even, in some instances, restless, busy, and quick; who tend, in their extreme varieties, wittingly or unwittingly, to imitation, affectation, and love of notice; who may also be fitful, or uncertain in mood, manner, greeting, and conduct; and who, while self-conscious, self-asserting, and self-approving, are given, so far as others are concerned, to discontent, disparagement, and candid criticism or censorious comment. . . . The men and women of this class, in addition it may be to other high qualities, have, not rarely, generous sympathies, emotions, and affections. These sympathies, emotions, affections are not usually deep, but when they are associated with high mental gifts and are helped out by strong reasoning powers, the resulting character is often altogether admirable. Sometimes the emotions and affections appear to be almost, if not entirely, absent; and if, at the same time, the mental gifts are but poor, the resulting character is not pleasing. The men and women of quite another class (called here, from its leading characteristic, the more reflective and more impassioned class) are those who tend to repose, tranquillity, gentleness, and who, under a placid demeanour, possess deep—if sometimes sleeping—sympathies, affections, and passions. These passions are sometimes worthy, and sometimes marked by turbulence or indolence, or sensuality, or moroseness, or cruelty." Jordan devotes a whole chapter to the "Bodily Characteristics of Temperament", pointing out that, in addition to many other features, "the more impassioned women and men also have, on the whole, a greater tendency to be lean". This tendency for introversion and leptomorphic body-build to go together we shall encounter again in several experimental studies summarized later on.

Far more influential than Jordan, whose work has been almost completely neglected until Jung devoted a whole chapter of his *Psychologische Typen* to it, was the Austrian psychiatrist Otto Gross, whose two books on *Die Zerebrale Sekundärfunktion* (1902) and *Über psychopathologische Minderwertigkeiten* (1909) introduced the concepts of "primary" and "secondary" function. These concepts are basically physiological, and refer respectively to the activity of the brain cells during the production of any form of mental content, and to the hypothetical perseveration of the nervous processes involved in this production. Thus a nervous process which succeeded in arousing an idea in the mind was supposed to perseverate, although not at a conscious level, and to determine the subsequent associations formed by the mind. Gross also postulated a correlation between the intensity of any experience and the tendency for that experience to persist secondarily and to determine the subsequent course of mental associations. Most intense and energy consuming, in his view, were highly affective and emotional experiences and ideas, and these would therefore be followed by a long secondary function, during which the mental content would still be influenced and in part determined by the perseverative effects of the primary function. (There is an obvious similarity between the concept of "secondary function" and that of "refractory period".)

According to the liability of a person to develop strong emotions, Gross then distinguishes two types—the deep-narrow and the shallow-broad. In the deep-narrow type we find characteristically a primary function which is highly charged with emotion and loaded with affect, involving the expenditure of great nervous energy, and requiring a lengthened period of restitution during which the ideas involved in the primary function go on reverberating and perseverating (long secondary function). In the shallow-broad type, on the other hand, a much less intense primary function, necessitating the expenditure of comparatively little energy, is followed by a short period of restitution (short secondary function).

Certain personality characteristics follow from the type hypothesis briefly described above. In the broad-shallow person, the short secondary function enables a much greater frequency of primary functions to take place within a given time; this constant readiness for brief actions and reactions suggests a certain superficiality, a distractibility, as well as a prompt reaction to external events (Jordan's "activity"). In the deep-narrow person, the long perseverative secondary function makes the integration of different sets of what Gross calls "themas" (sets of emotions, associations, determining tendencies, complexes, and sentiments centred around one idea which is the object of a primary function) more difficult, and leads to a sejunctive (dissociated) type of personality. (This concept of dissociation will be taken up in more detail in connection with Kretschmer's account.) Dissociation leads to a damming up of the available libido, to inhibition, and on the behavioural level to absorption in thought and social shyness.

Jung readily identifies the broad-shallow type with the extravert, the deep-narrow type with the introvert; his main difference from Gross lies in the stress he lays on the intensity of the primary function, whereas Gross stresses the length of the secondary function. "Introversion is characterized by general tension, an intensive primary function and a correspondingly long secondary function." Jung summarizes Gross's contribution by saying: "Gross deserves considerable praise for being the first to put forward a simple and unified hypothesis concerning the origin of these types."

One great advance of the formulation given by Gross over that given by Jordan appears to be that it lends itself extremely well to experimental verification. The first investigators to attempt such a verification were two Dutch psychiatrists, G. Heymans and E. Wiersma, who based a rather more complex system of typology on the notion of primary and secondary function, and who attempted to use objective tests of perseveration as measuring devices. They may be said to have anticipated the two main lines along which modern attempts at the verification of "type" hypotheses have proceeded. As will be shown in Chapter II, they used the method of intercorrelation of traits to demonstrate those sets of correlated qualities we have agreed to call types, and, as shown in Chapter IX, they used the method of objective test construction according to the dictates of hypothesis for the measurement of the functions allegedly underlying the sets of observed correlations. In their work they have slightly expanded and altered the descriptive account given by Gross; as Roback points out, what characterizes the "shallow-broad" type for these writers "is *change*, lightness, lack of endurance and ready susceptibility to objective stimulation", while the concept of the "deep-narrow" type "entails the qualities of seriousness, solidity, endurance, and great susceptibility to ideational stimulation". As a much more detailed account of the work of Heymans and Wiersma will be given below in connection with their experimental studies, no more need be said here.

Spearman (1927) took up the concept of perseveration and made it into a fundamental law, his famous "Law of Inertia": *Cognitive processes always both begin and cease more gradually than their (apparent) causes.* In this law he tried to combine the theoretical contributions of writers such as Gross (1902) and Jung (1921), and the experimental studies of perseveration by Müller (1900), Wiersma (1906), Heymans and Brugman (1913), and others. As his treatment cannot be divorced from the experimental studies on which his law is based, we must postpone consideration of his contribution to a later page, where the empirical studies of "perseveration" will be reviewed in detail.

We must now turn our attention to Jung (1921), whose views have already been alluded to many times. Basing himself on the work of Jordan and Gross, Jung sees the main cause of typological differences in the extraverted or introverted tendency of the libido, i.e. in the tendency of the individual's instinctual energies to be directed mainly towards the outer world (objects), or towards his own inner mental states (subject). "When we consider a person's life-history, we see that sometimes his fate is determined more by the objects which attract his interest, while sometimes it is influenced rather by his own inner, subjective states. . . . Quite generally one might character-ize the introverted point of view by pointing to the constant sub-jection of the object and objective reality to the ego and the subjec-tive psychological processes. . . . According to the extraverted point of view, the subject is considered as inferior to the object; the im-portance of the subjective aspect is only secondary."

Jung gives very extensive descriptions of the personality traits which characterize the introvert and the extravert respectively; these descriptions agree to a considerable extent with those of Jordan and Gross. The extravert emerges as a person who values the outer world, both in its material and in its immaterial aspects (possessions, riches, power, prestige); he seeks for social approval and tends to conform to the mores of his society; he is sociable, makes friends easily, and trusts other people. He shows outward, physical activity, while the introvert's activity is mainly in the mental, intellectual sphere. He is changeable, likes new things, new people, new im-pressions. His emotions are easily aroused, but never very deeply; he is relatively insensitive, impersonal, experimental, materialistic, and tough-minded. He tends to be free from inhibitions, carefree and ascendant. This brief description makes no pretence at being anything more than the most superficial summary of some of the characteristics of the extravert; they form a bare statement of a list of those traits which in Jung's opinion correlate together to define the extravert type. Our main interest will be in the empirical verifica-tion of Jung's conception, rather than in its detailed statement.

Jung links his description of extraversion-introversion with the distinction between the main neurotic disorders as given by Janet (1894, 1903). As is well known, Jung believes that the extravert in cases of neurotic breakdown is predisposed to *hysteria*, the introvert to *psychasthenia*. "It appears to me that much the most frequent neurotic disorder of the extraverted type is hysteria. . . ." On the other hand, speaking of the introvert, he maintains that "his typical neurotic disorder is psychasthenia, a disorder which is characterized on the one hand by marked sensitivity, on the other by great exhaustion and constant tiredness." Nowadays we would probably refer to "anxiety state", or "reactive depression" rather than to the obsolescent term "psychasthenia", which also held overtones of obsessional and compulsive tendencies. On the basis of a factorial study of 700 neurotics, referred to in the next chapter, Eysenck (1944) suggested the term "dysthymic" as a more modern equivalent to cover this syndrome of correlated affective disorders. (In literal translation, this term means mood-disorders, and appears to single out the hypothetical underlying emotional dysfunction or hyperfunction posited by Gross, Jordan, and Jung.)

Although Jung never formally elaborated this part of his hypothesis, it can be seen quite clearly that implicit in his scheme is a second factor additional to, and independent of, that of extraversionintroversion. This factor we may provisionally call "abnormality" or "neuroticism"; it is identified as that particular quality which hysterics and psychasthenics have in common as compared with normal persons. The independence of introversion and neuroticism is especially stressed by Jung: "it is a mistake to believe that introversion is more or less the same as neurosis. As concepts, the two have not the slightest connection with each other". If we wish to represent Jung's complete scheme, then, we must have recourse to two orthogonal factors or axes, one of which represents the extravertintrovert continuum, the other the normal-neurotic continuum. This additional factor of abnormality is also implicit in both Jordan and Gross; it is explicitly mentioned by Heymans and Wiersma, as will be shown later. Consequently there is considerable agreement here also between the authors so far considered.

Like Jung, Kretschmer (1948) took his prototypes from the psychiatric field, but unlike Jung he turned to the psychotic forms of disorder rather than the neurotic. Following Kraepelin and Bleuler, he distinguished two main psychotic syndromes or groups of symptoms: the schizophrenic on the one hand, the manic-depressive or cyclic type of psychotic on the other. Unlike most other psychiatrists, however, Kretschmer considered these disorders not as in any way qualitatively different from normal mental states, but merely as the extremes of a continuum, as exaggerated forms of behaviour patterns characteristic of normal persons. This hypothesis may perhaps be illustrated in terms of Fig. 3, showing the hypothetical distribution of the whole population in terms of a normal curve of distribution, ranging from one extreme (schizophrenia) to the other (manic-depressive insanity). All persons left of the mean would be *schizothymics*, meaning by that merely that their personality make-up had in common certain elements which are grotesquely exaggerated in those psychotic patients whom we label schizophrenics, whereas all those to the right of the mean would by *cyclothymics*, meaning by that that their personality make-up had in common certain elements which are grotesquely exaggerated in manic-depressive patients. Persons who are definitely abnormal but not yet psychotic Kretschmer would call schizoid or cycloid respectively, according to the side on which they fell, whereas the large number of persons in the centre of the distribution he would call syntonic if they were on the cyclothymic side, and dystonic if they were on the schizothymic

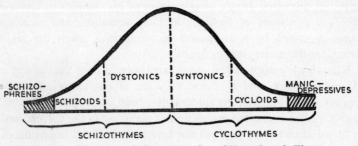

Fig. 3.—Diagrammatic Representation of Kretschmer's Theory.

side. (It is possible that Kretschmer would object to the use of a normal curve to depict the relation between schizothymes and cyclothymes, but little importance can in any case be attributed to the form of distribution when the underlying metric is unknown.)

Kretschmer's description of the cyclothyme has certain similarities to the types already considered. Like the extravert, the active-unimpassioned, and the broad-shallow type, the cyclothyme is objective, realistic, sociable, optimistic, hedonistic, trustful, co-operative, and frank; he is also subject to mood-changes without apparent cause. The schizothyme, like the introvert, the passive-impassioned, and the narrow-deep types, shows the opposite qualities to these. Kretschmer is suggesting, then, a definite dimension of personality similar to, but probably not identical with, those considered above. It would also seem to follow from his writings that another dimension is also implied, ranging from normality to psychotic disorder, and orthogonal to the cyclothymia-schizothymia dimension. Thus, as in the case of Jung, Kretschmer's theory would best be represented in terms of two orthogonal factors or axes, one measuring cyclothymia-schizothymia, the other normality-psychotic abnormality, or "psychoticism". (Indeed, if we were to follow him faithfully, we would have to add another two dimensions, namely the diathetic and the psychasthetic scales. In his view, cyclothymes vary among themselves on a scale ranging from humorous, vivacious, quick-witted, to the quiet, calm, serious—the so-called diathetic scale; whereas schizothymes vary from shy, nervous, sensitive, to dull, stupid, torpid—the so-called psychasthetic scale. As, however, there is no experimental evidence in Kretschmer's work regarding these scales, and as he makes little use of them and does not define their relation to each other in any way, we shall not deal with these scales in detail. In a similar manner, and for similar reasons, we have not discussed Jung's amplification of his theories in terms of the four functions of feeling, thinking, sensation, and intuition. Little is gained by a discussion of refinements when the major structures themselves are in doubt.)

Kretschmer's approach is more experimental than that of any of his predecessors, and a review of some of the empirical studies carried out by him and his students has been presented by Eysenck (1950). As his attempted proofs do not make use of the correlational or factorial methods, they will not here be considered in any detail; such factorial studies as have been carried out by psychologists outside his immediate circle will be mentioned in later chapters. Two points, however, call for notice. In the first place, Kretschmer attempts to anchor his typology on the firm facts of biological constitution, relating personality types and psychotic syndromes to types of body build. The schizophrenic, and accordingly the schizoid and dystonic person also, is believed to show in the majority of cases an asthenic, leptosomatic type of body-build; the manic-depressive, and accordingly the cycloid and the syntonic person also, is believed in most cases to show a pyknic, thick-set type of body-build. A review of factorial studies of body-build, and an evaluation of this claim, will be found in a later chapter; the hypothesis of this body-mind correlation had to be mentioned at this point because no account of Kretschmer's work could be complete without what he would consider his main contribution.

The second point to be considered relates to Kretschmer's psychological theories regarding the dynamic causes underlying the typology advanced by him. Kretschmer holds that the concept of *dissociation* (Spaltung) is of fundamental importance in understanding the mentality of the schizothyme, just as its opposite, integration, is important for the understanding of the cyclothyme mentality. By *Spaltung* he means "the ability to form separate and partial groupings within a single act of consciousness; from this results the ability to dissect complex material into its constituent parts". This concept of dissociation is very reminiscent of Gross's long secondary function leading to dissociation of "themas", and giving rise to the "sejunctive" type of personality. Kretschmer has added, and this is a most important contribution, a whole series of experimental tests for the measurement of this hypothetical trait of "dissociative ability". Unfortunately these tests have not yet been subjected to factorial study, and consequently their functional unity must remain unestablished; the extensive evidence reviewed by Eysenck (1950) suggests strongly, however, that the majority of these tests succeed in differentiating the cyclothyme from the schizothyme and the leptosomatic from the pyknic type of person.

The apparent similarity between the concepts of schizothymia and introversion, and between cyclothymia and extraversion, has led many psychologists and psychiatrists to identify the respective schemes of Jung and Kretschmer. In doing so, they have often overlooked certain consequences which are implicit in such an identification, but which are seldom if ever brought out in the purely semantic process employed in carrying out such identification. Fig. 4 gives a diagrammatic picture of some of these implications. It will be seen, in the first place, that in accepting such a view we are committed to the proposition that psychotic and neurotic disorders lie along one and the same continuum of "abnormality", a view explicitly held, among others, by Freud, who advances his hypothesis of "psychosexual regression" to account for differences in psychiatric patterns. In the normal person, there is hardly any regression to infantile patterns of psychosexual adjustment. In the conversion-hysteric, and even more so in the anxiety-hysteric, there is a considerable amount of such regression, while in the manic-depressive, and particularly in the schizophrenic, regression is almost complete. This hypothetical axis of "regression" would correspond quite well to the ordinate in our diagram. A similar assumption to Freud's is made by Kretschmer, although he does not invoke the concept of regression; for him also psychosis is merely a more advanced stage along the same road along which neurosis is an intermediate resting-place. Jung is less explicit in his views, but would probably not be found to differ essentially from the other writers mentioned.

One further assumption implied in Kretschmer's and probably also in Jung's system is indicated in Fig. 4 by cross-hatching certain parts of the diagram. If psychosis is the characteristic of persons at the *extreme* positions on the cyclothyme-schizothyme continuum, as Kretschmer appears to believe, then it should be impossible to find a psychotic whose position on the cyclothyme-schizothyme con-

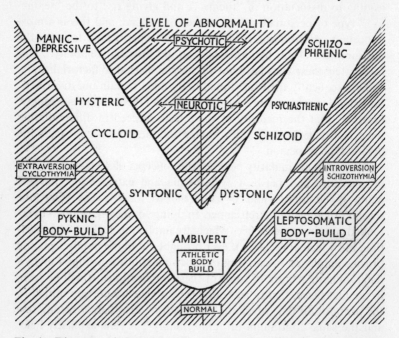

Fig. 4.—Diagrammatic Representation of Combined Jung-Kretschmer Theory.

tinuum was intermediate; conversely, it should be impossible to find a normal person whose position on this continuum was very far away from the centre. The regression of abnormality on cyclothymia-schizothymia, therefore, would be curvilinear, as indicated in the non-hatched part of the diagram; no actual cases should be found in the cross-hatched part of the diagram. The same argument would apply to Jung's view at the neurotic level.

There are, however, formidable obstacles to the easy acceptance of this view. These have been reviewed in detail by Eysenck (1952), who summarizes the available evidence and comes to the conclusion that experimental findings are solidly opposed to the hypothesis of one single dimension of abnormality, and that two such dimensions, orthogonal to each other and dealing respectively with neurotic and psychotic disorders, are required. Some of this evidence will be considered on a later page, but we may note that these experimental studies are in good agreement with orthodox psychiatric opinion, which is opposed to the "single continuum" hypothesis.

This objection may not be quite fatal to the identification of the two schemes. It might be possible to rotate the psychotic axis away from collinearity with the neurotic axis, while preserving the projections of points on both axes on the extraversion-introversion axis. Fig. 5 illustrates how this might be done. However, even this rotation does not do away with a second difficulty inherent in any attempt to bring the two schemes together. Jung speaks of an "essential relationship" between psychasthenia and schizophrenia; Kretschmer, on the other hand, links up schizophrenia with hysteria; "there is no doubt whatever that there are many 'nervous' and 'hysterical' individuals ... who are biologically nothing but schizoids".[1] A glance at Figs. 4 and 5 will show that there is a clear contradiction here between the Jungian and the Kretschmerian schemes which no amount of rotation can resolve. McDougall (1926) adds to the confusion when he writes: "There are ... two great categories of disorder under one or other of which we may attempt to place many of the cases, though without confidence in respect to many of them. . . . These two categories are the dissociative or the hysteric class, on the one hand; the neurasthenic or anxiety class, on the other. The liability to disorder of one or other of these two great types seems to be a matter mainly of innate constitution; persons of the extravert temperament seem more liable, under strain, to disorders of the hysteric or dissociative type; those of introvert ... temperament to disorders of the neurasthenic type." He thus links the concept of dissociation with hysteria and extraversion, where Kretschmer would link it with

[1] Pavlov (1941) would appear to agree with Kretschmer, rather than with Jung. In his view, hysterics are characterized by strong inhibitory and weak excitatory properties of the nerve cells; so are schizophrenics. Dysthymics, on the other hand, are supposed to be characterized by strong excitatory and weak inhibitory properties. Evidence from the work of Bender and Schilder (1930), Pfaffman and Schlosberg (1936), Shipley (1934), Welch and Kubis (1947), Taylor (1951), Spence and Taylor (1951), and many others would seem to support this hypothesis at a reasonable level of confidence. However, the evidence is somewhat indirect, as no investigator has attempted to set up a crucial experiment. In view of the obvious importance of the problem, and the objective nature of the test, such diffidence is difficult to understand.

schizophrenia and introversion. Quite clearly, there are too many contradictions in these various schemes to permit of any easy identification; we must turn to deductions which may be made from the various typologies, and the experimental testing of these deductions. Where clinical writers disagree so profoundly, even the most convinced advocate of the clinical approach may find it difficult to arrive at a rational conclusion without the aid of the hypothetico-deductive method.

When we are dealing with theories such as those discussed on the preceding pages, we can make essentially two kinds of deductions.

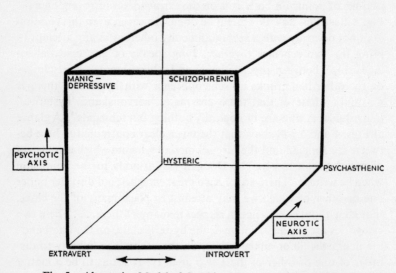

Fig. 5.—Alternative Model of Combined Jung-Kretschmer Theory.

These two kinds may be termed *direct* and *relational*, respectively. *Relational deductions* are based on the hypothesized system of inter-correlations which defines the alleged type, and involve the calculation of correlations between traits, and the factor analysis of the resulting matrix of intercorrelations. The deduction is verified if the hypothesized pattern of correlations is actually found, and a factor clearly corresponding to the alleged type is actually extracted. It is with this type of evidence that we shall in the main be concerned in the following pages. Verification of deductions in these terms does not of course *prove* the correctness of the hypothesis, because such proof is never possible in terms of the scientific method; all we are entitled to say is that the results support the hypothesis.

Direct deductions are seldom made by psychologists, although their verification is much less arduous, and much more convincing, than that given by relational deductions. In any complete investigation of personality organization, both methods should go hand in hand, and it may be helpful to give one or two illustrations of precisely what is meant by this "direct" type of verification.

Let us take as our starting-point Jung's hypothesis that the conduct of extraverts is more determined by objects and relations in the external world, while the actions of introverts are more determined by their inner subjective states. In order to test this hypothesis directly, we must do two things; we must obtain a group of extraverts and a group of introverts, and we must obtain a test of "objectivity-subjectivity" which should in terms of the hypothesis differentiate between our two groups in the predicted direction. We can find our two groups by reference to a subsidiary hypothesis of Jung's according to which he identifies hysterics with extraverts, and psychasthenics (dysthymics) with introverts. If we took groups of hysterics and dysthymics respectively, then we should be able to observe the predicted differentiation with special clarity.

As regards the test required, there is no dearth in the literature of measures which would satisfy Jung's definition; let us choose for our purpose the Level of Aspiration technique. In this test, a task (T) is presented to the subject who is made thoroughly acquainted with the requirements of this task. The score may be in terms of time taken, in terms of errors made, or in terms of number of correct solutions; it is desirable that there should be a marked but irregular learning curve on the task, and that the subject should have no certain knowledge of the score he has actually obtained. The tests are repeated, usually between five and ten times, and three measures obtained from the subject each time. These are: (1) his aspiration (A), i.e. a statement of the score he thinks he is going to obtain on the next trial; (2) his performance score (P), i.e. the actual score obtained by the subject but not communicated to him; (3) his judgment (J), i.e. his estimate of what score he has actually achieved on the trial. After obtaining these three measures, the subject is told his score (he may be told his true score or a made-up score), and the next trial is begun.

Two compound scores are calculated from these raw scores. One is the Goal Discrepancy score, in which the subject's actual performance is subtracted from his aspiration (A-P), so that he obtains a positive score if his aspiration outstrips his performance; and a Judgment Discrepancy score, in which the subject's judgment of his performance is subtracted from his actual performance (P-J), so that he obtains a negative score if he underestimates his own performance. It is known that normal people (non-neurotics, neither extravert nor introvert, i.e. neutral from the point of view of our hypothesis) tend to have slightly positive goal discrepancy scores and slightly negative judgment discrepancy scores. From these facts we are enabled to make up a very definite prediction regarding the scores of hysterics and dysthymics respectively; this hypothesis is represented diagrammatically in Fig. 6. The extravert is supposedly determined in his

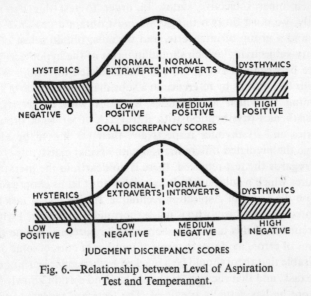

Fig. 6.—Relationship between Level of Aspiration
Test and Temperament.

conduct by external objects and relations; consequently his discrepancy scores (i.e. his deviations from external reality, as represented by his actual P scores) should cluster around zero. The introvert is supposedly determined in his conduct by internal states rather than by objective fact; consequently his discrepancy scores should be considerably removed from zero. Normal persons should be intermediate between these two extremes.

There is ample experimental evidence to show that in its essentials this deduction is borne out. Eysenck and Himmelweit (1946), Miller (1951), and Himmelweit (1947), using different tests and working in different countries, have testified to the correctness of the pattern illustrated in Fig. 6. Other deductions have also been verified in connection with the Level of Aspiration experiment; thus the lack of objective reference of the introvert's behaviour should lead him to act in a rather rigid, non-adaptive manner of making his aspiration and judgment estimates, while the close objective reference of the extravert's behaviour should lead him to a completely non-rigid conformity of his estimates with his objective scores. This prediction also has been shown to be borne out by experimental studies on hysterics and dysthymics (Eysenck, 1947).

One further example of this type of verification may be given, this time from the Kretschmerian system. Let us start with the hypothesis that schizothymes have an intense primary and a long secondary function. Again what is required is the selection of two groups, corresponding to the terms "schizothyme" and "cyclothyme", and a measure of primary and secondary function. The former may be found, according to Kretschmer's subsidiary hypothesis, by paying attention to the body-build of our subjects; pyknics should be predominantly cyclothyme, leptosomatics essentially schizothyme, and athletics intermediate between the others. As a test for the measurement of primary and secondary functions we may use the psychogalvanic reflex, a phenomenon believed to be closely related to strength of emotional arousal. We would predict, on the basis of the hypotheses outlined in the first part of this chapter, that pyknics would show slight deflections on the P.G.R. and quick return to resting level (short secondary function), while leptosomatics would show large deflections and slow return to resting level (long secondary function).

Kretschmer and Enke (1936) used 90 normal subjects, 30 of whom were of pyknic body-build, 30 of leptosomatic body-build, and 30 of athletic body-build. These were subjected to various stimuli (pleasant and unpleasant odours, pricks, and pistol shots), and the amount of P.G.R. deflection and the time taken for the P.G.R. to return to normal were noted. The results are given in Table 1; it will be seen that there is considerable support for the hypothesis, or rather the chain of hypotheses, under investigation.

TABLE 1
(*Maximum Deflection in mm.*)

	Pyknics	*Athletics*	*Leptosomatics*
Pleasant odour . .	17	18	33
Unpleasant odour . .	12	19	26
Prick	36	22	28
Pistol shot . . .	29	38	64

Return to Resting Level (in secs.)

	Pyknics	Athletics	Leptosomatics
Pleasant odour . .	61	93	101
Unpleasant odour . .	54	63	87
Prick	121	98	149
Pistol shot . . .	118	129	192

Many other examples of the direct method of investigation could have been given; a few will be found in the chapter dealing with tests of perseveration, persistence, suggestibility, and the like; others, dealing specifically with Kretschmer's views, have been summarized elsewhere (Eysenck, 1950). It is probable that a more determined effort to pursue this line of approach would have given us a considerable body of evidence on the basis of which to judge the various theories advanced; unfortunately the great theorists have seldom considered it necessary or even desirable to support their speculations with experimental proof, and experimentalists have tended to fight shy of the considerable difficulties involved in work of this sort. Much more energy has been expended on the relational type of deduction, although here, too, it must be admitted that several writers have advanced in a spirit of blind empiricism, rather than in that associated with the hypothetico-deductive approach. Nevertheless, enough evidence has accrued now to enable certain general statements about the organization of personality to be made, and to a consideration of this evidence we must now turn.

ADDENDUM

In describing the typological schemes of Jordan, Gross, Jung, and Kretschmer in the text, no mention has been made of two further schemes which have exerted a considerable influence on Continental psychologists, and which have given rise to a considerable body of experimental investigation. It seemed better not to disrupt the argument by making reference to the work of Pfahler (1936) and Jaensch (1938), which stands somewhat outside the direct succession of the writers mentioned in the text. Also, while factorial evidence is available in connection with the work of Jung and Kretschmer, none has yet appeared which would make it possible to judge that of Pfahler and Jaensch. However, no account of "typology" would be complete without brief mention at least of the contribution of the two last-named authors, and consequently the present note has been added.

Pfahler posits several dimensions orthogonal to each other as his major descriptive constants; it is the position of each person on these continua which determines his "type". These dimensions are: (1) *Apperceptive Mode*. This ranges from one extreme—"crystallized" apperception (objective, analytic, discrete, narrow, fixed range of attention, strong perseveration)—to the other ("fluid" apperception, subjective, synthetic, and global, wide, fluctuating range of attention, weak perseveration). (2) *Emotional Strength*. This dimension opposes strong emotionality to weak emotionality; in Pfahler's account it is somewhat mixed up with what should essentially be quite an independent component, namely (3) *Pleasure-Unpleasure*. He conceives of this polarity as constituting a definite tendency, one person's emotionality responding much more easily to pleasant, another person's to unpleasant stimuli. (4) *Vital Energy*. This concept resembles the Freudian libido, and may be considered to range from weak to strong.

By combining these dimensions as indicated in Table 2, Pfahler finally arrives at twelve types which he describes in great detail. It should be noted, however, that he also does not hold the concept of

TABLE 2

Classification according to Apperceptive Mode:	Crystallized Apperception (Narrow, fixed attentive range, strong perseveration)		Fluid Apperception (Wide, fluctuating attentive range, weak perseveration)	
Strong pleasurable emotivity.	A	D	G	K
Strong unpleasurable emotivity	B	E	H	L
Weak emotivity	C	F	I	M
Classification according to energy function	Strong vital energy	Weak vital energy	Strong vital energy	Weak vital energy

Pfahler: *Typological Scheme*

type criticized by so many American writers; he specially lays stress on the point that "man sich z.B. an Stelle der Rubriken A und D eine unendliche Kette ineinandergreifender Rubriken vorzustellen hat, deren Entfernung von A und Annäherung an D ein allmähliches

Abnehmen des Grades der vitalen Energie bedeutet. Irgendwo in einer Rubrik diesser Kette ist der Ort für die nach ihrem Erbgut zu charakterisierende Person". He thus clearly puts forward a theory of continuity of distribution, and nowhere makes any assumption regarding the form of that distribution.

Pfahler's dimensions strongly resemble concepts already discussed. Vital energy would appear to mark the opposite pole to neuroticism; the pleasure-unpleasure polarity would seem to correspond to extra-version-introversion; fixed as opposed to fluid apperceptive mode would correspond closely with Kretschmer's description of the schizothyme as compared with the cyclothyme. Of major interest in Pfahler's system are the attempts at experimental description and measurement of his various dimensions; as a detailed account of these would be out of place here, the interested reader must be referred to the original.

Much the same must be said of the system elaborated by the Jaensch brothers. Here also the experimental methods developed are of greater interest than the formal properties of their system, but it is the latter which will here be very briefly described. In doing so we can hardly do justice to all the changes and refinements which this system has undergone; only a rough outline is attempted. The main dimension around which Jaensch (1930, 1934, 1938) orders his typology is one of *integration*; human personality can be found to range from the pole of complete integration to the opposite pole of complete disintegration. However, again there is continuity— "zwischen den beiden Polen als Granzfällen stehen die manning-fachen Übergänge des Lebens". Secondary to this principle of differ-entiation is one of introversion and extraversion, i.e. a tendency to emphasize the inner or the outer world. (Jaensch himself does not use these Jungian terms, but the similarity of the concepts is clear.) A third dimension is indicated by the polarity of feeling and thinking. Various combinations of these three dimensions give rise to seven types, which are referred to by Jaensch in terms of capital letters and numerical subscripts. Four types are "integrated": B, J_1, J_2, and J_3. The first three types constitute a series going from the exaggeratedly integrated (B) through the normally integrated (J_1) to the partly and occasionally integrated (J_2); these are all orientated towards the outer world. J_3 is fully integrated, but orientated towards the inner world.

Of the three "disintegrated" types, S_1 and S_2 show failure of inte-gration either unredeemed (S_1) or compensated by a hyperdevelop-ment of intelligence which takes over functions rightly performed by feeling, as in the J types (S_2). A third type, called Svital by Jaensch, appears to occupy a position intermediate between the J types and the two S types on the integration scale, and is the only S type not considered degenerate. While a given person would be considered by Jaensch to have affinities to one or the other of these ideal types, he would also maintain that the natural development of any person is characterized by *phases* dominated by these type-concepts. Thus at the age of 4 the child goes through an S phase, from 6 to 12 through a J_1 phase, from 14 to 17 through a J_2 phase, to be followed by another S phase at 18, and finally by a J_3 phase.

While Jaensch's concepts often resemble those of other typologists —his concept of integration is very similar to Kretschmer's concept of dissociation, and attention has already been drawn to his debt to Jung's introversion-extraversion principle—and while he has originated many interesting and worth-while experimental procedures in his attempts to prove the correctness of his concepts (his stress on eidetic imagery as a typological test is probably best known here), his whole system is much less well structured than any of those discussed so far. The occasional brilliance which now and then penetrates the confused semantic diarrhœa of his writings indicates how much psychology might have gained from Jaensch's work had it not been for the mental illness which was his personal tragedy.

The reader may feel somewhat confused by this array of putative dimensions, and echo the feeling of Giese (1939) who writes: "Für die Typologie, deren Breitenwirkung heute eine besonders grosse und bei psychologischen Auslesen und Begutachtgaben auch praktisch sehr bedeutsame geworden ist, kann es nur förderlich sein, wenn wir an Stelle von Typologien *eine* Typologie bekommen". This demand for *one* typology instead of a whole collection of different typologies is, in essence, a demand for a scientific methodology which will enable us to test the claims advanced for any specific system; the essential incompleteness of the typologists' achievement lay in their failure to provide a technique of verification by means of which their claims could be subjected to genuine scientific validation. It is only through the method of factor analysis that such verification can come, and it may be surmised that a combination of the intuitive and often brilliant insight of the "typologists" and the precise and rigorous work of the statistician will in due course lead us to this *one* typology. The work described in the following chapters may serve as an indication that such a hope is at least not unreasonable.

*The reader would be more inclined to echo it he understood German

CHAPTER II

THE ANALYSIS OF RATINGS

THE PRECURSOR OF the large number of factorial rating studies which have been carried out in the last fifty years is a *Massenuntersuchung* carried out by two Dutch psychologists, G. Heymans and E. Wiersma (1909). This study differs somewhat from most of those which succeeded it in two ways. In the first place, it was based on a definite hypothesis; in the second place, it used statistical methods which, while they resemble factor analysis in their import, were yet rather simpler and more easily understood by the non-mathematical.

Both the hypothesis to be investigated and the method used are clearly brought out in what is essentially a preliminary paper separate from the main work. In this paper, Heymans (1908) analysed biographical material derived from 110 historical persons about whom a great deal was known. These persons were rated on a large number of traits which were considered to be interrelated in such a way as to give rise to three main factors, dimensions, or principles. These three principles are, first of all, *emotionality*, or emotional instability, secondly, *activity*, or general drive, and, thirdly, what we would now call a bipolar factor opposing dominance of the *primary function* to dominance of the *secondary function*.

This scheme was later on applied by Heymans and Wiersma (1906a, 1906b, 1907, 1908a, 1908b, 1909) to a rating study in which 3,000 doctors in the Netherlands were asked each to pick one family and rate each member of it by a simple method of underlining or double-underlining of a large number of traits. Four hundred doctors responded and sent in material on altogether 2,523 individuals. Most of the papers analysing this material are concerned with the interpretation of intra-familial similarities in terms of hereditary hypotheses; as such an interpretation is clearly arbitrary, and as in any case it is not germane to our own subject, nothing will be said here about it. It is in the last paper that we find a detailed analysis and justification for the threefold classificatory system adopted by the authors.

It is clear that if we consider each person to be either above or below the average with respect to each of the three factors, then there are eight possible combinations which might be considered to create separate types. This general scheme is shown in Table 3, together with a number of cases which were found by the authors to fall into each of the eight types.[1]

TABLE 3

	1 Emotionality:	2 Activity:	3 P- or S-Function	Type:	N:
1	−	−	P	Amorphous	98
2	−	−	S	Apathetic	94
3	+	−	P	Nervous	174
4	+	−	S	Sentimental	113
5	−	+	P	Sanguine	95
6	−	+	S	Phlegmatic	439
7	+	+	P	Choleric	257
8	+	+	S	Passionate	597
	Impossible to Classify:				656
	Total:				2,523

TABLE 4

Heymans and Wiersma	Ribot	Malapert	Queyrat	Martiny	Jung
Apathetic	Humble	Tempered	Equilibrated	Plastic	Sensitive introvert
Amorphous	Apathetic	Amorphous	Amorphous	Gregarious	Intuitive introvert
Phlegmatic	Active apathetic	Apathetic	Apathetic	Materialistic	Intuitive extravert
Sanguine	Active	Sensitive	Emotional	Primitive	Sensitive extravert
Passionate	Alive	Passionate	Passionate	Practical	Thinking extravert
Choleric	Calculating	Voluntary	Spontaneous	Social	Feeling extravert
Sentimental	Emotional	Affective	Sentimental	Aesthetic	Feeling introvert
Nervous	Contemplative	Calculating	Intellectual	Speculative	Thinking introvert

It may be helpful to quote the actual descriptions of the traits on the basis of which subjects were assigned a plus or a minus for the various factors. The score on the first factor was based entirely on the rater's answer to a single question regarding the emotional in-

[1] This eight-type scheme links up with the French rather than with the German and Austrian typologists. Table 4 shows its correspondence with the work of Ribot (1892), Malapert (1897), Queyrat (1896), and Martiny (1948). As the last-mentioned points out, it has certain affinities also to Jung's model when the four "functions"—sensation, intuition, thinking, feeling—are combined with the extravert-introvert dichotomy.

stability of the subject under investigation. The score on the second factor was, in fact, the average of the rater's endorsement of three traits; namely, (1) "Is always active in office, job, school, or household"; (2) "Usually busy in his spare time"; (3) "Usually attacks duties immediately and without delay". The subject's standing on the third factor was decided on the basis of the average of ten traits: (1) "Is quickly comforted"; (2) "Is easily reconciled"; (3) "Changeable in his likes"; (4) "Interested in new impressions and friends"; (5) "Easily talked around"; (6) "Desirous of change"; (7) "Easily changes job or subject of study"; (8) "Often busy with magnificent plans which come to nothing"; (9) "His actions are mainly determined by consideration of immediate results"; (10) "Often acts contrary to his own principles".

It should be noted that these three factors do not appear to be independent of each other. In Table 5, which gives percentages of cases showing various combinations of factors, it will be seen that emotionality and activity are relatively independent, but that strength of primary function is correlated with emotionality and lack of activity, whereas strength of secondary function is correlated with lack of emotionality and activity. (Note the bearing of these results on Jordan's hypotheses.)

TABLE 5

	A +	A −	
E +	75%	25%	
E −	74%	26%	$r_{tet} = + 0.020$
	P	S	
E +	38%	62%	
E −	27%	73%	$r_{tet} = - 0.205$
	P	S	
A +	25%	75%	
A −	57%	43%	$r_{tet} = - 0.500$

N = 1,867

The next step in the analysis consists of a detailed tabulation of percentage ratings of each of the whole list of traits submitted to the raters for members of the eight "type" groups. This shows which of these new traits belongs with each of the sets of traits on which the original choice of "type" was made, and while a correlational analysis would have been simpler and more straightforward, the method used is quite adequate for its avowed purpose. Thus, three larger sets of traits, sharing a certain type of "belongingness", are built up from the original hypothetical clusters.

These new and enlarged descriptions of the hypothetical factors will not be given in detail; they illustrate all too clearly that even without the aid of factor analysis, it was possible for psychologists to group together sets of adjectives, the psychological connections between which are very far from being apparent. Thus, while it may seem reasonable for the active person to be fond of movement, practical, self-reliant, abstemious, and courageous, it is not quite clear why he should be miserly, punctual, a collector of things, and patriotic and radical at the same time! [1]

Although the cluster of traits grouped around the "activity" factor does not therefore appear to have very much consistency, the same cannot be said of the other two factors, which we will find recurring again and again throughout this book. Without forcing their interpretation too much, we may say that *emotionality* resembles closely the factor of emotional instability, immaturity, or neuroticism, so frequently encountered, while *primary* and *secondary function* denote extraversion and introversion respectively. To illustrate this correspondence we may set down some of the traits found by Heymans and Wiersma to be characteristic of persons in whom the primary or the secondary function predominated. Those with predominantly primary function are impulsive, give up easily, are always on the move, jocose, superficial, vain, demonstrative, tending to exaggerate, given to public speaking, to telling jokes, and to laughing a lot. On the other hand, the person with predominant secondary function is quiet, persistent, grave, shut-in, reliable, given to introspective thinking, laughs little, has depressive tendencies, and is not given to indulge in the pleasures of the body.

[1] We do not intend to suggest that "activity" is not a useful descriptive variable in the psychology of personality; indeed, we will encounter it again in Guilford's factorial studies of inventory responses. We merely doubt whether the term can usefully be extended as widely as Heymans and Wiersma have done; in our view, this factor is located at the trait level, whereas "emotionality" and "primary" and "secondary" function are located at the type level. More will be said later about the difficulties of keeping these levels apart and the dangers resulting from mixing them up.

If our identification of these two factors is correct, we should expect that the emotional person, with predominant primary function (i.e. the *nervous* type of Heymans and Wiersma), would show the characteristics of the neurotic extravert, which if carried to an extreme would result in the diagnosis of hysteria, whereas the emotional person with predominant secondary function (the *sentimental* type) would resemble the neurotic introvert, or in its extreme manifestation the person suffering from anxiety and reactive depression, i.e. the dysthymic. We may quote, in somewhat free translation, the picture given by Heymans of those two types, the "nervous" and the "sentimental" respectively, and leave it to the reader to decide whether this identification is justified.

"The person of the nervous type is characterized by marked emotional instability, a small degree of activity, and an overwhelming strength of primary function, and is accordingly little inclined to regular work, has little persistence, and no tendency to get absorbed in his work. He is characterized by a high degree of sensitivity, emotional reactivity, and rapid change of mood. Such a person is characterized by inner contradictions and conflict between thought and action. He lacks self-sufficiency and fails to take a definite stand on matters of attitude. He is shy and there is a marked lack of inhibition. Among his primary interests, the most obvious is the erotic. Abstract virtues like punctuality, abstemiousness, honesty, reliability, and love of truth are largely absent in a person of this type. He shows a tendency to play a rôle; to pretend to be other than he is. The nervous person is lacking in judgment, practical sense, and suffers from an undevelopment of mathematical and systematic tendencies. Other characteristics are a tendency towards symbolism and a tendency to frequent change of address. The relatives of a nervous person frequently show neurasthenic or hysterical symptoms or are led by their uninhibited proclivities to commit crimes of one kind or another.

"Quite a different picture is presented by the 'sentimental' person. Of course, we find here again primarily those qualities which we have already found in the nervous person as characteristic of emotionality and lack of activity. Nevertheless, there are also considerable differences which throughout point to the inhibiting and regulating influence of the secondary function, which robs the passing moment of its omnipotence. Instead, we find those emotions which depend not so much on the passing emotion of the moment but on the after-effects of previous experiences, such as shyness, depression, and constant irritation. As in the field of emotion, so in the field of action: mobility as well as the tendency to regular work are at a minimum, but persistence, the tendency to get absorbed in one's work, may be above average. Instead of the frivolity and exaggerated openness of the 'nervous' person, we find in the sentimental person seriousness and reticence. The seriousness can also be found in many other manifestations: in the frequency with which abstract virtues, like conscientiousness, honesty, and reliability are found; in the strength of his tendency towards idealism, in the frequent appearance of specific religious or ethical ideals, in his lack of tolerance, in the rareness of his laughter, and the lack of attention he pays to social intercourse. The sentimental person is given to self-analysis and speculation; he likes music, while his interest for the real world is far below the average. When translated into abnormal behaviour, this person is characterized in the main by melancholy or paranoia."

Little need be said in criticism of the work of Heymans and Wiersma. Such faults as are implicit in their methodology have characterized most of the work of their successors; we will return to them at the end of the chapter. The particular concepts advocated by them have been relatively neglected by later investigators; occasional echoes can be found in the studies carried out by Biesheuvel in South Africa, and one or two papers directly relevant to this system will be reviewed later. In the main, however, their influence has been indirect rather than direct, and we would agree with Webb's (1915) judgment of their contribution. "The work of these investigators has broken new ground in some important particulars. Their large range of questions aimed at a fairly complete diagnosis of each individual personality, and it was an advance in method to collect large masses of data, from judges working independently, in such a way as to afford conclusions by means of statistical methods. They modestly conclude a report of their work with the remark: 'Mais ces recherches ne sont qu'une première ébauche, pour laquelle la postérité n'aura certes qu'un sourire compatissant'; but we may hope that posterity, having smiled, will be able to build much useful work upon the foundations they have laid."

Far more influential than any other single piece of research on the organization of personality has been the work of Edward Webb (1915), who was the first to use the method of factor analysis in the non-intellectual field, and while the statistics which he used are far from adequate by modern standards, they are definitely superior to those used by Heymans and Wiersma. From several points of view,

Webb's research, which was carried on under the guidance of Spearman himself, is methodologically superior to many that have followed in later years. This judgment is supported by the fact that his table of intercorrelations has been subjected to analysis by more powerful modern methods by a variety of later students. Some of these reanalyses will be described in detail later, as they are essential to a complete understanding of Webb's contribution.

The subjects of his enquiry were two groups of 98 and 96 students respectively, and four groups of schoolboys of an average age of 12, numbering 140 in all. Assessments were made by at least two judges, working as independently of each other as possible. These judges were in a position to make observations of their subjects under conditions relatively free from restraint. The subjects were made available for observation under a wide range of environmental conditions —in the lecture-room, common-room, the social gathering, the playing-field, at home, during holidays, etc. Subjects throughout were unaware that assessments were being made concerning them. Ratings were carried out by fellow students of the subjects in the two experimental student groups, and by two class masters in the case of the children. Thirty-nine traits were rated in the case of the students and 25 in the case of the schoolboys, grouped under the headings of "Emotions", "Self-qualities", "Sociability", "Activity", and "Intellect". Tests of intelligence were also administered and estimates of physique and records of examination ability obtained.

Reliability of the ratings varied between ·5 and ·7 on the average, with one or two occasional values dropping below the former or rising above the latter. Average reliability of ratings retained for the calculations was ·55, and product moment correlations were calculated between the averaged ratings. In addition to the raw correlations between all the traits, tables in which the correlations were corrected for attenuation are also presented.

Using Spearman's well-known method of inter-columnar correlations and tetrad differences, Webb proceeded to extract a general factor of intelligence, based primarily on the tests administered to the subjects, but which correlated quite highly also with ratings on such items as quickness of apprehension, profoundness of apprehension, originality of ideas, and power of getting through mental work rapidly. These correlations range from ·5 to ·6; there is also a correlation of ·67 between intelligence tests and examination ability. These data which Webb considers as supporting Spearman's theory of "*g*" are of no great interest, although the correlation between ratings and test results may perhaps be considered evidence of validity of the ratings. Webb goes on, however, to show that the correlations cannot be accounted for entirely in terms of this general factor, and shows that a second factor, independent of intelligence, can be extracted from the intercorrelations of the data. He is therefore led to put forward the hypothesis "that a second factor, of wide generality, exists; and that this factor is prominent on the 'character' side of mental activity (as distinguished from the purely intellective side)". This factor he considers to be in some close relation to "persistence of motives". He goes on to say "this conception may be understood to mean *consistency of action resulting from deliberate volition or will*. For convenience, we will in future represent the general factor by the symbol 'w' ".

The traits which characterize the person possessing a high degree of "w" are: tendency not to abandon tasks from mere changeability; tendency not to abandon task in face of obstacles; kindness on principle; trustworthiness; conscientiousness, and perseverance in face of obstacles.

This "w", or will factor, appears in many ways to be the opposite of Heymans and Wiersma's *emotionality*. In part it may perhaps represent a halo effect in the sense that it has often been shown that judges tend to group favourable qualities together because of their general like or dislike of the subject under investigation (Flemming, 1942). We will find ample evidence later, however, that this factor cannot be explained away entirely in terms of errors of rating, and there is no doubt that Webb in this study has made a significant contribution to the development of psychology. In many ways, his study is typical of what has become known at the London school; as P. Mabille (1951) puts it: "La caractéristique de l'école anglaise moderne semble bien être d'équilibrer harmonieusement les conceptions théoriques et les points de vue experimentaux, les nécessités cliniques et les exigences scientifiques de la statistique".

The first re-analysis of Webb's material, and the only one to make a genuine contribution to its understanding, was carried out by Garnett in 1918. His paper, which in its statistical development anticipates much of what was to become important later, such as the geometrical representation of patterns of correlations in terms of scalar products and the rotation of factor axes, used these methods to show that in addition to "g" and "w" another factor was contained in Webb's table of intercorrelations. This he called "c", because he conceived of this factor as being characterized by the trait of *clever-*

ness; seldom can brilliant mathematical treatment have resulted in a less appropriate naming of the factor discovered!

This will become apparent when we study the traits characteristic of "*c*" in both its positive and its negative aspects. On the positive side we have traits like cheerfulness, æsthetic feeling, sense of humour, desire to excel, desire to impose one's will, desire to be liked by one's associates, impulsive kindness, wideness of influence, and quickness of apprehension; on the negative side we have liability to extreme depression, unsociableness, lack of corporate spirit, tactlessness, little bodily activity, and pure-mindedness. This factor in many ways resembles the *primary* and *secondary function* of Heymans and Wiersma, or Jung's extraversion-introversion, and thus brings into fair agreement the results obtained by all the investigators mentioned so far.

Another re-analysis of Webb's data has been carried out by McCloy (1936), using the multiple-factor technique. He also carried out an independent factorial study of 43 traits on 31 students. The reliability of his ratings is claimed to be high. The first factor found in his own work is very similar to the first factor found in his re-analysis of Webb's data, and is closely related to "*w*". In his study, it is made up of the following traits: trustworthiness, vitality, thoroughness, sociability, respectful of rights of others, resourcefulness, courage, personality, perseverance, loyalty, leadership, integrity, and character. (The influence of the halo effect seems to be much more strongly in evidence here than in Webb's study.) The second factor in McCloy's study vaguely resembles the *c*+ traits of Garnett's analysis, being characterized by aggressiveness, initiative, self-confidence, adaptiveness, conviction, enthusiasm, energy, and lack of modesty.

Reyburn and Taylor (1939) also re-analysed Webb's data, using only 19 traits from Webb's student sample. They extracted four factors, of which, however, only the first two ("*w*" and "*c*") are very meaningful. "*w*" in their analysis is characterized on its positive side by a tendency not to abandon a task in the face of obstacles, or for mere changeability, trustworthiness, conscientiousness, and tendency to do kindness on principle. Absence of "*w*" is characterized by the absence of these traits as well as by a readiness to become angry, an occasional liability to extreme anger, and the lack of permanence of mood, i.e. by qualities to which Heymans and Wiersma would apply the term "emotionality". In its positive aspects, "*c*" is characterized by sense of humour, fondness for large social gatherings, a general tendency to be cheerful, a high degree of corporate spirit, and a high degree of bodily activity and pursuit of pleasure.

In its negative aspects, "*c*" is characterized by occasional liability to extreme depression and conscientiousness. This analysis is probably the best that has been carried out on Webb's data and, interestingly enough, it shows the closest similarity to the Heymans and Wiersma data, as well as to a great deal of work reported elsewhere in this book.

Another research must be mentioned here, as it was carried out at about the same time as Webb's. Unfortunately, the report of this study, which was carried out by Burt (1915), is far too short and incomplete to make any judgment of its value possible. It appears that 172 children from 9–12, as well as another group of 329 adults and children (which may or may not have included the original group), formed part of this investigation. They were rated on 11 traits, which were adapted from McDougall's list of primary emotions. The author claims that the data give rise to a factor of general emotionality, which presumably would be similar to Heyman's and Wiersma's factor of the same name, but it is impossible to place much reliance on this interpretation, as it is not clear whether age was held constant in the children's group, whether I.Q. was properly taken into account, and as the method of carrying out the ratings is not described in sufficient detail.

Burt has returned to a discussion of his system in a recent popular account (1939) in which he deals with the relation between this factor of emotionality, which he labels "*e*", and Webb's "*w*". He says: "So far as they overlap, my factor is the negative of his. Anything making for emotional instability must, *ipso facto*, hinder the steadiness or persistence of moral motives." Similarly, Gibb (1942) concludes from an examination of the evidence that "the major difference between '*w*' and '*e*' may be summed up by saying that '*e*' is the inverse of '*w*'. The former is emotional instability, the latter is stability or persistence."

Another study by the same writer (Burt, 1937) is of great statistical interest as it reports a comparison of the results of factor analysis by correlating persons and correlating traits. Eleven problem children were rated on 11 traits, again derived from McDougall's list of instincts: anger, assertiveness, sociability, curiosity, joy, sex, disgust, tenderness, sorrow, fear, and submissiveness, and correlations run between traits and also between persons. Three factors were extracted, the first of which was called *general emotionality*, the second appeared to be a bipolar factor opposing the aggressive to the inhibited emotions, and the third another bipolar factor opposing the pleasurable to the unpleasurable emotions. While these results would fit in quite well with the data we have analysed so far, it is difficult to accept them as they stand. The children were extremely highly selected from a larger group of 124 children, who themselves were selected from a still larger one of 500. We do not know what influence this high degree of selectivity may have had, nor do we know anything about the adequacy of the ratings which, in view of the somewhat outmoded list of traits presented to the raters, cannot be accepted without a certain degree of doubt. But one's major reservation must be with respect to the statistical treatment. It is clearly impossible, in view of the very high standard of errors of correlations based on 11 cases, to extract more than one statistically significant factor. Burt has tried to avoid this difficulty by taking his estimate of the probable error from the total group of 124 cases of which the 11 children analysed were claimed to be a representative sample. It is also claimed that inter-correlations for the total group of 124 children were similar to those of the 11. However, correlations for the larger group are not given, and it is impossible to evaluate this claim. Even if it were justified, however, it would clearly be inadmissible to base standard errors for the group analysed on the number of cases in a group not being analysed. It would clearly have been much more satisfactory to have given the straightforward analysis of the total group of 124 children, and the results given in this article must be regarded in the main as an illustration of a statistical method rather than as a contribution to the analysis of temperament.

Much the same must be said of Burt's report on "A Distribution of Temperamental Types" in his book *The Factors of the Mind* (1940). Here, again, the actual figures given refer to a group of 12 persons only. He extracts two factors, the first one identified as "general emotionality" or "emotional instability", the second marking the difference between the sthenic, aggressive, unrepressed, or extra-verted type, and the asthenic, inhibited, repressed, or introverted type. Burt, after giving the detailed figures, goes on to say: "It is interesting to note that in their concrete nature, the several factors obtained from the small group of adults tally with those of the larger group of children", and gives as a reference the article we have discussed above.[1]

[1] It is not quite clear how we can reconcile this reference to a *larger* group of children with the fact that the analysis was carried out only on a small sample of 11 children, i.e. one less than the small sample of 12 adults; presumably, Burt is referring here to the total group of 124 children, of whom the 11 are only a sample, but of course this larger group was only referred to in his paper and no actual figures regarding it are given.

Quite recently, Burt (1948) has published two tables of correlations dealing respectively with 328 neurotic or unstable children, and with 483 normal children. These children, the majority of whom were between 9 and 13 years of age, were rated again for a number of McDougall's "primary emotions", that of "comfort" apparently being added to the 11 mentioned above. These ratings were carried out in the main by teachers, although the exact procedure is not described. The results from this study appear to be in agreement with Burt's earlier conclusions; a first factor of general emotionality, or instability, is followed by a bipolar factor dividing the emotions into a "sthenic" (or demonstrative) group and an "asthenic" (or inhibited) group. A third factor, also adumbrated in previous researches, divides the emotions into those accompanied by pleasurable and unpleasurable feeling tone respectively. These are the results from the normal group; those from the neurotic group are claimed to be roughly similar but certain interesting differences appear. The instability factor only accounts for just over half as much of the total variance in the neurotic group, compared with the normal, and the relative size of the factor saturations shows a different order altogether. Burt suggests that: "These features could readily be accounted for as the effects of selection. Elsewhere I have shown that the most conspicuous feature distinguishing the psycho-neurotic child from the normal is his increased emotional instability. Evidently, therefore, in selecting psycho-neurotic cases we have been taking cases from the upper end of the scale of general emotionality. The effect of this must be to curtail the range of variation for the general factor; hence the factor coefficients are automatically diminished." This argument possesses a certain superficial plausibility as far as the change in percentage of variance accounted for is concerned, although it has usually been found that correlations increase rather than decrease when taken on neurotic as compared with normal samples. However, no recourse can be had to selection in explaining the failure of the factor saturations for the two samples to correlate significantly with each other, and it is difficult to see how Burt can identify two factors with each other when the correlation between these two factors is not significantly different from zero.[1]

His previous third factor, which distinguished pleasurable from

---

[1] One's faith in Burt's correct identification of his factors must be considerably diminished by his failure to take into account such obvious discrepancies. The trait having the highest saturation for one group actually has the lowest saturation for the other; yet Burt considers the two factors identical!

unpleasurable emotions, does not appear at all in this table in a statistically significant form. The extravert-introvert factor does appear again rather more strongly than before. Also, a new factor appears amongst neurotic children, to which Burt, however, does not give a name. These differences in analyses carried out on normal and neurotic children are interesting but difficult to interpret in view of lack of information regarding the methods used for obtaining the ratings. The failure of the two analyses to agree at all closely, except with reference to the introvert-extravert factor, must make one rather doubtful about the adequacy of the research design.

The next author whose work has important bearings on our general problem is Cattell (1933, 1934). We will discuss first his early contribution; his later work forms a separate section. Having made a thorough search of the literature, he put together 28 pairs of opposites denoting traits supposedly characteristic of introverts, schizothymes, anal neurotics, and persons suffering from inferiority complexes. He also added others from studies of "w" and "c", as well as an I.Q. test, ending up with 48 items in all. Four judges were used to rate subjects on these traits; reliabilities (2 vs. 2 judges) ranged from ·12 to ·72. His statistical analysis is a complex mixture of cluster analysis and Spearman's method of tetrads, and it may be said to have resulted in a confirmation of the "c" and "w" factors, as well as in his finding of a third factor which he calls "a" and which in his view resembles schizothymia. The traits characteristic of "a" are secretiveness, pessimism, stinginess, subjectiveness, effectlessness, lack of trust, formality, lack of emotionality, and extremism.[1] The "c" factor was renamed by him as a factor of "surgency", and its two aspects therefore received the designation of "surgent" and "desurgent".

Cattell tried to go beyond the field of ratings and link up scores on objective tests of perseveration with "w". We shall be concerned in more detail with the measurement of perseveration in a later chapter, so we may just note here that his work confirmed Pinard's (1932) demonstration of a curvilinear relation between "p" and "w", somewhat as shown in Fig. 7. Other objective tests used by him include tests of fluency; speed of writing, of decision, of walking, and of reading comprehension; oscillation (reversal of perspective); and the psycho-galvanic reflex. Correlations between personality factors and these tests tended to be low, with possible indications that the

---

[1] These traits resemble the "prepsychotic" factor discussed by Moore and his students; their work is reviewed on p. 253.

surgent type tended to be more fluent and to have higher speeds in the speed tests as well as quicker oscillation.

Much later than these early studies of Cattell's, but essentially in the same tradition, is a recent analysis by Howie (1945). This study of ratings of personal qualities on a group of 295 12–14-year-old schoolboys required teachers to make ratings on 10 traits: bodily activity, perseverance, excitability, quickness of intelligence, cheerfulness, mental activity, common sense, continuity of interest, initiative, and self-consciousness. Four factors were extracted by the author from the table of intercorrelations, of which the first one in his view is strongly coloured by the scholastic background in which the ratings took place. The second and third factors he identifies respectively with "w" and "c". The fourth factor, which is perhaps

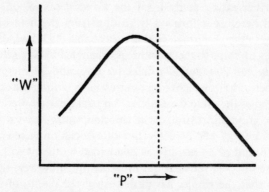

Fig. 7.—Curvilinear Relationship between "p" and "w".

of doubtful significance, contrasts, in Howie's view, excitability and placidity, and may remind the reader of Heyman's and Wiersma's "activity" factor.

Another study of children (50 children, 156 months of age on the average) was carried out in 1929 by Sister McDonough. The children were rated on 34 traits by three teachers with a mean average inter-correlation of ·72. They were also given the Woodworth-Cady questionnaire, which was found to correlate − ·38 with the ratings on stability. This study is noteworthy for its unusual carefulness in the organization of the ratings, although some of the traits rated, such as religiousness, are somewhat unusual and reflect the institutional background of the author. Using Kelley's method of analysis, Sister McDonough extracted four main factors, which were considered to represent *will*, *cheerfulness*, *sociability*, and *sthenic emotionality*. Brogden (1944) re-analysed her data and emerged with four factors, the first two of which were highly correlated however ($r_{12} = \cdot766$). In so far as these two correlated factors do not measure halo effect, they may be considered analogous to Webb's "*w*" factor, being characterized by such traits as reliability, will, self-control, stability, lack of emotionality, and lack of the following qualities: forwardness, quarrelsomeness, conceit, irritability, impulsiveness, expressiveness, and tendency to look for sympathy. The third factor was most highly loaded on intelligence and lack of credulity, and is obviously an intellectual one. The last factor is remarkably similar to Garnett's "*c*", surgency, or extraversion, being characterized by a tendency to be affectionate, sympathetic, sociable, cheerful, contented, humorous, and lacking in self-consciousness.

One further rating study from the London school ought to be mentioned here, as it forms a transition from the field of normal personality to the abnormal. In this study Sahai (1931) was interested in following up some of the hypotheses originated by Kretschmer, and accordingly had 200 mentally defective boys and 50 students rated on a number of traits which from Kretschmer's writings he considered to be typical of the cycloid character. The traits chosen were: "frank, humorous, grateful, trustful, cyclic emotion, warm-hearted, sociable, and enjoys gifts of life". Coefficients of association were calculated, and were found to be positive as demanded by the hypothesis. The tetrad criterion was satisfied but indifferently; however, the author concludes that the results have established the reality of a trait of "circular mentality" or extraversion. It would probably not be too fanciful to see a good deal of similarity between this pattern of traits and the uninhibited, sthenic, extraverted, *primary function* type. It should be noted that four other traits (suggestible, little tenacity of purpose, takes life easily, self-possessed), which had been hypothesized to form part of this syndrome, were found to give such low intercorrelations that they had to be excluded.

While Sahai's study is interesting in its use of psychiatric concepts, it fell to T. V. Moore (1930, 1933) to carry out for the first time "the empirical determination of certain syndromes underlying præcox and manic-depressive psychoses". Three hundred and sixty-seven patients were rated for the presence or absence of 41 symptoms. Tetrachorics were calculated between these 41 items, and the table analysed by a rather complex and cumbersome procedure. Eight factors in all were isolated; the names given to these, together with the main symptoms identifying them, are given below:

(1) Cognitive defect: reasoning, perception, memory, shut-in personality.
(2) Catatonic: mutism, negativistic, refusal of food, stereotypism of attitudes.
(3) Uninhibited: stereotypism of action; destructive, giggling, talking to voices.
(4) and (5) Manic: irritable, tantrums, destructive, euphoria. (This factor was divided in two by Moore, according to the presence or absence of euphoria.)
(6) Deluded-hallucinations: auditory hallucinations, bizarre delusions, disorientation, stereotypism of words.
(7) Constitutional-hereditary: lack of intelligence, depressed, tearful, previous attacks, insane relatives.
(8) Retarded-depressed: depressed, retarded, neurasthenic, suicidal.

These factors were themselves found to be intercorrelated, giving rise to two "second-order factors", as they would be called nowadays. One of these factors is made up of the catatonic, cognitive defect, uninhibited and deluded-hallucinated syndromes; the other of the retarded-depressed, constitutional-hereditary, and manic components. Presumably, the former second-order factor may be identified with schizophrenia, the latter with circular insanity. However, statistical methods of multiple-factor analysis were not sufficiently advanced in Moore's time to enable one to give much credence to all the details of his results.

Thurstone (1934) re-analysed Moore's data and arrived at a more satisfactory classification. He demonstrated the existence of five factors as follows:

(1) Catatonic: mutism, negativism, shut-in personality, stereotypism of actions, attitudes and words, giggling.
(2) Cognitive: logical fallacies, memory defect, perceptual defect, reasoning, disorientation.
(3) Manic: destructive, excited, irritable, tantrums.
(4) Hallucinatory: bizarre delusions, auditory and other hallucinations, speaking to voices.
(5) Depression: anxiety, depression, tearful, retardation of movement.

These factors are clearly more satisfactory than those advocated by Moore, and show that improvements in statistical technique can bring about clarification of personality description. It is a great pity that Moore's very stimulating and original work has not been repeated, using the outcome of his study (or rather of Thurstone's re-analysis of his study) as a starting-point for a number of rather definite hypotheses which could be confirmed or rejected.[1]

The only recent study comparable to Moore's original work is a paper by Wittenborn (1951) on symptom patterns in a group of mental hospital patients. Ratings were carried out on 140 patients, 50 rating scales being used in all. All of the patients were males, and varied considerably with respect to age, educational attainments, social status, cause of illness, and personality symptoms. Inter-correlations between these 50 sets of ratings were run and an ortho-gonal 7-factor solution produced. Wittenborn considers the solution relatively well defined and observes: "The fact that the clustering tendency is relatively clear-cut and that the factor loadings are high is encouraging to the purpose of this investigation, because it suggests that from an arithmetical standpoint it is possible to score an indivi-dual set of symptom-rating scales with respect to a limited number of factors."

Using only saturations above the arbitrary level of ·300, Witten-born found the following symptoms characteristic of factor one: unawareness of others' feelings; oppositional behaviour; deceptive behaviour; assaultive behaviour; incontinence; and inability to stick to a plan. Wittenborn identified this pattern with hebephrenic schizophrenia.

Factor two is considered reminiscent of Kraepelin's classical distinction between patients who are manic and patients who are depressed. There is a bipolar arrangement of the symptoms with respect to factor two, thus giving rise to two clusters. The manic cluster comprises the following symptoms: temper tantrums, loud-ness, attention-demanding behaviour, assaultive behaviour, fantastic thinking, exaggerated sense of well-being, feelings of persecution, and abrupt mood changes. The depressive cluster includes the following symptoms: gives in easily to others, avoids people, is incontinent, is very negative, shows little affective response, cannot make decisions, words not relevant to recognizable ideas, cannot stick to a plan, and has memory faults.

---

[1] A student of Moore's, J. T. Gannon (1939), has reported a rating study along similar lines on 123 normal students. His conclusions are difficult to interpret, however.

Guertin (1952) has also contributed an important analysis of 52 symptoms in 100 schizophrenics, finding six factors: excitement-hostility, psychomotor re-tardation and withdrawal, guilt-conflict, persecuted-suspicious, personality dis-organization, and confused-withdrawal. This paper appeared too late to be integrated with the text.

Factor three is characterized by conversion-type symptoms. "This combination of conversion-type symptoms with a *belle indifférence* and exaggerated affect is strongly suggestive of the type of patient diagnosed as hysterical or conversion hysteria." Factor four is identified as one of catatonic excitement and is characterized by the symptoms: spontaneous change in ideas, constant movement, compulsive acts, variations in rate of speech, memory faults, unrecognizable use of words, repudiation of earlier insights, insomnia, obsessions, unawareness of others, loudness, incontinence, delusional thinking, and hallucinations. The fifth factor is one of dysthymic disorder comprising as it does the following symptoms: insomnia, obsessive thinking, delusions of guilt, phobias, feelings of doom, subjectively experienced anxiety, suicidal attempts, fear of own behaviour, blocking and inability to carry out plans.

Factors six and seven are rather similar to each other, and are identified respectively as paranoid schizophrenia and paranoid condition. The main difference between factors six and seven is that in the latter obvious delusions and hallucinations are absent.[1]

This analysis is a clear advance on Moore's work, and is of considerable interest. In some ways it is regrettable that the author did not carry out an oblique solution with second-order factors, as this might have considerably clarified the factors emerging from his analysis. It is fairly clear that some of the factors, such as three and five for instance, may be subsumed under the more general heading of "neurosis", whereas other factors, for instance (1), (2), and (6), may be subsumed under the general heading of "psychosis". These more complex inter-actions could only be brought out by the type of analysis suggested, and are left rather in the air by Wittenborn's orthogonal method. In spite of these criticisms, Wittenborn's study is the most ambitious and the most acceptable of those dealing with ratings of symptom patterns in mental hospital patients.

Also dealing with abnormal subjects is a study by Eysenck (1944), which is based on a definite hypothesis derived from the studies reviewed so far and from the theories of Jung and McDougall. According to these writers, hysteria is a mental disorder to which extraverts are constitutionally predisposed; anxiety, reactive depression, psychasthenia, and other dysthymic traits are parts of a

---

[1] Two more recent papers by Wittenborn, Mandler, and Waterhouse (1951) and by Wittenborn, Bell, and Lesser (1951) show the applicability of this analysis to youthful mental hospital patients, but its insufficiency for organic patients of advanced age.

disorder to which introverts are constitutionally predisposed. Logically, this view may be broken down into two hypotheses: (1) people differ with respect to their position on a factor of extraversion-introversion, and (2) people differ with respect to their position on a factor of emotional instability or neuroticism. The hysterics, according to this view, would be the persons having a high score on neuroticism and a high score on extraversion; the dysthymics would be the persons having a high score on neuroticism and a high score on introversion.[1] Given a suitable set of ratings and subjects, it should be possible to verify the grouping of traits called for by this hypothesis.

Seven-hundred neurotic soldiers were selected from a total group of 1,000 by excluding all cases of epilepsy; cases where head injury formed part of the present illness; cases with previous organic illness of the central nervous system or with present signs of such illness; cases with organic mental syndromes; and cases where physical illness was an important factor. Ratings were obtained on 39 items, including one test of intelligence, and the intercorrelations between these items were submitted to a factor analysis. The first two factors extracted are plotted graphically in Fig. 8; it will be seen that we have here a clear verification of the hypothesis which inspired this study. The first factor, characterized by items such as badly organized personality, abnormal before illness, little energy, narrow interests, abnormality in parents, etc., is clearly one of emotional instability, or neuroticism, i.e. the opposite pole to "w"; the second factor opposes the introvert to the extravert group of traits, thus giving, in combination with the first factor, the typical picture on the one hand of the hysteric (conversion symptoms, sex anomalies, unskilled, hysterical attitude, degraded work history, low I.Q., narrow interests, little energy) and on the other of the dysthymic (anxiety, depression, obsessional traits, apathy, irritability, somatic anxiety, tremor, and effort intolerance). Two further factors of minor interest were obtained, but will not be discussed here.

An effort was also made by the same author (Eysenck, 1947) to verify another hypothesis, namely that distributions of people on these two factors were continuous and similar to a normal curve rather than bimodal. Distributions were plotted for 1,000 male and 1,000 female neurotics by a weighted combination of ratings for the various traits which go to make up these two factors. Distributions

[1] Hysterics would correspond to Heymans and Wiersma's *nervous* type, dysthymics to their *sentimental* type.

for both factors are closely similar to the normal curve of distribution, a result which is in good agreement with a similar demonstration by Burt on normal subjects (1940).

An independent confirmation of the existence of a neuroticism factor came in a study by Slater (1943), in which he intercorrelated, by means of tetrachoric correlations, notations on positive family history, childhood neurosis, poor work record, previous nervous breakdown, abnormal personality, and poor intelligence on 1,600 neurotic soldiers. Two factors were extracted, the first of which he

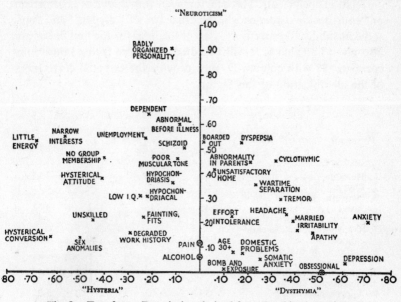

Fig. 8.—Two-factor Description derived from Psychiatric Ratings.

labelled "neurotic constitution"; this factor had loadings of ·82 on abnormal personality, ·66 on childhood neurosis, and ·59 on positive family history. The second factor was one of "inadequate intelligence" with loadings of ·49 on poor intelligence and ·59 on poor work record. (The hypothesis of neurotic constitution was further developed in another study by Slater and Slater (1944).)

The work of the Slater brothers was taken further in a large-scale study reported in three papers by Meyer Gross *et al.* (1949), Slater (1947), and Rao *et al.* (1949). Two hundred and one neurotic and 55 non-neurotic army officers were rated by a psychiatrist on 13 main behaviour "pointers"; ratings were confined to noting either the presence or the absence of the particular trait to be rated. A brief statement of the traits used is given in Table 6, together with the proportion of cases showing any of the traits in either the normal or the neurotic group. All the differences observed were found to be significant by means of a chi-squared analysis. Column D shows the observed differences in endorsements of each trait between the normal and the neurotic groups. A factor analysis was carried out on a table showing the frequency of concomitance of pairs of items, using a new method which does not require the conversion of these frequencies into correlation coefficients. Three factors were found, one of neuroticism or "constitutional adequacy", the other two of "shyness" and "episodic instability" respectively. Factor loadings for the first factor are also given in Table 6. It will be noted that these factor saturations correlate ·88 with column D, thus proving the essential correctness of the identification of this factor.

TABLE 6

Personality "Pointer" Rated:	Per cent Incidence:		D:	Factor Loadings[1]:
	Neurotics	Normals		
1. Heredity . . .	·41	·13	76	2·13
2. Physical ill-health . .	·27	·00	54	2·11
3. Neurotic traits in childhood	·45	·16	82	4·62
4. Former psychiatric illness	·37	·05	71	3·45
5. Shy, solitary, etc., in childhood . . .	·40	·11	74	3·96
6. Difficulty in making social contacts . . .	·33	·07	62	3·28
7. Emotional instability .	·73	·09	141	4·42
8. Obsessional features .	·37	·13	67	1·74
9. Apprehensiveness .	·59	·02	117	5·25
10. Dependence . . .	·53	·04	105	4·61
11. Unstable word record .	·23	·07	43	2·00
12. Marriage or sexual difficulties	·34	·05	65	2·81
13. Alcoholism . . .	·21	·00	42	·57

Scores were derived for the three factors extracted by noting the number of "pointers" of each class for each individual, thus obtaining three scores (a, b, and c) for each individual. These three variables were considered as defining a space of three dimensions in which any particular individual could be presented by a point. Groups of individuals could then be represented by a cluster of points around the mean value of that cluster.

[1] Values of p' $i\sqrt{n}$ obtained directly from a matrix of 2×2 tables on the assumption of a general factor and two group factors.

As the neurotic members of the sample used in this investigation had been diagnosed into one of five syndromes (psychopathy, obsession, hysteria, anxiety state, post-traumatic personality change), it was possible to use these psychiatric groupings in order to test the hypothesis that differences between these syndromes were due entirely to differences in severity of neurosis without any other principle of differentiation. The appropriate test for this hypothesis consisted in showing that the mean values of the groups in question were collinear in the three-dimensional test space, and tests of significance showed that this was indeed the case. Reasons for this failure to find any other factors may lie in the original choice of variables and the unreliability of the ratings, or in the condensation of 13 variables into only three factors. We do not consider that the failure of the writers to disprove the null hypothesis should necessarily be taken to mean that no differences exist between various psychiatric syndromes, except in severity of disorder. This view seems to be shared by the writers, because they went on to calculate from their material the first two canonical variates and to plot the position of the various groups in the two-dimensional space thus generated. The first component (severity of neurosis) ranks the groups in order from normal to obsessional and psychopathic. The second component, although not significant statistically, produces a grouping closely in conformity with the one suggested by preceding work. The main division indicated by the second component is between the hysteric, psychopathic group on the one hand and the anxious, obsessional (dysthymic) group on the other.

A repetition of this study on larger numbers of cases (there are only 17 cases in the obsessional group for instance and only 5 in the "personality change" group) would be of great interest, particularly as the method of canonical variates used by these writers differs in many ways from the factorial methods used by other authors, and has possibilities which ought not to be neglected. In its main outcome, this experiment supports the conclusions of Eysenck's study.

Up to this point we have been concerned almost exclusively with studies carried out by members of the London school. We must now turn to a variety of experiments reported mostly by adherents of the Thurstone school. In dealing with the exponents of multiple-factor analysis, we must, of course, expect a certain change in tone and emphasis. We would expect, for instance, to find a much larger number of factors extracted from each matrix; we must expect to find that the more general factors dealt with by the London school (neuroticism and introversion-extraversion) will emerge, if at all, only as second-order factors; we may expect, finally, that these studies will throw more light on the combinations of behaviour units at the trait level (i.e. the "group factors" as opposed to the "general factors") than has been the case in the studies already reviewed. However, it would not be correct to say that all the work to be discussed in the following pages has made use of Thurstone's methods of analysis; some of the most interesting contributions have been made by writers who used factorial techniques of a much less systematic type, mainly some variety of cluster analysis, and these writers have, on the whole, come closer in their emphasis to the work already described.

Historically, pride of place goes to Kelley (1934), who used tests and ratings for such traits as courtesy, anxiety, loyalty, mastery, poise, and fair-play with groups of children. Using his own method of analysis, he isolated two traits, one of social conformity, the other of individualism or assertiveness, which may or may not be identifiable with "w" and "c". The traits used are too unlike those of other investigations to arrive at any reasonable conclusion.

Simultaneously with Kelley's work was published an important paper by Thurstone (1934), in which 1,300 raters each rated one subject on 60 traits. Multiple-factor analysis disclosed five main factors: (1) friendly, congenial, broad-minded, generous, cheerful; (2) patient, calm, faithful, earnest; (3) persevering, hard-working, systematic; (4) capable, frank, self-reliant, courageous; (5) self-important, sarcastic, haughty, grasping, cynical, quick-tempered. This study, like Kelley's, appears to be mainly of historical interest. Its results are difficult to interpret, and might be more intelligible if the analysis were repeated using oblique and second-order factors.

Equally difficult to interpret are the results from another pioneer study. In the monograph which introduces his method of "orthometric analysis", Tryon (1939) has analysed a table giving the intercorrelations between 20 personality ratings on 170 12-year-old boys in which each child's score in a given trait is a pooled rating by his companions. Five clusters were isolated which he labels respectively "disordered aggressiveness, hyperactivity, buoyancy, ascendancy, and likeableness". These clusters leave over several *residual variables* which do not fit in well with any of the groups. A correlation table containing these clusters and residual variables was formed and analysed, showing that disordered aggressiveness and hyperactivity correlate highly together, while the other three traits also form a definite group. These two "second-order clusters" Tryon called "social tenseness" and "approved sociability". Tryon's method of analysis is not such as to make interpretation easy, and no attempt will be made here to assimilate his findings to those of other writers. It is hoped that his table of intercorrelations will be re-analysed by one of the more orthodox procedures, as it is one of the few examples of peer ratings among children.[1]

Another early study should be mentioned in this connection, although neither its design nor its results appear to shed very much light on the organization of personality (Tschechtelin, 1944). The Tschechtelin 22-trait Personality Rating Scale was administered to 300 children, and the average ratings of each trait for these 300 children by 8 classmates were used as a basis for tetrachoric correlations. Four factors were extracted from the table of intercorrelations and rotated. Factor I had relatively heavy loadings on good sportsmanship, entertaining, courtesy, dependability, boisterousness, punctuality, and intelligence. Factor II had loadings of six traits—sociability, pep, nervousness, intelligence, popularity, and disposition. Factor III seemed restricted to co-operativeness, with small loadings of sociability and punctuality: while Factor IV had one high loading only, namely for persistence. It had small loadings also for neatness, disposition, sense of humour, honesty, interest, and thoughtfulness. It is doubtful if these factors are very meaningful. No attempt will here be made to interpret them. The methodology of this study does not seem to make any crucial results appear very likely to emerge from the hodge-podge of traits rated or from the particular type of rating used.

A useful study by Rexroad (1937) is more strictly comparable with those analysed in the first part of this chapter. Ten traits were rated in 100 women students by faculty members, and the intercorrelations gave rise to three factors, of which the first one appeared to be one of general adjustment, corresponding to the "w" factor, whereas the second contrasted classroom interests with out-of-class situations, apparently an introvert versus extravert dichotomy. The actual traits involved in this dichotomy were, on the one hand, mastery of subject-matter, original ideas, independent working, seeing broader relations, of course material, as opposed, on the other hand, to social life, favourable impression socially, original ideas, and initiative out of class. The third factor, contrasting the "plodder" and the "gifted" scholar, is of doubtful significance and of little interest.

[1] A more accessible account of this study is given by Tryon (1943).

Of particular interest is a paper by Maurer (1941), using Thurstone's method to discover the patterns of behaviour of young children. Fifty women raters each rated one child (aged between 4 and 6) on a list of 50 adjectives. Tetrachoric correlations were run on 26 of these and three factors extracted. Thurstone's correction for uniqueness was applied and the clusters resulting from the analysis plotted. Fig. 9 shows the resulting diagrammatic picture of Maurer's result.

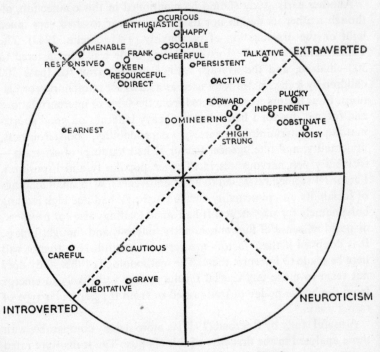

Fig. 9.—Representation of Maurer's Results.

Superimposed on her factor pattern, we have drawn two axes rotated through an angle of about 45°. When this is done, it will be seen that her results agree very closely with the general scheme found in so many other studies. The second quadrant contains qualities characteristic of "w", thus leaving the fourth quadrant as being characteristic of neuroticism. Qualities in the first quadrant (talkative, active, forward, independent, noisy, plucky) are typical of the extraverted, surgent, $c+$ personality, whereas those in the third quadrant (careful, cautious, grave, meditative) are characteristic of the desurgent, $c-$, introverted personality. It is of particular importance to find that these general dimensions of personality can be recognized and rated already at such an early age.

A quite recent study by Reyburn and Raath (1950) illustrates the possibility of arriving at factors similar to those discussed in the preceding pages by means of oblique and second-order factors. The total experimental population consisted of 160 ratees, evenly balanced with respect to sex and university education. Eighty-three observers were used to rate two subjects each on a five-point scale, covering altogether 45 well-defined personality traits. The actual ratings were

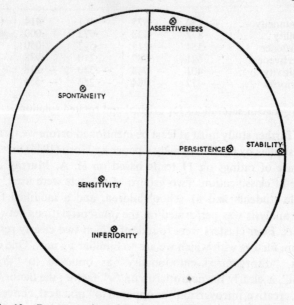

Fig. 10.—Representation of Reyburn and Raath Factorial Pattern.

gone over in each case with the rater by one of the experimenters to ensure proper understanding of the categories used. Oblique factors were extracted from the table of intercorrelations; these six factors show considerable intercorrelations. These intercorrelations clearly give rise to higher order factors, which have been extracted by Eysenck (1952). The results are set out in Fig. 10 and Table 7. The first factor has a saturation of ·972 for stability. This identifies it clearly with "*w*" and as the opposite end of neuroticism. Persistence is found closely associated with stability, and assertiveness also has a slight positive projection on this factor. Inferiority feeling and sensitivity are understandably loaded negatively on this factor. The second factor opposes assertiveness and spontaneity to inferiority and sensitivity. This agrees well with the hypothesis that the second factor is extraversion-introversion. We thus get a very interesting confirmation here for our view of "neuroticism" and "introversion-extraversion" as second-order factors in the orectic sphere, corresponding to Thurstone's second-order factor in the cognitive sphere.

TABLE 7

	I	II	I′	II″	h^2
1. Spontaneity .	− ·230	·575	− ·461	·414	·387
2. Stability .	·872	− ·428	·972	·000	·945
3. Persistence .	·554	− ·215	·592	·050	·353
4. Assertiveness .	·621	·789	·210	·978	1·001
5. Sensitivity .	− ·401	− ·044	− ·340	− ·218	·163
6. Inferiority .	− ·472	− ·384	−· 256	− ·554	·372

Factor saturations for original and rotated solutions.

One further study must at least be mentioned before we turn to the recent studies by Cattell, namely a paper by Horn (1944) in which he made use of ratings on 11 traits based on H. A. Murray's (1938) scheme of classification. Two groups of subjects were used, namely 28 male students and 41 schoolchildren, and a modified form of cluster analysis was performed on the intercorrelations between the 11 traits. Four clusters were found, of which two clearly resembled the main factors with which we are so familiar by now. One of these factors, "disorganized emotionality" as opposed to "organized control", is clearly the neuroticism or "w" factor; the factor "imaginative, creative, introversion" as opposed to "practical, conventional, extraversion" shows great similarity to the usual bipolar "c" factor. The two other clusters are more difficult to reconcile with previous work. One of them contrasts "creative expressiveness" to "apathetic conventionality", whereas the other is characterized by "unorganized expressiveness".

Among writers using ratings in order to arrive at a descriptive scheme of personality, none has been more persistent and ingenious in his quest than Cattell, and a detailed review and criticism of his work can hardly be avoided in a book such as this. To begin with, Cattell recognizes the difficulty which many other writers have glossed over in their attempts to discover the principal factors in terms of which human behaviour can best be described. "The first and greatest theoretical difficulty in the path of this enterprise consists in finding a basis for testing when the chosen population of traits is truly comprehensive. In what way can one ensure that all aspects of personality are taken into account in the trait-element list?" This question of sampling within the field of traits is probably as crucial as the problem of sampling within the field of subjects tested, yet it has received very little in the way of attempts at a proper solution. Cattell introduces the concept of the personality sphere which "may be considered to present a complete surface constituted by many small 'trait areas', each trait area defined by a trait term and abutting on traits most closely resembling it, the whole constituting an endless but finite continuum of behaviour meaning. If trait character is represented by direction as in factor-analytic representation, the sphere must be considered as one in n-dimensional space. There is no guarantee, in the axioms of this formal system, that the trait terms in languages will be absolutely evenly distributed over the spherical surface. Intercorrelation must decide the actual closeness of different trait-term areas. However, it is part of our assumption from the study of language that no large area is completely neglected by vocabulary, and that all dimensions of personality receive some representation."

Taking his departure from Allport and Odbert's (1936) list of some 4,500 trait terms in the English language, Cattell (1943), by throwing together "terms which any average user of the language would consider synonymous", reduced the list to about 160 terms. Various additions raised this total number to 171 traits, most of which were listed in the form of pairs of polar opposites. This list was further reduced to 50 nuclear clusters by a review of previous researches; Cattell is quite conscious of the fact that a good deal of subjectivity must enter into each of these steps, and particularly the last one. For his actual empirical study, Cattell further reduced the number of clusters to 35, which were then rated on a male population with a mean age of 30 years. The number of subjects included was 208; this large group was divided into 13 small groups of 16 men each. Ratings'and correlations were carried out independently for each of these groups, and the coefficients then averaged to obtain the correlation matrix for the factor analysis. This factor analysis resulted in what Cattell calls "the 12 primary source traits of personality".

Factor A: Cyclothymia versus Schizothymia. Good-natured, easy-going, natural, friendly, open, out-going, co-operative, adaptable, cheerful, good-tempered, as opposed to anti-social, surly, spiteful, tight-fisted, rigid, vindictive, unhappy, frustrated, dour, and hostile.

Factor B: Intelligence, General Mental Capacity versus Mental Defect. This is an intellectual factor and may presumably be equated with "*g*".[1] The main interest of this factor lies in the fact that the items stable, integrated character, are found to go together with intelligence; this correlation has been confirmed in other studies as well.

Factor C: Emotionally Mature, Stable Character versus Demoralized, General Emotionality. Realistic, stable, integrated, calm, self-effacing, emotionally mature, thoughtful, stoic, reserved, unemotional versus demoralized, changeable, characterless, infantile, demanding, self-centred, changeable, frivolous, emotionally maladjusted.

Factor D: Hypersensitive, Infantile, Sthenic Emotionality versus Phlegmatic Frustration Tolerance.

Factor E: Dominance versus Submissiveness.

Factor F: Surgency versus Agitated, Melancholic Desurgency. Cheerful, witty, sociable, hearty, talkative, responsive, genial, good-tempered, imaginative versus unhappy, melancholic, seclusive, shy, introspective, aloof, cold, and hostile.

Factor G: Positive Character Integration versus Immature Dependent Character. Mature, strong-willed, conscientious, realistic, emotionally mature, stable, integrated character versus dependent, impulsive, neurotic, changeable, infantile, dominant, self-centred, characterless, and unrealistic. (This factor is so similar to "C" that it is difficult to see any difference between them.)

Factor H: Charitable, Adventurous Cyclothymia versus Obstructive, Withdrawn Schizophrenia.

Factor I: Sensitive, Imaginative, Anxious Emotionality versus Rigid, Tough Poise.

Factor J: Neurasthenia versus Vigorous, "Obsessional Determination" Character.

Factor K: Trained, Socialized, Cultured Mind versus Boorishness.

Factor L: Surgent Cyclothymia versus Paranoia.

It will be clear that several of the factors described are simply renamed versions of those we have encountered before. Factors B and K may be identified as general intellectual ability; factors C and G as emotional stability, or the obverse of neuroticism; factors A, H, and L resemble the introvert-extravert dichotomy; factor E may also form part of this complex. These interpretations are supported by a re-analysis of the same data carried out by Cattell, in which he adopted a somewhat more rigid application of the simple structure

[1] This interpretation is borne out by objective tests of intelligence administered to 108 subjects out of the total group.

principle and arrived at a smaller number of factors. "G" and "C" coalesced into one factor, as did "B" and "K"; "A", "H", and "L" also coalesced into one factor. Cattell prefers the original analysis into 12 factors. The present writer, for reasons to be given presently, considers the later analysis to be more satisfactory.

It is possible, of course, that any attempt to identify these first-order factors of Cattell's with any of the more general factors isolated in previous work is doomed to failure, and that what we should be examining would be the second-order factors extracted from the intercorrelations of the 12 first-order factors. We are much more likely to find neuroticism and introversion-extraversion in such an analysis, just as Thurstone succeeded in finding an intellectual "g" factor, which emerged as a second-order factor from the inter-correlations between his primary mental abilities. A second-order factor analysis has been carried out by Cattell (1947), and the results bear out our anticipation. The first super-factor has much the highest loading on emotional stability, followed by dominance, character integration, and general ability. There can be little doubt that this represents "w", or the obverse of neuroticism. The second factor is not so clearly marked. "The second factor . . . is best viewed in its negative aspect. There it loads highly J (vigorous obsessional character), the simple and the paranoid-schizoid factors, A and L, trained mind, K, and desurgency, F, opposing are neurasthenic, cyclothyme, surgent, and possibly emotional stability. . . . The picture is that of a tense as opposed to a lax mind." This factor certainly has similarities with introversion-extraversion, but we cannot definitely assume identity.

In another publication Cattell (1948) has reported a rating study of 240 undergraduate women students of an average age of about 21 years. Eleven factors were extracted from the table of intercorrelations of 36 rated variables, one of which was an intelligence test. By and large, these factors are similar to those given in the previous analysis of male subjects. "C" and "G" appear again, but this time as factors 1 and 3, to mark the opposite pole to neuroticism. "A" and "F" again appear to make up the introvert-extravert dichotomy, and "K" and "B" show unmistakable similarities to general intellectual ability.

The analysis of these data was repeated by Banks (1948). She showed that four or at most five factors could significantly be extracted from the matrix of intercorrelations, and her interpretation of the factors extracted by her is as follows. The first factor she considers to be analogous to neuroticism [1] or emotional instability. Two bipolar factors are identified with extraversion-introversion and with a tendency to pleasurable or unpleasurable emotions respectively. The remaining two factors contribute little to the total variance and do not appear very meaningful.

These different sets of solutions to the problem posed by the observed matrix of intercorrelations may make the reader cautious and little inclined to accept any one of them as definitive, and he may wish to enquire as to the reasons for the seemingly disparate results. No conclusive answer can be given, but the following reasons appear to the writer sufficient to account for most of the discrepancies.

(1) Cattell's method of analysis, taken over from Thurstone, exaggerates the size of the communalities and consequently the number of the factors, a point acknowledged by Cattell himself. Some of the smaller of Cattell's factors might disappear if, instead of using the highest correlation in each column as indicating the self-correlation for the first factor, and the highest residual as indicating the required figure for later factors, Cattell were to keep communalities to the minimum values required to yield the minimum number of factors.

(2) The method used by Cattell results in oblique factors, i.e. in traits which are themselves correlated. Such an analysis is incomplete unless supplemented by a second-order factor analysis which accounts for the intercorrelations between primary factors. An analysis such as that carried out by Banks, on the other hand, extracts what are in effect approximations to these second-order factors first before extracting what may be regarded as approximations to Cattell's primary factors. A discussion of the relative value of these two approaches has already been given; it seems reasonable to assume that the two methods of analysis would have shown greater agreement if Cattell had extracted second-order factors in this study as he did in the previous one discussed above.

(3) In spite of marked differences created by the different approaches, there are consistent similarities between the solutions to which attention has been drawn throughout. Thus, the variables defining emotional instability, or neuroticism, appear almost identical in both solutions, and the same may be said of those variables defining introversion-extraversion. We cannot be certain of any of

[1]"Using that term in its ordinary sense to designate a lack of balanced personality arising from emotional causes."

the other factors, but with them also, a repetition of the work, together with a more complete analysis of the data, may bring a great deal of clarification.

We must turn now to a number of studies using various types of "cluster" analysis. One of the most systematic studies in this field has been that of Sheldon (1942). He began by collecting a list of 650 alleged traits of temperament, most of which were supposedly related to introversion or extraversion. After several revisions and a thorough study of some 30 students by means of a series of analytic interviews, the number of traits used was considerably reduced to 22, which appeared to fall into three main clusters. Traits in each of these clusters showed consistently positive intercorrelations among themselves and consistently negative correlations with the traits of each of the other clusters. Further traits were added to these clusters, until finally each cluster was made up of 20 traits altogether. These clusters were labelled "viscerotonia", "somatotonia", and "cerebrotonia" respectively, as they seemed to deal respectively with the functional predominance of the digestive viscera, the functional and anatomical predominance of the somatic structures, and the prepotency of the higher centres of the nervous system. (The linking up of the clusters of traits with bodily functions is apparent, and will be discussed in a later chapter.) The actual traits making up each cluster are given in Table 8.

TABLE 8

The Scale for Temperament

I VISCEROTONIA	II SOMATOTONIA	III CEREBROTONIA
( ) 1. Relaxation in posture and movement	( ) 1. Assertiveness of posture and movement	( ) 1. Restraint in posture and movement, tightness
( ) 2. Love of physical comfort	( ) 2. Love of physical adventure	— 2. Physiological over-response
( ) 3. Slow reaction	( ) 3. The energetic characteristic	( ) 3. Overly fast reactions
— 4. Love of eating	( ) 4. Need of enjoyment and exercise	( ) 4. Love of privacy
— 5. Socialization of eating	— 5. Love of dominating, lust for power	( ) 5. Mental overintensity, hyper-attentionality, apprehensiveness

TABLE 8—*continued*

I VISCEROTONIA	II SOMATOTONIA	III CEREBROTONIA
— 6. Pleasure in digestion	( ) 6. Love of risk and chance	( ) 6. Secretiveness of feeling, emotional restraint
( ) 7. Love of polite ceremony	( ) 7. Bold directness of manner	( ) 7. Self-conscious motility of the eyes and face
( ) 8. Sociophilia	( ) 8. Physical courage for combat	( ) 8. Sociophobia
— 9. Indiscriminate amiability	( ) 9. Competitive aggressiveness	( ) 9. Inhibited social address
— 10. Greed for affection and approval	— 10. Psychological callousness	— 10. Resistance to habit, and poor routinizing
— 11. Orientation to people	— 11. Claustrophobia	— 11. Agoraphobia
( ) 12. Evenness of emotional flow	— 12. Ruthlessness, freedom from squeamishness	— 12. Unpredictability of attitude
( ) 13. Tolerance	( ) 13. The unrestrained voice	( ) 13. Vocal restraint, and general restraint of noise
( ) 14. Complacency	— 14. Spartan indifference to pain	— 14. Hypersensitivity to pain
— 15. Deep sleep	— 15. General noisiness	— 15. Poor sleep habits, chronic fatigue
( ) 16. The untempered characteristic	( ) 16. Overmaturity of appearance	( ) 16. Youthful intentness of manner
( ) 17. Smooth, easy communication of feeling, extraversion of viscerotonia	— 17. Horizontal mental cleavage, extraversion of somatotonia	— 17. Vertical mental cleavage, introversion
— 18. Relaxation and sociophilia under alcohol	— 18. Assertiveness and aggression under alcohol	— 18. Resistance to alcohol, and to other depressant drugs
— 19. Need of people when troubled	— 19. Need of action when troubled	— 19. Need of solitude when troubled
— 20. Orientation toward childhood and family relationships	— 20. Orientation toward goals and activities of youth	— 20. Orientation toward the later periods of life

Note: The 30 traits with parentheses constitute collectively the short form of the scale.

Sheldon's prescription for the use of his scale is somewhat unusual. "The procedure recommended for using the scale for temperament is as follows: Observe the subject closely for at least a year in as many different situations as possible. Conduct a series of not less than twenty analytic interviews with him in a manner best suited to the situation and to the temperaments and interests of the two principals." Each trait is to be rated on a 7-point scale and the predominance of the three components—viscerotonia, somatotonia, cerebrotonia—is also indicated on a 7-point scale in such a way that for each person a formula is given containing three numbers, each measuring the strength of one of the three components. Thus, 1-1-7 would be a person almost entirely lacking in viscerotonia and somatotonia, with cerebrotonia completely dominant.

The final list of 60 traits is claimed by Sheldon to have been selected on the basis of intercorrelations among the ratings on 78 traits for a series of 100 male subjects. These correlations are given in his book; they are considerably higher than correlations between trait ratings usually are. Apart from his inspectional cluster analysis, Sheldon has not carried out any factorial study. Adcock (1948) has attempted such a study of Sheldon's figures, but in spite of several attempts found that he was faced each time with the problem of finding the root of a negative number. He remarks: "Obviously there is something peculiar about these intercorrelations", and goes on to attempt a rather complex interpretation.

Lubin (1950), who has made a statistical investigation of these intercorrelations, remarks that "the peculiarity is so great that one is forced to ask whether it may not be outside the bounds of mathematical possibility". He goes on to show that several of Sheldon's product moment correlations could not be simultaneously obtained from any actual set of measurements because they violate the well-known conditions for consistency. He concludes: "It follows that some at least of his figures must contain errors of arithmetical calculation." We may deduce from these observations that Sheldon's edifice is based on a somewhat insecure foundation, and any conclusions drawn from these figures should be regarded with great caution.

The three components isolated by Sheldon are not independent: viscerotonia correlates −·34 with somatotonia and −·37 with cerebrotonia; somatotonia and cerebrotonia intercorrelate − ·62. It is clear that a much more parsimonious description of the 60 traits rated would be possible in terms of two orthogonal factors rather than three correlated components[1]; in any case, it is clear that the intercorrelations among the components themselves must be accounted for in terms of some kind of Thurstonian second-order factor. This point is completely neglected by Sheldon.

One difficulty in the way of a ready acceptance of Sheldon's work must be the difficulty of repetition. Few psychologists can observe their subjects for a whole year and give each one 20 or more analytic sessions before making a rating. In several studies Sheldon has shown that moderately satisfactory correlations can be obtained between his own ratings and those of relatively inexperienced judges, making use of the short form of his scale. He has also developed a 20-minute interview technique which shows correlations of between ·8 and ·9 with his final ratings. The figures given by him are interesting, but like so much else in his work, they are given *en passant*, without very much information being vouchsafed regarding conditions of the experiment, the controls adopted, or any of the other attendant circumstances which must be known before a judgment can be made. Consequently, it is difficult to arrive at a proper conclusion regarding these devices.

More recently, Sheldon (1949), with the help of Wittman, has extended his work to abnormal mental states. Considering the psychotic syndrome in each case to be merely an exaggeration of the neurotic, he posits three main components of abnormality, which are again rated on a 7-point scale where the numbers are prefaced by the Greek letter ψ. The three psychiatric components in each case signify the *absence* or *lack* of one of the three normal components. Thus, cerebropenia (the suffix penic denotes lack of, or an abnormally low degree of, the component named) signifies the absence of cerebrotonia; visceropenia signifies the absence of viscerotonia; and somatopenia signifies the absence of somatotonia. Corresponding to these three "penias" we have three great neurotic and psychotic syndromes. Cerebropenia at the neurotic level leads to hysteria; at the psychotic level to manic-depressive psychosis. Visceropenia at the neurotic level leads to psychasthenia; at the psychotic level to paranoid schizophrenia. Somatopenia at the neurotic level leads to neurasthenia, and at the psychotic level to hebephrenic schizophrenia.

These various relations are illustrated in Fig. 11. The three corners of the triangle denote respectively the personality components viscerotonia, somatotonia, and cerebrotonia. The central part of the side of the triangle opposite each corner denotes visceropenia, soma-

[1] This has been demonstrated on Sheldon's own material by Ekman (1951).

topenia, and cerebropenia respectively. Distance from the centre of the triangle denotes degree of abnormality. The terms endomorphy, mesomorphy, and ectomorphy written in brackets at the corners of the triangle relate to body types, which in Sheldon's hypothesis are usually found with the temperamental types in question. A discussion of these types is given in a later chapter.

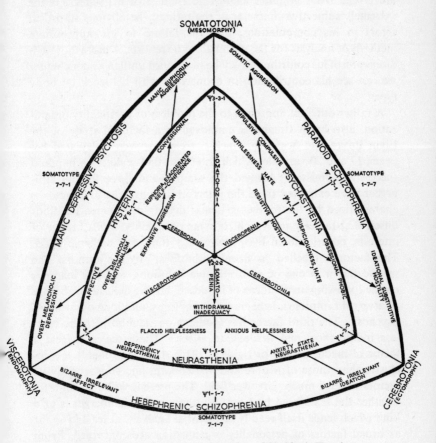

Fig. 11.—Diagrammatic Representation of Sheldon's Typology.

Most of the pioneering work in connection with this scheme has been carried on by Wittman (1948), who has constructed a check list of fundamental psychiatric behaviour reactions following the general scheme outlined, which is given at the end of this chapter. Interesting and suggestive as this instrument appears, the absence of correlational analysis of actual ratings makes it impossible to judge its value. Some supporting evidence is given by Sheldon and Wittman in their studies of body type, to be dealt with later.

In general, we may sum up Sheldon's contribution by emphasizing the novelty and comprehensiveness of his approach, the persistence of his endeavours, and the quantitative form in which his estimates are given. What militates against acceptance of his scheme is the extremely subjective character of the ratings, the obvious statistical errors in his computations, and the failure to use appropriate methods of analysis for the correlations he reports. A more thorough discussion of his contribution will be postponed until in a later chapter we can see his contribution in connection with his work on body types.

A rather different approach to the problem of personality organization, also by Wittman [1] is employed in a factorial study of the Elgin Prognostic Scale, in which correlations were calculated between 17 and 20 variables which enter into that scale. Two hundred successive admissions formed the sample, and three factors altogether were extracted from the intercorrelations. The first factor is characterized by the following items: defects of interest, insidious onset, shut-in personality, schizothyme personality, limited range of interests, constitutional bias, low energy tone, and asthenic build. This factor is labelled "schizoid withdrawal" by the authors. The second factor is one of schizophrenic delusions, and has loadings on the following items: ideas of influence, bizarre delusions, absence of atypical symptoms, hebephrenic symptoms, and long duration of psychosis. The third factor has loadings on: stubborn traits, careless indifference, and inadequate affect. "These scales suggest a factor of inadaptability or rigidity." This study is probably less inclusive than those of Moore and Wittenborn, and consequently its factors cover a much narrower field. The present writer is doubtful whether the scale used by Lorr, Wittman, and Schanberger is of a kind which lends itself readily to factorial analysis, at least in so far as broad factors of personality organization are concerned. From the point of view of prognostic indication, which determined the make-up of the scale, the usefulness of factor analysis is clearly doubtful, as a simple regression equation would presumably give at least equally good or probably better prediction than a combination of the three factors isolated.

The four studies next to be discussed all take their inspiration

[1] Lorr, Wittman, and Schanberger (1951).

from Harvard; although they are quite independent of each other in many ways, they share certain characteristics, such as excellence of psychiatric insight and wideness of scope, as well as a startling inadequacy of statistical treatment. The first of these studies is Murray's *Explorations in Personality* (1938), in which a large number of psychologists and psychiatrists used a great variety of procedures, many of them quite novel, on 50 Harvard undergraduates over a long period of time. As this book has become something of a classic in the literature of "personology", as Murray terms it, it will hardly be necessary to describe the many ingenious methods and techniques employed. From the point of view of the organization of personality, however, the yield is extraordinarily meagre. According to Murray, "the statistical analysis of the variables finally retained demonstrated that certain of them intercorrelated repeatedly to a significant degree. Most of these clusters seemed to correspond to our observations of people in everyday life. Hence, we concluded that they might be regarded as syndromes of functionally related factors which, for economy, could be used instead of the separate variables to portray character." To the reader whose appetite might be whetted by this announcement, it may come as a shock to find a footnote on the same page saying, "The chapter on the intercorrelations of variables and syndromes had to be omitted from this volume". He will instead have to make do with 100 pages of case-notes dealing with one subject ("The case of Earnst"), and a large amount of theorizing on the organization of personality by Murray and the other authors of this volume. It is fortunate that few other books eschew their duty to the conscientious reader who wishes to study the evidence for himself in so cavalier a fashion.

A very comprehensive rating study also is that of Sanford *et al.* (1943), which was clearly inspired by *Explorations in Personality*. 48 children altogether were followed up over a period of several years by a team of investigators who, in addition to ratings, used a number of techniques ranging from physical measurements and physiological determinations to projective techniques and studies of family background. In this chapter we will be concerned only with the personality ratings. Other results will be discussed in later chapters.

Sanford and his colleagues took over the general scheme outlined by Murray (1937). Ratings by three staff members on a large number of "needs" formed the basic data of the study; these ratings were "based on observations of the subjects in both free and controlled situations, ratings by teachers and parents, reports by teachers and by parents, and the results from a number of personality tests". 43 needs and traits were correlated with each other and syndromes constructed on the basis of a rather subjective form of cluster analysis. 20 such clusters were identified and intercorrelated with each other, but unfortunately no factor analysis was carried out on the resulting intercorrelations. The most clear-cut of the clusters is given the name "conscientious effort". "There is organized and persistent exertion to accomplish what is socially favored, and when obstacles are encountered there is renewed effort. There is the feeling that it is right to do these things and to some extent at least the subject takes pride in doing them. The syndrome denotes firmness, organization and persistence of action, and the capacity for living and working in accordance with standards. Underlying this factor, it may be supposed, there is considerable inner structure of personality." This cluster seems to represent most nearly the "w" factor, and, indeed, the similarity is quite striking. This syndrome correlates negatively with anxious emotional expressiveness and timid dependence, as well as with the syndrome called "sensation", "which seems to have a general tendency to seek for sensation or excitement".

Two opposed groups of traits resemble the extravert-introvert pattern, one made up of the items "good fellowship" and "social feeling"; the other made up of the items "self-sufficiency" and "counteractive endocathection".[1] Needless to say, these two groups of items intercorrelate negatively with each other.

An assessment of this study will be postponed until the other component parts of it are discussed in a later chapter. It would appear, however, that the excellence of the observational techniques and the rating methods are not matched by the quality of the statistical analysis, which appears subjective and almost perfunctory. It was considered at one stage that a factorial analysis of Sanford's table of intercorrelations of manifest personality syndromes might give interesting results, but it was found that out of 190 correlations, 10 were incorrect, by the simple check of comparing the two symmetrical halves of the table. Thus, the intercorrelations between "aggressive self-defense" and "good fellowship" are given variously as − ·48 and − ·28, and those between "aggressive self-defense" and "social feeling" as − ·59 and − ·39. "Counteractive endocathection" and "sensation" are correlated to the extent of either − ·52 or + ·52, different signs appearing in different parts of the table. Such errors

[1] "The liking for thought or emotion for its own sake. Preoccupation with inner activity."

must seriously disturb one's faith in the results given in any part of the book.

Another Harvard production—*What People Are*—by Heath (1945) proclaims itself to be "a study of normal young men". It is a report on the first few years' work by investigators working on the Grant study. The subjects were some 250 young men "who had general all-round normal reactions". Their academic work had to be at least satisfactory, and their health and college records had to indicate lack of physical or psychological abnormalities. Participants were around 20 years of age, ranging from 17 to 24. Each boy was studied for about 20 hours by means of interviews, physiological observations, anthropological examination of body structure and development, and psychological testing for the measurement of various mental functions. Details regarding his socio-economic status were obtained and further psychiatric interviews held. A great deal of information was thus elicited from the participants, but not a single correlation coefficient is given throughout the book. The statistical treatment given to the data is of a purely actuarial kind, and in view of the non-representative nature of the sample can be of very little interest.

The only exception to this general criticism is the attempt made by the authors to rate their subjects on the basis of "soundness" into three groups: "Group A contained young men who were 'thoroughly sound' in Webster's meaning of 'free from flaws', 'on a firm foundation'. . . . Group B contained boys in whom there was a question of a minor flaw. For instance, if a boy was lacking in warmth in his touch with people, or if he was erratic or showed degrees of sensitiveness, leading to minor frustrations, he would be placed in this group. . . . Group C contained boys whose history revealed a definite handicap. A good illustration would be swings of mood which interfered noticeably with function." Of the 252 men so classified, the "A Group" included 37 per cent., the "B Group" 45 per cent., and the "C Group" 18 per cent.

"After several years sufficient information had accumulated to set up a tentative and descriptive classification by certain outstanding and significant traits and activities. All descriptive terms contained in the histories were listed, and close study of these disclosed the existence of trait clusters, combinations that occurred with special frequency." A list of these trait groups, together with the occurrence of each in the total number of cases, and their occurrence respectively in groups rated A, B, and C on "soundness" are given in Table 9, together with the correlation of each trait with the "soundness" classification.[1]

It will be seen that some items, such as "vital affect", "friendly", "well integrated", "practical organizer", showed high correlations with "soundness", whereas others like "incompletely integrated", "asocial", "unstable autonomic functions", "lack of purpose and

TABLE 9

Distribution of Various Traits according to "Soundness"
(A, B, and C) Classification

| Trait Groups | Per cent. "Soundness" Classification in | | | | Co-efficient of Con-tingency $C =$ |
| | Total group | A | B | C | |
	Per cent. in 251 cases	Per cent. in 93 cases	Per cent. in 112 cases	Per cent. in 46 cases	
1. Vital affect	20	40	11	2	·36*
2. Friendly	22	39	14	7	·30*
3. Well integrated	60	83	56	22	·40*
4. Practical organizing	37	47	37	15	·23*
5. Humanistic	16	20	16	7	·13
6. Pragmatic	38	48	38	17	·22*
7. Political	17	19	20	7	·13
8. Just-so	13	11	18	7	·13
9. Bland affect	18	15	21	15	·08
10. Self-driving	14	10	19	11	·12
11. Cultural	22	18	25	20	·08
12. Verbalistic	18	19	15	24	·08
13. Inarticulate	14	11	17	15	·08
14. Shy	18	8	30	11	·27*
15. Physical science	12	11	12	17	·07
16. Sensitive affect	17	10	22	22	·16*
17. Creative and intuitive	6	3	9	7	—
18. Mood fluctuations	14	9	15	22	·13
19. Inhibited	19	6	30	15	·27*
20. Ideational	21	13	23	33	·17*
21. Self-conscious and in-trospective	25	12	32	37	·24*
22. Lack of purpose and values	20	8	19	50	·35*
23. Unstable autonomic functions	14	3	17	28	·26*
24. Asocial	10	0	11	26	·30*
25. Incompletely integra-ted	15	0	12	52	·46*

* Statistically significant.

[1] These correlations were calculated by the writer: the book itself is content to give instead a ratio between the percentage occurrences of each trait for groups A and C, a measure which is statistically meaningless and psychologically misleading.

values", "self-conscious", and "introspective" showed negative correlations. There is little doubt that this "soundness" rating corresponds to the factor of neuroticism, or rather its opposite pole, "w".

Another table is given by the authors, again in terms of percentages, showing the frequency of occurrence of various pairs of traits. This is summarized by Heath as follows: "Among individuals with *sensitive affect* there is an association with *creative* and *intuitive, cultural, verbalistic, unstable autonomic functions, self-conscious and introspective*, and *incompletely integrated*." It seems probable that if the general factor of "soundness" were partialled out from the intercorrelations of the traits, we would have here a description of the introvert as opposed to the extravert type. As it is, the description is a mixture of neuroticism and introversion and would appear similar to that given of the dysthymic type by Eysenck (1947). Nothing can show more clearly the need for a proper system of statistical analysis than this amateurish effort to sort out "how the traits group themselves together" by means of an inspection of percentage frequencies.

Some incidental findings are of interest. Some of the young men apparently had an almost perfect health record. "Their excellent health record often had its counterpart in good reports from the other examiners so that there seemed to be a link between good physical health and sound personality and adjustment, good balance of mental functions, freedom from structural defect, and normal physiology. The suggestion is sufficiently pronounced to warrant pursuit by further study."

In another publication, also by the Grant study (Woods, Brouha, and Seltzer, 1943), a figure is given showing the relationship between short interview ratings of mental health and a physical fitness index. This is reproduced below (Fig. 12), and shows a remarkable correlation between the two indices, taken on almost 2,500 officer candidates. At the opposite end of the scale we may note some figures given by Lovet Doust (1952), who showed that the incidence of various diseases was much higher in patients suffering from psychoses or neuroses than in normals; his figures are given in Table 10.[1] The old adage "mens sana in corpora sano" appears to derive considerable justification from these figures.

Follow-up data were available on over 200 of the young men studied by Heath, who went into the army, and a threefold classifi-

[1] 354 normals and 272 psychiatric patients with no gross physical disability filled in a questionnaire dealing with 110 disorders (38 symptoms and complaints, 72 actual diseases) from which they might have suffered in the past.

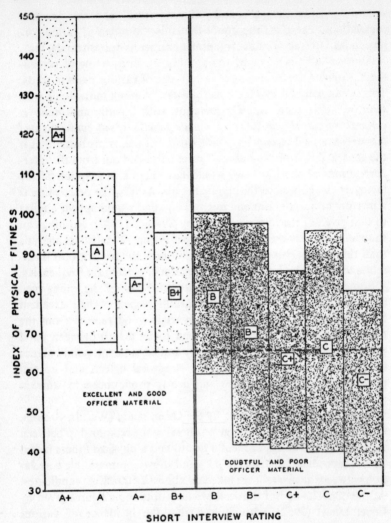

Fig. 12.—Relationship between Short Interview Rating and Physical Fitness Index.

cation of their adjustment was made into *excellent, normal,* or *difficult.* Of those in "soundness" classification "A", 31 per cent. were classed as excellent, 66 per cent. as normal, and 3 per cent. as difficult. Those who had been classified "B" were excellent in 10 per cent. of the cases, normal in 82 per cent., and difficult in 8 per cent. Those who had been classed "C" were never excellent, normal in 74 per cent. of the cases, and difficult in 26 per cent. The trait which distinguished best between those who in the follow-up proved excellent, normal, or difficult was the original rating on "well integrated".

TABLE 10

Psychiatric Diagnosis		Total Somatic Complaints		Total Somatic Diseases	
		M.	S.D.	M.	S.D.
Controls (N = 354)	. .	1·700	1·391	6·291	1·722
Psychopaths (N = 92)	. .	2·201	3·674	6·800	4·845
Neurotics (N = 120)	. .	3·491	6·552	8·907	2·799
Depressives (N = 59)	. .	8·334	2·176	13·654	4·447
Schizophrenics (N = 51)	. .	10·320	3·005	13·820	5·402

In so far as they go, then, these data agree well with the hypothesis of a general factor of neuroticism and seem to support the hypothesis of an introverted-extraverted factor. However, in the absence of proper statistical treatment of the data, it does not seem safe to draw any definite conclusion from them.

The last of the "Harvard studies" is only indirectly connected with Cambridge, Mass., by the fact that its orientation and much of its senior personnel came from that University. Entitled *Assessment of Men* (1948) and dealing with the selection of personnel for the Office of Strategic Services, it was written by the O.S.S. Assessment Staff, and in many ways carried forward the work begun by Murray in *Explorations of Personality* (1937). It makes use of an approach introduced by German military psychology, and later taken over by the British War Office Selection Boards, to be transplanted to the other side of the ocean in the selection procedures here outlined. The similarities of the approach to *Explorations of Personality* are obvious; we have again stress on psychiatric and semi-analytical interviews, on all sorts of projective devices, and quite generally on what is called "depth" or "dynamic" psychology.

Several hundred men went through this assessment process, each of them being observed by a large number of observers over quite a lengthy period; all of them were subjected to a great variety of tests, interviews, and other techniques, many of which showed again the typical ingenuity and skilled insight of the authors. The validity of the final ratings and the final recommendations made were assessed by correlating them with four types of appraisal: overseas staff appraisal, returnee appraisal, theatre commander's comments, and reassignment area appraisal. For the main camp (Camp "S"), where the men were investigated for three days in a very thorough-going fashion, these correlations were respectively ·37, ·19, ·23, and ·08, giving an average of about ·2 as an estimate of the validity of the procedures. In another camp (Camp "W"), where a very much shorter period of time was spent on each man, namely one day in all, the figures were ·53, ·21, ·15, and ·30 respectively, giving an average of almost ·3. It is interesting to note that the more information was obtained on the subjects of the rating technique, the less valid did the final rating seem to become. The O.S.S. staff do not consider that this result could have arisen because of differences in quality of subjects in the two camps or because of differences in the quality of the raters. They conclude a discussion of the problem by saying: "It would be profitable in the long run for us to assume that the additional information obtained by stretching the screening process from one to three days had diminished the validity of the final decisions and that this much more knowledge was a dangerous thing." (A similar point has been made by the authors of the Michigan Clinical Student Selection Programme (Kelly and Fiske, 1952), which is mentioned elsewhere in this book.)

Unfortunately, in spite of its great interest, *The Assessment of Men* does not throw very much light on the question of the organization of personality. The writers are so convinced of the truth of their "organismic hypothesis" that they have made certain that no data should be published in their book, or should be obtainable from the general set-up of their experiment, which could possibly throw any light on the relative virtues of this organismic approach, as compared with what they call the "elementalistic" method. They say: "The scheme employed by us may be called the multiform organismic system of assessment: 'multiform' because it consists of a rather large number of procedures based on different principles and 'organismic' (or 'Gestalt' or 'holistic') because it utilizes the data obtained through these procedures for attempting to arrive at a picture of personality as a whole; i.e. at the organization of the essential dynamic features of the individual. The knowledge of this organization serves as a base, both for understanding and for predicting the subject's specific behaviour." This of course is a reasonable hypothesis; it could easily be tested by comparing a prediction of final successes made on the basis of a statistical weighting of all the separate test results, ratings, etc., with the final rating based on such an organismic point of view. Such a procedure would have thrown a great deal of light on the process of organismic judgment formation itself, and would also have been something of a crucial experiment to test the organismic hypothesis. By assuming this hypothesis to be true, and by completely ostracizing any kind of statistical treatment which would have enabled them to test its validity, the authors have thrown overboard the possibility of convincing their theoretical opponents by proper scientific proof, and have, instead, relied on semantic argument. It has fallen to Kelly and Fiske (1950) in their recent study to show that when a study of this type is carried out in such a way as to enable a comparison to be made between the two methods of approach, then the organismic is decisively inferior to the elementalistic. The scientific reader will hardly need this additional evidence to show the superiority of actual proof over mere argument.

In view of this organismic bias of the authors, it is difficult to assess such intercorrelations as they have provided between ratings, as their method of arriving at these seems to make a halo effect even more certain than is usual in rating studies. They report intercorrelations for 133 men on such variables as motivation, energy, and intiative, effective intelligence, emotional stability, social relations, leadership, physical ability, security, observing and reporting, propaganda skills and overall ratings; they also report on a factorial study of this matrix of intercorrelation which gives rise to four non-orthogonal factors. The first of these is called adjustment, and is clearly again the "w" factor emerging in these rather novel surroundings. The second factor is called effective intelligence, and has high loadings on the ratings of effective intelligence, on observing and reporting, propaganda scales, and over-all ratings. The third factor, physical energy, is loaded on energy and initiative, leadership and physical ability. The last factor has only two loadings of any size ("energy and initiative" and "leadership") and is labelled "authoratative assertion". (The absence of an extravert-introvert factor is presumably due to the fact that none of the traits rated is relevant to such a factor.)

The four factors are highly intercorrelated. Thus, adjustment correlates ·58 with affective intelligence, ·70 with physical energy, and ·06 with authoritative assertion. Effective intelligence correlates ·37 with physical energy and ·48 with authoritative assertion. Physical energy and authoritative assertion are almost uncorrelated (R = ·09). No higher-order factor is derived, so that the study is manifestly incomplete.

It is interesting, however, to note that even in this organismic setting, a factor of adjustment or neuroticism emerges so clearly, particularly as it appears to give rise to what the writers seem to consider their main theoretical finding, namely that the "conception of the 'personality as a whole' points to goal-directed forces or conation as the chief unifying and integrating factor in personality". In this conclusion, of course, they are at one with Webb and many other members of the English school, although they make no reference to these earlier workers.

We must now turn to the more pedestrian but considerably sounder work reported by the group of psychologists connected with the Fels study. 30 rating scales of unusually high inter-rater reliability were constructed by the psychologists, and 40 nursery children rated on 29 of these scales. The intercorrelations between the scales are relatively high; when submitted to a factorial analysis by Richards and Simons (1941), they gave rise to three factors. Table 11 sets out the names of the scales used, the saturations for the

TABLE 11

Scale	Factor Loadings				Chron. Age	Binet I.Q.	Merrill-Palmer S.D. Score	Vineland Social Quotient	Joël Behav. Quotient
	I	II	III	h²					
Affectionateness				·07	− ·16	·00	·06	·28	·23
Aggressiveness	·64	·60		·82	·25	·18	·02	·21	·49
Cheerfulness	·35	− ·26	·70	·69	·07	·11	·07	·09	·32
Competitiveness	·80	·31		·73	·61	·36	·27	·12	·58
Conformity (non.)		·74	− ·32	·69	− ·22	− ·00	− ·34	·27	− ·28
Cruelty	·23	·81		·71	·00	− ·08	− ·08	·06	·08
Curiosity	·23	·29	·57	·46	·10	·08	− ·29	·18	·26
Emotional control (non.)		·79		·70	− ·14	− ·10	− ·24	·23	− ·11
Emotional excitability		·83		·71	− ·32	− ·02	− ·21	·23	·17
Fancifulness	·62			·43	·51	·50	·53	·15	·49
Frequency of gross activity	·68	·52		·77	− ·08	− ·09	− ·15	·33	·31
Friendliness	·71		·47	·74	·40	·15	·08	·18	·51
Gregariousness	·70	·36	·29	·70	·51	·02	·00	·04	·48
Intensity of emotional response		·71		·56	− ·02	− ·02	− ·16	·22	·17
Jealousy		·69	·55	·79	·51	·16	·14	·08	·26
Kindness	·52	− ·61		·69	·43	·10	·05	− ·04	·30
Leadership	·88			·84	·62	·41	·34	·20	·63
Obedience (non.)		·85		·74	·05	·01	·07	·28	·08
Originality	·72			·57	·33	·22	·02	·07	·31
Physical apprehensiveness (non.)	·27	·37	·62	·59	− ·09	·04	− ·00	·30	·27
Planfulness	·71	− ·28		·58	·55	·26	·38	− ·07	·41
Quarrelsomeness	·25	·89		·85	·09	− ·07	− ·11	·15	·11
Resistance		·86		·80	·26	·11	·05	·31	·05
Sense of humour	·44		·66	·63	·34	·14	− ·02	·18	·24
Sensitiveness	·54		− ·47	·51	·44	·15	·24	·07	·31
Social apprehensiveness (non.)	·35	·37	·72	·78	·13	·11	− ·19	·23	·24
Suggestibility (non.)		·73	·44	·75	− ·09	·11	·21	·16	·05
Tenacity	·40	− ·42		·33	·30	·20	·15	·03	·19
Vigour of activity	·66	·53		·76	·18	− ·17	− ·08	·35	·27

three factors, and the correlations of the scales with chronological age, with Binet I.Q., Merrill-Palmer sigma score, Vineland Social quotient, and the Joël behaviour quotient.

The interpretation of the factors is less certain than might be wished. "Inspection of these factor loadings suggests that Factor I has to do with desirability of behavior, in that desirable behavior at the nursery-school level is mature behavior. The pattern of coefficients is quite similar to that for the correlation of the scales with chronological age. But the pattern is also similar to that for the correlation of the scales with the Joël scale, where age was partialled out by using the Behavior Quotient. A name for this factor might be 'desirability of behavior' or 'maturity of behavior'." This factor is considered similar by the authors also to Richards' (1940) factor of "desirability" derived from the Merrill-Palmer Personality Rating Scales, and to Van Alstyne's (1936) factor of the same name established on young elementary schoolchildren. It is not believed that this factor resembles those extracted from correlations of ratings for adults.

"Factor II . . . seems to be one of independence or non-conformity, or even antagonism. It is in most saturation in *quarrelsomeness, resistance, disobedience, emotional excitability, cruelty, lack of emotional control, non-conformity*, etc. Its pattern is similar to that for the Vineland Social Maturity Scale. . . . The guess may be hazarded that this factor corresponds in part at least to neuroticism; in the absence of other nursery-school studies, and lacking follow-up investigations of the future adjustment of the children prominently saturated with this factor, such identification must remain extremely speculative. Yet it fits in well enough with general psychiatric theories of child development."

"Factor III is of greatest amount in *lack of social apprehensiveness* ('poise'), *cheerfulness, sense of humor, lack of physical apprehensiveness*, etc. It might be called a mood factor, or an extroverted factor, with sensitiveness and independence at the negative end. It may be similar to the 'surgency' factor. . . ." This interpretation in terms of extraversion appears reasonable to the present writer, although again the lack of comparative data from other studies, and the absence of longitudinal investigations, makes correct identification difficult.

Brief mention should perhaps be made in connection with this discussion of the Fels Child Behavior Scales of the Fels Parent Behavior Rating Scales. These 30 scales, discussed in detail by

Champneys (1941) and Baldwin, Kalhorn, and Breese (1945, 1949), were constructed with great care, and have been submitted to correlational analysis in four separate publications. In the first of these, Baldwin (1946) compared a sample of 74 sets of behaviour ratings of the parents of 3-year-old children with a sample of 79 sets of ratings of parents of 9-year-old children. (The ratings in each case were made by experienced home visitors.) Complete sets of intercorrelations were calculated, for the two age-groups separately; also calculated was a set of correlations between composite variables representing an average of the individual variables making up the composites. The correlations between these 13 composite variables are presented by the authors; unfortunately no factorial analysis was carried out to clarify the pattern of relationships disclosed.

This defect was made good by Roff (1949), who factor analysed correlations between all the 30 scales as given by Baldwin, Kalhorn, and Breese (1945). A summary of his results is given in Table 12. Roff labels the factors as follows: I. Concern for the child. II. Democratic guidance. III. Permissiveness. IV. Parent-child harmony. V. Solicitousness. VI. Activeness of the home. VII. Non-readiness of suggestion. (?) These factors themselves are intercorrelated, sometimes to a considerable extent ($r_{24} = \cdot64$; $r_{13} = \cdot36$; $r_{12} = \cdot37$), and it seems unfortunate that Roff has neglected to calculate second-order factors. If he had done so, his analysis might have approximated somewhat more closely to Baldwin, Kalhorn, and Breese's original work (1945), where they isolated three main factors by means of cluster analysis, called by them "Warmth", "Objectivity", and "Parental control".

Another failure which runs through the whole of the Fels work tends to make the scientific value of these excellent studies somewhat less than it might be. As we have seen, factorial studies of child behaviour give rise to factors descriptive of child behaviour; factorial studies of parental behaviour give rise to factors descriptive of parental behaviour. It seems strange that no attempt has been made to bring together these two sets of data, and to show to what extent parental and child behaviour are themselves related. Only in such an imbrication of the two separate types of study can the whole work find its proper fruition; in its absence we can only hope that in time this lack will be made good.

An excellent example of the enrichment of knowledge which may follow upon such a step is fortunately already available in the work of Hewitt and Jenkins (1946), to which we must turn next. This re-

ANALYSIS OF RATINGS 85

TABLE 12
Summary of Factor Loadings

	I	II	III	IV	V	VI	VII
Factor I: Concern for Child							
7 Contact duration	69						
21 Protectiveness	69						
20 Babying	63						
6 Child-centred	57						
25 Solicitous	53				− 36		
26 Acceptance	39			31			
4 Family sociable	− 37				70		− 41
9 Non-restrictive	− 37	32	35		32		
Factor II: Democratic Guidance							
12 Justification		64					
13 Democracy		62					
24 Explanation		62					
18 Non-coercive		61					
27 Understanding		43			33		
14 Clarity policy		38					
19 Accelerational		36				36	
23 Favourable criticism		34					
28 Non-emotional		33		33	− 35		
9 Non-restrictive	− 37	32	35		32		
Factor III: Permissiveness							
11 Non-severity			61				
10 Non-enforcement			51				
9 Non-restrictive	− 37	32	35		32		
Factor IV: Parent-child Harmony							
16 Non-friction				63			
15 Effectiveness				61			
3 Home non-discord				42	31		
22 Non-criticism				41			33
30 Rapport				40			
28 Non-emotional		33		33	− 35		
26 Acceptance	39			31			
Factor V: Sociability-adjustment of Parents							
4 Family sociable	− 37				70		− 41
1 Home adjustment					55		
25 Solicitous	53				− 36		
28 Non-emotional		33		33	− 35		
27 Understanding		43			33		
29 Affectionate					32		
9 Non-restrictive	− 37	32	35		32		
3 Home non-discord				42	31		
Factor VI: Activeness of Home							
2 Home active						76	
5 Co-ordination						53	
19 Accelerational		36				36	
Factor VII: Non-readiness of Suggestion							
17 Non-suggestion							58
4 Family sociable	− 37				70		− 41
8 Intense contact							− 34
22 Non-criticism				41			33

search is the only one to apply factorial method *both* to behaviour *and* to environment, and to link the factors derived from the one with the factors derived from the other. Taking their material from routine case histories, these authors studied 500 problem children, 78 per cent. of whom were boys and 22 per cent. of whom were girls. The average age of this group was between 11 and 12 and the mean I.Q. was 94. 45 traits were taken from the case histories, and inter-correlations calculated by means of tetrachorics. A modified form of cluster analysis was then performed in which traits were grouped together in such a way that all the group correlations were higher than ·30, while the correlations of one cluster with another were a good deal lower than this value. Three clusters were found in this way. The first one was called "unsocialized aggressive behaviour" and is made up of the following traits: assaultive tendencies, initiatory fighting, cruelty, defiance of authority, malicious mischief, and inadequate guilt feelings. The second cluster is called "socialized delinquency behaviour" and is made up of the following traits: bad companions, gang activities, co-operative stealing, furtive stealing, school truancy, truancy from home, and staying out late nights. The third cluster, "over-inhibited behaviour", is made up of the following traits: seclusiveness, shyness, apathy, worrying, sensitiveness, and submissiveness.

Corresponding to these three behaviour patterns there are three situational patterns built up in the same way by means of cluster analysis. The first of the situational patterns is called "parental rejection". It is made up of the following items: illegitimate pregnancy, pregnancy unwanted by father or mother, post-delivery rejection by father or mother, mother unwilling to accept parent rôle, mother sexually unconventional, mother-person openly hostile to child, loss of contact with both natural parents. The second cluster, called "parental negligence", is made up of the following items: interior of home unkempt, irregular home routine, lack of supervision, discipline lax, mother mentally inadequate, discipline harsh, mother shielding, sibling delinquency, deteriorated area. The third cluster is called "family repression" and is made up of the following items: father's discipline inconsistent, father hypercritical, father or mother unsociable, mother demanding, sibling rivalry, and mother-compensated rejection. A fourth cluster of "physical deficiency" was also established, but is probably of less psychological interest than the others: it is made up of items like central nervous system disorder, abnormal growths pattern, convulsions, auditory or speech defect, diseased tonsils or adenoids, chronic physical complaints. The inter-correlations between these four patterns are not high. Negligence correlates negatively with repression (— ·21) and with physical deficiency (— ·32), repression and physical deficiency correlate (·21), and parental rejection and repression correlate (·18).

We must now turn to the fundamental hypothesis underlying the work of Hewitt and Jenkins. This hypothesis they state in the following way: "Children who differ from each other in expressing fundamentally different patterns of behaviour of maladjustment . . . must have experienced fundamentally different patterns of environmental states; and conversely, children who are exposed to such fundamentally different patterns of situations will exhibit fundamentally different patterns of maladjustments." Proof for this hypothesis is sought in the table of correlations between the three clusters representing child behaviour and the four clusters representing situational patterns. This table is given below (Table 13), and it is certainly striking to observe the degree to which parental rejection is accompanied by unsocialized aggressive behaviour, negligence by socialized deliquency behaviour, and repression by over-inhibited behaviour (it is less surprising to find physical deficiency correlated positively with over-inhibited behaviour and negatively with unsocialized aggressive and socialized delinquent behaviour). Striking as these figures are, they cannot be taken as necessarily providing proof of the hypothesis advanced by Hewitt and Jenkins. Similar correlations might have been caused by the action of inheritance, which might be responsible both for the repressive behaviour of the parent and the over-inhibited behaviour of the child, or the negligent behaviour of the parent and the delinquent behaviour of the child, or even the rejective behaviour of the parent and the aggressive behaviour of the child, without assuming any direct causal relation between the behaviour of the parent and that of the child. The data given support the environmental view no more than they support the hereditary view; it is illusory to believe that the proof of the existence of a correlation between two variables can ever throw any light on the cause responsible for that correlation. Quite a different type of experimental design would be required to prove the hypothesis in question. In saying this we do not wish to detract from the interest and the importance of a piece of research which must be regarded as one of the most outstanding in the whole field of personality organization; the factorial findings remain quite unaffected by the criticism of the hypothesis regarding the origin of the observed interconnections.

TABLE 13

	Unsocialized Aggression	Socialized Delinquency	Over-inhibited Behaviour	Number of Cases
Parental rejection .	·48 ± ·07	·02	− ·20	101
Parental negligence	·12	·63 ± ·07	− ·17	78
Parental repression	·10	− ·12	·52 ± ·06	106
Physical deficiency .	− ·23	− ·31	·46 ± ·06	95

Support for some of Jenkins' and Hewitt's findings comes from another study of *Children's Behavior Problems* by Ackerson (1942). Taking a sample of 2,113 white boys and 1,181 white girls from the files of the Illinois Institute for Juvenile Research, this author selected a number of traits whose incidence seemed large enough to justify such procedures, and calculated tetrachoric intercorrelations between them. The number of traits used is quite large, amounting to 162. Two of the traits used are compound traits called "personality total" and "conduct total"; these terms refer to disorder manifestations either in the field of personality or conduct, and are, as it were, summed scores on a variety of sub-items.

Ackerson himself merely reports several thousand intercorrelations which result from his labour; he does not attempt to carry out a factorial study. This deficiency has been remedied by Himmelweit (1952), who selected 50 traits or notations from the total number given by Ackerson and carried out a centroid analysis. Fig. 13 gives a diagrammatic picture of the first two factors obtained from her analysis of the data for the boys in Ackerson's sample. The existence of a general factor of abnormality is quite marked, as is the division in the second factor between introverted items (sensitive, absentminded, seclusive, depressed, day-dreams, inefficient, queer, inferiority feelings, nervous, and changeable moods, to which must be added psychoneurotic, which notation in Ackerson's work appears to refer to dysthymic disorders only), and extraverted items (stealing, truancy from home and school, destructive, lying, swearing, disobedient, disturbing influence, violent, rude, and egocentric). As these two groups of items were used to establish personality total and conduct total respectively, it is not surprising to find that these two notations have clear projections on the positive and negative end of the second factor respectively.

These data support an explanation of extraversion-introversion, which has sometimes been made by followers of Freud, namely that

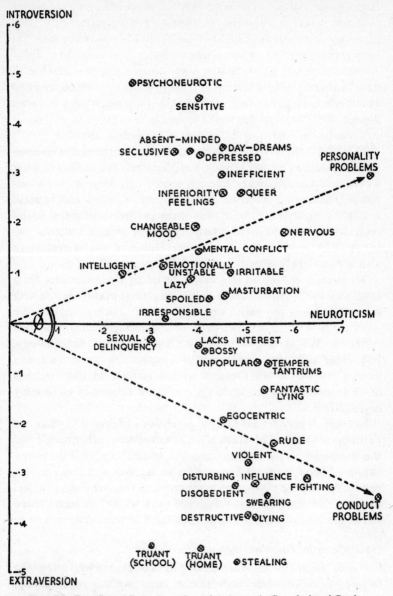

Fig. 13.—Two-factor Representation of Ackerson's Correlational Study.

introversion appears to reflect a predominance of super-ego over id activities, whereas extraversion reflects a predominance of id over super-ego activities. It should be possible to test a hypothesis of this kind experimentally; in the absence of such experimental proof it constitutes merely an alternative way of describing the same set of data. Altogether, identification of these two factors must be regarded as rather speculative in view of the fact that not much work has been done with children, so that we have very little to go on in arriving at any conclusion regarding the nature of the factors involved.

The third factor extracted by Himmelweit from the matrix is somewhat difficult to identify; it brings together items like inefficient, poor work, irresponsible, lacks interest, unpopular, lazy, dull, absent-minded, disturbing influence, fantastic lying, seclusive, and asexual. It might possibly be a forerunner of the psychoticism factor found several times in studies of adults; it also resembles Cattell's "*a*" factor and Moore's prepsychotic factor. However, this interpretation also is exceedingly tentative and little reliance is placed on it.

We have now finished our survey of rating studies, except for a small number of reports which have used ratings in conjunction with other techniques and which will be discussed in other chapters. We must try now to assess the value of the results which have been reviewed. We shall deal, not with the statistical methodology, but rather with an evaluation of the method of rating itself, and attempt to see to what extent we are justified in using ratings at all in our attempt to build up a scientific scheme of personality organization.

In a way, it may be said that the psychology of personality has two paths open to it, one of which is the observation of other people and the attribution to them of certain traits, while the other is the observation of one's own self and one's own motives and thought processes. While these two methods are primary, they are clearly subject to many dangers. The vast volume of work which has been carried out in the field of ratings shows what some of these dangers are.

(1) *Differential Understanding of Trait Names*

It is only too obvious when talking to two persons who undertake to rate others that their conception of terms, such as suggestibility, sense of humour, persistence, and so forth, varies widely and that on occasions quite contradictory meanings are associated with the same trait name. It is possible to reduce the influence of this factor by very careful discussions with each judge of the exact meaning of the term used; in the absence of such clarification of terms, it is almost impossible to attribute any meaning to the results of rating studies.

(2) *The Halo Effect*

It was observed quite early in the history of psychology that sets of ratings on different traits tend to show unduly high intercorrelations which, as Thorndike maintained in 1920, might be due to the general impression of the ratee possessed by the rater. This general stereotyped attitude would then colour all the judgments made of particular traits. As Vernon (1938) points out: "Most commonly, halo consists largely of our general liking for, or our dislike of the ratees, for it is usually found that the desirable or admirable traits give high positive intercorrelations and negative correlations with undesirable traits. Doubtless, this has some basis in actual fact; persons of fine character do tend to be high on all good qualities. Others do tend to be weak all round, but one is very liable to exaggerate this and to attribute unwittingly all the virtues to our friends, and the vices to our enemies."

(3) *Differences in Rating Ability*

Persons who rate others on personality traits may be presumed to differ with respect to their ability to carry out this task. Thus, for instance, Sheldon (1942) reports correlations between his own ratings and those of a class of graduate students, ranging from ·17 to ·94. Even if we refuse to accept Sheldon's own ratings as providing an objective standard of validity, and even if we consider that defective ratings may be due not only to lack of ability but also to other factors, such as lack of interest, lack of time, or lack of inclination, the fact remains that very marked differences are usually observed between raters, and that as long as no objective standard of validity can be applied, selection of raters must be relatively haphazard and may include the good and the bad indifferently.

(4) *Influence of Unconscious Bias*

The halo effect in a way is unconscious, but it may be reduced by acquainting judges with the existence of such a factor. Some bias, however, is very much more deeply rooted in the personality organization of the rater. Thus Sears (1936), in an elaborate study of raters and ratings, came to the following conclusions:

(i) "Those subjects who lacked insight into the amount of a given trait they themselves possessed tended, on the average, to attribute a greater amount of that trait to other people than did those subjects who possessed an equal amount of the trait but had insight."

(ii) "Projection [of this type] was not operative in influencing the judgments of all subjects on any given trait; its occurrence was apparently confined to those who lacked insight."

(iii) "In the group of subjects who possessed insight a negative correlation was found between amount of trait possessed and amount attributed to others. This suggests the operation of a dynamic process, tentatively entitled *contrast-formation*, which has an effect opposite to that of projection on judgments about others' personalities."

(iv) "Judgments about other people with respect to both acceptable and unacceptable [reprehensible] traits showed the influence of projection and contrast-formation."

These tendencies towards projection and contrast-formation in rating others were also found by Frenkel-Brunswik (1942) in her very important monograph on motivation and behaviour.

(5) *Influence of Acquaintanceship*

Vernon (1938) has summarized the literature to date to show that prolonged observation and close acquaintanceship do not necessarily improve ratings. Additional information on this point has since come to hand in very large-scale rating studies carried out by the O.S.S. (1948) and by the participants in the Michigan selection study (Kelley and Fiske, 1950). Contrary to the expectation of the psychologists and psychiatrists concerned in these studies, it was found again that relatively superficial knowledge gave better predictive accuracy than more thorough and detailed knowledge of subjects. These findings would seem to rule out what might appear to be one of the most promising methods for improving ratings, namely the use as raters of people having an intimate acquaintanceship with the ratees.

(6) *Rating of Observed and Inferred Behaviour*

It is often believed that more reliable and valid ratings can be obtained by restricting ratings to actually observed behaviour rather than to rate traits inferred from behaviour thought to be relevant to the trait. However, Newcomb (1931) has shown that ratings on observed items of behaviour are not significantly superior to ratings on behaviour which has only been inferred, and Frenkel-Brunswik (1942) has brought forward impressive evidence to show the superiority, under certain circumstances, of rating hypothetical variables far removed from behaviour rather than traits closer to overt observed behaviour.

(7) *Alternative Manifestations*

Frenkel-Brunswik (1942) has shown that "different classes of behavioral expressions were often related to one drive as alternative manifestations of that drive". She found that "one drive variable may circumscribe a family of alternative manifestations unrelated to each other: the meaning of the drive concept emerges in terms of families of divergent manifestations held together dynamically or genotypically, though often not phenotypically. And, on the other

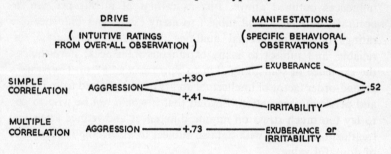

Fig. 13a.—Alternative Manifestations of the same Drive.

hand, one overt expression may be related to several underlying tendencies." Her findings are illustrated in Fig. 13a, where exuberance or irritability are taken to be alternative manifestations of the same drive of aggression.

(8) *Reliability and Validity*

When all the above-mentioned factors are taken into account, it will not surprise the reader to find the literature replete with indications of the low reliability of ratings, or to find that when reliabilities are high the explanation may be in terms of common bias or halo rather than in terms of validity. However, the picture is not altogether dark. Hartshorn and May (1928, 1929, 1930) found fairly high correlations between ratings and batteries of objective tests of honesty, self-control, and so forth, and many later writers have shown agreement between ratings on traits, such as neuroticism, and objective tests. Thus, it would be too radical a conclusion to say that ratings are entirely valueless, just as a too easy acceptance of the ratings must be deprecated as unlikely to lead to scientifically worth-while conclusions.

It will be clear from what has been said that a rating cannot be taken strictly as a description of the person rated; it is always quite inevitably an interaction between rater and ratee, and as such may, by appropriate methods of analysis, be used to throw light either on the ratee or on the rater, or on the interaction between the two, i.e. the process of rating itself. Most of the studies reviewed have failed to give due regard to the complexities of the subject, and if in spite of this there is such remarkable agreement at least on two main factors, namely emotional instability or neuroticism and introversion-extraversion, we must take this to indicate the great prominence of these factors which successfully penetrate the obscuring fog of the various influences outlined above. Just as ratings of intelligence are inaccurate, unreliable, and subject to many extraneous influences, so ratings of non-intellectual qualities are equally inaccurate, unreliable, and subject to many extraneous influences; nevertheless, the existence of something akin to Spearman's "g" or Thurstone's second-order factor of intellectual ability can be gleaned from ratings and personal observation. Beyond that it would not be wise to go; to lay too much stress on minute differences and refined statistical treatment in dealing with data so subject to disturbing influences is of doubtful value.

We may perhaps make two suggestions. In the first place, future studies using ratings should take into consideration all the difficulties involved and should attempt to set up the whole experiment in such a fashion as to obtain information, not only on the ratee but also on the raters and on the rating process. There is no justification any more for rating studies to neglect the contributions made by Sears, Frenkel-Brunswik, and others. If these more complex methods are adopted, we may hope to gain further insight into the organization of personality.

The second suggestion also relates to the design of experiments. Factor analysis has two main functions: (1) to explore a completely unknown territory and suggests principles of classification; (2) the setting up of explicit experiments on the basis of a clearly defined hypothesis which can be supported or refuted by the outcome of the experiment. The majority of the studies reviewed in this chapter are of the first type; surely the time has come when we can abandon an approach which can have merely suggestive results and take up instead an approach which follows more closely the hypothetico-deductive method so characteristic of the more developed sciences.

ADDENDUM

WITTMAN CHECK LIST OF PSYCHOTIC BEHAVIOUR REACTIONS

(1) Affective Exaggeration.
(2) Paranoid Projection.
(3) Schizophrenic Withdrawal.

(1) *Affective Exaggeration:* Exaggerated emotional tone associated with lowered threshold of emotionality; may be general as in emotional lability or selective and fixed at one of the two extremes, euphoric expansion or depressive constriction.

(2) *Paranoid Projection:* A compensatory reaction to extremes of suspiciousness and conceit. Usually characterized by the supercilious, domineering self-assurance associated with somatic aggression, but may be characterized by the opposite extreme of meekly accepting, submissive, and indecisive reactions associated with a compensatory type of ideational substitution.

(3) *Schizophrenic Withdrawal:* A regressive reaction characterized by apathy and withdrawal from social contacts, few if any interests, and marked lack of energy and initiative either with bizarre, irrelevant affect, or, at the opposite extreme, a paucity of affect and ideation.

The individual traits for each of the components listed are weighted on a 1- to 7-point scale, interpreted as follows:

(1) An extreme lack.
(2) Slight evidence.
(3) Present but not marked.
(4) A marked degree.
(5) Very marked degree.
(6) Extreme, colours the entire picture.
(7) Maximum, to the exclusion of opposing components.

The final weight for a given component is the average of the weights assigned for all the traits listed under that component. The subscripts A and B are used to indicate which of the two sub-types under a given component is the stronger. The subscript is omitted only when the total weights for A and B are equal or approximately equal, indicating a general reaction, i.e. affective lability, paranoid projection with somatic aggression and ideational substitution, or schizoid withdrawal with both bizarre, irrelevant affect, and paucity of ideation.

The sum of the three psychotic behaviour components has been empirically set at 10 points as designating a psychotic condition (at only 9 points if one component has the maximum weight of 7). A sum for the three components that is less than 10 points (unless one component is the maximum of 7) designates a psychoneurotic or nonpsychotic condition.

I. Affective Exaggeration

Euphoric Expansion (A)	*Depressive Constriction (B)*
(1) Vivacious and buoyant.	Dejected and hopeless in attitude and manner.
(2) Overactive and energetic.	Slow and retarded in movements.
(3) Distractible attention.	Narrowed interest and attention.
(4) Socially confident and assured.	Socially depressed and retarded.
(5) Flight of ideas.	Retardation of thought processes.
(6) Press of speech.	Retarded speech.
(7) Rhyming, punning speech, etc.	Monosyllabic or mute.
(8) Feelings of physical well-being.	Hypochondriacal complaints.
(9) Hypereroticism.	Hypoeroticism.
(10) Expansive ideation.	Ideas of unworthiness and guilt.
(11) Friendly and outgoing.	Self-absorbed and brooding.
(12) Lack of inhibitory control.	Inhibited in manner and control.
(13) Optimistic and independent.	Pessimistic and dependent.
(14) Noisy and loud.	Quiet and restrained.
(15) Histrionic and exhibitionistic.	Reserved and subdued.
(16) Blithe unconcern.	Overconcern with personal problems.

II. Paranoid Projection

Somatic Aggression (A)	*Ideational Substitution (B)*
(1) Assertive and aggressive manner.	Meekly submissive in manner.
(2) Overt recognition of own superiority.	Without overt superiority feelings.
(3) Self-assured and superior.	Dependence upon others.
(4) Superior and condescending in speech.	Self-depreciating in speech and manner.
(5) Rigid, inflexible judgments expressed.	Egocentric judgment only on probing.
(6) Egocentric attitude.	Egocentricity cloaked by obsequiousness.
(7) Forceful and energetic in speech and movement.	Weakly subordinated in speech and movement.
(8) Overt projection of unaccepted drives.	Ideational substitution for overt projection.
(9) Pedantic opinionated attitudes.	Indecisive, ambivalent attitudes.
(10) Conceited and grandiose.	Suspiciously apprehensive.
(11) Projection of erotic drives.	Repression of erotic drives.
(12) Openly critical and sarcastic.	Defensively accepting of authority.
(13) Exaggerated self-esteem.	Overt inferiority feelings.

(14) Indifferent disregard for others' opinion.

Sensitively protective of own ego.

(15) Irritable and irascible.

Accepting and conforming.

(16) Verbally or physically abusive.

Neither verbally nor physically abusive.

III. Schizoid Withdrawal

Bizarre, Irrelevant Affect (A)	Paucity of Affect and Ideation (B)
(1) Dissociated affect.	Apathetic and unconcerned.
(2) Incongruity of affect and ideation.	Apparent lack of affect.
(3) Physical inertia.	Mental and physical inertia.
(4) Bizarre delusional ideation.	Paucity of thought content.
(5) Silly laughter and grimacing.	Emotionally levelled.
(6) Lack of heterosexual contacts.	Lack of heterosexual interests.
(7) Collapsed flaccidity in appearance.	Extreme passivity in attitude.
(8) Irrelevant, rambling speech.	Monosyllabic or mute.
(9) Bizarre motor mannerisms.	Lifeless and automaton-like.
(10) Overt masturbatory activity.	Lack of any libido drive.
(11) Overt affective reaction to hallucinations.	Without auditory hallucinations.
(12) Ideas of influence and control.	Without ideas of influence or control.
(13) Bizarre somatic ideation.	Without somatic ideation.
(14) Autistic self-absorption.	Extreme indifference.
(15) Engrossed in delusional phantasy life.	No evidence of delusional ideation.
(16) Reversal of reality and phantasy.	Withdrawn from reality.

CHAPTER III

THE ANALYSIS OF QUESTIONNAIRES AND INVENTORIES

I F THE MAJORITY OF factorial studies making use of ratings have come from England, nearly all the questionnaire, inventory, and other self-rating studies have come from America. This fact has given rise to differences in the treatment of data which may at first appear confusing to the reader. As pointed out before, the London school, in their analysis of ratings, have followed, by and large, the principle of extracting the most comprehensive factors first and of keeping factors orthogonal; the Americans have rather followed the principle of extracting smaller "group" or "primary" factors first and letting these factors be intercorrelated. It is from the inter-correlations of these primary factors that they then proceed to extract the broader, more general factors which the English school would have extracted right at the beginning. As has been mentioned before, the two procedures do not involve any fundamental difference in the final outcome of the analysis provided they are both carried out competently by workers who are clearly aware of the difficulties and fallacies involved. However, sometimes the analysis is not carried to a proper conclusion—a member of the London school may only extract the most important one or two factors; the fol-lower of Thurstone may not complete his analysis by extracting second-order factors—and in that case there may be a superficial contrast between the two methods of analysis which may appear to give substance to the view held by some psychologists, namely that factor analysts agree with each other as little as do psychoanalysts.

The group of studies to be reviewed falls mainly into two periods, linked by a few researches which mark the transition. In the first period, attempts were made to use correlations between existing scales which were assumed to be separate measures of neuroticism, extraversion, ascendance, self-sufficiency, depression, etc., in order to discover either more parsimonious ways of arranging and scoring the tests, or of discovering more fundamentally meaningful psycho-logical variables. In the second period, analysis became more de-tailed and correlations were run between individual questions, no assumption being made about the factors which might be defined by these questions.

It may be said without fear of contradiction that the efforts of the first period ended in almost complete failure. As Vernon (1938) points out: "The attempts to classify test items or symptoms logically into distinct groups has not, we must admit, been successful. On the one hand, it is found that tests of presumably different traits inter-correlate very highly; on the other hand, different tests of nominally the same trait . . . tend to give very poor correlations with one another. It is doubtful, then, whether most of the traits at which the tests have been directed are unitary and discrete."

This overlap between hypothetically different traits is most apparent in attempts to measure neuroticism and introversion-extraversion. Vernon (1938) quotes the results of 40 experiments showing that the average correlation between different introversion tests, and the average correlation between introversion and psycho-neurotic tendency tests are practically identical, namely $+ \cdot 36 \pm \cdot 10$. A further 18 experiments with the Ascendance-Submission test showed an average correlation of $+ \cdot 30$ between submissiveness and introversion, or psychoneurotic tendency. Tests of inferiority feelings also agree quite closely with tests of introversion.

At first sight, such findings may appear to contradict explicitly the results arrived at in the last chapter. There, introversion and neuro-ticism were considered quite unrelated orthogonal dimensions of personality; now we seem to find evidence that they are not only related but identical. The answer to this problem is provided in an excellent paper by Collier and Emch (1938), who show that most questionnaire constructors have used Freud's conception of intro-version rather than Jung's. Freud tends to identify introversion with incipient neuroticism. According to him: "An introvert is not yet a neurotic but he finds himself in a labile condition; he must develop symptoms at the next dislocation of forces if he does not find other outlets for his pent-up libido" (1920). Jung's position, already quoted, is quite different. He considers that: "It is a mistake to believe that introversion is more or less the same as neurosis. As concepts the two have not the slightest connection with each other" (1921). This conceptual identification of introversion and neuro-ticism, so common in much recent work, rests on the misapprehen-sion of Jung's theory and does not invalidate our findings from the preceding chapter.

Two further difficulties were pointed out by Eysenck (1947). The first of these relates to the trait of "sociability", which is considered by many American writers to be the main characteristic of the extravert. Thus, Freyd (1924) considers the extravert to be "an individual in whom exists a diminution of the thought processes in relation to directly observable social behaviour with an accompanied tendency to make social contacts". Equally, there is much evidence that lack of sociability characterizes the neurotic; indeed, difficulty in making good social contacts is one of the outstanding traits of the neurotic (Russell Fraser, 1949). The implication of this statement of course is that "sociability" is not a univocal trait; in other words, in the two-dimensional space generated by the two orthogonal axes, neuroticism and introversion, the trait sociability does not lie on either axis but has projections on both. In this it is probably similar to other traits, such as persistence, and autonomic imbalance, which have been found to be correlated with both neuroticism and introversion. It follows that we cannot derive from ratings on sociability alone a score for either neuroticism or introversion. Yet this is precisely what many writers seem to have done. Their argument runs something like this: Introversion correlates with lack of sociability; neuroticism correlates with lack of sociability. Consequently, neuroticism = introversion. The arguments need only be stated to be seen to be erroneous.

The other difficulty in questionnaire studies of this type is brought out most clearly when we take the Jungian prototypes of the introvert and extravert respectively, namely the hysteric and the dysthymic patient. "The majority of symptoms listed in questionnaires are *affective* symptoms; indeed, it is almost insuperably difficult to design a questionnaire containing many hysterical symptoms. The dysthymic patient is troubled by the consciousness of emotional disturbances; it is easy to list a number of the more common of these disturbances, and a list of this nature is likely to cover most of the symptoms of which the patient complains. The symptomatology of the hysteric, on the other hand, is more *protean*; it relates to his attitude to associates rather than to individual symptoms, and is therefore much more difficult to put into the form of simple 'Yes' –'No' questions. Also, the hysteric has little insight into the pathological character of these attitudes, and is therefore unlikely to give very meaningful answers to a simple questionnaire" (Eysenck, 1947).

With a full appreciation of these difficulties we now turn to a detailed examination of the actual results obtained in the first period of the factorial analysis of questionnaire data.

The best starting-off point is a study by Willoughby (1932), in which 152 married couples and 144 female students filled in the Thurstone Personality Schedule. Willoughby on *a priori* grounds grouped the items in 6 sub-scales dealing with the following topics: (1) social; (2) extravert; (3) fantasy; (4) physical; (5) parental; (6) sex. Table 14 gives the intercorrelations between these six scales for husbands (top half) and wives (bottom half) respectively, as well as the results of two factor analyses carried out by the use of Thurstone's and Spearman's methods respectively. One factor was sufficient to account for all the intercorrelations, and it is interesting to note that this factor satisfied Spearman's tetrad criterion. Its identification as neuroticism is fairly obvious from the nature of the data used.

TABLE 14

	1	2	3	4	5	6	Thurstone Analysis Husbands:	Wives:	Spearman Analysis Husbands:	Wives:
1. Social .	—	·34	·59	·36	·46	·46	·77	·65	·69	·52
2. Extravert	·38	—	·57	·23	·40	·47	·70	·74	·60	·72
3. Fantasy .	·59	·55	—	·43	·60	·44	·84	·77	·86	·76
4. Physical .	·08	·22	·22	—	·34	·25	·63	·49	·46	·29
5. Parental .	·37	·39	·40	·19	—	·33	·72	·68	·65	·61
6. Sex .	·08	·32	·20	·17	·29	—	·68	·53	·59	·33

Perry (1934) gave three intelligence tests and nine personality questionnaires to 178 boys and 144 girls. These personality questionnaires, which included the Bernreuter, the Laird, and the Allport Ascendance-Submission Scales, gave rise to two main factors, one of neuroticism, the other of sufficiency, dominance, or ascendance. Two further factors were isolated—one of intelligence, the other seemingly very similar to the second factor. Identification of the first two factors with neuroticism and extraversion does not appear too far-fetched.

Not quite so clear is the interpretation of Flanagan's (1935) study of the intercorrelations between the four Bernreuter scales by means of Hotelling's technique. He finds two factors or components: the first of which he describes as "lack of self-confidence", whereas the second one is labelled "sociability". While it would be tempting again to identify these two factors in the same way as before, it is not really possible to do so in view of the fact that only four scales were included in the factor analysis.

Vernon (1938) analysed the replies to the Boyd Personality Questionnaire given by 50 men and 50 women. This test contains 120 items classified under 20 headings or general tendencies which, however, are not disclosed to the subject. The sets of scores on these "general tendencies" were intercorrelated and a factor analysis with rotation of axes performed. Three factors resulted, the first of which Vernon identified as "psychoneurotic tendency"; it contained such items as depression or melancholia; instability or temperamentalness; worry or anxiety; lack of self-control; shirking of responsibility; lack of self-sufficiency or confidence. The second and third factors, named respectively "carefreeness" and "scrupulousness", closely resemble the extravert and introvert types. The carefree person apparently shirks responsibility, is free from worry and emotional thinking, is not self-conscious, is free from tenseness, lacks definite interests, and is unable to concentrate. The "scrupulous" person is characterized by obsessional carefulness, suspiciousness, strong self-control of feelings, freedom from instability, from emotional thinking, and from inability to concentrate.

One of the latest studies using this type of approach is reported by Gibb (1942), who gave various personality inventories as well as tests of fluency, perseveration, and intelligence to 200 subjects. He arrived at four factors, the first of which he identified with Flanagan's lack of self-confidence or neuroticism; the others he labelled "fluency", "solitariness", and "concentration". Possibly a clearer picture is presented by his re-analysis of the data after the elimination of the Bernreuter scales. The first factor is very clearly one of emotional instability, which was found to correlate with low intelligence. The other factors are rather more complex, and too narrowly specific to be of great interest here.

Another recent example of a factorial study employing *a priori* scales is the work of Cook and Wherry (1950). They use as their variables scales from the Minnesota Multiphasic Personality Inventory, as well as a number of aptitude tests taken from the Navy Basic Battery. 111 naval enlisted submarine candidates constituted the experimental population. Six factors altogether were extracted from the battery, and labelled respectively: tendency to personality maladjustment, numerical verbal intelligence, tendency to overactivity, tendency to paranoia, mechanical coordination, and tendency to femininity of interest pattern. This study is not well conceived in that it includes too divergent types of test, and is not based on any kind of hypothesis which would integrate them in any way.

We must now turn to the studies which form our second group, i.e. those in which correlations are run not between scores on clusters of items selected on *a priori* grounds, but between individual items themselves. Pride of place here must go to J. P. and R. B. Guilford (1934, 1936, 1939), whose work has opened up an entirely new and important field of investigation. In their first study (1934), 36 typically introvert-extravert questions were administered to 930 students and intercorrelated. Four factors were extracted as the Spearman-Dodd test showed that a two-factor pattern would not apply to the data. These four factors were tentatively identified as (*a*) social introversion-extraversion, (*b*) emotional sensitiveness, (*c*) impulsiveness, and (*d*) interest in self. In 1936 the analysis was repeated, using more up-to-date methods of analysis, and three main factors were found and identified. Factor I is defined by the following items: inclined to keep in the background on social occasions; does not enjoy getting acquainted with most people; generally prefers not to take the lead in group activities; inclined to limit acquaintances to a select few. As the Guilfords point out, "the first factor is undoubtedly of a social character. . . . One might name this dimension social introversion-extraversion, sociability, shyness, or other similar designations." They label this factor S.

The second factor is characterized by the following items: has frequent ups and downs in mood; his feelings are rather easily hurt; inclines to worry over possible misfortunes; expresses his emotions readily; day-dreams frequently. "The second factor gives a rather neat picture. It is undoubtedly an emotional factor . . . running throughout the list of characteristics is a thread of emotional immaturity or emotional dependency. . . . We shall call this dimension factor E." The third factor is characterized by the following items: is a male; is not frequently absent-minded; likes to sell things; has not kept a personal diary of his own accord; is more interested in athletics than in intellectual things. "This suggests . . . the dimension of masculinity-femininity. . . . There is an element of aggressiveness in some of the items; this might be the oft-mentioned trait of dominance or of ascendance-submission. . . . One might name the factor the 'masculine-ideal'. However, for the present we shall name it with the more noncommittal letter M."

Two further factors were extracted, but were found rather difficult to define. The fourth one was tentatively labelled factor R, "the letter R standing for a word coined from the Greek, 'rhathymia', which means freedom from care". The fifth factor also was difficult to interpret. "The aspect emphasized is the liking for thinking and tackling problems requiring thought, versus a liking for prompt, overt action. We shall refer to this factor temporarily as factor T."

Scales were developed by the writers for the measurement of the first three factors and were applied to 200 new subjects. Instead of the hoped-for zero intercorrelations, S and E were found to be intercorrelated to the extent of ·463 and S and M to the extent of ·402. E and M intercorrelated to a negligible extent.

Two further factors were isolated, and the provisionally identified factors R and T were investigated more fully in a later paper by the same authors (1939). Thirty items were administered to 1,000 students and factor analysed. Nine factors were extracted. The first of these was one of depression (D); the second a factor of rathymia (R) previously noted; the fourth factor was the shyness or seclusiveness factor (S) isolated before; the sixth factor was labelled thinking introversion, and appears similar to the suggestive factor T isolated before; factor eight was called an alertness factor (A); factor nine was not found to be meaningful, and interpretations of factors three, five, and seven were not made with any degree of confidence.

Two further factors were isolated in another paper (1939), in which 600 subjects were given a questionnaire of 24 items. One of these was factor N (nervousness or jumpiness), the other factor GD (general drive, characterized chiefly by pleasure in action). This last factor may be compared with Heymans' and Wiersma's "activity" factor.

The Guilfords' factors are oblique, and unfortunately they have not carried out a second-order factor in order to clarify the relationship between their factors. In their 1939 paper they show that there are considerable correlations between factors D, S, and T, ranging from ·5 to ·7. "These relationships have distinct bearing on the question as to just what is introversion-extraversion . . . it would seem that there is some basis for lumping together some characteristics bordering on seclusiveness with some implying a thinking person, and still others that indicate depressed emotional tendencies and for calling the resultant picture the introvert. Because of the relationship between these three primary traits, it is easy to see how a more cursory inspection of personalities would lead to the conviction of a composite trait like introversion. The opposite composite of sociability, cheerfulness, and lack of meditative thinking would, of course, be the extravert picture. . . . The use of the term 'introvert', as we have indicated, to represent the person who is simultaneously on the side of the shy, depressed, and thinker, for the dimensions S, D, and T, would then seem to be justified by this statistical analysis."

This passage is very important. Guilford is frequently misquoted as having shown in his study that such type concepts as introversion are meaningless and conclusively disproved by his analysis into a number of independent traits. This is not at all a true picture of Guilford's contribution. What he has done rather has been to verify some of Jung's hypotheses relating to the correlation between certain traits (sociability, lack of depression, lack of desire to think), and to disprove others; if anything, it is the correlations between these "primary traits" which are impressive, not their independence.[1]

In more recent publications, Guilford has isolated further factors which again are not independent of each other or of those isolated before; those added to his previous list are: C (for cycloid disposition or stability of emotional reactions as opposed to "instability"); A (ascendance-submission); I (inferiority feelings as opposed to self-confidence); O (for objectivity as opposed to hypersensitiveness; Co (for co-operativeness); and Ag (for agreeableness as opposed to quarrelsomeness).

TABLE 15

Intercorrelations of Factor Scores

	S	T	D	C	R	G	A	M	I	N	O	Ag	Co
S	—	·423	·638	·439	·655	·379	·733	·101	·591	·384	·465	·140	·222
T	—	—	·645	·588	·300	−·070	·197	·212	·335	·391	·405	·169	·237
D	—	—	—	·901	·228	−·040	·481	·315	·740	·710	·746	·337	·442
C	—	—	—	—	−·021	−·188	·308	·330	·675	·701	·722	·351	·416
R	—	—	—	—	—	·559	·525	−·039	·270	·079	·207	−·084	−·019
G	—	—	—	—	—	—	·438	−·067	·088	−·231	−·059	−·314	−·169
A	—	—	—	—	—	—	—	·256	·570	·325	·460	·001	·200
M	—	—	—	—	—	—	—	—	·326	·348	·365	·006	·210
I	—	—	—	—	—	—	—	—	—	·674	·746	·350	·448
N	—	—	—	—	—	—	—	—	—	—	·720	·470	·529
O	—	—	—	—	—	—	—	—	—	—	—	·495	·616
Ag	—	—	—	—	—	—	—	—	—	—	—	—	·631
Co	—	—	—	—	—	—	—	—	—	—	—	—	—

Intercorrelations for these 13 factors were calculated on 122 men and 78 women by Lovell (1945); these correlations are given in Table 15. A factor analysis of this table of correlations between primary factors resulted in the extraction of a number of second-

[1] Emphasis on this correlation between primary factors may seem to many to be labouring the obvious, but misunderstanding has been frequent. Thus, Allport (1937) maintains "that the Guilfords' factor analysis of items included in many tests for extraversion-introversion shows that quite independent clusters of responses may be involved", but, as we have seen, these clusters of responses are really far from independent, and it is precisely on their intercorrelations that such higher order concepts as introversion-extraversion are built up.

order or super-factors. Six of these were extracted, although Lovell admits that a comparison of the standard deviations of the residuals with the standard error of the average correlation indicated that not more than three factors should be extracted. To the writer it is doubtful if any but the first two factors can be considered significant when proper extimates are made of the communalities in such a way as to reduce the number of factors extracted to a minimum, and

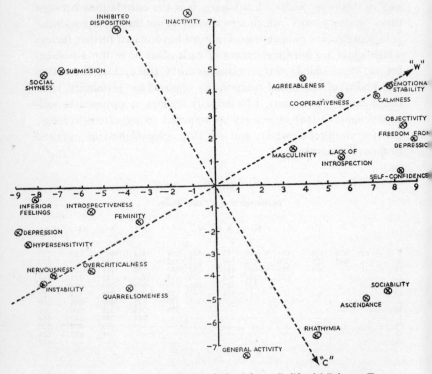

Fig. 14.—Two Second-order Factors derived from Guilfords' Primary Factors.

accordingly a plot has been prepared of the saturations of the 13 primary factors on the first 2 centroid super-factors (Fig. 14). When a rotation is carried out as indicated in the diagram, the resulting factors appear quite clear-cut and meaningful. The first factor is characterized by emotional stability, calmness, objectivity, freedom from depression, self-confidence, co-operativeness, lack of intro-spection, agreeableness, and sociability, as opposed to instability, depression, nervousness, hypersensitivity, inferiority feeling, over-criticalness, quarrelsomeness, introspectiveness, and social shyness.

The resemblance of this factor to "*w*" in its positive and to neuroticism in its negative aspect is striking.

The second factor is equally clear. It contrasts inhibited disposition, inactivity, submission, social shyness, inferiority feelings, and depression to sociability, ascendance, rhathymia, self-confidence, freedom from depression, and general activity. The similarity of this factor to "*c*", surgency or extraversion-introversion is again very marked.

These two factors also emerge from the rather more complex analysis carried out by Lovell (1945), and are indeed the only two clearly marked and meaningful factors among her six. Her first factor is tentatively identified "as a drive restraint variable". "Those factors with sizable loadings on it appear to have in common an active approach to experience. The person with high scores on them tends to engage in *vigorous overt action*, to give relatively *uninhibited expression* to impulse, to seek social contacts, and be a social *leader*." The items having high loadings on this factor are clearly the same as those which characterize the introvert-extravert factor in the writer's solution. Lovell's factor III "has been defined tentatively as an emotionality variable. At the low extreme on it would be the individual characterized by hampering emotional excess. At the other extreme . . . would be found the individual who is dependably cheerful and optimistic, free from constant analysis of himself and others, with some tendency to be (1) free of nervous habits, (2) lacking in hypersensitivity, (3) self-confident, sociable, and tolerant, and (4) lacking in domineering qualities." This factor is clearly the one labelled "*w*" or neuroticism in the writer's analysis. Lovell's super factors two and four appear very similar to each other, and seem to present no underlying principle which would make psychological sense. Both have high loadings on objectivity, tolerance, and lack of nervousness. Super factors five and six Lovell herself admits to be "too weak to be of any importance".

Similar to Lovell's work is that of North (1949), who administered the Guilford inventories for factors STDCR to 170 students, together with the Kuder Preference Record and an intelligence test. A factor analysis of the intercorrelations between the Guilford factors resulted in a two-factor pattern, which is reproduced in Fig. 15; the rotation indicated in this figure was carried out by North. It will be seen that the two factors I′ and II′ bear a striking resemblance to Neuroticism and Extraversion-Introversion. The former is characterized by C (emotional instability), D (depression), T (introspectiveness), and to some extent S (social shyness). The latter is characterized by R (happy-go-lucky carefreeness) on the extraverted side, and by S (social shyness) on the introverted side.[1]

Of some interest are the correlations between neuroticism and extraversion on the one hand, and the remaining variables measured by North on the other. Neuroticism shows a significantly negative correlation of $-\cdot25$ with intelligence (we will have occasion again and again to note such correlations of the order $\cdot2$ to $\cdot3$ between

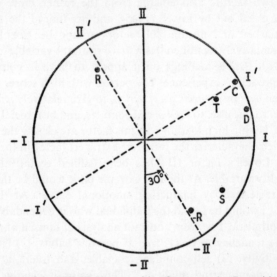

Fig. 15.—Plot of the STDCR Vectors with reference to the Centroid Axes I and II, and to the Orthogonally Rotated Axes I' and II'.

"w" and "g"); it also shows negative correlations with Kuder Preferences for mechanical ($-\cdot30$), computational ($-\cdot31$), and scientific ($-\cdot20$) activities, as well as a positive correlation of $\cdot23$ with literary interests. Extraversion correlates positively with the weight-height ratio ($\cdot17$); in a later chapter we will find a summary of the extensive evidence linking extraversion with the type of body-build indicated by this ratio. Extraversion also correlates negatively with

[1] If our interpretation of Lovell's and North's second factor as one of "introversion-extraversion" is correct, we should predict that hysterics would be differentiated from dysthymics by having high R and low S scores. In an unpublished research, Hildebrandt has shown that this prediction is borne out at a high level of significance. The possibility of making correct predictions of this kind considerably strengthens our faith in the soundness of the factorial argument.

computational ($- \cdot 16$) and positively with persuasive ($\cdot 35$) Kuder Preferences. These results are hardly surprising, and fit in well with the stereotyped picture of the extravert.

A somewhat different approach from that used by Lovell and North is that of Thurstone (1951). Basing himself on the intercorrelations between 13 sets of scores for the various Guilford factors, he showed that nine linearly independent factors could account for all the intercorrelations. These factors he named R (reflective), S (sociable), E (emotionally stable), V (vigorous), D (dominant), A (active), I (impulsive), X_1 (tentatively designated as confident), X_2 (left without interpretation). The correlations between these factors were quite considerable, the highest being $\cdot 52$ (E and S) and $\cdot 71$ (I and D), and a second-order analysis of this matrix was accordingly undertaken by Baehr (1951).

The first of her second-order factors had high positive saturations on Thurstone's S ($\cdot 79$), X_1 ($\cdot 73$), and E ($\cdot 62$). In addition, there was a small negative loading of $- \cdot 46$ on A. "The emotionally-toned responses in this factor are generally adjustive. The negative loading on Active suggests placidity or an absence of high-pressure or high-strung activity. The easy-going and uncomplicated behaviour evident here has caused us to designate this factor *Emotionally Stable*."

The second factor has two high saturations, namely on Thurstone's I ($\cdot 85$) and D ($\cdot 80$) factors. "The picture is one of impulsive, carefree, and general outgoing behaviour responses, all of which are facilitated by spontaneous reaction to stimuli. We designated this factor *Primary Function*." Primary Function, as we have seen before, is Heymans' term for extraversion, and we see therefore that here again the main two second-order factors which emerge from the analysis of the correlations between Guilfords' factors are neuroticism (or rather its obverse, emotional stability) and extraversion-introversion. The other two factors extracted by Baehr are labelled *Activity* and *Emotionally Unstable*; the latter, presumably, is the obverse aspect of her second factor, whereas the former is related by her to Heymans' postulated factor of the same name.

As a follow-up of this investigation, Baehr used a list of 22 behaviour items, employing a modified form of paired-comparison technique on 200 subjects. A factor analysis of the correlations between the 22 items resulted in four factors which she considered to allow of a clear interpretation, as well as two additional relatively meaningless factors. One of the interpretable factors she labelled emotional stability; it has positive saturations on cheerful ($\cdot 56$), even-tempered (·46), emotionally stable (·42), and negative correlations on high-strung (— ·60), impulsive (— ·56), and demonstrative (— ·41). Another factor which she labelled primary function, and which we may agree represents the extraversion-introversion dichotomy, is characterized by items "impulsive" (— ·56), demonstrative (— ·42), happy-go-lucky (— ·32), steady worker (·47), and persevering (·45).

Her third factor is again one of activity, while her fourth factor is called hypomania, and is considered to be "the resultant of a combination of some of the elements of primary function and emotional stability". Baehr's solution is not wholly acceptable; there are high correlations between these various factors (activity and primary function, for instance, intercorrelate — ·504), and no second-order analysis has been carried out. Nevertheless, in so far as it goes, this study fits in reasonably well in its main conclusions with those reviewed earlier.

On the whole, we may conclude our discussion of Guilford's contribution by saying that in so far as questionnaire responses can be admitted as evidence in our analysis of the organization of personality, a flood of light has been thrown on the principles of organization at the trait level, and that the higher-order constructs emerging from the intercorrelations of these traits confirm to a remarkable extent the results obtained previously by rating studies. Both these contributions are of outstanding importance; the first because analysis in terms of such very general factors as neuroticism and introversion lack the requisite applicability to many practical and theoretical problems, and the second because objections which may legitimately be made to questionnaire studies are entirely different from the objections which may legitimately be made to rating studies, and if it can be shown that to a considerable extent the main results from these two types of study agree, then the evidential value of the proof is very much increased.

Compared to Guilford's patient, long-continued, and fruitful work, most of the other researches in this field must be regarded as being of comparatively little interest, except in so far as they confirm or fail to confirm Guilford's findings. An exception to this appraisal may be made in the case of Cattell, who has tried to develop a system along somewhat independent lines, and who has also tried to link up factors found in questionnaire responses with factors at the level of ratings.

One of the most important studies confirming many of Guilford's findings is one carried out by Mosier (1937), who intercorrelated responses made by 500 male students on 39 items from the Thurstone neurotic inventory, and on the A.C.E. psychological examination. He found 8 factors, of which 3 were doubtful and not readily interpretable. The 5 factors readily identified were:

(1) Cycloid: ups and downs in mood, happiness to sadness, frequently in low spirits, often just miserable, worried over possible misfortunes, frequently grouchy.

(2) Depression: periods of loneliness, lonesome even with others, frequently in low spirits, often just miserable, difficulty in making friends.

(3) Hypersensitive: feelings easily hurt, cannot stand criticism, nervous, often in state of excitement.

(4) Inferiority: lack of self-confidence, easily discouraged, feelings of inferiority.

(5) Shyness: troubled with shyness, keeps in background on social occasions, feelings of inferiority, difficulty in starting conversations, not confident about abilities.

Mosier comes to the conclusion that "there is no single trait of neurotic tendency which can be postulated in a parsimonious description of behaviour", but this statement seems to reflect more the undeveloped state of multiple-factor analysis, which at that time had not advanced to the concept of second-order factors and oblique first-order factors, than the actual data analysed by Mosier. A reanalysis of his work by more modern methods would be of interest; it may be predicted with considerable confidence that such an analysis would, to a large extent, duplicate the results found by Lovell in her analysis of the intercorrelations between Guilford's primary factors.

Much in line with the results obtained by Lovell, North, and Thurstone is a research by Jenkins (1950). He posits two theorems. According to the first, "personality trait factors contain variances which comprise two independent basic factors or superfactors . . . these superfactors are neither antagonistic, oppositional, reciprocal, nor bipolar. In fact our evidence indicates that they are statistically independent behaviour tendencies, and hence neutral to each other".

The second theorem asserts that "*personality factors are unipolar*, and, by implication, constitutes a general denial of bipolar factors of personality. This theorem is not necessary for the truth of the first one, but it is important for its rationale as a part of a general theory of personality".

We will not here deal with the second theorem which, as far as the writer can see, is almost completely meaningless, but will instead examine the evidence given for the first. Unfortunately, this evidence is rather sketchy and depends essentially on correlations between nine traits which appear to fall into two groups. The traits within each group correlate positively with each other, but the groups do not correlate one with the other. Thus, we obtain two superfactors, referred to by Jenkins as factors C and A. (These letters stand for cholinergic and adrenergic respectively, although no evidence is given for this identification.)

The "C" factor is characterized by the traits of buoyancy, dynamism, emotional spontaneity, and carefreeness, i.e. a group of typically extravertive traits. Factor A is characterized by depression, lethargy, hypersensitiveness, anxiety, and feeling of social insecurity. The picture here presented is typical of the neurotic syndrome, or the obverse of factor "w". Also associated with these factors respectively, and well in agreement with our provisional interpretation of them as extraversion and neuroticism, are the following traits: for the "C" factor—feeling of strength, high activity level, feeling of well-being, spontaneity, and carefreeness; for the "A" factor—feeling of weakness, low activity level, hypersensitiveness, general inferiority, feelings of social insecurity, indecision, and procrastination.

It is to be hoped that Jenkins will publish his data in somewhat more extended form, indicating, among other things, the number of subjects used, and their selection, and that he will clarify the meaning of his second theorem. In so far as his research goes, however, it is not in contradiction to the general picture given by those previously cited.

TABLE 16
Factor Loadings according to the Centroid Method (1945 Group; Rotated Factors)

Variable	I	II	III	IV
1. Theoretical intelligence . . .	48	13	− 09	24
2. Practical intelligence . . .	00	70	19	16
3. Mechanical comprehension . .	30	66	− 11	25
4. Manual dexterity	− 15	78	39	− 06
5. Rote memory	64	− 28	28	05
6. Memory for contexts . . .	63	− 11	07	35
7. Perseverance, energy . . .	− 12	13	67	37
8. Readiness to assume responsibility .	− 28	21	27	70
9. Carefulness	33	07	51	12
10. Ability to take the initiative . .	− 11	01	30	79
11. Co-operativeness	11	21	57	37
12. Capacity for leadership . . .	26	15	18	75

The same may be said of a research somewhat more fully reported (Husen, 1951). Using self-ratings on 12 traits of 100 matriculants called up for the Swedish army, this author calculated intercorrelations and carried out a factor analysis the outcome of which is shown in Table 16. The four factors emerging from this analysis are fairly clear in their interpretation; two are cognitive, two orectic. The two cognitive factors correspond to Vernon's (1950) *v-ed* and *k-m* factors, i.e. the verbal-educational and the practical-mechanical; the former here is characterized by high loadings on "theoretical

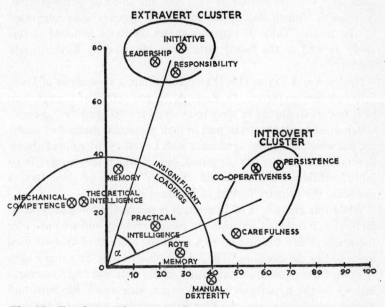

Fig. 16.—Two-factor Diagram showing results of Husen's Self-rating Scale.

intelligence", "rote memory", and "memory for contexts", the latter by "practical intelligence", "technical comprehension", and "manual dexterity".

The two orectic factors bear a marked similarity to extraversion and introversion respectively. The extraverted cluster is characterized by leadership, initiative, and readiness to assume responsibility, the introverted cluster by persistence, co-operativeness, and carefulness. All six qualities are "*w*" traits, and we might expect factors III and IV to be non-independent and to give rise to a "*w*" superfactor. That this is so can be seen from Fig. 16, which represents in diagrammatic form these two factors; the angle alpha between the two centroid vectors drawn through the two clusters is clearly less than 90°, and the two clusters can therefore be seen to be correlated. Husen himself agrees that we are here dealing with a "general character factor", which is a "second-order factor . . . situated behind factors III and IV".[1]

Reyburn and Taylor (1940) carried out a self-rating study in which 115 subjects responded to 10 items on a 5-point scale: also given was a perseveration test made up of three tests of the type used by Cattell. Three main factors were extracted of which the first is identified by them as "w", the second as "c", and the third as perseveration. A possible fourth factor of sociability appears also suggested by the results. Table 17 opposite shows the items included in this study as well as the factor saturations obtained by Reyburn and Taylor.

Reyburn and Taylor (1943) also contribute a re-analysis of Guilford's studies on factors, D, R, T, A, N, and GD. The most prominent factors to appear in their re-analysis are "c" and "w", a result which must be attributed in part to their particular method of analysis, but which is in good agreement with Lovell's work quoted above. Several other factors are suggested, one of which they name "flexibility", while another is named "tension"; some of these factors duplicate the primary factors of Guilford's.

While this analysis is of interest, it is not methodologically satisfactory, as it does not separate out clearly primary and second-order factors, and also because up to a point the method of analysis used tends to beg the question.[2] The former objection in the writer's view is more formidable than the latter; if the data are clearly contradictory to the hypothesis in accordance with which Reyburn and Taylor rotate their axes, results will be negative, whereas if the data can be made to appear congruent with the hypothesis which determines their rotation, this in itself is of some interest. However, this is a debatable point, and the author would not like to argue it with any conviction.

Layman (1940) has presented an analysis of intercorrelations of 67 items, which were subdivided into nine partially overlapping groups under hypothetical traits. Each table was factor analysed, and 51 items having factor loadings of ·5 or more on one or more factors

[1] Another paper, too late for detailed inclusion, which essentially supports the general outline emerging from the studies mentioned, is one by Banks and Keir (1952).

[2] Reyburn and Taylor rotate axes in accordance with an hypothesis regarding the most likely factors to be found.

TABLE 17

	2	3	4	5	6	7	8	9	10	p	Factor Loadings:		
											"w"	"c"	"p"
1. Makes friends easily	·07	·01	—·14	—·05	·03	·40	·08	·29	·02	—·04	·00	—·08	—
2. Easily hurt by remarks and actions of others		·02	·28	·22	·05	·00	·18	·06	·25	·05	—·25	·31	·29
3. Not suspicious of motives of others			—·03	—·05	—·08	—·06	·13	·16	—·25	—·09	·30	·12	—
4. Worries about possible misfortunes				·30	·16	—·17	—·08	—·09	·10	·15	—·30	·35	—
5. Indulges in self-pity when things go wrong					·33	—·15	·18	·03	·28	—·05	—·33	·62	—
6. Is easily rattled						—·04	—·01	·11	·16	—·10	—·09	·42	—
7. Takes prominent part in social affairs							—·09	·53	—·13	—·19	·06	—·28	·37
8. Does not criticize others and is careful of their feelings								·09	—·07	·24	·07	·18	—
9. Prefers working with others									—·17	—·18	·35	·29	—
10. Subject to change of mood without apparent cause										·19	·74	·00	—
11. p.										—	—·03	—·06	·48

were combined into one matrix and re-factored. Twelve factors altogether were extracted from this latter analysis; social inadequacy; social gregariousness; social initiative; social aggressiveness; self-sufficiency; impulsive action; changeability of interest; emotionality-moodiness; inferiority; emotionality-easily aroused; emotionality-introverted; inability to face reality. Some of these factors will be seen to be similar to Guilford's primary factors, but on the whole the work is clearly left in an unsatisfactory state as no second-order factors are extracted, thus making any detailed interpretation impossible. The study has one interesting feature, however, in that it appears to sub-divide a primary factor of sociability or social shyness into a number of components.

This possibility has been further explored by Brogden and Thomas (1943), who gave a questionnaire made up of 25 Bernreuter items relating to sociability to 365 students in order to discover "the primary traits in personality items purporting to measure sociability". Some of the five factors they extract are difficult or impossible to interpret, but others are relatively clear and intelligible. Factor I appears to be a factor of intellectual independence, and of liking for ideational activities, such as reading; factor two, which also occurred in Layman's analysis, is one of gregariousness; a third factor is interpreted as indicative of the need for primary emotional relationships. These results are very intriguing and of great potential importance. If the hierarchical scheme of personality organization outlined in the first chapter is correct, it follows not only that the most general traits like neuroticism and introversion-extraversion are made up of primary traits; it also follows that these primary traits themselves are made up of different clusters of reaction tendencies. Sociability lends itself particularly easily to further analysis in view of the fact that items supposedly characterizing it clearly relate to several different underlying tendencies, such as the three isolated by Brogden and Thomas. It is to be hoped that similar analyses will be carried out of all the other primary factors reported by Guilford, as in this way our knowledge will become more and more detailed.

In contrast to the Brogden-Thomas study of sociability, we have Pallister's (1933) work on the negative or withdrawal attitude. 209 women students were given a number of inventories, including the Leckey individuality record, broken up into eight categories (social confidence, co-operation, attitude toward family, nervous symptoms, optimism, physical symptoms, attitude towards sex, and work habits), a personal data-sheet, a vocabulary test, a set of ratings, and a number of physical measures. Correlations are given between the various Leckey categories, and by means of a tetrad analysis a generalized attitude of "withdrawal" established. Women having high withdrawal scores were, on the average, rated to be below the average for any of the characteristics rated (beauty, health, popularity, optimism, nervousness, temperament, attitude towards sex and family, work habits, and social confidence). Withdrawal attitude was related to verbal ability to the extent of ·28. This study, while it does not add much to our knowledge of sociability, does represent an interesting early application of factor analysis to personality study.

Most of the studies mentioned so far fail to make reference to psychiatric concepts. An outstanding exception to this rule is the work of Hsü (1943), who adapted Moore's approach to normal subjects. A 57-item questionnaire was given to 121 juniors and seniors from a Catholic women's college. Each item included examples of behaviour varying in number from 5 to 39. Certain groupings were arrived at on the basis of Yule's coefficient of association, and the method of tetrad differences used in connection with clusters forming a hierarchy. In this way a number of "fundamental character traits" were isolated. The nature of these is indicated by the descriptive titles given them: violent actions in anger, restricted sociability, staying by oneself in trouble, timidity, impracticability in using money, lack of interest in study, suspiciousness, tendency to depression, lack of self-confidence, timidity in social affairs, sulk and pout, sedentary recreations, active recreations, tendency to inactivity, and tendency to control temper. These primary factors were themselves intercorrelated, and what Hsü calls "super-factors" taken out. Eight such super-factors were extracted, which were labelled in psychiatric terms: "suspicion-depression", schizoid, præcox, laziness, paranoid, catatonic, manic-depressive, and social shyness. "Since several super-factors can be isolated in the present study, it may be interesting to see whether some supra-super-factor exists." Four super-factors were selected and intercorrelated and were shown to form a hierarchy which satisfied the tetrad criterion. Super-factor "manic-depressive configuration" is negatively correlated with the rest of the super-factors: "simple schizophrenic configuration", "paranoid configuration", and "catatonic configuration". "The fact that these three are . . . positively intercorrelated with each other seems to agree with the customary grouping of these three syndromes in psychiatry. Since these four super-factors resemble so closely the schizophrenic and manic-depressive syndromes, the nature of this supra-super factor can only be inferred as a factor of potency to psychosis."

While the statistical method used with its combination of features from Spearman and Thurstone is so clumsy as to make it almost impossible for the reader to reconstruct the various steps of the argument, and while terms such as "supra-super factors" call to mind Hollywood film advertisements rather than scientific concepts, some of the conclusions of this work do seem to point to a rather interesting similarity between psychiatric syndromes and trait clusters in normal people. Nor can the factor of "potency to psychosis" be dismissed too lightly, because we shall find ample evidence later to support the existence of such a factor.

We must now turn to a large-scale study carried out by Cattell (1950), in which he attempted to link up factors derived from his rating studies with factors from self-rating material. Using a carefully selected set of 80 items on 370 students, 19 factors, 4 of which he considers spurious or residual, were extracted; 12 of these are considered to have loading patterns consistent with factors previously isolated. Among these are factor one—general neuroticism or anxiety-depression; factor two—shyness; factor five—gregariousness; factor seven—sufficiency; factor eight—character stability; factor ten—rhathymia; factor twelve—masculinity.

The present writer is not entirely happy about the identification by Cattell of the factors extracted here with those derived in his rating studies; agreement seems occasionally forced and partly semantic rather than realistic. He is even more worried about the apparent overlap in this set of factors between primary and second-order factors; it seems clear that the analysis as it stands is not complete, and that until a proper second-order factor analysis is carried out it will be difficult to evaluate Cattell's contribution properly.

His belief in the similarity of factors derived from rating studies and questionnaire studies appears strengthened considerably, however, by a study of outstanding interest published by Fiske (1949). This writer made use of the data accumulated by the well-known research project on the Selection of Clinical Psychologists, which was sponsored by the Veterans' Administration and carried out at the University of Michigan (Kelley and Fiske, 1952). In this project, an extensive assessment programme was undertaken to evaluate students selected by Universities for first year positions in the V.A. Clinical Psychology Training Programme. 128 men constitute the sample of subjects. Three different modes of assessment were employed.

(1) A staff team of three experienced psychologists pooled their judgments, which were based on a mass of extensive and intensive material on each subject.

(2) Three team-mates, who had spent seven days with a subject, living and working together, rated him.

(3) The subjects rated themselves.

A rating scale of 22 items adapted from Cattell was used throughout.

Correlations were run between these 22 items for the three groups of data (A, B, and C) separately, and the three matrices factor analyzed independently. Five primary factors were extracted from each of the three matrices of intercorrelations, and thus it becomes possible to study the similarity of factors derived from questionnaires, ratings by peers, and ratings by clinicians.

Similarity of the factor patterns for the three groups can best be shown in the form of a diagram, and Fig. 17 is quoted from the original paper. Except for the fifth factor, agreement is surprisingly close, as is evident, too, from the average intercorrelations between the loadings on the primary factors, also published by Fiske. It is apparent that the three methods of evaluation give consistent results, a finding which may appear surprising to those who have tended in the past to condemn out of hand either or both of the methods of rating or self-appraisal.

Of most interest for our purpose are probably factor two, called by Fiske "*emotional control*", and factor three, "*conformity*". "Emotional control" apparently corresponds to the obverse of neuroticism; from his inspection of the most highly loaded item, Fiske concludes that "we can designate this ... factor as *emotional control* or *emotional self-possession*, keeping clearly in mind that this is probably a mature guidance of emotional expression in an inhibitive constricted pattern. Further explorations might well identify it more definitely as emotional maturity". Factor three is identifiable, though perhaps less clearly, with introversion. Items having high loadings in the various analyses are: serious, conscientious, submissive, silent, predictable, cautious, ready to co-operate, and slight overt interest in women. The picture is not quite consistent, as might be expected from the fact that these are primary factors which themselves are intercorrelated, although these intercorrelations appear to be relatively low. Nevertheless, without a second-order factor analysis we should not expect unambiguous identification of factors with those of our last chapter. Keeping this in mind, however, the general fit of this study, as compared with those described in the last chapter, is not too bad.

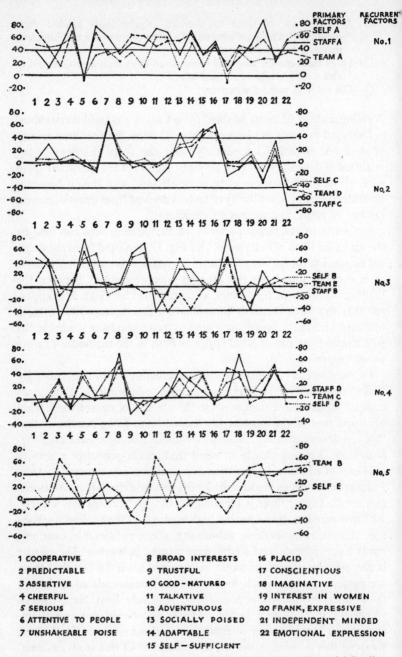

1 COOPERATIVE	8 BROAD INTERESTS	16 PLACID
2 PREDICTABLE	9 TRUSTFUL	17 CONSCIENTIOUS
3 ASSERTIVE	10 GOOD – NATURED	18 IMAGINATIVE
4 CHEERFUL	11 TALKATIVE	19 INTEREST IN WOMEN
5 SERIOUS	12 ADVENTUROUS	20 FRANK, EXPRESSIVE
6 ATTENTIVE TO PEOPLE	13 SOCIALLY POISED	21 INDEPENDENT MINDED
7 UNSHAKEABLE POISE	14 ADAPTABLE	22 EMOTIONAL EXPRESSION
	15 SELF – SUFFICIENT	

Fig. 17.—Diagram showing similarity of three Independent Factorial Studies.

We may briefly mention the interpretation given by Fiske to the other factors. The first he terms "*social adaptability*", the fourth the "*inquiring intellect*", and the fifth "*confident self-expression*". It will be seen from Fig. 17 just which items have high saturations on these factors. It might be thought that as the traits rated were taken from Cattell's list, the resulting factor should also be similar to his. Up to a point this expectation seems to be borne out. As Fiske points out, "These findings bear certain marked resemblances to those from Cattell's studies, although many discrepancies are also present. . . . A thorough study of these two sets of factors, one from Cattell and one from our ratings, leaves one with feelings of both optimism and discouragement. Even in the face of no complete congruence, the similarities support a belief in the possibility of eventual agreement upon the basic variables in personality. Yet, with such comparable rating scales and subjects, why are the results not more similar?" To the present writer the obvious answer to this question would lie in the absence of second-order analyses by the two writers, as well as in certain statistical differences between Fiske and Cattell in their method of rotation. Fiske attempted to maximize the number of "pure" loadings, whereas Cattell did not. Again, "Cattell uses unusually low loadings to help him identify his rotated factors"; Fiske "does not share this confidence in the significance of low loadings". The agreement found in spite of such differences in methodology is distinctly encouraging.

In all the studies mentioned in this chapter, it will have been noticed that factors identical with, or similar to, the concept of neuroticism have been invoked time and again; it would seem reasonable to enquire whether none of the investigators has taken the trouble to verify a hypothesis of this nature by testing both normal and neurotic groups and comparing their responses. By this we do not mean the kind of validation studies summarized by Ellis (1946) and Ellis and Conrad (1948), in which a particular personality inventory is considered valid if it discriminates between normals and neurotics at a reasonably satisfactory level. What we have in mind rather is the setting up of a definite hypothesis regarding the nature of the factor to be investigated, and a deduction from this hypothesis which can be verified by data collected from normal and abnormal groups. A fuller discussion of the type of analysis required and the type of reasoning underlying it will be given in a later chapter (cf. p. 148). Here we will only note two researches which have made use of questionnaire and self-rating material in a study of normal and neurotic groups.

The first of these studies was carried out by Bennett and Slater (1945) on 80 normal and 80 neurotic soldiers. The tests used by them were:

(1) A neurotic inventory divided into three sections dealing with questions related to the clinical syndromes of anxiety, hysteria, and depression.
(2) An annoyance test listing 60 possible annoying stimuli for situations of four kinds, 15 for each, the whole in random order. These four types of stimuli are: (a) frustration of self-assertion; (b) personal inadequacy; (c) dirt or untidiness; (d) noise.
(3) Three sections of the Pressey X-O Test, modified from the original, and dealing with (a) activities for which an individual should be blamed; (b) things about which he has ever felt worried, nervous, or anxious; (c) items which he likes or in which he is interested.

Scores on these 10 sub-tests were obtained and intercorrelations established for the two groups separately, as well as for the combined group of normals and neurotics. Biserial correlations were calculated between the normal-neurotic dichotomy for each of the 10 tests. These are reproduced under "D" in Table 18. Also given are first-factor saturations for the normal, the neurotic, and the combined groups.

TABLE 18

First Factor

		Neurotics	Normals	Combined	"D"
Inventory:	Anxiety	·77	·70	·77	·72
	Hysteria	·49	·55	·53	·43
	Depression	·78	·75	·70	·72
Annoyances:	a	·18	·03	·13	·25
	b	·46	·50	·47	·49
	c	·12	·21	·13	·10
	d	·63	·48	·54	·72
Pressey X-O:	a	·06	·02	·08	·19
	b	·43	·55	·49	·65
	c	·29	— ·23	— ·18	·56

It will be seen from Table 18 that there is a high correlation between column D and the first-factor saturation of the groups, whether separate or combined. This indicates quite clearly that a test which has a high power of discrimination between normals and neurotics also has a high saturation on the first factor extracted from a matrix of intercorrelations *of the normal, the neurotic, or the combined groups.* Similarly, a test having a low power of discrimination between normals and neurotics also has low saturations on the factor. Quite clearly, then, this correspondence between discriminant capacity of a test and factor saturation gives us considerable justification in labelling the factor one of neuroticism. We appear to get away in this fashion from the usual method of arbitrary and semantic labelling, which has been so severely criticized by many psychologists, and to go some way towards an objective method of defining and labelling factors.

Of equal interest is a second study to be mentioned in this connection (Stouffer, 1949). 15 scales were constructed according to the method of Guttman's scale analysis, dealing with a variety of topics which were thought to be relevant to neurotic disorder. These 15 scales were then applied to large numbers of normal and neurotic soldiers and intercorrelations calculated for normals separately, neurotics separately, and the combined groups. Also available was an estimate of the degrees to which each of the 15 scales discriminated between the normals and the neurotics, given in the form of a biserial correlation between scales and the dichotomy: normal versus neurotic. These correlations are given under the heading Criterion Column in Table 19, together with the factor saturations for the normal and neurotic groups respectively as calculated by Eysenck (1952). We find again the same phenomenon already described in connection with the work of Bennett and Slater: there is a close correspondence between the values in the criterion column and the first factor saturations both for the normal and for the neurotic group. Again, therefore, we have external validation for our identification of this factor as one of neuroticism. (The second factor appears almost identical for the two groups, and may be identified with extraversion-introversion, although there is the obvious disadvantage that without an external method of validation this identification is subjective and insecure. However, the items characterising this factor are sufficiently similar to those which in a previous study were used to identify the "c" factor to make this interpretation reasonable.)

Only one attempt to submit psycho-analytic concepts to factorial study, and to link up personality organization and developmental factors has been found in the literature. This is the work of Goldman-Eisler (1948, 1950, 1951). This writer makes use of the concepts of oral pessimism and oral optimism advanced by Abraham (1916, 1924, 1942), Freud (1938), and Glover (1924, 1925). "Oral character

TABLE 19

Title of Scale	Criterion Column	Factor Saturations, Normal Group		Factor Saturations, Neurotic Group	
		I	II	I	II
1. Psychosomatic complaints .	·66	·69	·15	·56	·16
2. Childhood neurotic symptoms	·38	·49	·09	·58	— ·01
3. Personal adjustment (—) .	·42	·67	·09	·68	·05
4. Over-sensitivity . . .	·33	·48	·45	·56	·50
5. Childhood fears . . .	·33	·42	·16	·52	·02
6. Acceptance of soldier role (—)	·35	·58	— ·15	·48	— ·29
7. Worrying	·27	·59	·02	·56	·09
8. Sociability (—) . . .	·33	·33	·03	·56	·08
9. Participation in sports (—) .	·28	·28	— ·14	·34	— ·26
10. Identification with war (—) .	·12	·40	— ·02	·31	— ·00
11. Childhood fighting behaviour (—)	·18	·30	— ·32	·17	— ·59
12. Childhood school adjustment (—)	·11	·15	·09	·19	·06
13. Relations with parents . .	·12	·10	·06	·20	·20
14. Emancipation from parents (—)	·08	·20	— ·34	·18	— ·24
15. Mobility	.09	— ·04	·31	·05	·24

traits are assumed to originate from repressed or deflected oral impulses which are dominant during the nursing period, and which have undergone transformation into certain permanent behaviour patterns by the processes of reaction-formation, displacement, or sublimation. Two main syndromes of bipolar significance seem to emerge from Abraham's and Glover's studies. . . . The basic conditions for the development and fixation in character of the one or the other syndrome are assumed to be the experiences of gratification or frustration attached to the oral stage of libido development." On the one hand, we have the orally gratified type, which is described by analytic writers as being distinguished by imperturbable optimism, generosity, bright and sociable social conduct, accessibility to new ideas and ambition accompanied by sanguine expectation. On the other hand, the orally ungratified type is characterized by a profoundly pessimistic outlook on life, sometimes accompanied by moods of depression and attitudes of withdrawal, a passive, receptive attitude, a feeling of insecurity, an ambition which combines an intense desire to climb with a feeling of unattainability, a grudging feeling of injustice, sensitiveness to competition, and dislike of sharing.

Clearly, two hypotheses are involved here; first, the existence of a syndrome of personality traits corresponding to that described above, and second, the correlation between this syndrome and early weaning. To investigate the first of these hypotheses, Goldman administered verbal self-rating scales for 19 traits, mentioned by psycho-analytic writers as having an oral connotation, to 115 adult subjects. Each scale contained between 6 and 10 items, and the reliability coefficients for the various scales were satisfactory. Inter-

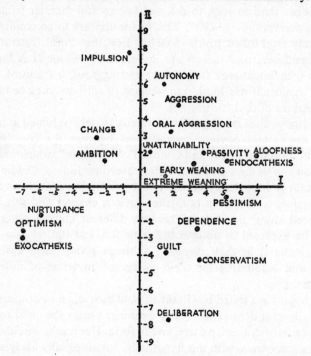

Fig. 18.—Plot of the Factor Loadings of nineteen tests as related to Variable "Early Weaning".

correlations between the scales were run, and two factors extracted from the matrix of intercorrelations. The resulting configuration of traits is shown in Fig. 18, which indicates quite clearly that the first factor to appear is one very similar to the hypothetical trait of oral optimism and oral pessimism. The trait "early weaning", which was defined as "having been weaned not later than at the age of 4 months", as contrasted with "having been weaned later", can be seen to have a saturation of ·337 on the "oral pessimism" side of this factor, thus confirming the hypothesis linking syndrome and orality. (This connection between syndrome and early weaning was also confirmed independently by means of analysis of variance procedures.)

The second factor is "characterized by extreme impulsiveness and a disinclination to wait or refrain from action (impulsion, ·761; deliberation, — ·766), by independence or a disinclination to conform (autonomy, ·560), by aggression, general and oral (aggression, ·479; oral-aggression ·303), and by a tendency to change, to seek the new, rather than to stick to the well-known and familiar (change, ·267; conservation, — ·436)". This factor appears to go counter to the firmly established psycho-analytic view that "oral frustration, oral impatience, oral sadism are inseparable"; factor II is highly loaded with impatience (impulsion) and aggression (sadism), but has no significant relationship to weaning (if early weaning be taken as a measure of oral frustration).

This study raises many problems which can only be hinted at here. There are certain obvious resemblances between the constituent traits of "oral optimism" and Guilford's "rathymia", which in turn was shown to be a good measure of extraversion. Indeed, Goldman's first factor is remarkably similar to the description of introversion-extraversion, as found in both the previous chapter and this one. This need cause no surprise because different clinical observers might be expected to observe the same fundamental relationships in the material at their disposal, although giving them different names and accounting for their emergence in terms of different hypotheses.

The hypothesis tested by Goldman is, of course, an environmental one; early oral deprivation (early weaning) causes the child to become pessimistic, aloof, passive, and so forth. Her results would seem to be in accordance with this hypothesis, but an equally likely alternative explanation should not be passed over too lightly. If we assume that introversion is an inherited quality, we might account for the observed correlation between early weaning and introversion by referring both the observed introverted behaviour of the child and his early weaning to the introverted tendency of the mother which leads her to an early interruption of weaning. The environmental explanation, of course, is the one preferred by Goldman, but her data do not offer any possibility of deciding in favour of one hypothesis as opposed to the other, and it would be quite unscientific to let one's choice be determined by personal preference. It should be possible, of course, to make deductions from these two alternative hypotheses which could be capable of disproof, but until such proof is forthcoming we must leave the decision between the environmentalistic and the hereditary view indeterminate.[1]

In assessing the evidential value of the studies reviewed in this chapter, we must of course also have recourse to such work as has been done on their validation. A very thorough review of some 350 studies by Ellis (1946) concludes "that group administered pencil and paper personality questionnaires are of dubious value in distinguishing between groups of adjusted and maladjusted individuals and that they are of much less value in the diagnosis of individual adjustment or personality traits". In a review of the validity of personality inventories in military practice, Ellis and Conrad (1948) come to a slightly different conclusion: "Military applications of personality inventories have yielded enough favourable results to command attention. In contrast, personality inventories in civilian practice have generally proved disappointing." In these evaluations Ellis has taken an unusually severe criterion of validity. He claims that he will in his review "usually evaluate the reported coefficients of correlation in terms of the conventional estimations given them in the consideration of psychological and educational tests. Thus, we shall say that r's from zero to ·19 indicate negative validity; from ·20–·39 mainly negative validity; from ·40–·69 questionably positive validity; from ·70–·79 mainly positive validity; and from ·80–1·00 positive validity". These standards can hardly be considered usual, and are very much more severe than those applied by most authors. Even so, the studies quoted by Ellis in his Table 2 indicate that some 35 per cent. give validation coefficients in excess of ·7, while only about 40 per cent. give validation coefficients lower than ·4.

These results to most psychologists would seem rather promising, particularly in view of the fact that they were obtained in civilian work, and that according to Ellis and Conrad military application of questionnaire results have even higher validation coefficients. In any case, it would seem inadmissible to take these coefficients at their face value. They validate questionnaires against criteria which are themselves imperfect, and consequently even a perfect measuring instrument could not be expected to give very high correlations with such imperfect criteria. All we can deduce from figures such as those given by Ellis is that there are high agreements between some questionnaires and some external criteria; to estimate the exact

[1] Those interested in the problem presented by the "oral character" in relation to correlational analysis may wish to consult the more recent papers by Blum and Miller (1952) and by Barnes (1952), which arrived too late for discussion.

validity of questionnaires would require the presence of a perfect criterion and in the absence of such a criterion must be impossible.

A different way of attacking the problem of evaluation has already been indicated elsewhere in this chapter. As has been pointed out there, the criticisms made justifiably of questionnaire studies are essentially different from those made equally justifiably of rating studies. If, therefore, the two methods of assessment give results which are identical, or at least essentially similar, we may have more confidence in the general picture provided by them. It has been shown throughout the chapter that in the main there is remarkable congruence between findings, and in at least one individual research (Fiske, 1950) this congruence has been demonstrated along strictly experimental lines independent of subjective estimation.

That is not to say that the position is a very satisfactory one. Quite clearly, the conditions under which questionnaires are filled in, the intelligence and co-operativeness of the subjects, their suggestibility and insight, as well as their mood and various unconscious factors of the type mentioned in connection with ratings, will powerfully affect and distort the results which may be expected in the use of questionnaires. Some of these difficulties can be overcome by the use of modern developments (the Humm-Wadsworth no-count, the Minnesota Multiphasic Personality Inventory lie and K scales, and similar empirical methods of improving forecasting efficiency), but on the whole it must be clear that questionnaire answers can never be taken at their face value. Only when their empirical relationships with other variables have been definitely established, under a reproducible set of conditions, will they take their place among other methods of investigation and throw important light on certain facets of the subject's personality (his own picture of himself, his degree of insight, his desire to give a good account of himself, etc.) which would be difficult to obtain by any other method. As in the case of ratings, questionnaires are a necessary but not sufficient means for arriving at a complete and adequate picture of a person's major traits and personality variables. Neither uncritical praise nor exaggerated blame would help in a proper evaluation of the usefulness of questionnaires in personality study.

CHAPTER IV

THE ANALYSIS OF OBJECTIVE BEHAVIOUR TESTS

AS IN EACH OF the previous chapters we found one particular group of studies outstanding in their psychological importance, their technical competence, and the excellence of statistical treatment, so here also we find one unified body of work which has rightly gained credit for its brilliance. We are referring to the three volumes in which Hartshorne and May (1929, 1930) have published the results of the famous Character Education Enquiry: *Studies in Deceit, Studies in Service and Self-Control*, and *Studies in the Organization of Character*. These three books may still be regarded as a landmark which has not been surpassed by later work. If in some ways we are forced to be critical of the theoretical interpretation of the results offered by the authors, we nevertheless wish to pay tribute to the scientific integrity which makes available all the data on which such criticism can be based.

The Character Education Enquiry was undertaken in the autumn of 1924 at the request of the Institute of Social and Religious Research "in order to carry out investigations which would relate to those experiences of children having moral and religious significance, and to apply the objective methods of the laboratory to the measurement of conduct under controlled conditions". After a detailed consideration of the literature, Hartshorne and May constructed a large battery of tests, which must be described in brief outline now to make intelligible the discussion of their results. They laid down certain general rules to which all tests should, as far as possible, conform. Thus, a test situation should be as far as possible a natural situation as well as a controlled situation; the test situation and the method of response should be such as to allow all subjects equal opportunity to exhibit the behaviour under investigation; the child should not be subjected to any moral strain beyond the usual, and the tests should not be allowed to put the subject and the examiner in a false social relation to each other; the tests should have "low visibility", i.e. they should not arouse the suspicions of the subject.

Various techniques were found to conform with these rules, such as, for instance, the "Duplicating Technique". The child is given any pencil-and-paper type of test; the papers are collected and a duplicate of the answers made in the office. At a later session of the class, the original papers are returned, and each child told to score his own paper according to a key supplied. Deception consists in illegitimately increasing one's score by copying answers from the key. Other tests made use of the "Improbable Achievement Technique". This consists in giving a test under conditions such that achievement above a given level is an almost certain indication of deception. Thus, a child who, when asked to put dots into the centre of a number of irregularly spaced circles on the blackboard with his eyes closed, succeeds in doing so well beyond what is known to be within the capacity of children may be presumed to have peeped.

Another type still is the "Double-testing Technique". In this method the children are tested twice on alternate versions of a given test; on one occasion conditions are such as to permit deception, on the other there is strict supervision and no opportunity to deceive. The difference between scores made on the two occasions is a rough measure of the tendency to deceive, i.e. either to copy answers from the key or to change answers to match the key. It is, of course, essential in this procedure that material be available in two equivalent forms having the same degree of difficulty at all levels. It may also be noted that, unlike the previous techniques, this one lends itself to showing deception in work done at home as well as in the classroom situations. It also lends itself to testing in another and different context, namely that of athletic contests, when the achievement of the child on such activities as "pull-up" or "chinning", the "standing broad jump", or dynamometer and spirometer tests can be measured when the test is given by the examiner and when it is self-administered, and the differences noted as evidence of cheating through inflated claims.

All these techniques for measuring cheating permit, of course, a large number of variations, and some of them may be applied in situations quite different from those originally envisaged. Thus, the authors found it possible to use tests of this kind in connection with parlour games, and on other occasions when motivation is high and when conditions are markedly different from those obtaining at school or in the home.

In contrast to these tests, all of which deal with cheating of one kind or another, there are others dealing with stealing and lying. In each case an opportunity was given for the child to steal or lie under conditions which made it seem unlikely to the child that he could be caught out, but which were so much under the control of the experimenters that a complete check was possible. Thus, for instance, in connection with the administration of one test, a little box was given to each pupil containing several puzzles not all of which were used. In each box was a coin ostensibly belonging to another puzzle which the examiner showed to the children but did not ask them to do. Each child returned his own box to a large receptacle at the front of the room. It was possible to check which children took the coin before returning the box by a system of numbering and distributing the boxes according to the seating plan of the class. Lying could be detected, for instance, by asking the children whether they had cheated on any of the tests; it was known, of course, whether they had cheated or not, and if they denied having done so the lie was apparent.

A large number of different populations were studied coming from different types of schools, institutions, urban and rural areas, and from variegated racial backgrounds. Altogether, some 170,000 tests were administered to over 8,000 public-school children and almost 3,000 children in private and standardized schools.

Attempts were made to find data outside the experimental situation which would throw light on the validity of the techniques employed. In the first place, ratings were used which showed a reasonable reliability of almost ·70 (first versus second ratings) and ·55 (one rater versus another). Correlations between behaviour tests and ratings were between ·35 and ·40, and increased to almost ·5 when corrected for attenuation. In view of the unknown validity of the ratings themselves, this correlation is encouraging.

We may now turn to the organization of personality as revealed in the intercorrelations of the different tests. Hartshorne and May give the intercorrelations of nine types of deceitful behaviour; the average intercorrelation of the nine tests is ·227. This would give a predictive reliability of ·725 and a predictive validity of ·851. In other words, the correlation between the nine tests in the battery and another nine tests of a similar character would be ·725; that of the battery with an infinite number of similar tests, i.e. with what we might call the theoretically "true" measure of dishonesty, would be ·851. Hartshorne and May calculate that it would take 31 tests of this type to give an internal validity of ·948.

The same techniques applied to the study of deceitful behaviour were also used in a study of socially approved behaviour. Hartshorne and May consider as socially desirable the tendency to do things for others rather than for oneself, and the tendency to work with others rather than to stand alone, a tendency which they believe "passes into and through a stage of *co-operation for the sake of organized competition* to a higher level of *co-operation for a non-competitive object*, the significance of which lies in the relation of the co-operating individuals to one another". In their attempts to devise test situations they have these two modes of response in mind.

Five tests were given to make up what are called the "service" tests.

(1) *The Self-or-class Test.*—A spelling contest was set up in which each pupil could compete for one of two sets of prizes, one for the winning classes and one for the winning individuals. No one could enter both contests. Each had to choose whether his score was to count for himself and help himself towards getting a prize or count for the class and help the class get a prize.

(2) *The Money Voting Test.*—In this test the class had to decide what to do with the money that might be, or had actually been, won in the previous contest. Scoring was in terms of the altruistic nature of the choice, ranging from (i) "Buy something for some hospital child or some family needing help or for some other philanthropy" to (ii) "Divide the money equally among the members of the class".

(3) *The Learning Exercises.*—This test attempts to measure the amount of drive induced by opportunities to work for the Red Cross, for the class, or for oneself, on a digit symbol matching test, using as scores gains from the basic unmotivated score of the first day.

(4) *The School Kit Test.*—Each child was provided with a pencil case containing 10 articles which came "as a present from a friend of the school". It was then suggested to them that they might give away any part or all of the kit in an inconspicuous way in order to help make up some kits for children who had no useful pretty things of this kind.

(5) *The Envelopes Test.*—The children were asked to find jokes, pictures, interesting stories, and the like for sick children in hospital, and were issued with envelopes in which to collect them. The number of articles collected was scored according to a complex scoring system.

Various other tests were also tried out, such as the Efficiency Co-operation test, in which work for self in a contest with other individuals was compared with work for one's class in an inter-class contest. In the Free Choice test carried out after the previous one, the choice was given as to whether the child wants to go on working for himself or for the class.

An effort was made again to test the validity of these tests by means of ratings, using a portrait-matching device, the guess-who technique, a check list, a conduct record, and a record of social service in school projects. The various validation scores had medium to low correlations ranging in the neighbourhood of ·3 to ·5. It was possible to make up a "total reputation for service" score which had a correlation with the theoretical "true" total reputation of ·77. Individual tests correlated with this total reputation score about ·2 to ·3. In combinations of two the tests correlated ·3 to ·5 with total reputation scores. Correlation between the total service score and the total reputation score was ·61. This is a very encouraging result in view of the well-known fact that correlations between ratings for intelligence test scores are seldom higher than this.

Turning now to the intercorrelations of the tests, we find an average correlation of ·201. The detailed figures are given in Table 20. The correlation of this battery with the "true score" would be about ·745. It would require 17 tests in all to give a high enough validity for individual prediction.

TABLE 20

Intercorrelations of Final Service Tests—Populations X, Y, and Z

	2	3	4	5
1. Free choice . . .	·20 ± ·02	·17 ± ·02	·13 ± ·03	·20 ± ·02
2. Efficiency co-operation .	—	·27 ± ·02	·32 ± ·02	·21 ± ·02
3. Money vote . . .	—	—	·27 ± ·02	·12 ± ·03
4. Kits . . .	—	—	—	·12 ± ·03
5. Envelopes . . .	—	—	—	—

In addition to the battery of service tests described above a number of tests of self-control were also developed. In particular an attempt was made to measure persistence and inhibition. Persistence tests will be described in some detail in a later chapter, and therefore we will not give any detailed account of those used by Hartshorne and May. Inhibition tests, however, are not discussed elsewhere. Six techniques altogether were tried out:

(1) The Story Inhibition Test.
(2) The Safe Manipulation Test.
(3) The Puzzle Manipulation Test.

(4) The Ruggles Distraction Test.
(5) The Picture Inhibition Test.
(6) The Candy Inhibition Test.

In the first of these, each child has a copy of a story which is read aloud by the examiner up to the climax. The child is then asked to turn the sheets over and write on the back of the last page how he thinks the story will end. The child is thus expected to inhibit the drive to know how the story ends and instead has a guess at it. If he chooses to guess, he is not told how the story comes out.

In the second test a small toy safe with a combination lock is put on each pupil's desk. He is instructed not to touch it for a lengthy period, during which a paper and pencil test is given; self-control consists in inhibiting the tendency to touch and play with the safe.

In the third test a box is passed to the children containing a peg test, as well as five small puzzles, definitely attractive to children, with which they are asked not to play. Inhibition consists in leaving these puzzles alone and concentrating on the major task.

In the Distraction test an arithmetic test is set out on a page covered with distracting and interesting drawings. Self-control consists in not giving way to the temptation of looking at these.

The Picture Inhibition test is similar to the Distraction test, and the Candy Inhibition test resembles the Safe Manipulation test.

Reputation for self-control was canvassed in a similar way to that used for service. This has a theoretical validity of ·86 for persistence and ·76 for inhibition. The correlations of reputation with the persistence test are not very large; neither are those between inhibition tests and reputation. The theoretical validity of the persistence tests is ·78 (obtained from their average intercorrelation of ·239). That of the inhibition tests is ·65, based on an average intercorrelation of ·16. These low and somewhat unsatisfactory correlations may be due to the fact that group tests were used; it is doubtful if group testing is well suited to this type of problem. A number of individual tests of persistence and inhibition were applied and gave somewhat higher intercorrelations, particularly as far as the tests of inhibition were concerned (average intercorrelation of 6 tests = ·225). Hartshorne and May conclude their brief discussion of these measures, which were unfortunately confined to a very small group of children, by saying that they "are very suggestive of the possibilities of individual testing in this field and offer a most promising research problem".

The entire battery of tests of honesty, service, and self-control was given to three groups of children, populations X, Y, and Z, totalling about 850 children. To these children were given 64 tests of behaviour and opinion, 37 performance tests of the type described, 20 paper-and-pencil tests, and various schedules and data sheets of one kind or another. Correlations between different types of test are given in Table 21; the raw intercorrelations are in the upper right section, correlations corrected for attenuation in the lower left section. Reliabilities are given in brackets.

TABLE 21

*Intercorrelation of Total Conduct Scores—Populations
X, Y, and Z Combined*

Test	Honesty	Service	Inhibition*	Persistence
Honesty .	(·86)	·303	·361	·129
Service . .	·439	(·56)	·276	·049
Inhibition .	·487	·472	(·61)	·123
Persistence .	·166	·083	·202	(·61)

*Omitting the Picture Inhibition test.

Moral knowledge tests of various kinds were also given to these children and correlated with conduct scores. Corrected for attenuation, these correlations turned out to be ·464 with honesty, ·300 with co-operation, ·373 with inhibition, and ·336 with persistence. Moral knowledge, therefore, seems to be to a moderate extent related to moral conduct.

Reputation scores of the type discussed above were also available for the children in this study; correlations found between objective test scores and reputation scores, corrected for attenuation, were ·48 with honesty, ·63 with service, ·62 with inhibition, and ·50 with persistence, giving a grand average of ·558. Reputation and conduct may therefore be considered to be related to quite a considerable extent.

We must now turn to what is perhaps the most important analysis carried out by Hartshorne and May, namely their study of integration. Most definitions of personality use this term, although they seldom attempt any adequate operational definition of it. Interpreting the term "integration" as "consistency of performance", they maintain that the integrated or consistent person gives responses that are organized in such a way that the person's conduct can be predicted. "On an altitude scale they may have excellent or bad characters, but . . . they may be depended upon to function consistently on their own level. . . . Heretofore we have been placing children on a vertical scale and ranking them high or low. We shall now attempt to place them on what may be called, for convenience, a horizontal scale, and shall arrange them according to the consistency with which they function on their given level . . . Our definition of integration as consistency of performance holds fairly close to a widely used meaning of the term. By *integration* is often intended a certain dependability or stability of moral conduct. Conversely, the individual lacking in integration is at the mercy of the varying temptations of every situation. His conduct is inconsistent, undependable, unpredictable, or even contradictory."

Taking as their point of reference the mean of the population to which the child belonged, Hartshorne and May calculated a modified form of standard score to make deviations from the mean comparable from test to test. Using such scores for 21 tests, they then calculated for each child separately the amount of variability (standard deviation) for his 21 scores. This means that the more consistent the child the more closely would his 21 scores be grouped together round the mean and the smaller would the standard deviation be. Similarly, the more inconsistent the child the more variable his scores about the mean and the larger his standard deviation. The distribution of these "integration indices" were not very different from the normal curve of distribution. The reliability of this integration score was found to be only ·4.

Integration, as defined, shows a considerable correlation with honesty. In the Y population, the correlation between honesty and integration is ·522, which rises to ·882 when corrected for attenuation. The correlation for the Z population, for various reasons discussed by the authors, is rather lower, but the two populations combined still give a corrected coefficient of correlation of ·776. These correlations cannot be taken too seriously in view of the heteroscedastic nature of the scatter diagram, but we must agree with Hartshorne and May that the observed correlation "indicates the presence of a genuine association between level and consistency of achievement". Among the variables correlated with integration, perhaps the most interesting is intelligence. For the various groups, these correlations are ·314, ·219, and ·266. These correlations are almost identical with the best estimates available of the correlation between "w", or lack of neuroticism, and intelligence, suggesting the possibility that this quality of integration isolated by Hartshorne and May may be closely linked to integration as understood by the psychiatrist, i.e. as the opposite of neuroticism. This interpretation is strengthened by the fact that Hartshorne and May found ratings of emotional stability (admittedly of doubtful validity) to show a highly significant correlation of ·28 with integration. Also, persistence and resistance to suggestion showed correlations with integration of ·435 and ·367; it will be noted in later researches that both lack of persistence and suggestibility appear again and again as defining "neuroticism".

Nowhere do Hartshorne and May carry out factorial analyses of their data. One of the associates working with them for part of the time, J. D. Maller (1934), has used some of the intercorrelations reported by them between the four types of test used (honesty, co-opera-tion, inhibition, persistence) to carry out a Spearman-type analysis. He found tetrad differences not significantly different from zero and concluded therefore that all the intercorrelations could be accounted for in terms of one general factor which, it is quite clear from the correlations presented by Hartshorne and May, cannot be identified with intelligence. He concludes that "the factor common to the various character tests, which may be referred to as factor C, is a readiness to forgo an immediate gain for the sake of a remote but greater gain". Unfortunately, the tests used in these studies are too different from those used by other authors to make identification of this factor very easy, but in view of the high correlations of these tests with "integration" the present writer feels that the possibility of identifying Maller's "C" with Webb's "w" cannot be gainsaid. An experimental proof of this hypothesis should not be too difficult to arrange.

While the Hartshorne and May studies are included in this volume because of their great general importance and theoretical interest, and in spite of the fact that the data were not in any consistent way treated factorially, the pioneering work of Oates (1929) deserves its place as effectively the first factorial study of objective behaviour tests. This work is of interest in many directions. It may be noted here particularly because, unlike so many more recent studies, it sets out with a clear-cut hypothesis which is testable by means of factorial analysis, and which is decisively disproved. Instead of resting content, however, with such a negative conclusion, Oates goes on to show that his data are compatible with an alternative hypothesis, which is in fact identical with that discussed in the previous two chapters.

The tests used by Oates, as well as the original hypothesis tested, are those put forward by June Downey (1919). Her "will-temperament" tests, which had a great vogue in the years immediately after the First World War, had the misfortune of being both incontinently praised and equally incontinently criticized. Their history is amusingly told by Symonds (1931), whose very full account, unfortunately, leaves out Oate's research, which is the only direct attack on the problem posed by June Downey.

Briefly, Downey presents twelve tests divided into three groups. Each of these is composed of four tests designed to measure (a) "fluidity" or speed of response; (b) "forcefulness" or decisiveness of action; and (c) "carefulness" and persistence of reaction. The tests used to measure these three variables were largely drawn from graphology, and there is no doubt about the ingenuity with which Downey has adapted graphological principles to test construction.

The four tests designed to measure "fluidity" are:

(1) *Speed of Movement.*—This is simply the speed at which the subject writes the words "United States of America".

(2) *Freedom from Load.*—On the hypothesis that some people habitually write near their maximum speed while others are subject to "load", or inhibition, and therefore write considerably below their maximum, the subject is instructed to write "United States of America" as rapidly as possible; the ratio between speeded and normal writing constitutes the score.

(3) *Flexibility.*—The subject is instructed to write "United States of America", changing the style of writing as much as possible.

(4) *Speed of Decision.*—This is the speed with which judgments are made on 22 pairs of opposite traits which the subject has to check as characterizing himself.

The four tests to measure "forcefulness" are:

(1) *Motor Impulsion.*—The subject writes his name in his usual manner, and then under distraction. The assumption is that persons high on motor impulsion, or muscular tension, tend to speed up and enlarge their handwriting when working under distraction.

(2) *Reaction to Contradiction.*—This measures the subject's reaction to being contradicted by the examiner on a point on which the subject is right.

(3) *Resistance to Opposition.*—The subject's behaviour when a small obstruction is placed in front of his pen point whilst the subject is writing his name with his eyes closed.

(4) *Finality of Judgment.*—The subject rechecks the list of traits on which he earlier rated himself, and the time consumed in rechecking constitutes the score.

The four tests to measure "carefulness" are:

(1) *Motor Inhibition.*—The subject is told to write "United States of America" as slowly as possible.

(2) *Interest in Detail.*—The subject copies some handwriting from the test booklet. This is done twice, once as rapidly as possible, then as exactly as possible. The score is a combination of the difference in speeds and the degree to which the model is approximated.

(3) *Co-ordination of Impulses.*—The subject has to write the words "United States of America" on a line just over an inch in length, taking care to write very rapidly but not to run over the line. The score is the number of letters omitted or which run over the line, as well as the degree to which the time approximates the time for normal writing.

(4) *Volitional Preservation.*—In the "disguised handwriting" test the subject is given a certain amount of time for practice. The present test gives him a score according to the length of time spent on practising.

Here we have a very clear-cut hypothesis, according to which the tests when intercorrelated should group themselves in three groups of four, such that within each group the correlations should be high, and between one group and the others, low or zero. Downey explicitly denies the existence of a general factor, so the "between-group" intercorrelations should not be significantly different from zero, whereas all the "within-group" correlations should be significant. Oates gave the 12 tests in this scale to 50 secondary schoolboys, to whom he also administered 10 intelligence tests; examination results, too, were available to him. The pattern of correlations which he found is entirely different from that called for by the hypothesis. In factorial terms it can be represented not by three independent group factors but rather by one general and one bi-polar factor. The general factor has high loadings on freedom from load or inhibition, speed of decision, co-ordination of impulses, interest in detail, speed of movement, and finality of judgment. This general factor is identified by Oates as one of temperament, and in his view appears very similar to Webb's "w". He tries to point this analogy in a very interesting manner by comparing the intercorrelations of total score on the Downey tests (which of course would be a rough measure of the general factor) with intelligence and scholastic ability, with similar correlations obtained by Stead (1925) on character ratings (persistence, trustworthiness, conscientiousness, general excellence, etc.), with intelligence and scholastic ability. These various combinations of three traits (character or temperament, scholastic ability, intelligence) taken two at a time, are given in Table 22, as well as the partial correlations, with the third trait in each case partialled out. It will be seen that the correlations are remarkably similar, showing that total score on the June Downey test is related to scholastic ability and intelligence in very much the same way that the character ratings of "*w*" qualities used by Stead are correlated with the same variables.

TABLE 22

		Oates		Stead	
		r	partial r	r	partial r
Scholastic ability and intelligence:	.	·573	·548	·573	·568
Scholastic ability and temperament	.	·357	·298	·335	·243
Intelligence and temperament	.	·205	·001	·250	·067

The second factor is identified by Oates as opposing speed to inhibition. The former he considers diagnostic of unrepressed or extraverted personality, the latter of introverted personality. Thus, this first factorial study of objective behaviour tests from the London school supports in remarkable fashion the conclusions derived from ratings and questionnaire studies.

The same may be said of another study directed by a former student of Spearman's and carried out in Canada, in which, for the first time, we find factorial analyses carried out on objective test scores obtained from both normal and abnormal subjects. In the first of these studies Line and Griffin (1935) gave a battery of 10 tests, of which, however, 4 were questionnaires, to "a group of some 50 individuals chosen to show in a very marked and obvious way the functional gradient in which we were interested. About one-third of the group were graduate students at the University of Toronto, and were selected as carefully as possible on the basis of obviously sound mental health . . . individuals whose mental health, while not obviously bad, seemed at least to be in a slightly precarious state, comprised the middle third of our group . . . the rest of our subjects were in-patients at the psychiatric hospital. Many of them were certified insane, and all of them required full-time supervision". (It is not quite clear to the writer just how many subjects were included altogether, or how they were distributed among these three groups, because the figures given in various tables by the authors do not agree.)

The tests included in this battery were:

(a) Kent-Rosanoff Word Association test; average reaction time.
(b) Variation in reaction time.
(c) Total number of responses on 10 Rorschach ink-blots.
(d) Oscillation or variation in output in such tasks as addition of pairs of digits.
(e) Speed test: the score here is the total number of responses made in the oscillation test.
(f) Speed of response: total number of symbols written during test (g).
(g) Perseveration: 6 tests averaged.
(h), (i), (j), (k) are the neurotic, introvert, self-sufficiency, and dominance scales respectively of the Bernreuter Personality Inventory.

The intercorrelations of the tests for the total group, as well as factor saturations for two factors, are given in Table 23. The first factor is called "objectivity" by Line and Griffin; they believe that "it may be closely related . . . to the 'w' factor investigated by Webb with normal subjects". Nearly all the tests have high scores on this factor, which characterizes a person who makes neurotic, introverted, submissive answers on the Bernreuter scales and is not self-sufficient; who has a long word reaction time and shows considerable variation in his speed of reaction; who oscillates markedly in his work, perseverates, is slow in speed tasks and gives few responses on the Rorschach. The second factor is characterized according to them by fluency. Its highest loadings are a number of words given in response to the Rorschach cards, the speed tests, self-sufficiency, and dominance. In view of data already mentioned or to be summarized in later chapters, it seems likely that this factor bears some relation to extraversion.

TABLE 23

	B	C	D	E	F	G	H	I	J	K	"Objectivity" I	"Fluency" II
A	·92	−·44	·29	−·39	−·64	·27	·29	·35	−·39	−·30	·76	−·01
B	—	−·51	·33	−·40	−·68	·32	·50	·38	−·51	−·34	·84	−·04
C	—	—	−·27	·34	·24	−·26	−·33	−·35	·39	·38	−·52	·50
D	—	—	—	−·77	·49	·16	·14	·16	−·09	−·06	·58	−·06
E	—	—	—	—	·61	−·30	−·17	−·23	·16	·19	−·55	·42
F	—	—	—	—	—	−·38	−·07	−·07	·10	·02	−·58	·19
G	—	—	—	—	—	—	·04	·12	−·19	−·27	·54	·07
H	—	—	—	—	—	—	—	·94	−·61	−·73	·70	·04
I	—	—	—	—	—	—	—	—	·60	−·78	·71	−·01
J	—	—	—	—	—	—	—	—	—	·65	−·58	·37
K	—	—	—	—	—	—	—	—	—	—	−·60	·31

This pioneering research is obviously open to several criticisms. The groups investigated are not characterized sufficiently to make a repetition of the research possible; neurotics and psychotics are indiscriminately thrown together into the abnormal group; the influence of age and intelligence has not been held constant, thus leaving a spurious factor to disturb the pattern of intercorrelations. Some of these criticisms are obviated in a paper by Line, Griffin and Anderson (1935), in which four homogeneous groups were given tests similar to or identical with those already used. These groups were:

(1) 42 men in the Ontario Reformatory at Mimico.
(2) 120 University students.
(3) 70 teachers in the Ontario public schools.
(4) 40 women engaged in social service work.

Some of the additional tests used consisted of the Thurstone Neurotic Inventory, the Army Alpha, and the Chant Optimism-Pessimism Scale. It is difficult to summarize all this work; on the whole, it would appear that in each group a factor of "objectivity", or, as the authors are now inclined to call it, "stability", can be found, although the average loadings tend to reflect a curtailment in range of stability such as might be expected on theoretical grounds.[1] Thus, for the original mixed group, the average loading on this factor is ·62, for the Ontario Reformatory Group Test ·52; at the other end for teachers and University students it is ·47 and ·42 respectively. It is noteworthy that in the only group in which an intelligence test was included, it has a relatively high saturation (·46) for this factor of stability, suggesting that there is a certain degree of contamination with intelligence. As will be shown later, "stability" and intelligence, while not completely unrelated, tend to show considerably smaller correlations than that.

In putting forward these criticisms, we do not wish to detract from the importance of the work described. Perfection is not to be expected in pioneering efforts, and the lack of adequate methods of analysis at the disposal of the investigators is a handicap not often appreciated by later writers who have available more powerful methods. It is unfortunate that until quite recently the field of investigation opened up by Line has not been followed up by others; of those discussed in this book it is perhaps one of the most promising.

Quite a different type of research, which, nevertheless, also comes under the heading of "objective behaviour", is the work of Koch (1934, 1942) on "certain measures of activeness in nursery-school children". In her first article Koch carried out a multiple-factor

[1] Justification for the use of the term "stability" can be found in the writers' demonstration that the factor score differentiates at a high level of significance between the normal and abnormal groups from which the intercorrelations were derived.

analysis of correlations between 9 different measures of activeness, resulting in three factors:

(1) Strength or maturity.
(2) Nervousness or emotionality.
(3) Spontaneous activeness or aggression.

The second factor from her description is clearly identifiable with neuroticism, and the third, not quite so clearly, is similar to extraversion.

In her later paper an improvement in methodology makes these factors come out much more clearly. Two observers carried out a time-sampling study of pre-school children, using 400 half-minute units of observation. Thirty-eight variables were intercorrelated, ranging from laboratory tests, such as the psycho-galvanic reflex, to nervous habits (genital, pedal, ocular, scalp, hair, aural, nasal, respiratory, digital, and corporal) and behaviour items (crying, daydreaming, bossing others, etc.). Three main factors were found from the intercorrelations of the 38 items used. One of these is a "tension" factor, which is loaded positively with the nervous habit items and constipation, as opposed to "persistence of speed"; this bears a marked resemblance to "w" as opposed to neuroticism. Another factor is called "social introversion", contrasting the individual who "mobilizes his energy well, is relatively uninhibited and socially outgoing" to the individual who fails to show these traits. A third factor is called "lack of vigour", and may correspond to the "strength or maturity factor" in Koch's earlier work. (It may be the opposite of Heymans' and Wiersma's "activity factor".) The other factors isolated by her are difficult to interpret. However, those already mentioned will suffice to show that the most marked factors in the behaviour of nursery and pre-school children are similar to those which we found so clearly marked in the behaviour of normal and abnormal adults.

More recently, Brogden (1940) has reported a "factor analysis of 40 character tests" administered to 100 white boys. Many of these tests were questionnaires and opinionnaires; 10 tests were sub-tests of the Otis measure of intelligence. Most of the character tests were similar to those used by Hartshorne and May. In spite of the rather homogeneous and biased sample of tests used, it is noteworthy that the first of the eight centroid factors extracted is clearly identifiable with Webb's "w", being highly loaded on resistance to suggestion, conscientiousness, and lack of perseveration. The other factors are labelled respectively "honesty", "persistence", "general intelligence", "self-control" or "inhibition", "achievement", and "compliance to moral code". Of these, the self-control or inhibition factor bears some similarity to introversion, but it is impossible to be certain of this identification in view of the unusual nature of the tests employed in this case, and the failure to extract second-order factors.

It will be clear to those who have made an attempt to identify factors derived from intercorrelations between objective behaviour tests that such interpretation is markedly subjective, and has certain dangers and difficulties different from, but no less marked than, those encountered in connection with ratings and self-ratings. It appears certain that the most meaningful results will be obtained when we get away from the habit of including only one type of material in a given study, but try instead to cross-validate factors over all the different fields of material available. The need for such cross-validation has been seen most clearly perhaps by R. B. Cattell (1946), whose attempt to match factors derived from ratings and self-ratings has already been mentioned. In his first study in the field of objective behaviour tests, Cattell (1948) used 50 test scores obtained from 130 men and 240 women. Testing was partly group and partly individual, and the tests used covered a great variety of different techniques. Included were tests of intelligence, perseveration, fluency, reaction-time, speed of judgment, psychomotor speed, perceptual speed, dark adaptation, oscillation, fluctuation of attitudes, honesty, suggestibility, endurance, persistence, sense of humour, colour-form tendency, repression, mirror drawing, criticalness, self-confidence, mysticism, level of aspiration, psycho-galvanic reflex, work curves, and various others.

Correlations between these tests present rather an arid picture of near-zero coefficients. This is partly explained by Cattell on the grounds "(1) that the tests are deliberately chosen to represent the whole range of the *personality sphere* and are thus mostly remote from one another, and (2) that the tests, being intended to be exploratory, are uniformly brief and of proportionally low reliability". The correlation matrix was factored by Thurstone's grouping method, 10 factors being found significant by Tucker's rather lenient criterion.

Identification of these factors is extremely difficult. Most of the saturations which are used to define factors are very low, and only one of Cattell's final 11 factors is identified by more than two tests having factor saturations of above ·3; 4 factors have no saturations at all above this level. Nor does it seem easy to identify the factors isolated with those emerging from Cattell's previous studies. A determined attempt to do so is made by Cattell, but to the present writer these tentative identifications, while suggestive, certainly do not appear conclusive. While we may agree with Cattell that "this research can claim to have achieved only a low degree of definition of the factors" we rather doubt whether he is right in claiming that "the catholicity of the tests, their deliberate spacing with regard to primary personality factors, and their representation of previously found objective test factors perhaps justifies the conclusion that the factors found here cover the main structure of personality—at least in groups of this age".

A similar, essentially negative conclusion must follow a perusal of Cattell and Saunders' paper (1950). In this study, 370 students were rated, 405 completed the questionnaire used, 358 took part in the group sessions in objective testing, 140 completed the individual objective testing, and 35 the assessment by special physiological measures. All subjects were undergraduates in the proportion of about two women to one man. Thirty-seven variables altogether were included. It would be difficult to discuss the results in any great detail because of the large number of variables involved and of the necessity of discussing Cattell's terminology and use of concepts. His own conclusion seems quite acceptable to the present writer. He says that if this factorization "is doing what we intended it to do, only one conclusion is possible, i.e. except for two or three instances, the known personality factors, contrary to our hypothesis, are not out-crops of the same factors in different media. This does not mean that every factor may not have a manifestation in all three regions; it only means that the examples we have taken from each region do not coincide. If we accept tentatively the matches that are made above, we have left over, unmatched and unrepresented, three rating factors, nine questionnaire factors, and three objective test factors. . . . Where factors are unmatched we should expect to obtain factors among them that are second-order factors. Thereby we are delivered into the nightmare statistical situation of having first- and second-order factors intermixed in the same study, with all the difficulties of interpretation which that involves." These negative results should not be taken to mean that the goal which Cattell has set himself is impossible to reach or that his failure to cross-identify factors is inherent in the material. On the other hand, it would be idle to pretend that these results do not present a powerful barrier to easy acceptance of Cattell's set of factors.

As Thorndike (1950) has pointed out, "the reader may be somewhat hesitant to accept Cattell's characterization of the different factor dimensions and may be somewhat disturbed at the complexity of the correlated and descriptively quite complex factors, and may be rather less prepared than the author to accept the factors in different studies as identical". Admittedly, the analyses of objective tests published by Cattell are exploratory, but, as Thorndike goes on to say, they do "raise the question of how low reliabilities and communalities may be and still permit a factor analysis which can yield clear and interpretable results. The writer has a feeling that with communalities as low as those found in this study, the small amount of variance which is represented by common factors is almost sure to be obscure and unclear. In these studies, Cattell has ambitiously undertaken to plot out the whole sphere of personality variables, and the representation of any sector of this sphere has necessarily been limited. It is to be hoped that more intensive exploration of more limited segments will serve to refine and, if necessary, to revise the picture which has been sketched for us".

An even more general criticism may be made of Cattell's contribution, which may serve at the same time to link up the discussion of his work with the more recent contributions of the London School. In his discussion of the problems of factor analysis, Cattell (1946) deals with the choice which has to be made among the unlimited number of factorial solutions possible for any given matrix. Quite rightly, he points out that the scientist "will want to find the set of factors which corresponds to a set of psychologically real influences because he is interested in understanding the psychological meaning of his predictions and because he is curious to gain truth for its own sake. In that case, he may (1) devise possible ways of over-determining the analysis of the given correlation matrix, so that only the one set of true factors will emerge, or (2) start from the opposite shore and propound, on psychological grounds alone, a hypothesis about what source traits are operative in the variables. Then he will see if these factors correspond to any of the possible mathematical factors found in the matrix". Cattell goes on to endorse the former and reject the latter possibility. "This latter procedure is a very common and respected one in science. Typically the researcher invents a hypothesis and tests it against measurements, but unfortunately, in the present situation, this scientific habit of working is far from being a happy one. For, in the first place, personality study has so few other reliable avenues for arriving at or even suspecting the basic source traits, that hypotheses are likely to be erratic. In the second place, the mathematical solutions to any set of correlations are so numerous and varied that unless the hypothesis can be studied in very precise quantitative terms, the proof of it is easy—so easy as to be worthless."

In thus rejecting the hypothetico-deductive method and leaning exclusively on the concept of statistical over-determination as expressed in simple structure, Cattell has gone to one extreme of a continuum, the other end of which is represented by those who maintain what might be called the "engineering" approach. If we want to discover the validity of a test which has been constructed to measure a given trait, we have traditionally two methods of doing this. We can find an estimate of validity by correlating the test with an outside criterion; this may be called a test of "practical validity". Or we can correlate it with other tests, presumably measuring the same trait, intercorrelate these tests, and carry out a factor analysis; the factor saturation of the test in question with that factor will then be a measure of its theoretical validity. Both methods have obvious disadvantages. We seldom have a tested criterion available for truly significant psychological variables, such as neuroticism, introversion, persistence, suggestibility, intelligence, etc. (Sometimes, of course, we have a large number of different criteria available, which correlate only slightly or not at all with each other. Our problem then is to find a criterion for selecting a criterion, and we are thus being confronted with an infinite regress.) The difficulties of the other approach are possibly most apparent to those who have a healthy scepticism of an exaggeratedly mechanical and statistical approach to psychological problems; while these objections in the writer's view are less fundamental than those to the first approach, relating as they do largely to imperfections of present-day methods, they are, nevertheless, at the moment very real and make exclusive reliance on theoretical validity a very dangerous precept.[1]

[1] The dilemma presented by the apparent "forced choice" between these two courses of "practical" and "theoretical" validity, and the solution to the problem here presented, recall Bacon's words in the *Novum Organum*: "They who have handled the sciences have been either empirics or dogmatists. The empirics, like the ant, amass only and use; the dogmatists, like spiders, spin webs out of themselves. But the course of the bee lies midway—she gathers materials from the flowers of the garden and the field, and then by her own powers changes and digests them. Nor is the true labour of philosophy unlike hers. It does not depend entirely, or even chiefly, on the strength of the mind, nor does it store up in the memory unaltered the materials provided by natural history and mechanical experiments—but changes and digests them by the intellect."

Under these conditions, an attempt has been made by Eysenck (1947, 1952) and his colleagues to combine these two methods of validation into one approach which, as far as possible, should follow the dictates of the hypothetico-deductive method. This approach and some of the results obtained from it will be described in the succeeding paragraphs.

From the literature so far surveyed, it appears that the one factor in the non-cognitive personality field on which there is almost universal agreement is the factor of "w", or stability, as opposed to instability or neuroticism. We may set up a hypothesis regarding this factor, namely that human beings can be ranged along a continuum from one extreme (the very stable, mature, well-adjusted type of person) through the average, normal sort of person—to the other extreme (the highly neurotic, unstable, poorly adjusted sort of person). We may further add the hypothesis that a person whose position on the continuum is close to the unstable extreme will be quite likely to be brought to the attention of a psychiatrist, or himself seek psychiatric aid. Thus we might obtain two groups, those seeking psychiatric aid for reasons fundamentally related to emotional instability, and those not seeking such aid. We would not need to hypothesize that degree of instability was the only variable determining the position of a person in either group, nor would we need to make the assumption that the psychiatrist's decision as to whether a given person was suffering from instability or from other causes had a very high reliability. It is sufficient, from our point of view, that a group, the members of which had never been to see a psychiatrist, would, on the average, have a different position on the neuroticism continuum from a group, the members of which had visited a psychiatrist. We may call members of the first group "normal" and members of the second group "neurotic", realizing full well, of course, that there is likely to be a great deal of overlap on the basis of such a very rough-and-ready criterion as the one we have employed.

The degree of overlap existing between "normals" and "neurotics" is not always realized. It is very likely considerably greater than the overlap which can be found along a different dimension of personality, namely that of intelligence, between the mental defectives and the normals. As Tizard and O'Connor (1950) have shown, in a typical high-grade mental defective population several individuals can be found to have I.Q.s above 100 and the average I.Q. of such a population is in the neighbourhood of 75. On the other hand, in the "normal" population will be found many individuals with I.Q.s as low as 65, or even 50 and below. Nevertheless, when we compare the average institutionalized population with the average non-institutionalized population, we will undoubtedly find a marked difference in the position of the two means on the hypothetical continuum of intelligence; we will also, of course, find a great deal of overlap. Thus in the intellectual field the position is precisely analogous to the hypothetical position outlined above with respect to the "w" factor. Russell Fraser (1946) has, for instance, shown that a "normal" group of this kind contains a fair percentage of severely neurotic and an even higher percentage of slightly neurotic people who would benefit from a visit to a psychiatrist, and conversely, everyone working in a mental hospital is well aware of the fact that many people who come to seek the help and advice of a psychiatrist are suffering from disabilities not closely related to lack of emotional stability.

Let us next assume the existence of a set of tests $T_1, T_2, T_3, \ldots T_n$, all of which have a linear regression on the hypothetical neuroticism factor. It will be immediately obvious that each of these tests will differentiate between groups of normals and neurotics. It will also be obvious that the degree of success with which the test differentiates between normals and neurotics is a function of its correlation with the hypothetical factor of neuroticism. We may calculate an index for the purpose of showing the degree of differentiation achieved by each test by correlating (biserial or tetrachorics) the test with the normal—neurotic dichotomy. Let us call these correlations "criterion correlations" and the set of correlations obtained in this way the "criterion column". If our hypothesis is correct, then the criterion correlation should be exactly proportional to the correlations of the tests with the hypothetical neuroticism continuum.

The only method of verifying this deduction consists in intercorrelating our n tests, factor analysing the matrix of intercorrelations and using the resulting factor coefficients as approximations to the correlations of our tests with the hypothetical neuroticism factor. If these saturations are proportional to the criterion correlation, then we may consider the various hypotheses outlined above verified, and we may safely and without sematic argument identify the factor thus isolated as one of emotional instability, or neuroticism. The crucial test of the original hypothesis then lies in the correlation between the factor saturations and the criterion correlations; we would not expect this correlation to be unity because some of the assumptions of linearity of regression, and so forth, are not likely to be fulfilled exactly by most existing test data; proper refinement of these tests, however, should lead us closer and closer to a perfect correlation.

If we are willing to follow the argument outlined above, it will be clear that we have an excellent method for selecting tests for defining our factor of neuroticism. According to the hypothesis, tests which fit into the general pattern would all significantly differentiate between normal and neurotic groups, and consequently a large number of experiments have been carried out in an attempt to select tests differentiating at an acceptable level of significance between normals and neurotics (Eysenck, 1947). Thus, it was found, for instance, that normals have better dark vision, are less suggestible on the body-sway test, have better motor control, have smaller goal and judgment discrepancy scores on the level of aspiration test, show greater flexibility on the aspiration tests, have better manual dexterity, quicker personal tempo and greater fluency, are more persistent, tend to be less extreme on perseveration tests, and recover more rapidly on stress tests. They also give fewer neurotic answers on an inventory of neuroticism.

If these tests were given to groups of normals and neurotics, we should be able to make three perfectly definite predictions on the basis of our hypothesis. In the first place, we can predict the direction of the difference between the two groups on each test. In the second place, we can predict that if all the tests are scored in such a manner that the normal response obtained the plus score and the neurotic response the minus score, then all the intercorrelations of the tests within the normal group, or within the neurotic group, should be positive. Thirdly, we can predict that if a factor analysis is carried out on this table of intercorrelations, a general factor of neuroticism with positive saturations throughout should make its appearance, and the saturations of each test with this factor should be proportional to the criterion correlations, i.e. the correlations of each test with the normal-neurotic dichotomy.[2]

An experiment to test this hypothesis was carried out by Himmelweit, Desai, and Petrie (1946). 105 male Service patients constituted the experimental group; they were returned prisoners-of-war from

[1] The method of analysis outlined above, which has been called "criterion analysis" (Eysenck, 1950), is rather more complex than this, and involves rotation of factors into maximum conformity with the criterion column. It also, at a later stage, calls for a readjustment of the criterion itself in accordance with a double maximization principle. These refinements are not necessary, however, for the understanding of the underlying logic of this method, and as they are somewhat technical they have not been included in this brief account.

[2] Formal development of these deductions will be found in Eysenck's (1950) paper on Criterion Analysis.

Germany who had shown difficulties in adjustment and had been sent to the special psychiatric section of the hospital for treatment. In order to make the demonstration more convincing, relatively mild cases of neurosis were chosen to make up this group. The control group was made up of 93 surgical cases who were chosen from the same environment in order to equalize the effect of hospitalization. The two groups were matched with respect to age and educational background. A detailed analysis of the data was carried out by Eysenck (1950), who calculated product-moment correlations between 16 tests individually administered to the group. The number of subjects was only 64, as not all had taken each test. All these 64 were normal in the sense that they were not under psychiatric treatment at the moment. (It is important to realize that by restricting the analysis to the normal group only we make the test of our hypothesis much more stringent. If each test included in the battery discriminates between the normal and the abnormal group, it follows automatically that if we calculate intercorrelations over both the normal and the abnormal group, then a general factor of neuroticism must emerge which would almost inevitably be proportional to the criterion correlation. There is no reason to expect such an outcome when we restrict ourselves to one of the groups only, either the normal or the neurotic, unless we accept the hypothesis which the experiment was designed to test.)

The outcome of the experiment was quite clear. There were no significant negative correlations in the table of intercorrelations. All the tests differentiated in the expected direction, although not always at an acceptable level of significance, and all the factor saturations for the first factor were positive. In addition, there was a correlation of ·574 between the criterion column and the general factor.

The list of tests employed is given below.

A. Maudsley Medical Inventory—40-item neuroticism questionnaire. Score = number of questions answered "No" (non-neurotic).
B. Dark Adaptation—U.S. Navy Radium Plaque Adaptometer. Score = goodness of dark vision.
C. Non-suggestibility—body-sway test. Ability to resist suggestion to sway forward.
D. Motor Control—absence of static ataxia; given as preliminary test to C.
E. Goal Discrepancy Score—*smallness* of level of aspiration scores on O'Connor Tweezers test.
F. Judgment Discrepancy Score—*smallness* of judgment discrepancies on O'Connor Tweezers test.

G. Index of Flexibility—number of shifts in aspiration scores on O'Connor Tweezers test, irrespective of size or direction.

H. Manual Dexterity—best score of nine trials on tweezers test.

I. Personal Tempo—speed of writing 2, 3, 4 repeatedly for two trials of 15 seconds each.

J. Fluency—number of *round things* and of *things to eat* mentioned during 30-second periods.

K. Speed Test (1)—speed of tracing when instructed to be both quick and accurate. (Choice conditions.)

L. Speed Test (2)—speed of tracing prescribed path on track tracer under instruction to be quick.

M. Persistence Test I—length of time during which leg is held in uncomfortable and fatiguing position.

N. Persistence Test B—holding breath as long as possible, without inhaling or exhaling.

O. Stress Test—ability of S to recover previous scoring rate on pursuit-meter type of test after special stress period.

P. Non-perseveration—extremes of perseveration (SZ test), either very high or very low, are scored low, while scores nearer the average are scored high.

Also given is a diagram (Fig. 19), showing the relative position of the various tests in a two-factor space. Number 1 represents the first centroid factor extracted from the intercorrelations; $\hat{D}$ represents the same factor rotated into maximum agreement with the criterion column. I', and II', indicate the best possible "simple structure" rotations, which will be seen to give no very intelligible or meaningful results.

The second factor which emerged from this analysis gave rise to a grouping of tests which "is in conformity with what in previous investigations had been shown to be characteristic of the introvert-extravert (dysthymic-hysteric) dichotomy. Thus, introverts (dysthymics) have been shown to be more persistent, extraverts (hysterics) to show less judgment discrepancy, and somewhat less suggestibility, as well as better dark adaptation. However, not all the tests are in agreement with this hypothesis, and little emphasis is laid on the possible identification of this second factor."

It is interesting to note that out of 16 tests, only three failed to have saturations of ·30 or above with the factor of neuroticism, one of these three being the questionnaire. Two tests, Body-sway Suggestibility and Static Ataxia, have loadings above ·65; another five tests have loadings of ·5 or above. When it is realized that the tests with the higher saturations are precisely those which in previous work, as well as in this particular research, gave the best discrimination between normals and neurotics, there remains very little doubt about the identification of this factor.

In a more recent experiment, Eysenck (1952) has duplicated many features of the original one. Two groups of male soldiers, one neurotic and the other normal, again formed the experimental and control groups respectively. The total group was made up of 200 men in the normal and of 120 in the neurotic group. These were submitted to a battery of individual and group tests, including examples of all types of personality tests, although, unfortunately, it was impossible for every test to be given to every subject. The tests used included tests

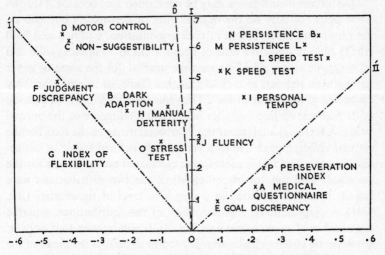

Fig. 19.—Two-factor Representation of Objective Test Results.

of intelligence and vocabulary, various questionnaires, such as scales from the M.M.P.I., the Maudsley Medical Questionnaire, the Word Connection List, and Annoyances, Worries, Likes, and Dislikes tests. Also given were Manual Dexterity tests, Persistence, Tapping, Speed of Decision, Level of Aspiration, Oscillation, Writing Pressure, Suggestibility, Word-association, Motor Disorganization, Abstraction, Concentration, Dark Vision, Flicker Fusion, Perseveration, Speed, Expressive Movement, and Group Rorschach tests. Results are far too numerous to be discussed at any length, but it was again found that the tests differentiated in almost every case in the expected direction between normal and neurotic groups.

Twenty-eight tests were intercorrelated for the normal group and a factor analysis carried out. A very clear factor of neuroticism emerged again, and an attempt was made to estimate the accuracy with which this factor could be measured by the various tests used. The method of multiple R, although it gave a satisfyingly high value in the neighbourhood of ·9, was rejected, as it is well known that this method capitalizes on chance differences. Instead, a score was derived from 16 tests which had been designated before the experiment was carried out, giving equal weight to all the tests and thus making no use whatsoever of the statistical finding of the analysis itself. Using this combination of scores, a validity estimate for the sum of these tests of approximately ·80 was established.

One further investigation may be mentioned here because it throws some light not only on the organization of personality but also on the origin and development of such organization. Eysenck and Prell (1951) gave 17 objective tests of neuroticism to 50 monozygotic and 50 dizygotic twins, all of whom were normal "in the sense of never having been patients at a child guidance clinic, or in any other way suspected of mental disorder". The same tests were given to a group of 21 neurotic children, similar in age and intelligence to the normal twins. A factorial analysis of the intercorrelations of the tests for the normal children gave rise to a very clearly defined factor of neuroticism, and when factor scores were calculated on this factor for the "normal" and the "neurotic" children, the two distributions were found to be differentiated at a very high level of significance ($p <$ ·001). A diagrammatic representation of the distributions, equated for number of cases, is given in Fig. 20. It will be seen that none of the neurotic children had normality scores as high as the mean of the normal children, and that some of the normal children had scores as high as 14σ above the mean of the neurotic group. There can be little doubt, therefore, that the factor isolated can be correctly identified as a factor of neuroticism (Eysenck and Prell, 1952).

On the hypothesis that neuroticism is inherited, we would expect factor scores on neuroticism to be much more alike in monozygotic than in dizygotic twins, and this deduction is borne out by the data. The intra-class correlation between monozygotic twins is ·851; that between dizygotic twins is ·217. Calculation of Holzinger's h^2, which is presented by him as an estimate of the degree to which a given score is determined by hereditary factors, shows that $h^2 = $ ·81. While Eysenck and Prell are somewhat critical of this statistic, in view of that fact that some of the assumptions involved in its derivation are clearly not fulfilled in actual practice, it should be borne in mind that some of these questionable assumptions will lead to an over-estimate, others to an underestimate, of the true value of h², so that on the whole the obtained figure of 81 per cent. represents the best available estimate of the contribution of heredity to neuroticism. This compares well with the figures obtained in the field of intelligence, and suggests that neuroticism is inherited to at least as marked an extent as are cognitive abilities.

One point should be noted here because it is of considerable importance in any estimate of the value of factor analysis in arriving

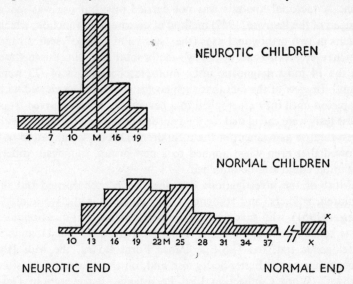

Fig. 20.—Objective Test Discrimination between Normal and Neurotic Children.

x 2 sets of normal twins are respectively 8 and 14 times the neurotic S.D. removed from the neurotic mean, so that their proper scale positions would fall outside the limits of this diagram.

at psychologically meaningful factors. Eysenck and Prell found that the factor score on neuroticism showed an hereditary determination to a greater extent than did scores on any of the individual tests, which contributed to the factor in proportion to their correlations with each other. It would appear to follow from this that the factor of neuroticism must have some degree of biological reality and be more than a mere statistical artefact, as otherwise it is difficult to see how the factor could be determined hereditarily to a greater extent than its constituent parts. This demonstration is important because it appears to be the first time that an experimental answer has been given to one of the most frequent criticisms made of factorial studies.

Yet another study, carried out by Himmelweit and Petrie (1951), uses the general method outlined above. 50 neurotic children and 50 normal children in the age range from 9–14 were tested by means of a large battery of objective, projective, and questionnaire tests, many of them specially designed for the investigation by the writers. The groups were matched for age and I.Q. By and large, the detailed findings agreed well with those found in earlier work; in the case of newly designed tests differences were usually in the expected direction. A factorial analysis was not carried out, but use was made instead of the Penrose (1947) method of discriminant function, which results in two orthogonal axes (the "size" and "shape" scores), and which resembles in some ways a two-factor solution. Using this method on the 14 most diagnostic tests, multiple correlations of ·73 were found. In view of the fact that such coefficients must be viewed with suspicion until they are applied to a new group, scores derived from these tests were calculated for the neurotic group and correlated with a psychiatric assessment of these children. This cross-validation test showed that even when applied to a new group, significant differentiation could still be obtained.

Most of the investigations described have been carried out on children, soldiers, and students. Quite different is the work of A. Heron (1951), who gave a battery of performance and questionnaire tests to 80 unskilled workers. Tests used included the Dominoes Intelligence test, the U.S.E.S. Paper Form Board, the Mill Hill Vocabulary test, a Letter Series test, and, on the non-cognitive side, Crown's Word Connection List, Persistence, Perseveration, Dexterity, Static Ataxia, and Aspiration tests, as well as Worries, Annoyances, Interests, and Food Dislikes inventories. Also included in the factor analysis was Work Adjustment as rated by a panel of six raters, and a psychiatric rating. A diagrammatic representation of the results is given in Fig. 21, showing the relation of the various tests to two factors extracted (rotated positions). The differentiation of the intelligence and the neuroticism factors will be seen very clearly.

Intelligence is defined by Dominoes, Letter Series, Vocabulary, Paper Form Board, and various writing tests. Neuroticism is defined by Static Ataxia, Annoyances, Worries, Interests, poor job adjustment, non-persistence, and so forth. It seems clear that in this population, too, a factor of neuroticism can be demonstrated which is defined by much the same tests as previously. A third factor also emerging from this study is possibly similar to extraversion-introversion, although not much reliance can be placed on this identification.

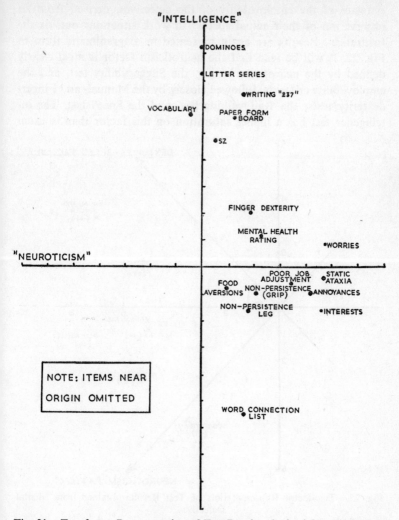

Fig. 21.—Two-factor Representation of Test Results obtained from Unskilled Workers.

Quite a different population again was used in the work of Tizard and O'Connor (1951). Basing themselves on 104 high-grade defectives, they used the Matrices test of intelligence, a four-point rating of stability, which was based on the social behaviour of the defectives, and Suggestibility, Rail-walking, Manual-dexterity, Finger-dexterity, and Speed tests. Also available was a carefully constructed estimate of the employability of the defectives, derived from an observation of their actual success in work situations outside the Institution. Results are again presented in diagrammatic form in Fig. 22. It will be seen that the neuroticism factor is most clearly defined by the neuroticism rating, the Suggestibility test, and the employability criterion, followed closely by the Manual- and Finger-dexterity tests, the Rail-walking test, and the Speed test. The intelligence test has a higher saturation on this factor than is usual

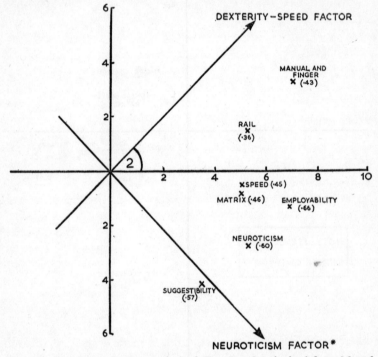

Fig. 22.—Two-factor Representation of Test Results obtained from Mental Defectives.

(·46); there is of course no reason to expect the correlation between intelligence and neuroticism to be identical in samples which deviate so very markedly from the normal.

The last experiment to be discussed in this chapter goes somewhat beyond the pattern set by the two preceding chapters, and relates directly to a query raised by the two experiments of Line reported earlier. It will be remembered that he found a factor of "stability" by contrasting normal with neurotic and psychotic groups. This raises the question of whether it is justifiable to lump together different types of abnormality. Psychiatric opinion tends toward the belief that psychosis and neurosis are characterized by fundamentally different reaction tendencies, and if that were true, of course, no meaningful result could be expected from an experiment in which those two reaction types were thrown together. On the other hand, writers like Freud believe that psychosis is merely a more advanced state of regression than is neurosis, so that we could represent those two types of disorder as lying on one and the same dimension. Yet another possibility, of course, would be represented by the view that psychosis is a disorder qualitatively different from normal states of behaviour, and consequently not represented on any continuum, but either present or absent. An attempt to provide data to settle this controversy was made by Eysenck (1952).

The method of analysis used was again that of criterion analysis, which has been briefly explained above. The set-up of the experiment was very simple. Three groups of patients were tested—a normal group, a schizophrenic group, and a manic-depressive group. The normal group was made up of 100 subjects; the psychotic groups each contained 50 subjects. No chronic cases of psychosis were included and no one was tested during acute psychotic episodes. Manic-depressive patients were tested exclusively during their non-manic states. Altogether, 84 different sets of scores were obtained from a somewhat smaller number of tests, and an F test of significance was carried out on each score for the three groups. Of the scores, 27 were non-significant, 6 were significant at the 5 per cent. level, 12 at the 1 per cent. level, and 39 at the ·1 per cent. level. These values show fairly conclusively that on the basis of objective tests, the three populations tested were not chance samples from a single universe, but significantly differentiated from each other. Twenty tests were selected from the whole battery and product-moment correlations calculated between them for the normal and psychotic groups separately. Also calculated were biserial correlations of each test with the following dichotomies: normals versus depressives; normals versus schizophrenics; schizophrenics versus depressives; normals versus psychotics.

The two tables of correlations (one for the normal and one for the psychotic group) were factor analysed by means of Thurstone's centroid method, and two significant factors extracted. On the hypothesis of a normal-psychotic continuum, we would expect the factors for the two analyses to be proportional to each other, and this was indeed found to be the case. Correlations between factors from one group and those from the other came to ·868 and ·746. We would also expect, on the basis of this hypothesis, that the first factors should be proportional to the criterion correlations of the tests with the normal-psychotic dichotomy. These correlations were ·895 and ·954, so that again we may say that the deduction has been verified. Apparently, psychotic states do in fact form a continuum with normal mental states, and cannot be said to be qualitatively differentiated from the normal.

An attempt was also made in this study to find evidence for the hypothesis usually associated with Kretschmer, namely that there exists a fundamental personality variable of schizothymia-cyclothymia, which in its most extreme form is characterized by the distinction between schizophrenics and manic-depressives. The possibility that the second factor obtained in the analysis of the intercorrelations between the 20 tests might be identifiable with schizothymia-cyclothymia was canvassed, and correlations run between the saturations for this factor and the criterion column made up of the correlations between each test and the schizophrenic-manic-depressive dichotomy. These correlations turned out to be quite insignificant (·029 and ·085), so that we find no support for this hypothesis whatsoever. These data should not be taken to mean that Kretschmer's hypothesis is conclusively refuted; it is possible that with a better selection of tests a more positive result could be attained.

That such an outcome is not very likely is shown by a recent study in which Brengelmann (1952) gave a number of objective behaviour tests which, according to Kretschmer, were diagnostic of the schizothymia-cyclothymia dimension, to 100 normal subjects. The tests included one of Personal Tempo (Tapping), on which schizothymes should obtain higher scores; a Tremometer test, in which schizothymes should make fewer mistakes and take less time than cyclothymes; the Muller-Lyer Illusion, in which cyclothymes should evince higher degrees of illusion than schizothymes; a Colour-form test, in which schizothymes should be form reactive, cyclothymes colour reactive; and a Reading test in which the tachistoscopically presented stimulus words should be apprehended by the schizothyme by an analytic method, and by the cyclothyme by a Gestalt method. Reliabilities of these tests were found to be satisfactory.

The intercorrelations between these tests are given in Table 24. Only one correlation is significant at the 1 per cent. level, and this is contrary to expectation. One further correlation is significant at the

TABLE 24

Tests	1	2	3	4	5	6	7	8
1. Personal tempo . . .	—	−·086	−·122	−·166	·183	−·056	·139	·093
2. Tremometer mistakes . .	—	—	−·522	·056	−·040	·157	·046	·121
3. Tremometer time . . .	—	—	—	−·106	·102	−·128	−·190	·045
4. Muller-Lyer Illusion Total .	—	—	—	—	−·063	·086	−·009	·084
5. Muller-Lyer Illusion Difference	—	—	—	—	—	·083	·054	·017
6. Colour form (spontaneous) .	—	—	—	—	—	—	(·455)	·203
7. Colour form (special instruction)	—	—	—	—	—	—	—	·072
8. Tachistoscopic Reading test .	—	—	—	—	—	—	—	—

Values in parentheses derived from tests not experimentally independent.

5 per cent. level, namely that between the two colour-form tests; all the other correlations are insignificant, and so variable that they cannot be interpreted to support in any way the Kretschmerian hypothesis. We must conclude that tests, all of which are declared by Kretschmer to measure the dimension cyclothymia-schizothymia in normal people, do not, in fact, produce a pattern of intercorrelations which would support the hypothesis. Here, then, we have another example of definite disproof of a hypothesis by factorial methods. Taken together with the previously mentioned research, these data must throw considerable doubt on the existence of a schizothymia-cyclothymia dimension, although a good deal of further experimental work should be required to finalize such a conclusion.

It has been demonstrated above that a normal-psychotic dimension appears to be called for by the results of the experimental tests and the intercorrelations. The question has not yet been answered whether this dimension is identical with that of neuroticism, or whether it is in fact quite separate and different. A long discussion of this problem is given by Eysenck (1952), who quotes several original experiments to show that two dimensions at least are required to accommodate the three populations of normals, neurotics, and psychotics. We need not here go into the statistical basis of this argument beyond noting that it is essentially dependent on the fact that those tests which discriminate successfully between normals and psychotics do not on the whole discriminate between normals and neurotics. Thus, the Body-sway Test of Suggestibility, which has always given a very good discrimination between normals and neurotics, does not discriminate at all between normals and psychotics; neither do tests of persistence, perseveration, oscillation, or word association. It is difficult to reconcile data of this type with the Freudian hypothesis of one dimension of "regression" from the normal, through the neurotic, to the psychotic, and consequently it appears probable that in addition to a factor of neuroticism we must also recognize the existence of what ought perhaps to be called a factor of psychoticism, although the term has an unusual and unattractive sound, which may make it difficult of acceptance.

We may now summarize the results of work carried out with objective behaviour tests. As far as the "w" factor (neuroticism) is concerned, there can be little doubt that these tests have strongly supported the evidence available from ratings and self-ratings, and have added considerably to our understanding of the nature of this factor. They have also enabled us to measure it with considerable accuracy and to make predictions regarding it which can be tested and verified. These contributions are particularly important, in that they are made on an objective basis and are not dependent on subjective interpretation of mental states, either one's own or someone else's. Consequently, most of the objections to ratings and self-ratings are not applicable to objective behaviour tests, and for any thorough understanding or description of personality we consider it essential that tests of this type should be included. With respect to extraversion-introversion, there is no clear-cut evidence derived from objective tests along factorial lines. There are many indications, as is shown, for instance, in a review of the literature by Eysenck (1952), that quite a number of tests can be found which can discriminate at a high level of significance between hysterics and dysthymics, i.e. between the groups which, according to Jung, are the prototypes of extraversion-introversion respectively. This would appear to be a very promising field of research, but until direct evidence is available, nothing further can be said about the definition of extraversion-introversion by means of factorial studies.

It must, of course, be admitted that the use of objective behaviour tests raises problems different from, but no less real than, those raised by the other approaches mentioned. The most urgent of these is the problem of interpretation of factors. The reader may best see the difficulties involved by trying to find a meaningful psychological label for the following conglomerations of tests characterizing one or two of Cattell's factors:

(1) Low Perceptual Closing Speed; large mean P.G.R.; high aspiration level; absence of questionable preferences.

or (2) High Fluency; high total information; high two-hand co-ordination score; high ideo-motor speed; a high rate of cube fluctuation and low use of C.M.S. circles.

It appears to the writer that these problems of interpretation cannot easily be brushed aside, nor do they permit of a simple semantic solution. The method of criterion analysis affords one possible way of unambiguously identifying factors, but it can only be used when tests are selected and groups of subjects tested according to a very definite and clear psychological hypothesis. When there is no such hypothesis, the method is not applicable. This fact may be illustrative of what, to the writer, seems the main conclusion to be drawn from much of this work, namely that like most other statistical methods, factor analysis cannot with advantage proceed in the dark, but should always be related quite definitely to a hypothesis, and each experiment should be set up in such a way that the hypothesis under investigation can be supported or disproved. In the absence of such an approach, there will always be dispute and semantic confusion; with it, there is hope of ultimate agreement on the main dimensions of personality.

CHAPTER V

THE ANALYSIS OF PHYSIQUE (BODY BUILD)

THE BELIEF THAT constitutional factors play an important part in personality is held very widely. Unfortunately, there are few areas of psychology in which a greater superstructure has been built on so small a factual foundation. A salutary check to the endless speculation of psychologists, physiologists, phrenologists, psychiatrists, anthropometrists, endocrinologists, and others was provided in 1930 by the publication of Patterson's *Physique and Intellect*. In this book he made a thorough survey of the available literature, and came to the conclusion that: "our detailed survey of available quantitative evidence has demonstrated that prevalent notions regarding the intimacy of the relationship between physical traits and intellect have been greatly exaggerated. . . . The suggestion is frequently encountered that physical traits may be found associated to a greater extent with temperament than with intellect. Even here, however, little optimism is justified. An intimate connection between body build and temperament has not been disclosed." A good deal of research has been carried on since Patterson's monograph appeared, particularly with respect to body build and its relation to personality, and we must investigate with particular care the validity of the claims advanced by various recent writers that the dearth of positive findings reported by Patterson was due to faulty methods of investigation rather than to a lack of relationship between constitution and personality.

This is not the place to give an historical review of attempts to set up constitutional typologies. We shall merely note the main landmarks and otherwise refer the reader to Table 25, which sets out briefly the various systems advanced by a large number of writers. As is appropriate, the first name in that list is that of Hippocrates who, about 430 B.C., described two antithetical types of body build which he called the *habitus apoplecticus* and *habitus phthisicus*. The former was thick-set, strong, and muscular; the latter thin, delicate, and weak. While many later writers followed this dichotomy, others interpolated a third type intermediate between these extremes, as did, for instance, the Frenchman Rostan (1828), with his digestive, muscular, and respiratory-cerebral type; the German Beneke (1878), with his phlegmatic, athletic, and asthenic-cerebral types; the Italians Viola (1933) and DiGiovanni (1919), with their microsplanchnic, normosplanchnic, and macrosplanchnic types; and the American Wells (1869), with his motive or mechanical system, vital or nutritive system, and mental or nervous system.

TABLE 25

BODY TYPE

Author	Eurymorph	Mesomorph	Leptomorph[1]
Hippocrates (430 B.C.)	Habitus apoplecticus	—	Habitus phthisicus
Halle (1797)	Abdominal	Muscular	Cephalic
Rostan (1828)	Digestive	Muscular	Cerebral-respiratory
Walker (1852)	Nutritive	Locomotive	Mental
Carus (1852)	Phlegmatic	Athletic	Cerebral-asthenic
Wells (1869)	Vital	Motive	Mental
Beneke (1878)	Hyperplastic	Normal	Hypoplastic
Huter (1880)	Food-type	Strength-type	Sensation-type
Virenius (1904)	Connective	Muscular	Nervous-epithelial
Sigaud (1914)	Digestive	Muscular	Cerebral-respiratory
Mills (1917)	Hypersthenic	Sthenic	Asthenic
Viola (1933)	Megalosplanchnic	Normosplanchnic	Microsplanchnic
Stockard (1923)	Lateral	Intermediate	Linear
Bauer (1924)	Hypersthenic	Sthenic	Asthenic
Kretschmer (1948)	Pyknic	Athletic	Leptosome (Asthenic)
Sheldon (1940)	Endomorph	Mesomorph	Ectomorph
Burt (1947)	Pachysome	—	Leptosome
Martiny (1948)	Entoblastique	Mesoblastique	Ectoblastique

Many other writers apart from those mentioned in Table 25 were ringing changes on the same general theme, some of them putting forward hypotheses also regarding the connection between their various physical types with temperament. It was not, however, until Kretschmer (1925) published the first edition of his rightly famous *Körperbau und Charakter* that psychologists and psychiatrists became seriously interested in this general field. Kretschmer took over essentially Rostan's three types, calling the thick-set, round type the

[1] The terms used in the heading of this Table to describe the three main body types were suggested by Rees and Eysenck (1945), and are used here because they are purely descriptive, operationally defined, and do not carry overtones of any particular system. Eurymorph, mesomorph, and leptomorph are defined in terms of observed distributions of body-build indices, calculated according to the Rees-Eysenck formula; "mesomorph" refers to indices lying within $\pm$ 1 S.D. of the mean, "eurymorph" to indices lying more than 1 S.D. in the pyknic direction, and "leptomorph" to indices lying more than 1 S.D. in the asthenic-leptosomatic direction.

pyknic, the thin, lean type the *asthenic* or *leptosomatic*, and the intermediate type the *athletic*. He also added another concept, that of the *dysplastic* type of body build, which essentially denotes an incompatible mixture of different types in different parts of the body.

To this essentially threefold division on the physical side he added an essentially threefold division on the mental side. In the first editions of his book, the temperamental typology was a twofold one based on the two main groups of functional psychoses, the schizophrenias, and the manic-depressive disorders respectively. Schizophrenics were found to be largely leptosomatic in body build, manic-depressives largely pyknic. In later years he has come more and more to regard (on the physical side) the athletic type as not being intermediate between the other two but as being quite separate from them in many ways. Similarly, on the level of personality description, he has taken the epileptic as his third prototype, postulating a special set of traits as characterizing the epileptic personality, and linking this type with athletic and dysplastic body build. Table 26 shows the distribution of some 8,000 cases of schizophrenic, manic-depressive illness, and epilepsy with respect to their body build; while these figures are subject to much criticism (lack of correction for age, subjectivity of body-type ratings, subjectivity of clinical diagnosis, different standards of different investigators), they nevertheless illustrate a conclusion which is forced on the reader after a careful survey of the whole literature (Eysenck, 1947), namely that when all is said and done there is a genuine difference in body build between schizophrenics and manic-depressives; the conclusion with respect to epilepsy is much less certain and is still subject to discussion.

TABLE 26

Distribution (in per cent.) of Body Type for Schizophrenic,
Manic-depressive, and Epileptic Groups

	Schizophrenics: 5,233 *cases*	Manic-depressives: 1,361 *cases*	Epileptics: 1,505 *cases*
Pyknic . .	13·7	64·6	5·5
Athletic . .	16·9	6·7	28·9
Leptosomatic .	50·3	19·2	25·1
Dysplastic .	10·5	1·1	29·5
Doubtful .	8·6	8·4	11·0

While the demonstration of the correlation between body build and psychosis might be of interest to psychiatrists, Kretschmer's real contribution to psychology lies rather in his hypothesis regarding the "schizothymia" and "cyclothymia" types as constituting a fundamental dimension of personality, of which the schizophrene and the manic-depressive were merely the exaggerated prototypes. He devoted a great deal of ingenuity and considerable psychological insight to the experimental proof of this proposition. A survey of most of the available material has been published by Eysenck (1950), who draws attention to three main points. In the first place, Kretschmer in his proof is considerably handicapped by lack of statistical sophistication. While most of the experiments reported by him with respect to differences of groups of manic-depressives and schizophrenics, or between normal people of leptosomatic and pyknic body build, give results which are significant when the proper tests are carried out, his overall methods of verifying his general hypothesis are faulty although ingenious, and cannot prove or disprove his case. In the second place, the tests designed by Kretschmer in order to measure the various traits postulated by him to characterize the schizothyme or the cyclothyme respectively are of the very greatest interest and importance and deserve a through investigation by means of more advanced statistical and experimental methods. In the third place, both Kretschmer's hypotheses and his methods have been very much misrepresented in the non-German literature, due perhaps to the fact that no translation has been made of any of the later editions of his book in which he incorporated the experimental evidence as it accumulated and in which he modified his theories and hypotheses accordingly.

As most of the studies carried out by Kretschmer and his students are not factorial or even correlational, except for those by Sahai (1931), Brengelmann (1952), and one or two others mentioned already, we will not again summarize this literature, but instead turn to factorial studies of body build as the first step in the factorial investigation of the importance of constitutional factors in personality.

First in this, as in so many fields, is a study by Spearman (1927), who analysed some data on bodily dimensions and anthropological measurement by means of his method of tetrad differences. His conclusion, which has been substantiated by every subsequent research, was that the existence of "type" factors in this field could not be gainsaid; this position he contrasted with what he thought to be the case in the cognitive field where he considered such "type" factors to be non-existent.

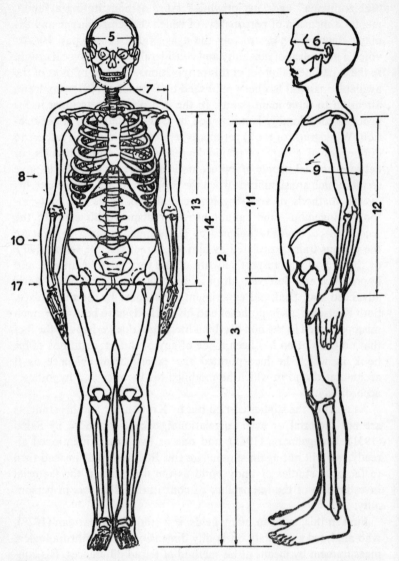

Fig. 23.—Diagram indicating Anthropometric Measurements used by Rees and Eysenck.

It would be tedious to enumerate in detail the numerous investigations which have been carried out, since nearly all agree in finding two very strongly marked factors which contribute between them some 60 per cent. to the common factor variance; in addition, numerous relatively restricted factors have been reported, to which we will return later. Table 27 gives the results from a number of investigations, reporting percentage of variance contributed by the first and second factors respectively, the number of subjects, and the number of measures used.

TABLE 27

Investigator	Factor I	Factor II	n Subjects	N Measures
	per cent.	per cent.		
Dearborn and Rothney (1941)	59	8	533	8
Hammond (1942)	31	9	100	12
Cohen, 1 (1938) . .	44	24	50	14
Cohen, 2 (1940) . .	46	19	64	14
Cohen, 3 (1941) . .	35	25	62	12
Rees and Eysenck (1945) .	34	12	200	18
Burt (1947) . . .	55	14	528	17
Burt and Banks (1947) .	55	14	2400	9
Mullen (1940) [1] 1 . .	43	5	189	17
Mullen (1940) [1] 2 . .	41	5	212	17
Mullen (1940) [1] 3 . .	48	4	230	17
Mullen (1940) [1] 4 . .	39	9	219	17
Mullen (1940) [1] 5 . .	32	11	305	17
Mullen (1940) [1] 6 . .	29	12	165	17

To illustrate the meaning of the results and the type of measures employed, we will quote an investigation employing the largest number of measures on a satisfactorily large number of subjects. Rees and Eysenck (1945) collected 18 measures on 200 soldiers. Fig. 23 shows the measures used in diagrammatic form.[2]

The interpretation of the factor can best be demonstrated by a diagram plotting the respective position of the various measurements in a two-dimensional factor space. This has been done in Fig. 24, which gives the factorial solution for the male sample discussed; for the sake of interest we have also given the results from a more recent analysis by Rees (1950) of 200 women, using very much the same measures. The similarity between the two solutions will be clear. The

[1] In order of age, from 7-year-old through 9, 11, 13, 15-year-olds to 17-year-olds.
[2] This figure is quoted by kind permission of Professor L. L. Thurstone (1946), who carried out a re-analysis of the Eysenck and Rees data and used it as an illustration. The results of this re-analysis will be discussed below.

first factor has positive correlations with all traits, and is clearly a general factor determining body size. The second factor has positive saturations for length measurements, and negative saturations for breadth, width, and circumferential measurements. It is this opposition between the thin, elongated, leptomorph individual and the

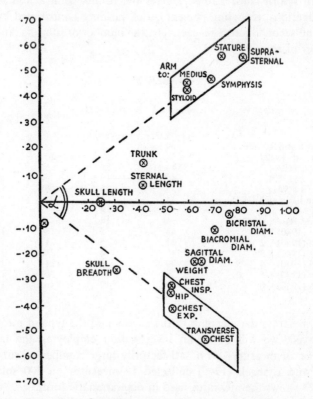

Fig. 24a.—Saturation of Anthropometric Measurements with General and Type Factors: Men.

thick-set, round eurymorph individual which lies at the base of all the typologies enumerated in Table 25.

We may now look at the suggestions for further factors which emerge from some of the analyses. When several measures of a particular type of the body, such as a head or the hand, are included, separate factors emerge relating to that particular part of the body. Such factors are of relatively little interest. Rather more important is the finding of a factor by Thurstone (1946) in his re-analysis of the

Rees-Eysenck data representing "chest depth as distinguished from . . . chest width."[1]

Nearly all the researches quoted have used centroid factors without rotation into simple structure; the exceptions are two papers by

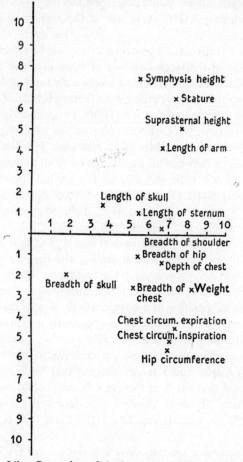

Fig. 24b.—Saturation of Anthropometric Measurements with General and Type Factors: Women.

Thurstone (1946, 1947), re-analysing data published by other workers. His rotations are not always compelling, but they do indicate quite

[1] There is some suggestion in the work of Rees and Eysenck (Eysenck, 1947) that it is lack of chest *depth* which is related primarily to the schizophrenic group of disorders rather than lack of chest *width*, which appears to be more closely related to dysthymia-introversion. However, not enough cases have been used to establish this hypothesis.

clearly that great advances could be made in this field by (*a*) using much larger numbers of measures and (*b*) carrying out a proper multiple-factor analysis on these measures. His data also suggests quite strongly that second-order factors are likely to emerge from such an analysis, which would correspond to the "size" and "shape" factors which reappear in every one of the researches summarized in Table 27.

This view is supported by two analyses, which are of special interest because of the large numbers of cases involved and the fact that the subjects measured were at a very early level of development. Carter and Krause (1936) carried out a factorial study of certain data published by Bakwin and Bakwin (1934). These investigators "made careful measurements of various dimensions of new-born babies, and then presented two tables of correlations. The first showed the intercorrelations between all possible pairs from among 18 external dimensions of 608 male new-borns. The second showed the same sort of intercorrelation figures obtained from measurements of 609 female new-borns. . . . These measures included gross bodily dimensions, body weight, and various facial details".

Thurstone's multiple-factor method was applied to these data; two separate analyses were carried out dealing with the data on males and the data on females respectively. "The first factor reflects the mild but general agreement of all the external dimensions. The first factor loadings are all positive and comparatively heavy for each of the eighteen variables . . . factor one is apparently a measure of size in general." The remaining factors, while showing good intercorrelations between the two analyses, are not readily intelligible, a fact admitted by Carter and Krause, who say that "it is not necessarily to be expected that the later factors will reveal clear-cut pictures of familiar trends". It seems possible that departure from orthogonal factors might have contributed to make these factors more easily intelligible.

A more extensive analysis covering several age levels is that by McCloy (1940), who took nineteen measurements on groups of college men and women, and on boys and girls respectively, at ages of 9 days, and 4, 6, 8, 10, 12, 14, and 16 years. "In each of these groups the computations were carried out to five factors, and, if the fifth factor seemed at all promising, to the sixth factor. In the final analysis, however, none of the factors beyond the fourth seemed significant. In each age-group the same three factors appeared, and in almost all the groups the fourth factor was evident."

The first factor was clearly marked in each case by the measurements of fat and subcutaneous tissue. "These four measurements stood out in one factor and were almost always well grouped." This factor was called one of "growth in fat". "The second factor is that which is weighted highest in the linear measurements, such as in height and sitting height. In other studies on adults . . . this factor is also high in lengths of upper-arm, forearm, lower leg, foot, etc. . . . We were tempted to call it a linear-growth factor. In view, however, of the fact that it is present in almost all variables except fat, we shall tentatively call it a 'general growth factor'."

The third factor is labelled a "cross-sectional factor"; it is most heavily loaded in the girths, widths, and depths.

The fourth factor is less clear and consistent, and McCloy does not attempt to label it.

The many detailed analyses and tables given by McCloy cannot be discussed here further. It seems likely that the factors extracted by means of orthogonal rotational techniques, although they are in general agreement with the conclusion drawn from our survey of earlier work, could with advantage be replaced by a system of oblique and second-order factors. It is to be hoped that such an analysis will be carried out on McCloy's data. In its absence we can add little to his own interpretation.[1] One important feature of all the analyses reported should be noted, namely that none of them gives any support to the triangular kind of conceptual scheme as advanced by Rostan, Kretschmer, Sheldon, and others. The only possible exception to this generalization lies in Sheldon's data, which will be discussed below. Before turning to Sheldon's contribution, however, we must note a few at least of the studies carried out by other workers using factorial techniques or related concepts.

We have already mentioned Sahai's (1931) research, in which he found evidence on the basis of intercorrelational patterns for the existence of a factor of introversion-extraversion. This author carried out a number of physical measures on his subjects, and calculated

[1] Too late for proper inclusion comes a report by Heath (1952) of an investigation which fulfils these conditions. A second-order factor analysis was carried out by her on correlations between 29 variables on 4,128 women, with age held constant. Five first-order factors were extracted and interpreted as A—length of bones, B—cancellous bone size, C—lower-body girth, D—girth of extremities, E—upper-body girth. Second-order factors X and Y are obviously closely related to the usual length- and breadth-factors; X has loadings on C, D, and E, while Y has loadings on A and B. There is a correlation of ·33 between X and Y, interpreted as "an indication of general growth" (p. 94). The similarity of this solution with that diagrammed in Fig. 24 is obvious.

ratios from these. His data support the existence of a "pyknic" type of body build, and this he found correlated with extraversion to the extent of ·20 ± ·04, a value which when corrected for attenuation reached the respectable size of ·35 ± ·04. His suggestion that extraverts are somewhat more eurymorph in body build is confirmed by Burt (1937), who found the following correlations of eurymorph body build with temperamental type:

		General Instability	Extraversion	Cheerfulness
Children	N.			
Abnormal group	131	—·23	·26	·19
Normal group	197	—·11	·08	·17
Adolescents				
Abnormal group	13	—·33	·16	·30
Normal group	100	·04	·18	·14
Adults	180	—·13	·32	·16

Burt's data also suggest that neuroticism or emotional instability is less frequent, and cheerfulness more frequent, in persons of eurymorph build.

Support for the proposition that extraverts are more eurymorph can also be found in the monograph by Sanford et al. (1943), to which reference has already been made. Using 18 individual measurements on 48 children, intercorrelations were prepared and subjected to a somewhat unsatisfactory form of cluster analysis. The outcome of this analysis can best be stated in the author's own words: "We have distinguished four syndromes of body build, the first two being based on high positive intercorrelations among the several anthropometric measures, the last two being based on the relationship between the measures on syndromes one and two for the individual subjects:

(1) Wide, heavy build.
(2) Tall, narrow build.
(3) Large build (i.e. tall, heavy, wide).
(4) Short, wide build."

These partly overlapping clusters are awkward to work with and much more unsatisfactory than proper factor measures would have been; however, in spite of this difficulty the results obtained are clear enough. The person of tall, narrow build, i.e. presumably the leptomorphic type, when compared with the person of short, wide, or wide heavy build, i.e. presumably the eurymorph type, is characterized by the following manifest personality syndromes: conscientious work, counter-active endocathection,[1] guilt and remorse, self-sufficiency, orderly production, and sensitive, imaginative creation; all these are introverted qualities. The person of eurymorph body build, on the other hand, is characterized by the opposite qualities to those mentioned above, as well as by good fellowship and social feeling, i.e. particularly extraverted qualities. A similar picture emerges between the physical syndromes and fantasy syndromes derived from the T.A.T. The person of leptomorphic body build is particularly characterized by lack of social themes and lack of love themes; the eurymorph person by self-assertion themes and social and love themes.

Regarding the correlation between physical syndrome and what Sanford calls "family press", i.e. general family background, the main correlations are between leptomorphic body build and tight control, cultural stimulation, and artistic temperament. Those between eurymorph body build and "family press" are mainly with erotic stimulation, lack of tight control, and of cultural stimuli and artistic temperament. Thus, family background again fits in with the general picture of the introvert and the extravert. Correlations between physical syndromes and intellectual abilities show the leptomorph to be characterized by spatial, number, reasoning, comprehension, abstract, manual manipulation, memory, verbal and vocabulary, non-verbal, and all the other abilities measured or rated, whereas the eurymorph is inferior on all of them. This is again in line with a great deal of evidence showing the introvert (and the leptomorph) slightly superior on scholastic tests of general intelligence and knowledge.

In spite, therefore, of the somewhat unsatisfactory cluster technique used by Sanford, we obtain from his very detailed study, which extended over several years and involved a close investigation of all the children along clinical lines, a picture very similar to that described before, namely a marked tendency for leptomorph children to be introverted and for eurymorph children to be extraverted.

[1] The cathection of thought or emotion for its own sake, preoccupation with inner activities.

These studies have all dealt with normal subjects. Eysenck (1947) extended the scope of this type of investigation to neurotics, again using a hypothetico-deductive approach. If the writers previously mentioned are correct in believing that introverts tend to be leptomorph in body build and extraverts eurymorph, and if Jung is correct in assuming that the hysteric is the prototype of the extravert and the psychasthenic or dysthymic is the prototype of the introvert, then it would follow that in a group of adult neurotics, those of eurymorph body build would be characterized by hysterical symptoms, whereas those of leptomorph body build would be characterized by dysthymic symptoms. Taking a sample of 1,000 unselected neurotics all measured for body type by means of a formula derived from the Rees-Eysenck factorial study, 120 were found to be eurymorphs, 150 leptomorphs, and 730 mesomorphs, i.e. intermediate between the extremes. The following items were found to characterize the eurymorphs as compared with the leptomorphs: hysterical personality, hysterical attitude, hysterical conversion symptoms, diagnosed conversion hysteria, intelligence average or below, muscular tone good. Leptomorphs, on the other hand, were characterized by the items: vocabulary above average, anxious, obsessional, depressed, suffering from headaches, dyspepsia, tremor, irritability, and loss of weight. They also tended to be single and teetotal and to be seclusive.

Most of these differentiations were statistically significant, and in almost every case mesomorphs were found to be intermediate between the extreme groups. It would appear, therefore, that the hypothesis under investigation has been borne out and that hysterics and dysthymics respectively may be justifiably considered to be the neurotic prototypes of the extravert and the introvert respectively.

Rees (1950) carried out a similar study on 60 leptomorph, 77 eurymorph, and 263 mesomorph women using an index of body build derived from his own factorial analysis. Eurymorph women were characterized by hysterical personality, very marked hysterical traits, hysterical motor and sensory conversion symptoms, and backwardness in school; whereas the leptomorph women were characterized by anxiety, depression, irritability, touchiness, suspiciousness, shut-in, weak, and dependent personality, as well as autonomic symptoms, effort intolerance, and above average vocabulary test scores. These results closely confirm those obtained by Eysenck (1947), and leave little doubt that the hypothesis under investigation is at least partly valid. The results are particularly impressive when it is considered that psychiatric diagnoses are notoriously unreliable, particularly on war-time cases, seen only for a limited period of time and under considerable stress of work, and when it is also considered that many of the psychiatrists who took part in this work were relatively inexperienced.

So far we have dealt only with body types relating to the second factor extracted in the variance analysis; obviously, the first factor of body size is also of some interest. Again, it is possible to devise an index based on the factorial studies which would identify the microsomatics (those having a small body), the macrosomatics (those having a large body), and the mesosomatics (those having an intermediate body size). As in the case of the eurymorph, leptomorph, and mesomorph groups, we are dealing of course not with separate types but with a continuous distribution; the extreme groups are simply those who are more than one standard deviation from the mean in either direction.

Eysenck (1947) compared 156 microsomatic, 156 macrosomatic, and 688 mesosomatic male neurotic soldiers, and found the microsomatic person characterized by the following items: unskilled civilian occupation, elementary education, sexually inhibited, narrow hobbies, teetotal, poor physical health, weak and dependent, inert, non-aggressive, anxious, hypochondriacal, depressed, poor muscular tone, low intelligence, poor vocabulary. "Altogether both mentally and physically he is what is popularly called a poor specimen." These results suggest that general body size may be of greater importance for personality than body type, although a repetition of the research would be needed before any such general conclusion could be drawn.

We must now turn to the work of Sheldon, which is much more extensive than that of any other investigator with the exception of Kretschmer, and which has incorporated a number of ideas from other writers and some somewhat novel techniques which have made it of great interest to many psychologists. The first of the general ideas which characterize Sheldon's scheme is derived from such writers as Bessonet-Favre (1910), Bauer (1923), and Castellino (1927), who try to link up the different types of body build with the three germinal layers in the embryo. As is well known, there are three of these—the ectoderm, endoderm, and mesoderm, to which should perhaps be added the mesenchyme (Hertwig, 1881), which acts as a kind of "packing tissue" between the other germinal layers and gives rise to the connective tissues, the myocardium and the visceral musculature, the endocardium and the endothelium of the blood vessels, the lymph glands, lymph vessels, and the spleen. Body types resulting from over-development of either of these components would correspond approximately to Kretschmer's pyknics (endoderms), athletics (mesoderms), and leptosomatics (ectoderms). Fig. 25 presents such an embryological scheme as developed by Martiny (1948), whose biological arguments are somewhat more plausible than Sheldon's.

In his inspection of some 4,000 male bodies, Sheldon found three extreme types of variants which corresponded closely to Kretschmer's three types. In the first of these, Kretschmer's pyknic type, Sheldon found that "the digestive viscera, especially the gut, held a more or less predominant position in the organic economy. In these people the most manifest external characteristic is a conspicuous laying on of fat, which is an indication of predominance of the absorptive functions—the functions of the gut—over the energy-expending functions." He goes on to say that: "The functional elements of the digestive system are derived embryologically almost entirely from the endoderm, the innermost of the original three embryonic layers. We can quite naturally therefore refer to the extremes of type one as those exhibiting a condition of *endomorphy*."

In a similar way, bones, muscles, connective tissue, and the heart and blood vessels were seen to predominate overwhelmingly in the variants of type two, which correspond to Kretschmer's athletics. This type he therefore called the *mesomorph*, as these functions are derived predominantly from the mesoderm, the second embryonic layer. As regard the third type, Kretschmer's leptosomatic or asthenic type, "the principal derivatives from the embryonic ectodermal layer are the skin itself, hair and nails, sense organs (exteroceptors), and the nervous system, including the brain. Relative to total bodily mass, all these organs are conspicuous in the bodily economy of the extreme variants of type three. . . . Hence, we have named them *ectomorphs* or persons exhibiting ectomorphy".

Having thus adopted the Continental ideas of embryological determination of body type, Sheldon introduces another idea borrowed from Plattner (1938), namely that of considering these three genetic "factors" as components of total body build, each having a certain determinable influence. This influence is rated by Sheldon on a seven-point scale so that each body type may be represented by a set of three numbers denoting respectively the influence of each of the three components. Thus, 117 would be a person characterized

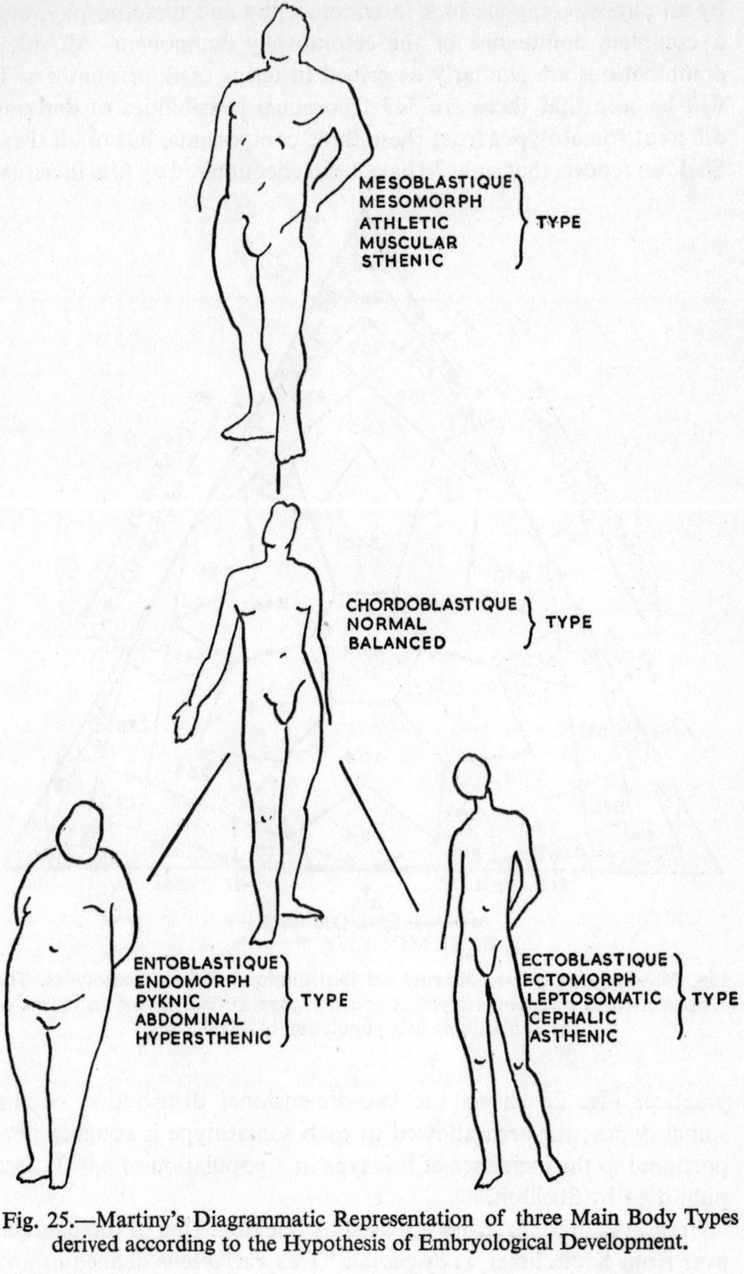
MESOBLASTIQUE
MESOMORPH
ATHLETIC
MUSCULAR
STHENIC
TYPE
CHORDOBLASTIQUE
NORMAL
BALANCED
TYPE
ENTOBLASTIQUE
ENDOMORPH
PYKNIC
ABDOMINAL
HYPERSTHENIC
TYPE
ECTOBLASTIQUE
ECTOMORPH
LEPTOSOMATIC
CEPHALIC
ASTHENIC
TYPE

Fig. 25.—Martiny's Diagrammatic Representation of three Main Body Types derived according to the Hypothesis of Embryological Development.

by an almost complete lack in endomorphy and mesomorphy, and a complete dominance of the ectomorphy component. All other combinations are similarly described in terms of three numbers. It will be seen that there are 343 theoretical possibilities of deriving different somatotypes from these three components, but of all these Sheldon reports that only 76 have been encountered by him in actual

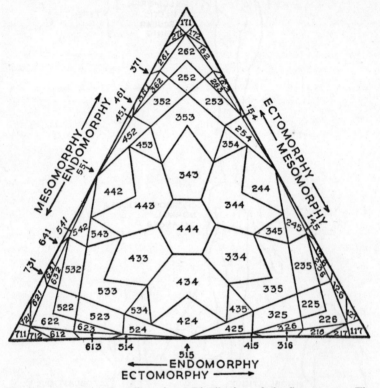

Fig. 26.—Showing a Two-dimensional Distribution of the Somatotypes. The area allotted to each Somatotype is roughly proportional to the incidence of the Somatotype in a population of 4,000 cases.

practice. Fig. 26 shows the two-dimensional distribution of the somatotypes; the area allowed to each somatotype is roughly proportional to the incidence of this type in a population of 4,000 cases published by Sheldon.

Several additional scales are used by Sheldon. One of these, taken over from Kretschmer, is *dysplasia*. "This variable is defined as any inconsistent or uneven mixing of the three primary components in different regions of the body." This Sheldon refers to as a "*d*" index. It is derived in the following way. The whole body is split up into five regions, the first dealing with the head, the second with the trunk (breadth), the third with the arms, the fourth with the trunk (thickness), and the fifth with the legs. Somatotype ratings are made of each of these five regions, and the sum of the disagreements constitutes the "*d*" index.

Another index, the "*g*" index, is concerned with gynandromorphy, i.e. the extent to which a physique presents traits ordinarily associated with the opposite sex. Lastly, yet another index, the "*t*" index, is found, which relates to textual variations among persons, ranging from coarse to fine. The description of this index in Sheldon's work is not at all clear, but Sheldon reports a re-rating reliability on 1,000 cases of ·93.

The only really novel contribution which Sheldon has made to this field is his technique of anthropometric measurement. He makes use of a photographic technique in which each subject is photographed identically posed from three different angles; all measures and ratings are then taken from these standard photographs. There are obvious advantages in this method, although one would like to know a good deal more about repeat reliabilities and correlations of measures so obtained with those derived from more orthodox procedures.

Assessment of Sheldon's contribution so far is difficult. Most of his ideas are derivative rather than original, although there can be no doubt that he has popularized the constitutional type of study in the U.S.A., where this field had been relatively neglected. It is probable that, as far as description of human physique goes, his method, if carefully followed, would give a more accurate and more complete picture than any other yet available. However, a number of questions arise which would have to be answered before his system can be adopted. Most important of these is that of the lack of independence of his three components. On p. 138 of his book, Sheldon gives scatter diagrams showing correlations between his components for 2,000 men and 1,000 women. Correlations between the first and second components are relatively low ($-$ ·32 and $-$ ·11 respectively for the men and the women). Between the third and the first components, correlations are considerable ($-$ ·27 and $-$ ·70). For the correlations between the third and the second components coefficients are again considerable ($-$ ·64 and $-$ ·41). It is quite clear that Sheldon's three types could be described much more parsimoniously in terms of two orthogonal factors, as indeed would seem inevitable in view of the factorial results summarized earlier in this chapter.[1]

This conclusion is subject, of course, to one important proviso. On a purely descriptive basis, two factors may do all that Sheldon's three types can do. If, however, it could be shown that these three types are real derivatives from certain embryological layers and are functionally continuous with these layers, then the observed inter-correlations among the types would be a cheap price to pay for the gain in understanding obtained through this relationship. It would still, of course, be necessary to postulate some causative agency responsible for these intercorrelations, a point completely neglected by Sheldon; nevertheless, no one would deny that wherever there is a conflict between statistical factors and physiological, anatomical, or genetic determination, it is the statistical factor which should be thrown overboard rather than these more palpable influences.

When we look at the evidence presented by Sheldon in favour of his scheme, we find that it is rather unsatisfactory. Apart from neglecting the considerable complexity of the development of the germ layers (the interested reader may refer to Hamilton, Boyd and Mossman, 1945, for a concise account of the known facts regarding embryological development), Sheldon has at no point attempted to make deductions from his hypotheses, which could be used to verify or refute his theory. Many such deductions are suggested by a careful reading of the relevant literature. The ectoderm is concerned with the development of the enamel organ germs of the permanent teeth, various parts of the eye, and the sensory epithelia of the olfactory and auditory organs. It would seem to follow that the ectomorphic person should show measurable differences with respect to quality of teeth, sensory acuity of eye and ear and nose as compared with the other types. Similar deductions could be made for the other somatotypes. It should be possible to make detailed developmental studies on animals, possibly even including genetic changes, which might

[1] This has been shown very clearly by Ekman in two important contributions (1951). As he points out: "Our principal task has been to find out whether Sheldon's morphological system could not be simplified by reducing the dimensions from three to two. It would appear that this question can be answered very definitely in the affirmative" (p. 87). Ekman goes on to show that a similar simplification is possible in the psychological field, where Sheldon's three dimensions can equally well be reduced to two. He also proves that the correlations between body build and temperament, using Sheldon's material, is not lessened by this transformation. Altogether, Ekman's treatment is much more sophisticated and definite than Sheldon's, and students of the problem of human physique should benefit considerably from a perusal of his contribution.

lead to a verification of this embryological hypothesis. In the absence of such evidence, the whole scheme remains entirely speculative, and must therefore be considered inferior from the point of view of simplicity of description to the factorial one outlined above. Unless the embryological hypothesis can be substantiated and unless some causal factor can be found to account for the negative correlations in the development of the three components, Sheldon's whole system must remain an interesting but speculative attempt to probe beyond the observed interconnections to some hypothetical underlying causes.[1]

One remaining question relates to the permanence of the somatotype. In 1940 Sheldon wrote that: "It has been possible to follow the development of several hundred individuals over a period of about a dozen years, and while many have shown sharp fluctuations in weight, we have discovered no case in which there has been a convincing change in the somatotype." In 1949, Sheldon appears to retract what to most readers will be the clear import of that statement by saying: "I have not yet seen a case which seems to present, after careful study, a change in the somatotype, but I have seen cases in which I changed my mind as to how the somatotype should be read. In other words, I have seen later (and earlier) photographs of individuals that seem to introduce new evidence as to the strength of one or more of the primary components, and have thus been led to a revision of a former estimate of somatotype. . . . When I wrote that no case had been discovered in which there had been a convincing change in the somatotype, I meant that in all cases where there *seemed* to be a change I had been convinced on re-examination of both or all photographs that I (or someone) had made an unnecessary error in the first judgment." It is quite clear, then, that the somatotype *as rated* may change, although Sheldon may be right in his contention that the morphogenotype, which he defines as "the three-dimensional trajectory through time along which an organism will travel under basal conditions", does not change. That, of course, is a personal opinion, and he attempts no proof in its favour.

We are now ready to consider correlations between body type, as rated by Sheldon, and temperament type, as rated by him also. 200 young students constituted the sample, as will be remembered from

[1] What is so conspicuously missing from Sheldon's writings is the careful, controlled genetic work which alone can make his theories acceptable. As an example of this type of work, cf. Brues's (1950) original use of linkage in the investigation of genetic factors in body build.

our discussion of Sheldon's rating experiments in Chapter II. The correlations between endomorphy and visceratonia was ·79; between mesomorphy and somatotonia ·72; and between ectomorphy and cerebrotonia ·83. "These are higher correlations than we expected to find, and they raise some questions of great interest. If we were to regard the product moment correlation as a measure of the degree to which two variables are made up of common elements, correlations of the order of ·8 would suggest that morphology and temperament as we measure them may constitute expressions at their respective levels of essentially common components." Correlations are also given by Sheldon between the three temperamental components and several other bodily indices. Thus, the "g" index (gynandromorphy) correlates ·39 with viscerotonia and ·28 with cerebrotonia, but — ·63 with somatotonia. The "t" index (textural component) correlates ·36 with cerebrotonia, but only insignificantly with the other two components. I.Q. and sexuality also correlate positively with cerebrotonia but hardly at all with the other two components. One might expect from these correlations that the "t" component would correlate with I.Q., which it does (·39), and with æsthetic intelligence (·58) and sexuality (·40).[1]

Much could be said about these results. We have noted in a previous chapter the serious statistical errors apparent in Sheldon's table of correlations from which the temperamental syndromes were derived. We must note here the even more important experimental error of having the same observer rate personality and body build in his subjects when it is almost certain that his hypotheses will influence his ratings. The correlations actually found are much higher than those reported by any other investigators (when corrected for attenuation, on the assumption of any reasonable reliability for ratings, they very closely approach perfection). Such results obviously have to be checked and repeated before very much credence can be given to them. We have encountered only one independent study of Sheldon's claims—that by Fiske (1944). The number of significant findings in this study of adolescent boys is not conspicuously greater than chance expectancy. The use of Sheldon's improved procedure for classifying physique yielded "the same paucity of significant relationships to physique that has been found in earlier studies". This conclusion deserves particular emphasis as the somatotyping of the subjects in this study was done by Sheldon himself, and as a con-

[1] Perhaps relevant here is the work of Sills (1950) dealing with the relationship between body components and performance of motor skills.

siderable variety of procedures was used for the purpose of personality measurement. In addition, the statistical procedure employed (analysis of variance) was superior to any employed in Sheldon's own studies.

Some support of Sheldon's scheme is given in a comparatively objective study by Child (1950), who used 414 Yale students, who had been somatotyped by Sheldon himself, as subjects. A special questionnaire was constructed for this study based on Sheldon's description of the various personality correlates of his somatotypes and chi-squared analyses made of tables relating body type to questionnaire items. Altogether, 96 predictions were made, based on Sheldon's views. Of the relations empirically observed, 74, i.e. 77 per cent., were in the predicted direction, 20 reached significance at the 5 per cent. level, and 10 at the 1 per cent. level. Of the 21 correlations contrary to prediction, only 1 was significant at the 5 per cent. level, none at the 1 per cent. level. "The three dimensions of physique differed in the confirmation of predictions. The measured difference is that many fewer predictions are confirmed at acceptable levels of statistical significance for endomorphy than for the other two dimensions of physique."

Child also made an attempt to study the magnitude of relationships between physique and self-rated behaviour by constructing scales of viscerotonia, somatotonia, and cerebrotonia, from the most significant items, i.e. those showing the highest correlation with body build. These scales were derived from half of the population and applied to the other half. The resulting correlations are set out in Table 28. As will be seen, the correlations between viscerotonia and endomorphy (·13), somatotonia and mesomorphy (·38) and cerebrotonia and ectomorphy (·27) are in the predicted direction, but

TABLE 28

Correlations between Dimensions of Physique and
Sets of Self-ratings Described in Text.

	Dimension of Physique		
	Endomorphy	Mesomorphy	Ectomorphy
Self-ratings:			
Viscerotonia .	+ ·13	+ ·13	− ·15
Somatotonia .	+ ·03	+ ·38	− ·37
Cerebrotonia .	− ·03	− ·38	+ ·27

are about as low as correlations between body type and temperament have usually been found to be. "It is thus possible but not certain that appropriate measures based on ratings, such as were used here, have quite a sizeable relationship with dimensions of physique. It is reasonably certain that this relationship does not at all approach the magnitude of the relationships reported by Sheldon between dimensions of physique and his measures of temperament."

It will be remembered that Sheldon extended his scheme of temperament analysis to include psychotic and neurotic manifestations and a survey of his work in this field can be found in Chapter II. Here we are concerned with the relationship between the morphological components and psychiatric diagnosis, as based on the work of Wittman (1948). 155 psychotic male patients constituted the experimental group and were somatotyped by Sheldon himself. Wittman made a rating for these patients on the traits from her check list,[1] thus obtaining an average rating for each of the primary psychiatric components. This rating procedure apparently had a good deal of reliability, as correlations of her ratings with those of an independent rater averaged ·86. Correlations were then run between these ratings and the morphological components. The first psychiatric component (manic-depressive) correlated ·54 with endomorphy, ·41 with mesomorphy, and − ·59 with ectomorphy. The second psychiatric component (paranoid) correlated − ·04 with endomorphy, ·57 with mesomorphy, and − ·34 with ectomorphy. The third psychiatric component (hebephrenic) correlated − ·25 with endomorphy, − ·68 with mesomorphy, and ·64 with ectomorphy. These correlations are rather high, and as the two parts of the study (psychiatric ratings and morphology ratings) were apparently kept separate, they are of considerable interest.

Sheldon claims that these correlations would be higher still if account were taken of the rather more complex scheme which is presented in Fig. 11, p. 71, in this book. His verbal presentation is by no means clear, but it would appear to be reducible to the following outline.

If we represent the three main body types as the three corners of a triangle, then a line drawn from the centre of this triangle to each of the three corners will represent respectively the viscerotonic component (leading to the endomorph body type), the somatotonic component (leading to the mesomorph body type), and the cerebrotonic component (leading to the ectomorph body type).

[1] This list is given in detail in Chapter II, p. 95.

Neurosis and psychosis are represented not by the "tonia" of the visceral somatic and cerebral processes respectively, but rather by their "penia", i.e. not by their development but by their absence. Consequently, the three main neurotic and psychotic types will lie in the middle of the three sides of the triangle at opposite ends to the viscerotonic-endomorphic corner (psychasthenia, paranoid schizophrenia), the somatotonic-mesomorph corner (neurasthenia, hebephrenic schizophrenia), and the cerebrotonic-ectomorph corner (hysteria, manic-depressive psychosis). Sheldon attempts to support his hypothesis that the primary psychiatric components are located opposite the morphological poles by means of correlating ratings on primary psychiatric components of the 155 subjects carried out by him while doing the somatotyping, with the same components according to hospital records. These correlations are indeed somewhat larger than those in the Wittman study, but that may be due to the fact that, in addition to body build, Sheldon also had the patients' behaviour to guide him in his ratings. It is difficult, consequently, to accept them as proving his point.

While these studies are experimentally much better controlled than Sheldon's work on normals, they still leave much to be desired. The main outcome, however, is well in line with previous work showing the relationship between manic-depressive psychoses and eurymorph body build, schizophrenia and leptomorph body build, with patients suffering from paranoid delusions being intermediate in body build between the other two, and showing considerable relationship with the mesomorphic body type.[1]

In summary, it may be said that Sheldon's results wherever they are comparable with the work of his predecessors agree fairly well with their conclusions. His studies suffer from methodological and statistical weaknesses which make it difficult to accept some of his claims, particularly in so far as they relate to the size of correlations observed between somatotype and temperament. Correlations with objective tests (Fiske, 1942; Smith, 1949; Janoff *et al.*, 1950) are extremely low, even where they are in the expected direction. In spite of their messianic ring his contributions cannot be dismissed, but neither can they be accepted at face value. They probably contain sufficient truth and insight to be worthy of proper scientific investigation.

[1] For a direct comparison of the factor-analytic with the Sheldonian approach, the work of Moore and Hsü (1946) may with advantage be consulted.

CHAPTER VI

THE ANALYSIS OF PHYSIOLOGICAL MEASURES

COMPARED WITH THE number of studies using body build as a variable, there is a dearth of studies dealing with physiological differences. Nevertheless, the few investigations which have been carried out suffice to show that in this borderland between mind and body there is a rich harvest to be reaped, and few of the studies reviewed in this book are of greater fundamental importance than those which relate psychological traits to physiological functioning.

The pioneer study in this field is the work carried out by Darrow and Heath (1932) on "Reaction Tendencies Relating to Personality". Their work bears the mark of that early period both in the statistical method of analysis employed and the type of psychological test used; nevertheless, it would ill become us to smile at this early attempt, which in many ways still constitutes an example of objective procedure and insightful analysis.

On the psychological side, the Thurstone Neurotic Inventory and the Northwestern University Introversion-Extraversion test were used on the 80 or so students who constituted the experimental group. On the physiological side, Darrow and Heath say that the laboratory test used by them "was formulated for the purpose of eliciting behaviour of psychological significance, such as anticipation or anxiety, relief, adaptation to repeated stimuli, summation of responses to repeated stimuli, conditioning to indifferent stimuli, and rate of extinction of the conditioned responses. These terms are, of course, only general designations of the kinds of physiological activity on which information was sought". A polygraph recording was made of blood pressure, arm movement, respiration, and the P.G.R. "The stimuli employed in this study consisted of verbal warnings of the impending shocks, verbal information concerning periods of rest with no shocks, the clicks of the pendulum and pendulum release (part of the time mechanism governing the duration of the shocks), and a standardized electric shock acting on the flexor muscle of the thumb."

It would be impossible to describe here in any detail the actual procedures used, nor would it be possible to give the many tables relating physiological activity to individual questions on the questionnaire. We must instead turn to the factorial analysis which was carried out along rather original lines. First of all, single questions were combined into composite scores, the groupings of personality items being empirical groupings, "depending on relationships intrinsic to the material with which we have to deal. Empirical or intrinsically determined groupings of personality and physiological reaction tendencies have been arrived at by tabulating instances where our original list of histograms showed regressions between various physiological measures and specific personality items. Where several of the physiological measures appear related to two or more of a group of questions, each of which was, in turn, related to two or more of the related physiological measures, we have inferred that there was possibly a significant personality-physiological interrelationship to be studied."

When these personality constellations had been determined, the subjects were given scores on each on the basis of the number of questions answered in a "neurotic" manner. Correlations were then determined between constellation scores and the standard scores on the physiological measures. These correlations were then arranged in such a way that there was the least possible scatter of the larger coefficients, both along the ordinate of Table 29, on which the physiological measures are listed, and along the abscissa, where the personality constellations are given. "The groupings and their order are, in other words, empirically determined by internal relationships and not by theoretical considerations. By this method of presentation it is possible to observe at a glance the amount of overlapping of the various personality-physiological relationships. It is also possible, where overlapping occurs, to find some logical unity relating neighbouring groups of personality constellations and to apply a more or less general term of designation to the adjacent measures." This table is of the greatest possible interest, and will repay considerable study in detail.

Darrow and Heath summarize their results by saying that the data of Table 29 "show a marked tendency for a group of personality constellations including (1) 'socially inactive tendencies', (2) 'neurasthenic tendencies', (3) 'hyper-sensitivity', (4) 'depression', and (5) 'anxiety' to correlate highest with the following group of physiological measures: (1) the recovery-reaction quotient; (2) the resistance rise during two minutes of rest after stimulation; (3) the percentage of association of the conditioned with the conditioning stimuli, and (4) the conditioned blood-pressure rise. We have called this group of personality constellations, all relating more or less to the same physiological measures, the 'neurotic' constellation because it comprised the larger part of what we judged to be the truly 'neurotic' tendencies. We have tentatively designated the four physiological measures the 'neurotic syndrome' because of their relationship to this 'neurotic' constellation." This "neurotic syndrome" correlates ·304 with socially negative tendencies, ·330 with neurasthenic tendencies, ·303 with depression, ·338 with anxiety, ·346 with hypersensitivity, ·238 with excitability, ·299 with total score on the neurotic inventory, and ·066 with intelligence. The data leave little doubt that we are dealing here again with "w", or neuroticism, though in a somewhat unusual form.

Darrow and Heath also find in their table a tendency for the measures "which are correlated with anxiety to be correlated with neurotic scores on the inventory used". They also found that practically none of the measures which were in any degree functions of "neurotic" tendencies gave better than near zero correlations with extraversion-introversion. They conclude that "in a general way extraversion appears to correlate with large physiological reactivity in measures where this reactivity is not measurably affected by "neurotic trend." The writer does not feel entirely happy with this conclusion in view of the rather low correlations reported and in view of the doubtful validity of the measure of extraversion-introversion used. While physiological verification of this factor could be of very great interest [indeed, this study requires repetition (perhaps on groups of hysterics and dysthymics) before the interpretation of Darrow and Heath can be accepted.

Like most pioneers, Darrow has failed to be appreciated properly by psychologists, who instead of following up his trail-blazing study stubbornly persisted in working with the meritritious questionnaire and the ambiguous rating. It is perhaps only right that we should quote Darrow's recommendations for further work which appear at the end of his paper: "There is evidence that the various measures we have used may become more valuable (1) as we improve on our classification of the various personality variables, (2) as we study individuals on whom we have other data than those available by the questionnaire method, (3) as information is accumulated governing extreme or limiting conditions, and (4) as data accumulate on psychopathological cases."

Another study which deals with physiological variables is the work of Sanford *et al.* (1943), described in the book on *Physique, Personality, and Scholarship*, which was referred to in a previous chapter. Intercorrelations are given for a large number of variables, such as creatinine excretion, osseous development, endrogenes and estrogenes, as well as B.M.R., calory output, and other variables. Most of the data are of interest more to the study of development, the subjects being children and adolescents, rather than to that of the inter-relationship between physiology and psychology. Also given by him is a table of intercorrelations of a number of autonomic variables. While few of these are significant, "a syndrome was defined for further study consisting of flushing, sweating, skin-stroking intensity, odour, acne, and palpable thyroid. This has been called the parasympathetic response syndrome. . . . On the other hand, pupillary size, pella, skin stroking, colour, sinus arrhythmia, blood-pressure variability, do not correlate highly with any of the variables in the above syndrome".

Correlations were run between the response systems thus defined and various personality and phantasy syndromes. The parasympathetic response appears to be positively correlated with conscientious work and counteractive endocathection, and negatively with passive timidity, good fellowship, and social feeling. Sympathetic response is positively correlated with willing obedience, timid withdrawal, and anxious emotional expressiveness. In view of the small number of cases, none of these correlations can be taken very seriously as none of them are as high as ·4 even. Of the correlations between physical syndromes and phantasy syndromes only two are suggestive. The phantasy syndrome "strong character" correlates ·44 with parasympathetic response and —·65 with sympathetic response. As both mental age (positively) and male sex (negatively) are correlated with parasympathetic response, and as these factors are not partialled out from the other correlations, it is difficult to interpret these findings in any consistent fashion. Altogether, this study is too unsystematic and too little guided by any kind of hypothesis to be of much value in linking up psychological and physiological variables.

The same comment applies to another pioneering study in this field, namely that of Darling (1940). Using 58 children over the age of eight from the Institute for Juvenile Research in Chicago as his subjects, this writer obtained six ratings and ten autonomic measures. The ratings had rather low inter-rater reliabilities in the neighbourhood of ·35; the traits rated can be found in Table 30. The autonomic measures taken were pulse-rate, systolic and diastolic blood pressure, the differences between these two pressures, blood-pressure change from first to second visit to the laboratory, P.G.R. resistance, conductance, change, and startle reaction, and continuous blood-pressure recording. The six ratings and five autonomic measures (some of them combinations of the simple recordings mentioned above) were intercorrelated, and a factor analysis performed. The resulting four factors are shown in Table 30, together with Darling's interpretation of these factors.

TABLE 30

Tests	Factor Loadings			
	I	II	III	IV
1. Attention	·047	·822	− ·107	·049
2. Co-operation	·051	·802	·010	− ·069
3. Alertness	− ·120	·844	·262	− ·084
4. Boldness	− ·104	·668	·297	·096
5. Excitement	·008	·626	·565	·058
6. Hyperactivity . . .	·030	·497	·577	− ·055
7. Cholinergic activity (Cond. react. − S.B.P.) . .	·796	·149	− ·082	·013
8. Conductance reactivity . . .	·705	·048	·101	·696
9. Conductance level . . .	·298	− ·133	·286	·119
10. Sympathetic activity (Cond. react. − S.B.P.) . .	·021	·038	− ·094	·795
11. Systolic blood pressure . . .	− ·721	− ·083	·005	·544

Tentative interpretation of factors:	Cholinergic (parasympathetic?) activity	Attention-alertness	General motor activity	Sympathetic (adrenergic) reactivity

It will be seen that factors I and IV are named cholinergic (parasympathetic) and adrenergic (sympathetic) respectively; these two factors are quite orthogonal to each other, not opposite poles of one factor, as one might have anticipated. Factors II and III have loadings exclusively on the ratings, just as the other two factors have loadings of any size exclusively on the autonomic measures; they are labelled attention-alertness and general motor activity. The only bridge between ratings and autonomic activity is provided by the fact that factors I and II correlate to the extent of $r = ·310$. If this correlation, whose significance is of course extremely doubtful, can be taken seriously, it would seem to indicate a tendency for alert children to be cholinergic. But in view of the smallness of the correlation, the extreme unreliability of the ratings, and the lack of independence of the autonomic measures this work must be considered suggestive rather than conclusive. If we are willing to regard the qualities which go to make up factor II as "w" qualities, we might find in this study an adumbration of Wenger's finding that neuroticism was significantly correlated with adrenergic (sympathetic) reactivity.

Much more systematic is a whole series of studies by Wenger, which shows most clearly how valuable the factorial approach can be when guided by a definite hypothesis. Taking his lead from the well-known Eppinger and Hess (1917) theory of "vagotonia", Wenger (1942) set up the following two hypotheses: "(A) The differential chemical re-activity and the physiological antagonism of the adrenergic and cholinergic branches of the autonomic nervous system permit of a situation in which the action of one branch may predominate over that of the other. This predominance of autonomic imbalance may be phasic or chronic and may obtain for either the adrenergic or the cholinergic system. (B) Autonomic imbalance, when measured in an unselected population, will be distributed continuously about a central tendency which shall be defined as autonomic balance."

It will be noted that Wenger follows Dale rather than Eppinger and Hess in stressing the chemical rather than the anatomical differentia-tion of autonomic nerves. "For most practical purposes, the terms 'adrenergic' and 'sympathetic', or 'cholinergic' and 'parasympathetic' may be considered as synonyms."

In his first study, Wenger (1941) used 62 elementary schoolchildren, aged between 6 and 11, to whom was given a battery of autonomic tests, each of which was selected on definite hypotheses regarding its relation to autonomic innervation. These tests were intercorrelated, age was partialled out, and a factor analysis undertaken. Two main factors appeared, of which one was considered to be an autonomic factor, the second a muscular-tension factor. "The first factor is defined chiefly by sparcity of saliva, high percentage of solids in saliva, fast heart rate, little sinus arrhythmia, much palmar and volar sweating, high basal metabolic rate, and low blood pressure." Factor saturations are given in Table 31 below. It will be seen from the signs and the high factor loadings, as well as from the description just given, that the syndrome isolated is one of sympathetic or adrenergic predominance. (The second factor, labelled "muscular tension", while of great interest from the research point of view, is not strictly relevant to our main theme, and will here be disregarded. A brief discussion of it will be found in Chapter IX.)

TABLE 31

Measure	Autonomic Factor	Muscular Factor
Short dermographic latency . .	− ·06	·31
Short dermographic persistence .	·20	− ·28
Low salivary output . . .	·56	·05
Per cent. solids in saliva . .	·52	·17
Short heart period . . .	·42	·62
Little sinus arrhythmia . .	·46	·51
Reaction time	·02	·31
Change in palmar log conductance .	− ·07	·74
Muscular relaxation . . .	·02	·18
Little restlessness (rating) . .	·02	·21
Standing palmar conductance .	·48	− ·03
Reclining palmar conductance . .	·50	− ·42
Non-palmar conductance . .	·30	− ·08
B.M.R.	·36	·17
Small sigma respiration amplitude .	− ·07	·19
Respiration rate . . .	·07	·30
Change in systolic blood pressure .	− ·11	·06
Systolic blood pressure . .	− ·29	·26
Diastolic blood pressure . .	·19	·50
Low pulse pressure . . .	·35	·23

A regression equation was derived from seven of the measures having reasonable saturations on this factor, and it has been found that, on repetition of the investigation over periods varying from six to twelve months, retest correlations for the factor scores would run between ·5 and ·7 for the various groups. The factorial solution itself seemed to be very stable. When the whole investigation was repeated and a new regression equation derived from the new factor saturations, this was found to be remarkably similar to the original one. Factor scores derived from the two equations correlated ·84 and ·85 for the two sets of data. "The relationship between the two equations approximates the reliability of measurement of either one. For both solutions, the autonomic factor may be regarded as relatively stable and therefore basically valid" (Wenger, 1942). This device of repeating the whole procedure of testing, intercorrelating of measures, and factor analysing the resulting table in order to test the stability of factors provides a much more impressive proof of the stability of factors than could be derived from any theoretical argument. Unfortunately, this is a technique that is relatively rare, and it may be hoped that in the future more workers will follow the example set by Wenger.

Before turning to his large-scale studies on adults, we may note just one further observation contributed by Wenger. He considered that children with scores indicating parasympathetic predominance were less emotional, showed more controlled behaviour, and were more shy than those with scores showing sympathetic predominance. This description would seem to link up the adrenergous-sympathetic type with extraversion, and the cholinergic-parasympathetic type with introversion, with deviation from the mean towards either extreme perhaps being considered as a measure of neuroticism.

This plausible hypothesis, however, is not supported by Wenger's later work. Essentially, in these later studies, Wenger (1948) contrasted samples of normal aviation students with other groups suffering from operational fatigue or neurosis, on the hypothesis that excessive sympathetic functioning is characteristic of neurotic malfunctioning. Almost 500 normal cadets and aviation students constituted the control group, and 298 patients suffering from operational fatigue constituted the experimental group. The results of the study in terms of the ability of various tests to discriminate between the two groups are given in Table 32, column 1 setting out the critical ratios for the various comparisons. For the second experiment an identical design was used comparing the same control group with an experimental group made up of 98 psychoneurotic patients coming from a similar Army aviation background. The critical ratios for the

TABLE 32

Item	I CR, Normal v. Operational Fatigue	II Factor Saturations, Normal Group	III Factor Saturations, Operational Fatigue Group	IV CR, Normal v. Neurotics
Salivary output . .	2·86	·25	—	8·13
Salivary pH . . .	2·50	—	·48	4·23
Dermographic latency .	1·00	·17	—	0·38
Dermographic persistence .	0·93	·11	− ·01	0·61
Palmar conductance .	4·84	·19	·45	0·47
Log conductance change .	1·06	·31	·23	3·36
Volar conductance .	1·43	·19	·14	—
Systolic blood pressure .	6·52	—	·37	4·46
Diastolic blood pressure .	8·60	·30	—	4·60
Heart period . . .	7·82	·60	·36	6·65
Sublingual temperature .	2·50	·47	·45	2·00
Finger temperature . .	3·08	·03	− ·02	3·81
Tidal air mean . .	5·92	—	—	2·47
Tidal air sigma . .	0·42	·15	—	1·58
Oxygen consumption .	0·80	·13	·35	3·43
Pupillary diameter . .	—	—	—	—

same tests are given in Table 32, column 4, where it will be seen that most of them give satisfactory discrimination between normals and neurotics.

Factor analyses were also carried out on the intercorrelations of the tests for the normal group and for the operational fatigue group separately. Saturations for an autonomic factor extracted from both these studies are also given in Table 32, columns 2 and 3. These various columns of factor saturations show a distinct tendency to be proportional to each other, and it is apparent that those tests having the highest factor saturations are also the tests discriminating best between normals and neurotics, or between normals and operational fatigue cases. On the whole, it will also be seen that the factor saturations are similar to those obtained from the groups of children, thus lending additional support to Wenger's general hypothesis. "It may be concluded . . . that we are dealing here with a fairly stable physiological pattern. The important tests and relationships are Salivary Output (high), Palmar Conductance (low), Volar Conductance (low), Heart Period (long), and Oxygen Consumption (low); with Pulse Pressure (high) and Diastonic Pressure (low) significant for children, and probably both Systolic and Diastolic Pressure (low) significant for adults. Dermographic Persistence (long) seems to be significant at the child level, but not at the adult level; Sub-lingual Temperature (low) undoubtedly is important, at least at the adult level. . . . It is concluded, therefore, that the factor represents the functional status of the autonomic nervous system, and that it is valid at both the child and young-adult levels of physiological development."

The results quoted so far show a distinct tendency for Wenger's factor of autonomic imbalance to be significantly correlated with neuroticism, as judged psychiatrically. In another part of his study Wenger attempts an interesting correlation between personality factors and physiological factors. Having obtained a factor score for the autonomic factor on 264 normal Army Air Force cadets, he administered the thirteen Guilford Personality Inventory Scales, discussed in a previous chapter, to these cadets and correlated scores on the questionnaires with the autonomic factor scores. None of these correlations is very high, but they present a very clear picture. The highest positive correlations are given by factors D (Depression), C (Emotional Instability), S (Shyness), and T (Thinking Introversion). The highest negative correlations are given by Co (Co-operative), O (Objectivity), Ag (Agreeable, Good-natured), and N (lack of

Nervous Tenseness and Irritability). None of the other correlations exceed ·1 and may therefore be omitted. Reference to Fig. 14 (p. 106), in which we set out the two second-order factors derived from the intercorrelations of Guilford's primary factors, will show that these traits are precisely the ones having the highest saturations for neuroticism. There is thus a considerable agreement between the factor saturations of the thirteen Guilford questionnaires for neuroticism, and the correlations of these thirteen questionnaires with the autonomic factor. (The regression line between these two variables, when plotted, is curvilinear, but can easily be straightened out by transformation of the raw r values into their inverse hyperbolic tangents.) To put it briefly, then, the Guilford tests, having a high saturation on neuroticism, also have high correlations with Wenger's autonomic factor, and the tests having low saturations on neuroticism have low correlations with Wenger's autonomic factor. This is precisely what would be expected on the basis of the hypothesis that Wenger's autonomic factor is a measure of neuroticism, and constitutes striking proof for this contention, as well as providing added proof for the validity of Guilford's inventories.

Wenger's contribution is of considerable interest and importance, although it inevitably leaves several questions unanswered and raises doubts on certain points of interpretation. To take the latter first, the occasional inversions of prediction encountered in his work are very much more damaging than is usually the case in this type of work because of the definiteness of the hypothesis under investigation. Thus the prediction of an association between high sub-lingual temperature and sympathetic stimulation was not borne out in fact. Pupillary diameter, which theoretically should have high loadings on the factor, is practically unrelated to the other variables. There are several other inconsistencies, and although Wenger's arguments in defence of his position cannot be dismissed, they are not always convincing. However, when all is said and done, the number of inconsistencies is relatively small and the number of agreements very much larger than would have been expected on any alternative hypothesis.

Regarding the relation of this factor with personality, Wenger often speaks of autonomic imbalance as being related to neurotic disorder, but, in effect, what he has related to neuroticism is sympathetic predominance. It is not at all clear from his writings whether the opposite of the neurotic sympathetic-adrenergic person would be someone having no autonomic imbalance either way, or perhaps rather the person having parasympathetic-cholinergic predominance. This point is quite crucial to an adequate understanding of the relation between autonomic functioning and personality, yet nothing is said about it in Wenger's publications. Possibly, later work will throw some light on this point. Until it is cleared up, however, we cannot altogether dismiss the hypothesis advanced in connection with our discussion of Wenger's work on children, namely that neuroticism is correlated with deviation from autonomic balance in either direction, while extraversion and introversion are related to the direction of the deviation from autonomic balance.

A series of autonomic measures different from those in Wenger's battery was used by Theron (1948) and Van der Merwe (1948) in their attempts to use peripheral vasomotor reactions as indices of basic emotional tension and lability. In the first of these two studies, Theron carried out a factorial investigation of 50 normal students at the University of Stellenbosch. Plethysmographic records were taken according to a method described by Van der Merwe and Theron (1947), while the subject was relaxed, while his left hand was immersed in a cold-water bath, while the subject inhaled deeply and held his breath as long as possible, and while the subject was given mental arithmetic problems to solve. 12 scores entered into the final table of intercorrelations, namely (1) room temperature; (2) temperature of hot-water bath, in which the subject held both his hands before the beginning of the experiment; (3) pulse volume during relaxation; (4) pulse volume immediately before the cold-water test; (5) pulse volume immediately before deep-breathing test; (6) volume before the arithmetical tasks; (7) the rate of change in finger volume with the cold-water test; (8) rate of change in finger volume with the deep-breathing test; (9) the rate of change in finger volume during the arithmetical tasks; (10) the Bell Inventory emotional stability score; and (11) the Bell Inventory total score; (12) the rate of change in finger volume during tasks when the pulse volume before tasks was made statistically equal for all subjects.

Three rotated factors extracted from the matrix of intercorrelations are given in Table 33. Factor 1 is called "emotional stability" by Theron, and is clearly similar to "w" or the inverse of neuroticism. It is highly loaded on the two Bell Inventory variables and on the rates of change in finger volume (variables 9 and 12). Variables 3, 4, and 6, .e. the three pulse-volume measures, have negative loadings with this factor, indicating that the labile subjects with larger Bell and finger-volume scores tend to have smaller pulse volumes than

TABLE 33

| Variable | Matrix of Multiple-factor Loadings | | | |
	K^1	K^2	K^3	h^2
1	·114	·116	·341	·142
2	·023	·234	− ·031	·057
3	− ·429	·778	·141	·809
4	− ·368	·883	− ·039	·917
5	− ·212	·879	·210	·860
6	− ·319	·848	·120	·835
7	− ·470	·437	·207	·455
8	− ·174	·442	− ·194	·263
9	·420	·413	·812	1·005
10	·882	·024	− ·112	·792
11	·904	·134	− ·113	·848
12	·584	·136	·649	780

the stable. Variable 7, the rate of change in finger volume with the cold-water test, also has a negative loading on this factor. A factor score was computed using variables 3, 4, 6, 7, and 9, which gave a multiple correlation with the factor of ·788. Factor measurements of the 50 individuals correlated ·653 with the Bell emotional scores.

The second factor was labelled "basic emotional tension" by Theron and was highly loaded in all the physiologic variables (3–9) and especially high in the different pulse volumes. Theron concludes his discussion by saying: "This factor could therefore be designated as basic emotional tension and is quite probably similar to the autonomic factor . . . found by Wenger." (It is difficult to accept this identification as Wenger's factor correlates highly with neuroticism; Theron's not at all.) Theron obtained factor measures by combining variables 3, 4, 5, and 6; the multiple correlation between these variables and the factor was found to be ·923.[1]

Van der Merwe (1948) applied the factor measures as determined by Theron to 8 patients with anxiety symptoms (dysthymics) and 12 hysterics. The results are presented in the form of two diagrams. Fig. 27 shows that the *emotional lability* scores of the hysterical and anxiety groups combined differ significantly from those of the normal group; the difference between the two clinical groups was not significant. Fig. 28 shows that on *basic emotional tension* hysterics deviate from the normal group in one direction (showing an imbalance or shift to parasympathetic predominance), while the anxiety

[1] The third factor is of no importance or nterest here.

group differs in the opposite direction from the normals, showing a shift in the direction of sympathetic predominance. The combined hysteric-anxiety group is not differentiated significantly from the normal group.

These results tend to support the hypothesis put forward in connection with Wenger's data regarding the differential predominance of sympathetic and parasympathetic function in introverts and extraverts. They cannot, however, be admitted as in any sense definitive,

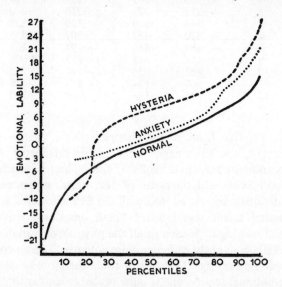

Fig. 27.—Percentile Curves showing the Emotional Lability Scores of Hysteria and Anxiety Patients as compared with Normal Subjects. (Curves slightly smoothed.)

as the number of measures used is not large enough to allow of any definite identification of the factors with the main autonomic systems. Repetition of this study with the inclusion of some of Wenger's variables would be of very great interest indeed.

Similar to Wenger's work, and in many ways complementary to it, is that of Jost and his various collaborators.[1] Where Wenger is concerned with the resting level of autonomic functions, Jost is interested in autonomic reactions to frustration, and his work gives a clear indication that the changes following upon frustration are

[1] Jost succeeded Wenger as psychologist to the Fels Study. In a later chapter we shall encounter further examples of work done by this very active group of investigators.

closely related to personality factors of an important kind. Only one of the studies reported by him is factorial (Sherman and Jost, 1942), but the others are so closely relevant to the problem discussed there that they will also be mentioned. In this factorial study, two groups of 18 children were tested. The control group consisted of children known to be extremely well adjusted. The experimental group included 15 neurotic and 3 psychotic children.

"The physiological reactions in 7 situations were measured in each

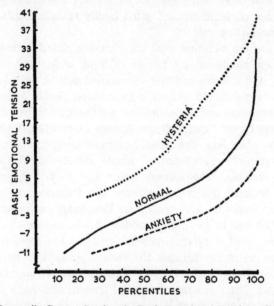

Fig. 28.—Percentile Curves showing the Basic Emotional Tension of Hysterical and Anxiety Patients as compared with Normal Subjects. (Curves slightly smoothed.)

of the subjects and remeasurements were taken in order to confirm the observations. These situations were used: attention to a learning situation, the process of learning in a frustration situation, the process of recall, sensory stimulation, and a final period of rest. The reactions during the rest period were employed to represent the basal physiological levels. The attention-to-learning periods were used in order to obtain measurements of the physiological changes of the subjects during mild tension situations. The sensory stimulation was produced in order to compare the physiological reactions during a sudden stimulation with the reactions during frustration; that is, the reactions during actual physical stimulation were compared with the reactions during ideational and emotional stimulation. The sensory stimuli were bright light, a loud noise, and a painful stimulus produced by pinching."

Frustration in these situations was produced by instructing subjects to learn a sequence of digits by the anticipation method; the first few series were easy, but later ones were so complex that failure followed inevitably. Physiological measures taken included the galvanic skin response, respiratory rate, and amplitude pulse rate, blood pressure, hand tremor, gross bodily measurements, and the electro-encephalogram.

Twenty of the measures used were intercorrelated for both groups of children combined by means of rank order correlation coefficients, and a factor analysis was carried out on the 14 measures which were considered to be the most stable. Table 34 reproduces the measures used and the saturations for the three factors extracted.[1]

The first factor "included the ratings of emotional stability as made by observers, the electro-encephalograph findings, hand tremors, respiratory differences, initial galvanic response, blood-pressure changes. The second factor was tentatively called the 'central' because the items included the measures of heart and respiratory function. The items were the changes in pulse rate, the per cent. change in galvanic response, blood-pressure changes, and the frequency of respiration per half-minute. The third factor was called the peripheral because the items appeared to be measures either of muscular movements or of changes due to specific sensory stimulation. The items included hand tremor, change in pulse rate during frustration, change in galvanic resistance during frustration, and hand tremor during sensory stimulation."

Rotation of factors into simple structure might have given a more meaningful picture, and the second and third factors at least are not at all clear as they stand. The first factor, however, is an approximation to emotional stability ("w") with comparatively high loadings on quite a number of physiological measures. It is doubtful if we

[1] Also given in the table are critical ratios for these measures taken from another paper by Jost (1941). Subjects in this experiment were 18 emotionally unstable and 20 very stable children. It is not quite clear whether these children are partly identical with those taking part in the Sherman-Jost research described above. Some of the measures in the factor analysis could not be identified in Jost's table of critical ratios. It will be seen that there is a clear tendency for the measures having high saturations on the factor of emotional stability to have high critical ratios, and vice versa.

TABLE 34

Factor Loadings

Measure	Contributions			
	F_1	F_2	F_3	C.R.
1. Rating of emotional stability . .	·92	− ·19	·34	—
2. Per cent. change resistance (frustration) .	·48	− ·66	·29	3·70
3. Initial resistance	·52	− ·13	·41	3·06
4. Equation of galvanic response . .	·44	·28	·55	—
5. Blood-pressure change (stimulation) .	·48	− ·42	− ·16	3·90
6. Electro-encephalogram . . .	·76	·19	− ·09	—
7. Sigma respiratory curve . .	·54	·41	− ·05	2·86
8. Hand tremor (first rest period) . .	·74	·31	− ·54	3·34
9. Hand tremor (last rest period) . .	·65	·11	− ·28	5·45
10. Per cent. change pulse-rate (attention) .	·37	·63	·08	2·30
11. Vineland emotional stability schedule .	·35	− ·12	− ·12	—
12. Number of respirations per half minute .	·28	·39	− ·22	2·00
13. Per cent. change pulse rate (frustration) (−)	·08	− ·78	− ·50	2·44
14. Per cent. change resistance (learning) .	·39	− ·20	·02	3·52
	4·11	2·27	1·40	
Total		7·78		

can regard the results as proving the hypothesis that frustration induces differential reaction physiologically in normal and neurotic children, as the two measures of frustration reaction included in the factor analysis (numbers 2 and 13) have rather low saturations on the "stability" factor. It would seem rather that the second factor can be regarded as somewhat specific to frustration reactions, as the two measures just mentioned have the highest saturations on this factor. The third factor appears in some ways similar to Wenger's factor of muscular tension, although the identification is by no means clear.

In spite of these criticisms, we may agree with the main conclusions of the authors. "The physiological measures showed that the neurotic individuals reacted more intensively to the frustration situation; the initial reactions, that is during rest and during the attention and learning periods, were also more intense in the neurotic children . . . frequency of the hand tremors was much greater in the neurotic children than in the normal, both before and after frustration . . . the pattern of physiological reactions was significantly different between the two groups. . . . The schizophrenic children presented a very stable physiological picture . . . [this] may mean . . .

that their mental condition precludes their being disturbed by situations which ordinarily produce tensions in normal individuals and especially in neurotic persons."

The generalization suggested in this summary, namely that the neurotic child is much more unstable physiologically than the normal, while the psychotic child is more stable than the normal, was taken up in another paper by Sherman and Jost (1945). Using 25 well-adjusted boys, 16 neurotic, and 4 psychotic children, they again took a number of physiological measures (brain potentials, blood-pressure changes, respiration, galvanic skin resistance, heart rate, and hand tremor), using measures at resting levels, during a word-association task, and during the frustration task consisting of increasingly difficult arithmetical problems. Scores on all the measures were transformed into standard scores so that the normal children would be at the 50th percentile on the average on all measures. According to the hypothesis, the neurotic children should then have mean scores at a higher and the psychotic children mean scores on a lower percentile than the normals. This prediction was borne out at a high level of confidence. Out of nine scores the neurotics were at a much higher percentile on eight measures, while the psychotics were at a lower percentile than the normals on eight measures also.

These results, which are more systematic, but in essence similar, to those reported by Odegard (1930), Hoch (1944), Whitehorn and Richter (1937), and others, clearly support the conclusion, quoted in an earlier chapter on the basis of objective behaviour tests, that the hypothesis of a single continuum going from the normal through the neurotic to the psychotic, cannot be maintained, but that instead we are dealing with a two-dimensional problem and must therefore posit two factors at least to account for the observed facts.

Where Wenger used physiological measures of the resting organism and Jost physiological reactions to frustration, G. L. Freeman (1948) lays special stress on physiological recovery after stress. This emphasis derives from his basic hypothesis, namely "that all behaviour is an attempt to preserve organismic integrity by homeostatic restoration of equilibrium". According to him: "Total behaviour dynamics is a study of an energy system undergoing change. ... As a biological energy system, man has a remarkable facility for maintaining his identity and for organizing himself, and even the world about him to that end. ... The basic construct for ordering the behaviour of an energy system is *homeostasis* or the maintenance of essential *constant states*. The latter term refers to a pattern or distribution of energies which the system is so constructed to restore when such states are disturbed."

This stress on the theoretical concept of homeostasis or restoration of the original state after disturbance, naturally leads to the investigation of physiological recovery from stress as the experimental model for investigating this hypothesis. "The typical homeostatic response curve can be treated somewhat in isolation. The human subject is brought into the laboratory and 'relaxed down' until a measure of basal tissue activities 'levels off' to indicate the more persistent background conditions of quiet rest. From this *basic energy level* the subject is 'displaced' by an external stimulus of controlled intensity and duration. The equilibratory sequence has three phases: (1) *mobilisation*, wherein bodily energies are internally aroused to meet the stimulus-induced displacement; (2) *discharge*, wherein the aroused energies are externally expressed by overt response; and (3) *recovery*, wherein the organismic system returns toward its pre-stimulus condition."

Freeman relates stimulus intensity to organismic arousal by quoting the work of Darrow (1937) and himself to show that "systematic studies of the skin-conductance measures have shown that as stimulus intensity is arithmetically increased, this index of energy mobilization varies as a logarithm of its base". From this Freeman derives his recovery quotient (RQ): $\dfrac{B - C}{B - A}$, in which B is arbitrarily defined as the level reached on the P.G.R. one-half minute after stimulation; point C as the level reached five minutes after peak mobilization (B); and A as the level at which the stimulus is applied. "With time relations of A, B, and C in this constant ratio, the degree of homeostatic recovery is reliably indicated by dividing the per cent. discharge decrement by the per cent. mobilization increment that occurred in the standardized periods of measurement. This fundamental integrative measure of neuromuscular homeostasis was given the name *physiological recovery quotient*."

We cannot go further into Freeman's hypothesis, but must turn to his experimental studies to discover how far they can aid us in our description of the organization of personality. In the one factorial analysis reported, Freeman and Katzoff (1942) used 24 college men as subjects. Measures were obtained under four conditions aside from rest. These conditions were: (1) Startle; a blank cartridge fired without warning; (2) Motor Conflict: wrong or delayed responses on pushing keys in accordance with a stimulus light were punished by electric shock delivered through reaction key; (3) Verbal Associations to critical and non-critical words; (4) Sensory Discrimination going from easy to difficult pitch discriminations and including distractions. In addition, questionnaires and ratings were used, and time samples of nervous movements obtained.

Thirty measures were intercorrelated and subjected to factor analysis. Of these, 10 were measures of covert physiological activity, 11 were measures of overt behaviour, and 9 were ratings and personality tests. Factor analysis carried out on these variables produced four factors. (Factor saturations are those obtained after rotation with orthogonal axes to simple structure.)

The interpretation of factor one is relatively clear. It is characterized by the psychiatric rating for emotional stability, three different recovery quotients (startle, verbal, and motor), variability in basal movements, motor-movement increment, main basal movement, and the voice level R.Q. Freeman called this factor a control factor, and it is reasonable to suppose that it is the physiological equivalent of Webb's "*w*". It presents conclusive evidence in favour of Freeman's view of the recovery quotient as a suitable physiological measure for this fundamental personality variable.

When we turn to factor two, interpretation is somewhat less certain. "The measures with significant loadings on the second factor are clearly concerned with 'per cent. conductance increment' or the extent to which any given individual is physiologically aroused by the experimental situations. . . . We may identify the second as an 'arousal factor'."

There is some question as to the identity of factor three in Freeman's opinion. "The major variables with high loadings are self-ratings on various aspects of emotionality ('general neuroticism', 'nervousness', 'visceral disturbance', etc.). The principal exceptions are 'time sampling of nervous movements' and (possibly) 'variability of basal movement'. We might therefore conclude that this as a factor represents S's stereotype of how he reacts—a kind of 'rated emotionality'. Certainly the factor is heavily weighted with pencil and paper tests." A similar factor was found by Eysenck (1952), and identified in an identical manner. The fourth factor in Freeman's study has only two significant loadings and we may agree with him in regarding it as a "specific".

This analysis has given rise to a general picture of personality organization which Freeman presents in the form of a personality sphere showing the three major axes of differentiation. This is reproduced in Fig. 29. (In this reproduction a number of dots will be found which make the personality sphere look as if it had measles. The dots represent the position of people in Freeman's three-dimensional representation, and are used by him to illustrate an argument irrelevant to our presentation.) "The uniqueness of the individual personality pattern is conceived . . . to depend upon the interaction of quantitative gradations in such factors as *discriminate capacity*, *drive arousal*, and *discharge control*. A visualization of such patterns should somehow relate these major axes of differentiation with each

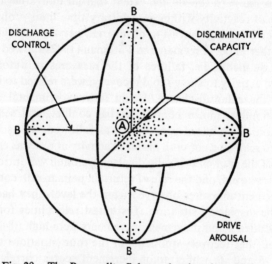

Fig. 29.—The Personality Sphere, showing three Major Axes of Differentiation.

other and make it possible to show each individual's position with reference thereto." It is clear that Freeman's "discriminative capacity" is identical with Spearman's "*g*" or Thurstone's second-order factor of intellectual ability. Can we identify the factors of "discharge control" and "drive arousal" in a similar way? We must turn to Freeman's various experimental studies for our answer to the question.

In one study, for instance, Freeman (1939) used as *stress* the inhibition of micturition, and determined galvanic skin response, blood pressure, and muscle-action potentials under resting or *pre-load* conditions, under *load* conditions (when the subject following water intake reported that the urge could be delayed no longer), and under *post-load* conditions, i.e. after micturition had taken place. Other stress conditions used included the time that painful electric shock could be endured. Ratings and self-ratings on neuroticism were also available. "The result of the various approaches described above seem to be in the same direction. In meeting experimentally induced frustration, the human organism mobilizes bodily resources in varying amounts. When the tension load is removed . . . the speed with which the organism returns to its resting reactivity level correlates with objective indices of success, in withstanding the stress imposed, and with ratings of neurotic tendency. Assuming the experimental loading is standard for all, the extent that an individual returns to his pre-load reactivity within an arbitrary time limit probably constitutes the best single measure of inherent nervous stability."

In another paper, Freeman and Pathman (1942) showed that low-recovery quotients, i.e. failures of the measures of autonomically controlled activity to show rapid recovery, were related to inhibition of overt muscular discharge. Using four experimental situations (startle stimulus, motor conflict, verbal conflict, and sensory discrimination), a standard procedure was followed. The subject was allowed to relax in a cot until his basal activity at rest was established and one of the four emotionally displacing stimuli was introduced. It was then removed, and the rate of return in palmar-skin conductance and movement measures observed from the levels they had reached during the displacing situation. Test-retest reliabilities for both recovery quotients and movement increments were high (.8–.9), and it was found that recovery quotients in the four situations correlated between .5 and .6, while motor increment scores correlated .6–.8. Recovery quotients and motor increments over all the tests correlated to the extent of approximately .53. "The results provided tentative confirmation of the hypothesis that within the limits of these tests individuals tend to recover internal equilibrium most rapidly who readily discharge aroused excitation by overt muscular action, even though this is apparently unadaptive."

In yet another study, Freeman and Pathman (1943) investigated the reactions of 15 manic-depressives and 11 schizophrenics to experimentally induced displacement. No differences were found between psychotics and normal subjects in terms of basal physiological activity, and while manics showed a greater internal arousal and greater overt discharge than normal subjects, schizophrenics failed to show the hypothesized lack of internal arousal and lack of overt discharge. Schizophrenics and manics were found not to be defective with respect to neuromuscular homeostasis; they failed to show lower physiological recovery quotients when compared with normals. Altogether, it was found that physiological reactions to experimentally induced displacement were more diagnostic of the duration of the psychosis than of its classification.

It seems established, then, that quick recovery on the physiological side and an increase in motor movement over the resting level characterize the normal as opposed to the neurotic person; there is no differentiation by these measures as between the normal and the psychotic, a finding well in line with those mentioned previously in connection with the work of Jost. Can we, then, interpret Freeman's factor of discharge control and drive arousal with any of the factors isolated before? In principle this seems unlikely. Freeman's factors are derived almost entirely from physiological measures and within broad limits fulfil the demands of simple structure. They must, therefore, be regarded as primary factors whereas both neuroticism and extraversion-introversion are second-order factors. Discharge control and drive arousal may therefore correlate with, but cannot be identical with, these second-order factors.

The studies summarized above seem to show fairly conclusively that Freeman's discharge control factor is closely related to neuroticism and is likely to constitute an extremely good measure of it. The factor of drive arousal, however, appears to be much less definitely established and its relationship to our two second-order factors remains difficult to disentangle. It should be realized that the factorial analysis on which Freeman bases himself was carried out on only 24 subjects, and that it seems quite unwarranted to take out four factors from a correlation matrix having the extremely high standard errors associated with correlations based on such small numbers. This consideration must also influence, of course, the acceptability of the rotation. Freeman claims "that there are no significant negative loadings in the final factors". It should be realized, however, that for a correlation to be significant at the 1 per cent. level with an N of 24 cases, it would have to be ·515, or even higher since the S.E. of *rho*, the coefficient used, is greater than that of *r*. It will be remembered that Spearman was able to claim fulfilment of the tetrad criterion in his earlier work because he analysed tables derived from very small numbers of subjects so that the standard errors were sufficiently large to swamp any deviations from the hypothesis. Until Freeman's work is repeated on much larger numbers, we find it difficult to accept his factors, other than the first, as firmly established building stones, and must rather regard them as plausible hypotheses of great intrinsic interest and value.

It should be noted that Freeman in his own interpretation is somewhat more ambitious than this. In a table of his, Freeman (1948) identifies his arousal factor with Wenger's factor of emotional lability, or autonomic imbalance, and with Jost's emotionality factor; he also identifies his discharge control factor with Wenger's muscular tension and Jost's so-called central factor. This identification does not rest on a secure basis. Fortunately we have an objective test for its adequacy. The discharge control factor is based very largely on recovery quotient measures, and has high correlations with ratings on emotional instability or neuroticism. Similarly, the emotional lability-autonomic imbalance factor of Wenger and the emotional factor of Jost showed high correlations with neuroticism. In consequence, if there is to be any identification of factors for these various workers, surely it would be along the lines indicated by the above correlations, i.e. discharge control would be identified with emotional lability-autonomic imbalance, and with emotionality. Freeman's arousal factor has no significant correlation with neuroticism. It is difficult therefore to see how he can identify it with Wenger's and Jost's factors having high correlations with neuroticism.

We do not claim that this brief discussion of factor identification can have any finality. Until all the measures used by these various workers are included in one battery, it will be impossible to give an adequate appraisal of Freeman's hypothesis. However, in so far as the data have been presented, they seem to contra-indicate Freeman's identification and support the one suggested above. Here indeed is a most fruitful field of research, full of great possibilities, and it would be ungenerous to end this account of Freeman's outstanding work on a note of minor criticism. His contribution is one of the very few in the field of personality organization which follows the dictates of scientific method, beginning as it does with a clearly defined hypothesis and going on to verify deductions made from this. If at times the reader may find it difficult to agree with some of the assumptions made (the writer, for instance, finds it difficult to accept the proposition that as stimulus intensity is arithmetically increased the skin conductance index of energy mobilization varies as a logarithm of its base), he is always enabled to set his mind at rest by direct experimental proof. Hitherto, unfortunately, Freeman's contribution has been somewhat neglected by clinical psychologists, who appear to prefer the unverified and often unverifiable claims of "organismicists" and projective techniques experts to the demonstrated validity of at least some of Freeman's procedures. Future scientists may regard this phenomenon as an odd misplacement of energy, and it is to be hoped that the balance will soon be restored.

In coming to a general conclusion regarding the value of the work presented in this chapter, several points should be emphasized. In the first place, it does not seem to the writer that the factors isolated by Wenger, Jost, Theron, Freeman, and so forth can be identified directly with each other, as several of these authors have tried to do. It is quite likely that there is a certain amount of communality between tests of autonomic function taken in the resting state, taken during frustration or under stress, and taken during the period of recovery, but as each of the authors mentioned has concentrated almost entirely on one of these different methods, the factors isolated cannot be generalized to cover all of them. In view of the fact that each author has demonstrated considerable correlation between neuroticism, as assessed either clinically, or by ratings, or inventories, and one of the factors isolated, it follows that either the multiple determination of neuroticism by all these methods combined will have very high validity indeed, or, of course, that all these methods would correlate highly together. The truth will probably be found to be intermediate between these extremes; the various factors isolated will probably be correlated to a fairly appreciable extent, giving rise to a second-order factor, and the determination of neuroticism by a combination of these various methods will be considerably better than its measurement by any one of them.

In the second place, it seems to the writer unfortunate that only one of the experimenters mentioned, namely Van der Merwe (1948), has made an attempt to take measures of autonomic imbalance separately on different clinical groups within the general classification of neurosis. His demonstration that the factor of "basic emotional tension" discriminates very well between hysterics and anxiety states but does not discriminate between neurotics (i.e. hysterics and anxiety states in one group) as opposed to normals, may indicate why a number of correlations between autonomic measures and neurosis have been found to be insignificant. In future work it is to be hoped that clinical groups, both in the neurotic and in the psychotic fields, will be kept separate so that more detailed information regarding the nature of each factor may be possible. Great advances in our knowledge are likely to accrue from such a procedure.

In the third place, it seems to the writer that the number of cases used in the factorial studies mentioned has usually been rather inadequate, the only exception to this rule being the work of Wenger. This writer has established his conclusions beyond cavil in two ways: (1) by repeated measurements, factor analysis, and determination of factor scores several times on small samples, showing that each time results were very similar; and (2) by using really large groups of between 400 and 500 people in his work. It is only by such long-continued experimentation and demonstration of repeatability of results that factor analysis can overcome its inherent difficulty of not possessing adequate tests of factorial significance.

Altogether, it is the writer's opinion that while only a beginning has been made in this field of study, this beginning is so promising that a great deal of research endeavour should be devoted to clarifying some of the issues involved. The obvious promise of a method which would enable us to establish a person's degree of neuroticism or introversion-extraversion by means of quite objective physiological measures will not be gainsaid by anyone; we are clearly dealing with constitutional factors of the greatest importance, and even in the present state of development these methods can without a doubt be usefully applied in military psychology, clinical psychology, and possibly also in the industrial field.

CHAPTER VII

THE ANALYSIS OF INTERESTS AND ATTITUDES

THE TERMS "INTERESTS" and "attitudes" in non-technical usage refer to rather similar concepts. Interests are attitudes having positive valences, or, to put it rather more simply, interests are attitudes held with respect to objects or classes of objects towards which we feel a certain attraction. Lack of interest is usually taken as an indication of a negative or unfavourable attitude; the man who is not interested in women may be regarded as being unfavourably disposed towards them. This simple manner of looking at these two concepts leaves out of account all the complications introduced by such factors as ambivalence, or reaction formation; it is also out of line with the way in which "interest" and "attitude" are being used in contemporary psychology. The former refers almost exclusively to vocational or occupational preferences; the latter to opinions held on social or political matters. The older term "sentiment", introduced by McDougall (1923) to cover this whole area of affective and conative constellations around some central idea, has gone out of fashion; it might perhaps with some advantage be revived to denote what the more recent terms have in common. In the absence of such a unifying term, or of any unified treatment of the data derived from investigations of occupational and socio-political preferences, we must discuss interests and attitudes separately.

Super (1949) points out that "there have been four major interpretations of the term interest, connected with as many different methods of obtaining data". The first type of interest he calls *expressed interest*, which he defines as the verbal profession of interest in an object, activity, task, or occupation; the subject simply states that he likes, is indifferent to, or dislikes the activity in question. The second he labels *manifest interest;* this is synonymous with participation in an activity or occupation. "Objective manifestations of interest have been studied in order to avoid the subjectivity of expressions or to avoid the implications that interest is something static." The third type he calls *tested interest*, using this term to refer to interest as measured by objective tests as differentiated from inventories which are based on subjective self-estimates; the assumption underlying the resulting type of test is that interest is likely to manifest itself in action (e.g. accumulation of relevant information) which can be made objectively measurable.

The fourth type Super calls *inventoried interest;* it "is assessed by means of lists of activities and occupations which bear a superficial resemblance to some questionnaires for the study of expressed interests, for each item in the list is responded to with an expression of preference. The essential and all-important difference is that in the case of the inventory each possible response is given an experimentally determined weight, and the weights corresponding to the answers given by the person completing the inventory are added in order to yield a score which represents, not a single subjective estimate as in the case of expressed interests, but a pattern of interests which research has shown to be rather stable". It is with inventoried interests, more particularly with those obtained by means of the Strong Vocational Interest Blank (1943), that we shall in the main be occupied in this chapter.

This Blank is a device by means of which patterns of interests characteristic of members of different trades and professions may be determined. It consists of 400 items, to each of which the subject responds by indicating whether he likes, dislikes, or is indifferent to that item. One hundred items have reference to occupations; the remainder refer to amusements (golf, fishing), school subjects, activities, and peculiarities of people. Other parts of the Blank call for an indication of most and least liked activities from a given list; preference judgments between alternate choices; and estimates of one's abilities and characteristics. Different forms are used for men and women. Scoring is entirely empirical, weights for a given occupational interest being derived from the actual responses of persons working in that particular field, as contrasted with "men in general". A score "indicates not the *amount* of interest possessed but the *likelihood* that the person has or does not have the interests of men in the given occupation. A high score means that the individual has the interests of the occupation in question, while a low score means that he does not have such interests". In view of the fact that mean raw scores differ considerably from one occupation to another, they are transformed into standard scores, ratings (A, B +, B, B −, C +, and C), or percentile scores.

A superficial cluster-analysis of the intercorrelations of 36 occupations, based on 285 college seniors, led Strong to group occupations into 11 sets. The basis of classification was that each occupation should correlate ·60 or higher on the average with the members of its group, and lower than this with the members of all other groups. (There are three exceptions to this rule, none of great importance.) The resulting classification is produced below, in Table 35. It will be

TABLE 35

Classification of Occupations

Group	Occupation
I . . .	Artist Psychologist Architect Physician Dentist
II . . .	Mathematician Physicist Engineer Chemist
III . . .	Production manager
IV . . .	Aviator Farmer Carpenter Mathematics-physical science teacher Printer Policeman Forest service
V . . .	Y.M.C.A. secretary Y.M.C.A. physical director Personnel manager City school superintendent Minister Social science teacher
VI . . .	Musician
VII . . .	Certified public accountant
VIII . . .	Purchasing Agent Office worker Accountant Banker
IX . . .	Real estate salesman Life insurance salesman Sales manager
X . . .	Lawyer Author-journalist Advertising man
XI . . .	President of manufacturing concern

seen that four groups contain only one member—production manager, musician, certified public accountant, and president of a manufacturing concern. Interpretation of these clusters is difficult, although many of the relations depicted would be readily acceptable to common sense.

Factorial studies have been carried out by several writers to establish a more fundamental basis of classification. Thurstone (1932) was the first to venture into this new field. His original analysis was carried out on 18 of Strong's scales. It was found that the observed correlations could be accounted for in terms of four factors, which he labelled (1) interest in science; (2) interest in language; (3) interest in people; and (4) interest in business. A certain amount of argument is centred around the identification of the factors; as we shall see, Strong, in his analysis, has refused to name his factors at all. As Thurstone points out, "this matter of naming the factors is entirely extraneous to the statistical analysis. The statistical work may be correct, while considerable argument might conceivably be made about the naming of the factors . . . when multiple-factor analysis is undertaken there is absolutely no guarantee that the resulting factor loadings will so arrange themselves that they can be readily named". In spite of these warnings, Thurstone's interpretation appears reasonable to the present writer and it is of some interest to see the factorial composition of certain interest scores to illustrate the meaning of these factors. Psychology, for instance, has a loading of ·77 in science, of ·47 in language, of − ·04 in people, and of − ·28 in business. To those who have noted the preoccupation of psychologists with semantic problems and their preference for rats to human beings, the second and third of these correlations will not come as a surprise, just as the average income of psychologists is probably a just reflection on the last of the saturations mentioned. Table 36 sets out in full Thurstone's results, and it can be left to the reader to form his own impression on the correctness of his naming of these factors.

Four further analyses have been carried out by Strong (1943), based on 25, 30, 32, and 36 variables respectively; results from these more extensive later studies show striking agreement with each other, and with Thurstone's original analysis.[1] Only the last and most comprehensive of all these studies will be discussed in detail. Strong presents an unrotated and a rotated solution, both containing four de-

---

[1] All these studies were carried out on adult subjects. A report by Carter, Pyles, and Bretnall (1935) gives similar results with respect to high-school students.

TABLE 36

Name of Profession	Four Interest Factors				
	I Science	II Language	III People	IV Business	h^2
Advertising	− ·48	+ ·66	− ·21	+ ·22	·76
Art	+ ·45	+ ·70	− ·18	− ·31	·82
Certified public accountant	− ·04	+ ·32	·00	+ ·56	·42
Chemistry	+ ·98	− ·21	− ·15	+ ·06	1·03
Engineering	+ ·84	− ·36	− ·22	+ ·16	·91
Law	− ·23	+ ·77	− ·12	+ ·44	·85
Ministry	+ ·09	+ ·51	+ ·62	− ·30	·74
Psychology	+ ·77	+ ·47	− ·04	− ·28	·89
Teaching	+ ·36	+ ·15	+ ·68	− ·22	·66
Life insurance	− ·82	− ·02	+ ·27	+ ·45	·95
Architecture	+ ·83	+ ·26	+ ·16	+ ·05	·78
Y.M.C.A. secretary	− ·23	·00	+ ·90	− ·37	1·00
Farming	+ ·71	− ·54	+ ·01	+ ·18	·83
Purchasing agent	− ·05	− ·79	+ ·01	+ ·44	·82
Journalism	− ·15	+ ·84	− ·28	+ ·25	·87
Personnel	− ·30	− ·26	+ ·66	− ·19	·63
Real estate	− ·76	− ·07	− ·06	+ ·58	·92
Medicine	+ ·71	+ ·33	− ·26	− ·09	·69

finite factors and a doubtful fifth factor. Taking the unrotated solution first, we find factor one characterized by the following occupations: Psychologist, Dentist, Mathematician, Physicist, Chemist, Printer, Mathematics-Science Teacher, and Musician. Factor three loads on Strong's original groups III, IV, and VIII, as well as on a masculinity scale. Factor four loads highly on group VI, while factor five has hardly any high loadings. Interpretation of these factors is a little uncertain, but would presumably be in terms of interest in science (factor one), interest in people (factor two), interest in business (factor three), and interest in material things (factor four).

The rotated solution presents a slightly more obscure picture. Factor one is again characterized by interest in scientific subjects; factor four by interest in people. Factor three appears to represent interest in material things (an alternative possibility is that this factor simply groups together low-level occupational interests). Factors two and five are by no means clearly defined, and have no very high saturations to guide in interpretation.

Analyses of female interest patterns have been made by Strong (1943) and by Crissy and Daniel (1939). Both reveal very similar patterns, and Strong has made use of the rotation carried out by Crissy and Daniel on their material. The four rotated factors have been named by these authors: "interest in people", "interest in language", "interest in science", and "interest in male association". Strong "fails to see any gain by naming the factors resulting from rotation . . . naming a factor is largely guessing today". With this remark the present writer would on the whole be in agreement, provided it is confined to factorial studies in the field of interests. There is little trace in these various analyses of any attempt at setting up specific hypotheses regarding the nature of a given factor, and predicting on the basis of such hypotheses the factorial composition of new scales not included in the original analysis. Factor analysis has been used to suggest such hypotheses regarding the classification of interests; what is lacking is any attempt to test the correctness of the hypotheses derived. The design of experiments along such lines would probably be rather complex and difficult, but until the attempt is made the results so far achieved cannot be taken too seriously. From the simple point of view of practical usefulness factor analysis is not likely at the moment to improve on the predictive accuracy of the existing single scales. From the scientific point of view, however, we must formulate some kind of theory to account for the observed intercorrelations, and thus to bring order into an extremely confused field. To refuse to "name" factors may be an act of scientific caution, but clearly the matter cannot be allowed to remain there. Some underlying principles of classification are clearly present in the field of "interests"; until these are found and measured, we can hardly rest content.

Relevant to this general problem of classification of interests is the work of Kuder on his *Preference Record* (1939), although no factorial analyses were carried out by this writer. However, the internal consistency criteria adopted, and the relative independence of the scales which make up the final record, effectively amount to something very similar to a factorial study, and consequently the resulting classification may with advantage be quoted here. Ten main areas are recognized by Kuder: outdoor, mechanical, computational, scientific, persuasive, artistic, literary, musical, social service, and clerical. Intercorrelations between scores in these areas are relatively slight; only three are above ·4 (outdoors versus persuasive = − ·49; outdoor versus clerical = − ·40; scientific versus persuasive = − ·42). There is clearly some overlap with Strong's factors, but Kuder's list would appear rather more comprehensive. Possibly a factor analysis of the correlations between Kuder's 10 areas (which would correspond to primary factors) would result in second-order factors of some interest.

Much more satisfactory than the purely empirical findings discussed so far is the work to be discussed next. This is clearly based on a definite hypothesis, which can be supported or disproved; it thus follows closely the traditional hypothetico-deductive approach of science. The hypothesis referred to originated with the German psychologist Spranger (1927), who based his typology on the contrasting patterns of interests or values held by his six *types of men*: theoretical (rational, scientific), economic (utilitarian, useful), æsthetic (beauty, harmony), social (people, human relations), political (power, dominance), and religious (unity, communion). Allport and Vernon (1931) constructed a self-administering test of preference-judgments to measure the degree to which respondents were influenced by these various values or interests; this test they called the Study of Values. Use was made in the construction of the different scales of the internal consistency technique, although no factorial study was carried out until Lurie's paper (1937) appeared to make good this deficiency.

This author used 203 students as subjects, all of whom had filled in the Study of Values forms. Tetrachoric correlations were run between 24 scores obtained from the 144 items of the Allport-Vernon test, and a Thurstone-type factor analysis carried out, using oblique factors. Four main such factors are isolated. "Factor I is clearly *social* and altruistic, a factor having to do with the valuing of human relations as such. . . . The second is complex, involving items supposed to correspond to Spranger's economic and political types, and inversely to the æsthetic type; one might call this pattern the *Philistine* type, aggressive, go-getting, utilitarian, anti-cultural. Factor III is plainly *theoretical*. . . Number IV is the *religious* type, probably more closely connected with doctrine and practice than the vague mystical unity with the cosmos that Spranger envisaged." Conformation of the relatively independent existence of these four types comes from a more recent study by Coates (1950), who constructed scales for the measurement of the religious, æsthetic (i.e. opposite to Philistine), theoretical, and social types, and showed by internal-consistency methods the relative independence of these types.

There are obvious connections between these studies and the work of Strong and Thurstone. Lurie's theoretical corresponds to Thurstone's scientific type; Lurie's social corresponds to Thurstone's "interest in people". The Philistine factor probably corresponds to "interest in business". These identifications are merely *a priori*, of course; more solid evidence is provided in some studies by Ferguson,

Humphreys, and Strong (1941), Sarbin and Berdie (1940), van Dusen, Wimberley, and Mosier (1939), Duffy and Crissy (1940), Burgemeister (1940), and Tussing (1942). These various authors have shown conclusively that definite trends exist which connect the Strong scoring categories with the Allport-Vernon types. As Strong (1943) points out, "these relationships between the Allport-Vernon values and occupational interests indicate general trends and aid in interpreting both sets of data. Unfortunately they are not high enough to warrant using either test for the other, since scores in one test cannot be transmuted into the other with sufficient reliability for use in individual diagnosis".

Rather different from the preceding investigations, although still relevant to the problem of classification of occupational interest, is a recent paper by Vernon (1949). A list of 58 occupations was drawn up by him and given to some 50 judges. These were asked to judge the degree of similarity or dissimilarity of pairs of occupations on a seven-point scale; on the average five judges rated each of the 1,653 possible combinations of two occupations. Correlations were then calculated to show the resemblance of the total pattern of interests in each pair of occupations, and a factorial analysis performed. Four factors emerged:

I. Gregarious versus Isolated.
II. Social Welfare versus Administrative.
III. Scientific versus Display.
IV. Verbal versus Active.

Vernon identifies some of his factors with both Strong's and Spranger's types. Thus factor II he considers to correspond to Spranger's social versus political types; Strong's group 2 he relates to the scientific, 4 to the active, 5 to the social welfare, 8 to the administrative, 9 to the display, and 10 to the verbal type. It is to be noted that Vernon identifies his factors both from the positive and the negative end; this seems a reasonable procedure in a field where negative factor saturations cannot be avoided. Possibly Strong's factors could with advantage be treated in a similar manner. Certainly the impossibility of avoiding bipolar factors makes a simple taking over of methods of analysis and interpretation from the field of cognitive testing somewhat hazardous, and may ultimately lead to new techniques more easily adapted to this type of problem.

Lacking even more in psychological hypotheses than the work of Strong, and even more strongly empiricist in outlook than his, is a study by Adams and Fowler (1946) and Kelley (1946). These writers collected a list of 40 "rubrics" (rather specific interest types) which were then used to construct preference items each of which covered several "rubrics". Correlations were run for 800 men on 35 of these rubrics, and five factors extracted from the matrix. These factors were not rotated or in any way interpreted, but were simply given meaningless names based on the initial letters of the rubrics having high loadings on each factor. As summarized by Vernon (1949), the five factors are:

(1) MIMSEC—masculine, mechanical versus social, effeminate.
(2) PEPGAP—persevering, pioneering, economic, practical versus adventurous, physical activity.
(3) PAMRIM—power, aggressive, money, physical activity versus religion, industrious, music.
(4) RODPOD—routine, domestic, religious versus pioneering, outdoor, daring.
(5) NEVCOM—nature-loving, religious, salesmanship versus power, mechanical, spatial, orderliness, verbal, music.[1]

Vernon comments: "So far no convincing examples of the practical applicability of these heterogeneous types have been published, and we are entitled to doubt whether such extreme empiricism actually works." Indeed, it would seem that in this field particularly the use of factor analysis can only be justified if it advances our psychological understanding; as Thomson (1939) has pointed out: "When vocational guidance proceeds by giving to a candidate a number of tests which have previously been given to persons already engaged in the occupations, the use of factor analysis has no mathematical justification whatever."

Somewhat different from all the foregoing analyses, both in the activities included in the questionnaire and in the method of analysis are two studies by Chisnall (1942) and Hammond (1945). Both deal with leisure-time interests among adolescents attending a Youth Centre, and both agree in finding, first a general factor and then a bipolar factor. "Analysis of the interests showed that some had a very specialized appeal attracting members who showed little interest in other aspects of the Centre (e.g. darts, table tennis, reading), whilst others drew upon a more general interest. This latter kind of interest is the one which is most likely to promote a community

[1] The haunting beauty of these five names recalls Lewis Carroll and Lear.

spirit." The bipolar factor which followed this general factor "fitted in with the usual idea of an athletic type, interested primarily in physical activities in contrast with a more sedentary type having artistic and intellectual interests". This second factor might be identified with extraversion-introversion, but it might with equal justice be regarded as a sex factor—boys tended towards the athletic, girls towards the artistic pole. Altogether, interpretation in more general terms is difficult of these two researches because of the narrow range of activities included.

One further research may be mentioned which confirmed Chisnall's and Hammond's second factor on an all-male sample of 1,000 Navy recruits. Vernon and Parry (1949) carried out a factor analysis of 20 interest items in a biographical questionnaire, and extracted two general factors, one of which contrasted interests having high cultural loadings (discussion, photography, acting, and reading) with interests in physical activities (boxing, football, metal-work, and cooking). The other general factor was of no interest, as it merely represented a tendency to tick many or few interests. Four group factors were also found, however, after the elimination of the two general factors, which Vernon identified with mechanical, athletic, social, and domestic interest types. The narrow range of items again makes this analysis not quite comparable with those of Thurstone, Strong, and Lurie, although it would not be possible to deny certain similarities.

Altogether, we may agree with Vernon's (1949) conclusion when he writes: "Interests can be classified into groups or types at a rather general level. In spite of the different approaches of different typologists, and the very different kinds of test material analysed by different factorists, there is a fair amount of overlapping or concordance between their results. Similar groupings tend to emerge also whether actual occupational interests or leisure-time pursuits are considered." The amount of agreement found is promising, but it is far from sufficient to make one feel that anything like finality has been reached in these efforts at finding a basis for classification. A parallel might be drawn between the present state of this field and the state of personality questionnaire analysis before the Guilfords' attempt to get away from correlation between *a priori* clusters, and to analyse instead correlations between items. No large-scale study of such intercorrelations between items has yet been carried out, and there is little doubt in the writer's mind that only by such a study, using oblique and second-order factors if necessary, can a really firm foundation be laid for a proper system of classification of interests and values.

After this discussion of the organization of interests and values, we must turn to the problem presented by attitudes. Here, as in so many other fields, the pioneering study is due to Thurstone (1934). Eleven attitude scales were given to almost 400 students, whose scores on an intelligence test were also known. These 12 variables were correlated and two factors extracted from the resulting matrix. Fig. 30 shows in two-dimensional projection the position of the various scales, to-

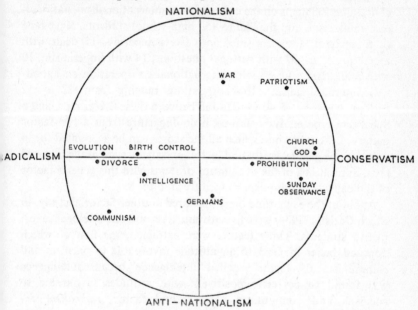

Fig. 30.—Factor Study of Radicalism with Attitude Scales by Thelma Gwinn Thurstone.

gether with the interpretation of the two factors as given by Thurstone. No detailed criticism of the results of this study need be given here; we may note, however, that the second factor can hardly be identified as a "nationalism" factor in view of the fact that the "patriotism" scale has a higher factor saturation on "conservatism" than on this putative "nationalism" factor, although in ordinary speech these two terms are almost interchangeable. Also it should be noted that the position of the axes is somewhat arbitrary, as there is clearly no simple structure to be derived from this particular analysis. As will be shown later, a slight rotation of this arbitrary axis pattern brings Thurstone's results into good agreement with those of later workers.

While we may doubt the exact identification of the factors or the precise position of the axes, Thurstone's study must, nevertheless, be regarded as giving strong support to the view, the correctness of which had been adumbrated by Lundberg (1926), George (1925), Likert (1932), and others, affirming the existence of a general radicalism-conservatism factor.[1] Confirmation of his results was given in a study by Kulpe and Davidson (1934), who administered a questionnaire containing 108 items on the issues of race, internationalism, nationalism, militarism, and the like to 150 high-school students. Sixty-nine of these items were classified into five categories—15 dealt with racial questions, 17 with national questions, 14 with imperialism, 10 with militarism, and 13 with international co-operation and good-will (internationalism). Intercorrelations ranging from ·22 to ·52 with an average r of ·40 were found between these five groups, and a Spearman-type analysis showed little departure from a two-factor pattern, i.e. a pattern in which all the scores can be accounted for in terms of one general factor and factors specific to each of the separate tests. Saturations of the five groups of items with this general factor of radicalism-conservatism ranged from ·5 to ·8.

At about the same time there appeared another factorial study, in which Carlson (1934) gave five attitude tests and one intelligence test to 215 students. Three factors were extracted, the first of which opposed belief in God to an attitude favourable to pacifism and communism; this factor he called "intelligence" because intelligence was found to correlate positively with attitudes favourable to pacifism and communism. His second factor, *radicalism-con-servatism*, opposed belief in God to attitudes favourable towards prohibition and communism; while his third factor opposed belief in God to an attitude favourable towards birth control and was called "*religious*". These groupings, and also the names given to them, could be criticized in detail; the main difficulty seems to be that no convincing interpretation is possible with such a very small number

[1] Among the earliest attempts to find generality in the field of social attitudes was the study by Lentz, who took six *a priori* groups of questionnaire items: education, religion, government, sex, non-social, and general. There were 190 items in the six groups and 579 college students constituted the sample. Reliabilities for the six sub-tests averaged about ·6 and the intercorrelations between the six sub-tests averaged around ·45, a value which was considerably increased when the correlations were corrected for attenuation. No factor analysis was carried out, but Lentz concludes that his results "argue strongly for the validity of the concept of general conservatism". Cf. also Stayner (1936, 1942).

of attitudes. It will be shown later that Carlson's results can be fitted in well with those of Thurstone and later writers, and consequently no further discussion of his data will be given here.

The studies of Thurstone, Kulpe, Davidson, and Carlson were conducted on a relatively small scale. The work of Rundquist and Sletto (1936) on *Personality in the Depression* was carried out on a much larger scale. A considerable number of subjects, including university students, high-school students, and employed and un-employed workers of various types, were used in an effort to study "the effects of the depression on the personality and family life of young people". This purpose dictated the choice of variables. "Loss of morale, development of feelings of inferiority, disharmonic family relationships, increased disrespect for law, economic radicalism, and disillusionment concerning the value of education, are among the effects most commonly alleged to result from unemployment." Consequently, scales were constructed by means of internal con-sistency techniques, dealing with morale, inferiority, family, law, economic conservatism, and education. Correlations were calculated between these variables on nine different groups containing between 50 and 500 subjects.

No factorial analyses were carried out; the authors relied instead on partial and multiple correlations. Of particular interest here will be the correlations of conservatism with the other scales. Correlations with morale for the various groups are around the ·3 level. With education they tend to lie in the neighbourhood of ·1. With attitude towards the family, correlations are at about the same level as with education, whereas with attitude towards the law they tend to be rather higher, i.e. between · 4 and ·5. On the whole, morale was found most closely associated with the other variables measured, and conservatism least closely associated. "The fourth order partial co-efficients between economic conservatism score and score on each of the other scales were computed for 500 men. Their size ranged from — ·041 (economic conservatism versus family) to ·119 (economic conservatism versus morale). These are obviously not significantly different from zero." It is difficult to interpret this result in the ab-sence of a proper factorial study. If Kulpe and Davidson's findings of a general factor of conservatism could be applied to the present data, then all fourth-order partials would be likely to vanish, so that this particular finding is of no great significance. In addition, the whole study suffers from the fact that what is intercorrelated are not indivi-dual items but scales put together partly on an *a priori* basis, although in fairness to Rundquist and Sletto it should be said that the method of internal consistency validation employed by them partly obviates this criticism. Nevertheless, the writer doubts if any general conclusions can be drawn from their work, the importance of which, from the point of view of its primary objection, namely the changes induced in personality by the depression, is, of course, not in question.

The work of Rundquist and Sletto (1936) was followed up by Darley and McNamara (1938, 1940). These authors gave the Rundquist and Sletto scales, as well as four adjustment inventory scales (home, health, social, emotional) and the Minnesota Inventory of Social Attitudes to 100 men and 100 women, calculating correlations separately for the two groups and separately for test and retest applications. Five factors were isolated: factor one, a measure of adjustment to society; factor two, a measure of the individual's effectiveness in social situations; factor three, one of family adjustment; factor four, one of neuroticism; factor five, one of radicalism-conservatism. Correlations between these factors were found to be relatively low, the highest being ·45. New scales were made up on the basis of these findings to measure the factors concerned, but little use seems to have been made of these scales, and the whole analysis does not appear to advance our knowledge to any considerable extent.

More in line with the earlier factorial studies than *Personality in the Depression* is a series of analyses by Ferguson (1939, 1940, 1941, 1942a, 1942b, 1944a, 1944b, 1946). In the first of these studies, Ferguson pointed out that the results of Thurstone and of Carlson "did not yield unequivocal definitions of the factors found to be required for the explanation of the intercorrelations among tests with which they were concerned". Using tests of the equal-appearing interval type for the measurement of attitudes towards war, reality of God, patriotism, treatment of criminals, capital punishment, censorship, evolution, birth control, law, and communism, he administered these instruments to 185 students and factor-analysed the resulting matrix of intercorrelations. He failed to find simple structure with the entire battery of tests, but when scales for the measurement of attitudes towards censorship, law, patriotism, and communism were dropped, he obtained an excellent fit to simple structure and succeeded in locating his axes uniquely.[1] Factor one he found to be characterized by scales dealing with the reality of God, as opposed to belief in evolution and birth control. Factor two was described by scales

[1] This is not a very difficult feat, of course, when almost half the variables have been dropped and only 6 remain!

measuring attitudes towards the treatment of criminals, capital punishment, and war. These two factors he called "religionism" and "humanitarianism", and in his second paper, scales were constructed for the measurement of these two attitudes. In 1941 the experiment was repeated by administering the same scales to another set of 178 students, and the same two factors "religionism" and "humanitarianism" emerged. In 1942 a third factor of "nationalism" was added to the others by re-analysis of the original data so that Ferguson now claims to have established the existence of three "primary social attitudes", as he calls them: religionism, humanitarianism, and nationalism. In 1944 another repetition of the original experiment was carried out, using some 600 cases altogether. In this experiment, Ferguson showed again that the same factors could be extracted from the matrix of intercorrelations. In his other studies, he has tried to relate these various factors to such variables as sex, religion, education, and so forth.

In 1944 Eysenck made an attempt to integrate the findings of Thurstone, Carlson, and Ferguson, as well as those of an analysis carried out by him on some 700 replies to a questionnaire containing 32 propositions. It was found that when the original two centroid axes in each of the various analyses were superimposed on each other, similar items from the different researches fell into the four quadrants. Thus, the first quadrant was characterized by such items as favourable attitudes towards patriotism, war, capital punishment, law, and harsh treatment of criminals. The second quadrant was characterized by favourable attitudes towards evolution, divorce, abortion, birth control, and divorce reform. The third quadrant was characterized by pacifism, anti-ethnocentrism, and favourable attitudes towards sex and race equality, and the fourth by favourable attitudes towards religious issues, such as the existence of God, Sunday observance, church-going, and so forth.

The first axis or factor was interpreted as one of radicalism-conservatism; "the *radical* attitudes—communist, favourable towards easy divorce, birth control, and evolution—are opposed to the *conservative* attitudes—patriot, favourable towards religion, capital punishment, law, and so on". The second factor was rather more difficult to interpret. "On the one side we have the practical, materialistic, extraverted person, who deals with the environment either by force (soldier) or by manipulation (scientist). On the other side we have the theoretical, idealistic, introverted person who deals with problems either by thinking (philosopher) or by believing (priest). ...

The *practical* attitude is that of James' "tough-minded" man . . .; the *theoretical* attitude is that of the 'tender minded'."

This interpretation was considered less of the nature of a conclusion but rather as an hypothesis to govern further research, and accordingly an experiment was set up to test the validity of the interpretations made and the reproducibility of the factors isolated. This attempt at validation was governed by two main principles, both of which would appear to contain a methodological advance on previous work: (1) it was considered that confirmation of the correct identification of a radicalism-conservatism factor could only come by reference to a tested criterion, namely an actual survey of opinions held by known conservatives and radicals respectively; (2) it was considered that the nature of the second factor could be clarified most by stating hypotheses regarding its nature and including items which would present a test of the accuracy of these hypotheses. The second of these two principles governed the selection of items, the first determined the sample to whom the questionnaire was given. A set of 40 items was prepared and is reproduced below in Table 37. 750 subjects constituted the sample, which was selected in such a way that 250 were socialists, 250 liberals, and 250 conservatives. Party affiliation was decided on the basis of the vote cast in the last election. Groups were equated for age, sex, and education. Tetrachoric correlations were calculated between all the items, and a factorial analysis carried out which gave rise to two main factors. Fig. 31 shows the distribution of the various items which characterize the two factors. The first factor was called R (for radicalism-conservatism), the second factor T (for tough-minded versus tender-minded).

Proof for the correct identification of the R factor is obtainable by reference to actual attitude statements of the socialist and conservative groups respectively. Differences in item endorsements between these two groups were calculated for each of the 40 items, and the following hypothesis set up. An item having high positive saturation for the R factor should also have a markedly higher endorsement by the socialists as compared with the conservatives. Items having high negative R saturation should show considerably higher endorsement by conservatives than by socialists. Items having zero loadings on the R factor should show no difference in endorsement between the two political groups. Intermediate items should show intermediate differences in endorsement. This deduction can be put to the proof by correlating the column of factor saturations on R with a column of endorsement differences for the 40 items. This

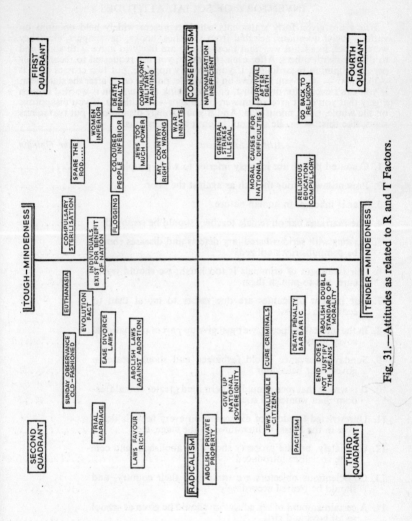

Fig. 31.—Attitudes as related to R and T Factors.

FIRST QUADRANT

SPARE THE ROD.....

WOMEN INFERIOR

DEATH PENALTY

COLOURED PEOPLE INFERIOR

COMPULSORY MILITARY TRAINING

FLOGGING

JEWS TOO MUCH POWER

MY COUNTRY RIGHT OR WRONG

WAR INNATE

CONSERVATISM

NATIONALISATION INEFFICIENT

FOURTH QUADRANT

GENERAL STRIKES ILLEGAL

SURVIVAL AFTER DEATH

MORAL CAUSES FOR NATIONAL DIFFICULTIES

GO BACK TO RELIGION

RELIGIOUS EDUCATION COMPULSORY

TOUGH-MINDEDNESS

COMPULSORY STERILISATION

EUTHANASIA

INDIVIDUALS EXIST FOR BENEFIT OF NATION

TENDER-MINDEDNESS

EVOLUTION FACT

SUNDAY OBSERVANCE OLD-FASHIONED

EASE DIVORCE LAWS

ABOLISH LAWS AGAINST ABORTION

ABOLISH DOUBLE STANDARD OF MORALITY

DEATH PENALTY BARBARIC

CURE CRIMINALS

END DOES NOT JUSTIFY THE MEANS

GIVE UP NATIONAL SOVEREIGNTY

JEWS VALUABLE CITIZENS

TRIAL MARRIAGE

LAWS FAVOUR RICH

ABOLISH PRIVATE PROPERTY

PACIFISM

SECOND QUADRANT

RADICALISM

THIRD QUADRANT

229

TABLE 37

INVENTORY OF SOCIAL ATTITUDES

Below are given forty statements which represent widely held opinions on various social questions, selected from speeches, books, newspapers, etc. They were chosen in such a way that most people are likely to agree with some and to disagree with others. After each statement, you are requested to record your personal opinion regarding it. If you strongly approve, put two crosses after it —like this: + +. If you approve on the whole, put one cross after the statement. If you can't decide for or against, or if you think the question is worded in such a way that you can't give an answer, put a zero—like this: O. If you disapprove on the whole, put a minus sign. And if you strongly disapprove, put two minus signs, like this: — —. Be sure not to omit any questions.

Attitude Statements	*Your Opinion*
1. Coloured people are innately inferior to white people	....
2. Present laws favour the rich as against the poor	....
3. War is inherent in human nature	....
4. The marriage bar on female teachers should be removed	....
5. Persons with serious hereditary defects and diseases should be compulsorily sterilized	....
6. Our treatment of criminals is too harsh; we should try to cure, not to punish them	....
7. Our present difficulties are due rather to moral than to economic causes	....
8. In the interests of peace, we must give up part of our national sovereignty	....
9. Sunday-observance is old fashioned and should cease to govern our behaviour	....
10. It is wrong that men should be permitted greater sexual freedom than women by society	....
11. Unrestricted freedom of discussion on every topic is desirable in the Press, in literature, on the stage, etc.	....
12. Ultimately, private property should be abolished, and complete socialism introduced	....
13. Conscientious objectors are traitors to their country, and should be treated accordingly	....
14. A certain amount of sex education should be given at school to all boys and girls	....
15. The laws against abortion should be abolished	....
16. Only by going back to religion can civilization hope to survive	....
17. Marriages between white and coloured people should be strongly discouraged	....
18. Jews are as valuable, honest, and public-spirited citizens as any other group	....

Attitude Statements	*Your Opinion*

19. Major questions of national policy should be decided by reference to majority opinion (e.g. by referendum) . . . .

20. There should be far more controversial and political discussion over the radio . . . .

21. The present licensing laws should be altered so as to remove restrictions on hours of opening . . . .

22. All human beings are born with the same potentialities . . . .

23. Divorce laws should be altered to make divorce easier . . . .

24. Patriotism in the modern world is a force which works against peace . . . .

25. Modern life is too much concentrated in cities; the Government should take steps to encourage a "return to the country" . . . .

26. Crimes of violence should be punished by flogging . . . .

27. The nationalization of the great industries is likely to lead to inefficiency, bureaucracy, and stagnation . . . .

28. It is right and proper that religious education in schools should be made compulsory . . . .

29. Men and women have the right to find out whether they are sexually suited before marriage (e.g. by companionate marriage . . . .

30. The principle "Spare the rod and spoil the child" has much truth in it, and should govern our methods of bringing up children . . . .

31. Women are not the equals of men in intelligence, organizing ability, etc. . . . .

32. Experiments on living animals should be forbidden . . . .

33. The Jews have too much power and influence in this country . . . .

34. Differences in pay between men and women doing the same work should be abolished . . . .

35. Birth control, except when medically indicated, should be made illegal . . . .

36. The death penalty is barbaric, and should be abolished . . . .

37. There will be another war in twenty-five years . . . .

38. Scientists should take no part in politics . . . .

39. The Japanese are by nature a cruel people . . . .

40. Only people with a definite minimum of intelligence and education should be allowed to vote . . . .

Personal Details

It would be appreciated if you would fill in the following details:

41. Age. . . . . 42. Sex. . . . . 43. Weekly income (self or husband). . . . . .
44. Type of work. . . . .

(From Eysenck, 1947)

correlation turned out to be $+ \cdot 98$, which is sufficiently close to unity to be regarded as adequate proof of the original hypothesis.

Regarding the second factor, unfortunately no such outside criterion was available, and consequently inspection of the variables having high saturations on it becomes necessary. Such inspection, taken together with the provisional hypothesis formed on the basis of the previous tentative identification of that factor, led to the abandonment of the terms "practical" and "theoretical" and to the adoption rather of the terms "tender-minded" (instead of theoretical) and "tough-minded" (instead of practical). The reasons for this renaming will be obvious from an inspection of the items included in Fig. 31.

Scales were constructed from items having high saturations with these factors for the accurate measurement of both R and T. These were found to have almost zero intercorrelation with each other, and to be relatively independent of sex, age, and education. Two exceptions to this general statement may be noted. Women showed a distinct tendency to be more tender-minded, and well-educated subjects showed a distinct tendency towards greater radicalism. Scores on the R factor have on several occasions been found to distinguish at a high level of significance between different political groups, whereas scores on the T factor have usually failed to do so.

One exception should be noted to this rule. In a recent paper, Eysenck (1951) tried to clarify the concept underlying the T factor by putting forward two hypotheses: (1) working-class subjects are more "tough-minded" than middle-class subjects; (2) communists and fascists, although at opposite ends of the continuum with respect to the R factor, are both more "tough-minded" than are the socialists, liberals, and conservatives. Both predictions were fulfilled at a high level of confidence. When middle-class socialists, liberals, conservatives, and communists were compared with working-class socialists, liberals, conservatives, and communists, respectively, the latter were found in each case to be more tough-minded than the former. When communists and fascists were compared with members of the other three groups, they were found to occupy positions in the first and second quadrants respectively, i.e. the fascists tended to be conservative and tough-minded, whereas the communists tended to be radical and tough-minded. Both groups were considerably more tough-minded than the three democratic parties of whom the liberals were found to be the most tender-minded.

The analysis of social attitudes into two main factors may thus be regarded as having a considerable degree of validity. It reconciles the data from analyses by all the writers mentioned hitherto, and it appears to be relatively independent of the country in which the analysis is carried out or the particular items or scales employed. Some recently published investigations have shown that a very similar pattern to the one discussed above emerges in such widely different cultures as the American, Swedish, and the German, where the set of questions used in the previous analysis was given to large middle- and working-class samples of nationals in each of these countries respectively (Eysenck, 1953).

One question arises, however, which demands an answer. When the results depicted in Fig. 31 are compared with Ferguson's analysis, it will be found that agreement is striking with respect to the actual position of the various items, but that his two main factors, "religionism" and "humanitarianism", are rotated from R and T through an angle of about 45 degrees. Thus, "humanitarianism" is characterized by the items in the tender-minded-radical quadrant, and "anti-humanitarianism" by the items in the tough-minded-conservative quadrant. Similarly, "religionism" is characterized by the items in the conservative-tender-minded quadrant, and anti-religionism by items in the tough-minded-radical quadrant. Indeed, it would seem that the sets of items in each of these quadrants define a particular type of person. Items in the first (tough-minded-conservative) quadrant define the fascist, and, as pointed out above, when R and T scales are given to members of the fascist party, their scores cluster in this neighbourhood. Similarly, the second quadrant tough-minded-radical) shows a cluster of items characteristic of the communist, and, again, actual experiment has shown that the R and T scores of communists tend to cluster in this quadrant. The third quadrant (radical-tender-minded) is characterized by items which would define members of the Society of Friends, pacifists, members of the Independent Labour Party, and other similar organizations. Items in the fourth quadrant (conservative-tender-minded) all refer to religious beliefs and practices, and would therefore characterize the active church-goer.[1]

[1] One interesting point should be noted here. The analyses of social attitudes reported bear a striking relation to Lurie's (1937) work on the "study of values". His social-altruistic factor corresponds to the tender-minded radical; his philistine type to the tough-minded conservative; his religious type clearly corresponds to the tender-minded conservative; while the theoretical, scientific factor bears a somewhat less close relation to the tough-minded radical type. This identification is based on the rather remarkable resemblance in description between these various studies; it should be an easy matter to decide by experiment whether such cross-identification is empirically justified.

There is no absolute preference attached to a description of the relations between attitudes in terms of R and T compared with a similar description in terms of Ferguson's two factors. Both would reproduce the observed correlations with equal accuracy, and both give a psychologically meaningful interpretation. The writer's preference for the R and T solution arises from the social importance of the radicalism-conservatism dichotomy, which enables us to assign a position to the R axis which is quite unique and invariant by simply maximizing the correlation between factor saturations on R and per cent. differences between endorsements for the statements included in the analysis by known socialists and conservatives. On the other hand, it must be admitted that a similarly unique position can probably be assigned to Ferguson's factors by reference to simple structure. There are certain doubts attaching to this possibility, however, as Ferguson worked with a very small number of variables indeed; in analysing a large table of correlations like Eysenck's, it would be much more difficult to reach any form of simple structure. Ultimately, the decision must be made on psychological rather than on statistical grounds, and it is here that the R-T analysis seems to the writer more promising than Ferguson's. It seems more reasonable psychologically to regard communism as a mixture of radicalism and tough-mindedness, or fascism as a mixture of conservatism and tough-mindedness, than it is to consider radicalism as a mixture of humanitarianism and anti-religionism or conservatism as a mixture of religionism and anti-humanitarianism.

This conclusion agrees well with one of the few factorial studies in the area which were guided by a definite hypothesis. Hatt (1948) was concerned with the problem of ethnic attitudes and elaborated a research design to make possible the study of two frequently mentioned hypotheses. The first of these assumes that attitudes towards ethnic groups are positively correlated with attitudes towards the lower class; this position has found political expression in socialism, communism, and several liberal and progressive movements. Essentially what is implied is a class relationship as the essence of attitude patterns. The other hypothesis maintains that attitudes towards minorities are a function of some universally applicable standard of ethical morality and unrelated to class attitude. This view has often led to the belief that favourable attitudes towards the minority are the expression of a breadth of education likely to be characteristic of the middle and upper classes. However, many who accept this second view do so without any class implication whatsoever. Using three separate groups (university students, high school students, and upper class adults), Hatt constructed and administered six attitude scales measuring antagonism towards the upper class, the middle class, the lower class, Negroes, Jews, and the foreign born. Inter-correlations were run between the six scales for the three groups separately, and a factor analysis, using Hotelling's method of principal components, was carried out. The first principal component accounted for 53 per cent. of the variance, and inspection of its relationship with the several scales revealed at once that it agrees markedly with the hypothesis that attitudes towards minorities vary directly with each other, directly with attitudes towards the lower class, and inversely with attitudes towards the upper class. The types resulting from this factor "represent the polar patterns earlier described as inherent in the first view of the class nature of attitudes towards ethnic minorities; the 'progressive, class-conscious partisan of the lower class', and the 'reactionary and class-conscious upper-class supporter' ".

The second principal component accounts for an additional 20 per cent. of the total variance. "This pattern is definable almost exactly in the terms of the second approach mentioned at the beginning of this paper. It is composed of the same basic inter-class relations as in factor one, the negative correlations of considerable magnitude between attitudes towards upper and lower classes. In this component, however, the association of class attitudes with attitudes towards ethnic groups is reversed. Here antagonism towards the upper and favourable attitudes towards the lower class are associated with antagonism towards the minorities. The other end of this pattern represents a favourable attitude towards minorities associated with favourable attitudes towards the upper class and a negative attitude towards the lower class. This is the syndrome of attitudes which would justify a 'tolerance' approach based upon ethical enlightenment and brotherhood and void of the direct class appeal. In this factor the 'broadly educated, high principled altruist' and 'ignorant, narrow opportunistic bigot' of the second hypothesis are apparent. Both original hypotheses have thus been empirically verified as applicable to the samples, though with different degrees of importance."

The two factors isolated in this admirable study resemble very closely the radical-conservative, and the tough-tender-mindedness factors described previously; as we have shown before, ethnocentrism is correlated both with conservatism (Hatt's first factor) and also with tough-mindedness (Hatt's second factor), which in turn is found much more conspicuously in working-class than in middle-class samples. Here, then, we have another independent proof along quite original lines of the essential soundness of the analysis of social attitudes in terms of the R and T factors.[1]

A striking confirmation of the findings reported by Ferguson, Eysenck, and Hatt is contained in a recent study by Adorno, Frenkel-Brunswik, Levinson, and Sanford on *The Authoritarian Personality* (1950). This brilliant contribution to the study of attitude and personality takes its starting-point from the phenomenon of anti-Semitism. As a first step, five scales were constructed "dealing respectively with imagery (opinions) of Jews as personally *offensive* and as socially *threatening*; with attitudes concerning what should be done to or against Jews; and with the opposing views that Jews are too *seclusive* or too *intrusive* (assimilative)". These sub-scales have reasonable reliabilities and correlate quite highly together, co-efficients ranging from ·74 to ·86; if corrected for attenuation they would all be well over ·9. While no formal factor analysis was carried out these results are in good agreement with a factorial study by Eysenck and Crown (1949) in which 24 statements relating to anti-Semitism were intercorrelated and the resulting matrix factor analysed. A very prominent general factor was found leaving residuals of no more than doubtful significance. A Guttman-type analysis of the scale indicated a reproducibility of 85 per cent. There appears little doubt therefore that anti-Semitism qualifies as a consistent social attitude.

The next step of Adorno *et al.* was the construction of an ethnocentrism scale, referred to as the "E" scale. (The anti-Semitism scale is referred to as the A-S scale.) This E scale is made up of three sub-scales "dealing respectively with Negroes, various other minorities, and patriotism (extra-national groupings)". Correlations between these three sub-scales were again quite high, ranging from ·74 to ·83; if corrected for attenuation, these correlations would all be above ·9. Anti-Semitism was found to correlate ·80 with the total E scale and ·74, ·76, and ·69 respectively with the three sub-scales (Negroes, minorities, and patriotism). "Anti-Semitism is best regarded, it would seem, as one aspect of this broader frame of mind; and it is the total ethnocentric ideology rather than prejudice against any single group which requires explanation."

[1] Essentially similar in their conclusion to the R-T studies are a number of papers by Sanai (1950, 1951, 1952). Sanai's main contribution appears to be a renaming of the R and T factors.

Next, a scale of politico-economic conservatism (PEC) was constructed. "No attempt was made, in the construction of the PEC scale, to cover all the forms in which conservatism and liberalism are currently expressed. The main focus was, rather, on some of the more underlying—and therefore more stable—ideological trends which appear to characterize conservatism and liberalism as *contrasting approaches* to *politico-economic* problems." Four main ideological trends were used: (1) support of the American *status quo;* (2) resistance to social change; (3) support of conservative values; and (4) ideas regarding the balance of power among business, labour, and government.

Conservatism was found to correlate with anti-Semitism, to the extent of ·43 (average of four groups totalling 295 subjects). Ethnocentrism and conservatism showed a correlation of ·59 for these groups. This correlation is very close to that obtained for a total of 1,568 subjects ($r = $ ·57), and indicates quite clearly the marked relationship between conservatism and ethnocentrism. If conservatives tend to show more prejudice, then we should expect, on the basis of the work previously outlined, to find the more religious also to show more prejudice. This is borne out in fact; it is found that "subjects who profess to some religious affiliation express more prejudice than those who do not".

After these various scales had been constructed, an attempt was made to create yet one further scale for the measurement of implicit anti-democratic trends. "There gradually evolved a plan for constructing a scale that would measure prejudice without appearing to have this aim and without mentioning the name of any minority group. . . . It was clear at the time the new scale was being planned that anti-Semitism (A-S) and ethnocentrism (E) were not merely matters of surface opinion but general tendencies, with sources, in part at least, deep within the structure of the person. Would it not be possible to construct a scale that would approach more directly these deeper, often unconscious forces? If so, and if this scale could be validated by means of later clinical studies, would we not have a better estimate of anti-democratic *potential* than could be obtained from the scales that were more openly ideological?" The items in this anti-democratic or "fascist" scale (called the F scale) include statements such as the desirability of a double standard of morality; that obedience and respect for authority are the most important virtues children should learn; that sex criminals ought to be publicly whipped; and that there will always be war and conflict, human nature being what it is. It will be seen that these items are practically identical with those appearing in the tough-minded-conservative quadrant in Fig. 31; the anti-democratic, or authoritarian, character defined by this scale appears precisely similar to the fascist character outlined there, and as the opposite of Ferguson's" humanitarianism".

It may be interesting to state briefly the explicit generalizations regarding this authoritarian or "force" character which guided Adorno and his co-workers in their selection of items. The variables which they used to make up the basic content of the F scale were conventionalism, or the rigid adherence to conventional middle-class values; authoritarian submission and aggression, i.e. the tendency to be submissive towards ingroup authorities and aggressive towards people who violate conventional values; anti-intraception, defined as opposition to the subjective, the imaginative, the tender-minded; superstition and stereotypy; power and "toughness"; destructiveness and cynicism; projectivity, i.e. the projection outwards of unconscious emotional impulses; and an exaggerated concern with sexual "goings-on".

"These variables were thought of as going together to form a single syndrome, a more or less enduring structure in the person that renders him receptive to anti-democratic propaganda. One might say, therefore, that the F scale attempts to measure the potentially anti-democratic personality." According to this hypothesis, we would expect substantial correlations with the anti-Semitism, ethno-centrism, and conservatism scales, and such are indeed found. The correlation between the F and the A-S scales is ·53; that between the F and the PEC scales is ·52, and that between the F and the E scales is ·73. This last correlation, if corrected for attenuation, would rise to about ·9.

We have already commented on the startling similarity between the results of the study under consideration and those of the studies previously reported, to which, curiously, Adorno, Frenkel-Brunswik, Levinson and Sanford make no reference. That relationship is pictured in Fig. 32. The vertical and the horizontal axes respectively represent the R and T factors; the diagonal lines represent Ferguson's humanitarianism and religionism factor; the concentric circles in the first quadrant represent respectively the anti-Semitism, ethno-centrism, and fascism scales. The PEC scale would be identical with the radicalism axis. Such close agreement between different investigators, using quite different procedures and methods of analysis, is comparatively rare in social psychology, and may be taken as an indication of the firmness with which this attitude-structure is marked in contemporary Western culture.

Criticism of this concept of the "authoritarian personality" will be deferred until after a consideration of the attempt made by the authors of this book to link the concept with a detailed investigation of personality dynamics. In the main, interview procedures were used

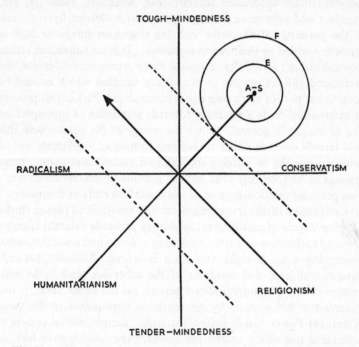

Fig. 32.—"The Authoritarian Personality" as related to R and T Factors.

for the purpose of obtaining more information on personality variables, but projective techniques were also used. The selection of the subjects was determined by their responses on the A-S or the E scale. Most of the interviewees belong either to the uppermost or to the lowermost quartile, the proportions of high-scoring and low-scoring subjects being approximately equal. This basis of choice has been indicated in Fig. 32 by means of two parallel lines drawn at right angles to the humanitarianism factor in such a way that about 50 per cent. of the total population would lie between these lines, with 25 per cent. lying above the upper and 25 per cent. below the lower of the two lines. Comparing these extremes, it was found that certain personality variables appeared to be consistently related to this dichotomy.

These variables in the main appeared to be the following: (1) Repression versus awareness: the prejudiced individual showed a failure on the whole to be aware of unacceptable tendencies and impulses in himself. This failure made it impossible for him to integrate these tendencies (mainly fear, weakness, passivity, sex, impulses and aggressive feelings against authorititive figures, such as the parents) satisfactorily with the conscious image he had of himself, and led to their being repressed. (2) Externalization versus internalization: as a defence against these repressed tendencies, the prejudiced subject resorts to projection, i.e. that which cannot be accepted as part of one's own ego is externalized. Part of this process of externalization is a tendency towards avoidance of introspection and of insight in general. "Since the energy of the person is in this case largely devoted either to keeping instinctual tendencies out of consciousness or to striving for external success and status, there appears to be relatively little left for genuine libidinization of one's own personal relationships or of one's work as ends in themselves." (3) Conventionalism versus genuineness: the prejudiced person shows a higher degree of conformity; seemingly he needs external support given by authorities or public opinion in order to find some assurance concerning what is right and what is wrong. Attitudes towards parents, children, and members of the other sex tend to be conventionalized. The unprejudiced person, on the other hand, is not governed in his attitude by conventional approaches to the same extent. (4) Power versus love orientation: the prejudiced person is orientated towards a search for power, "the comparative lack of ability for affectionate and individualized interpersonal relations, together with the conception of a threatening and dangerous environment must be seen as underlying the prejudiced individual's striving for the attainment of power, either directly or by having the powerful on his side". (5) Rigidity versus flexibility: one of the most characteristic aspects of the prejudiced individual is his rigidity. "This must be seen as a consequence of the features discussed so far. In order to keep unacceptable tendencies and impulses out of consciousness, rigid controls have to be maintained, as any loosening of the absoluteness of these controls involves a danger of a breaking through of the repressed tendencies." However, repression does not cause these impulses to lose their dynamic strength; quite on the contrary, abrupt or unsuccessful repression prevents rather than helps in their control and mastery. An ego thus weakened is more in danger of becoming completely overwhelmed by the repressed forces. Greater rigidity of defences is necessary to cope with such increased threat. "In this vicious circle, impulses are not prevented from breaking out in uncontrolled ways. Basically, unmodified instinctual impulses lurk everywhere beneath the surface, narrowing considerably the content of the ego so that it must be kept constantly on the lookout. Rational control extends to a small sector of the personality only."

These descriptions of the authoritarian personality presented by Frenkel-Brunswik with a wealth of supporting detail are extremely convincing, and should be read in full by the student, who may feel that the very abridged summary above does not do justice to the complex theory under discussion. Evidence of the essential correctness of the hypothesized correlation between personality and attitude structure is further given by the fact that after an interview covering the personality aspects only, it was possible, with considerable success, to forecast the attitude-scale scores of the subjects. "The defining criterion of selection, extremely high versus extremely low standing on the overt anti-Semitism or ethnocentrism scale shows a per cent. agreement of about ·85, with both the overall intuitive ratings and the composite standing on the interview. (This figure is an average of an agreement of about 95 per cent. achieved by one rater, whose material happened to include the most complete interviews, and an agreement of 75 per cent. achieved by the other rater, whose data were more fragmentary.)"

While fully realizing the importance of the contribution made by Frenkel-Brunswik, Levinson, Sanford, Adorno and the other authors of *The Authoritarian Personality*, the writer believes that their work is subject to one very damaging criticism. The proper way to approach a problem of this type would appear to be (*a*) to isolate the fundamental dimensions involved, and (*b*) to investigate the personality correlates of these dimensions. The authors of the book under review started in quite a different manner. Taking their point of departure from one specific issue in the field of social attitudes, they effectively proceeded to construct a dimension which passes through this point without enquiring (*a*) how many dimensions were involved in the field under investigation, or (*b*) enquiring into the proper location of the axes defining this field. Many of their findings, accordingly, are ambiguous. Let us return to Fig. 32. Essentially, Frenkel-Brunswik, in her interviews, compared persons from quadrant one with persons from quadrant three, calling them respectively "prejudiced" and "unprejudiced". In doing so she has unwittingly selected persons who would have high and low scores respectively on Ferguson's "humanitarianism" factor. The outcome, as regards this one factor, is quite clear. The question remains what would happen to the person, say, in the second quadrant, i.e. the person holding communist beliefs. Would he also be contrasted with the prejudiced authoritarian type of person in quadrant one, or would he show many qualities in common with him? Clearly, the existing stereotype of the communist would lead one to assume the second hypothesis. In that case, the characteristics with which Frenkel-Brunswik endows the person in the first quadrant would be shared by the individual in the second quadrant; in other words, the personality pattern painted by her would be characteristic of the tough-minded as opposed to the tender-minded, instead of the "fascist" as opposed to the "humanitarian".

This example may illustrate the importance of a proper dimensional analysis before proceeding further towards the complex interrelationships obtaining between such dimensions and outside variables. It is possible that Frenkel-Brunswik is right in identifying the authoritarian personality with the tough-minded conservative. Such a belief, however, requires proof and cannot rest on mere assumption. There is much evidence, although in the nature of the case it can only be indirect evidence, in the very pages of *The Authoritarian Personality* to support the view that the authoritarian personality pattern is characteristic of the tough-minded group as a whole, not only of the tough-minded conservative. It will require a repetition of the work described, with a change in experimental design, before we shall be able to tell definitely what the relations are between personality and social attitudes. At the moment, the evidence is ambiguous, due to disregard of the fundamental requirements of dimensional analysis.

There is little need to summarize the system of classification arising from the researches reviewed in this chapter, as they appear to agree remarkably well in their broad outlines; although a good deal of filling in at an intermediate level would seem to be required. One point, however, should be raised at this juncture. Regarding the general picture presented, as in the case of personality structure, we are in the case of attitudes dealing with four main and distinct layers. At the lowest level the attitude expressed is entirely specific in its content or is determined entirely by the specific features of the situation. We reach a higher level when such statements of attitude are repeated on separate occasions, thus showing a certain reliability which is the minimum requirement for any kind of organization. Such views, voiced repeatedly in different situations and having a certain degree of repeat reliability, we shall call opinions. Thus, if a person is heard repeatedly in different circumstances to voice a belief that "Negroes ought to be kept down" or "The Government is run by Jews", we may count that as an opinion, whereas an occasional, never repeated exclamation provoked by some unfortunate experience, such as, for instance, "a woman driver, of course!" would not be counted as an opinion but would remain at the lowest level of the hierarchical structure because of its specific nature and its lack of reliability.

When it is shown that certain opinions tend to correlate together, we reach a third level—that of attitude measurement. If, for instance, a set of twenty or thirty statements regarding the Negro or the Jew, all dealing with different aspects of the racial question, are answered in a consistent manner, then we may justifiably speak about an anti-Negro or an anti-Jewish attitude. Lastly, we reach the highest level when it can be shown that attitudes thus are intercorrelated, thus giving rise to higher order constructs. For instance, as we have seen, anti-Negro prejudice, war-mindedness, favourableness to institutionalized religion, dislike of socialism, dislike of soft upbringing of children, liking for industrial discipline, and many more attitudes are intercorrelated in a conservative pattern; conservatism therefore represents an even wider integration of opinions than does a simple attitude subsumed under it.

These four stages of organization emerge fairly clearly from current research, although it cannot be gainsaid that intermediate stages are possible. Thus, for instance, the concept of ethnocentrism would be intermediate, in its power to integrate and generalize opinions, between the concept of anti-Negro or anti-Jewish attitude and the higher-order concept of conservatism. However, the general principle of organization from the very large number of low-level verbal statements through the fairly large number of opinions, and the much smaller number of attitudes to the very small number of really high-order general concepts, like conservatism, will be reasonably clear. The technique of factor analysis enables us in a given context to assign to a given statement in a given population the percentage of the total variance contributed by error factors (first level), specific factors (second level), group factors (third level), and general factors (fourth level). Thus we can obtain for any given question or statement an equation setting out clearly the relative importance of the four levels discussed above (Eysenck, 1951).

Factor analysis has been used almost exclusively to derive concepts at the highest level of all; at the level of attitude measurement other forms of consistency analysis, such as the equal-appearing interval scale construction method of Thurstone or Guttman's scalogram analysis, have been used. These methods are plausible alternatives to full-scale factor analysis, but as Eysenck and Crown (1949) have shown, they cannot really replace factor analysis, when the possibility of group factors being present cannot be ruled out.

Research in social attitudes, then, does not essentially constitute an exception to our general finding that a solution by means of oblique primary factors, giving rise to second-order factors, is the most acceptable at the present stage of development of factorial analysis. The stage of obtaining oblique primary factors is usually omitted, either by constructing a scale for each of these primary factors (anti-Semitism, war-mindedness, pro-Church attitude, etc.) by means other than factorial analysis, and then intercorrelating a number of sub-scales (Ferguson) or else by taking one statement from each scale having high correlations with the total scale, and intercorrelating statements of this kind taken from a large number of different scales (Eysenck, 1947). In either case, these "primary factors" show high intercorrelations, and give rise to second-order factors such as R and T, or "religionism" and "humanitarianism".

A last question relates to any further "second-order" factors that may be present in the field of social attitudes. A careful survey of the whole literature covering non-factorial as well as factorial studies fails to reveal any strong claimants, apart from the two factors already discussed, and while, of course, the possibility can never be ruled out that further factors may be found, it is not apparent to the present writer just what ground would be left for these factors to cover. Consequently, it is believed that we have at hand a fairly complete description of the total content of the universe of social attitudes.

CHAPTER VIII

THE ANALYSIS OF CORRELATIONS BETWEEN PERSONS

ALL THE RESEARCHES discussed so far deal entirely with cor-relations between tests. In this chapter we shall be concerned with factorial studies in which correlations are run, not between tests but between persons, or, alternatively, even within a single person from one occasion to another. The general possibilities and inter-relationships of these different approaches are well illustrated by Cattell's Covariation Chart, which is given below as Fig. 33. This diagram

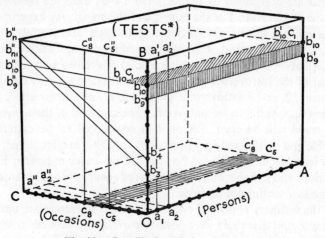

Fig. 33.—Cattell's Covariation Chart.

presents a system of rectangular co-ordinates in three dimensions, arbitrarily truncated. The co-ordinates do not represent continua, but rather a population of points arranged in serial order. Along OA lies a series of persons, a_1, a_2, etc. ; along OB lies a series of personality tests, b_1, b_2, etc. ; and along OC lies a series of occasions of testing, c_1, c_2, etc.

Cattell discusses in great detail the possible types of correlation to which this general scheme can give rise, but in fact the only three which have been used are correlations between tests, correlations between persons, and correlations between occasions. It is the latter two types of correlations with which we shall here be concerned.

Before turning to a discussion of the various researches employing these methods, it will be necessary to devote a few lines at least to a discussion of the principles underlying these new methods. Such a discussion is necessary in the first place because text-books on statistics hardly ever deal with the possibility of correlating persons or occasions, and, secondly, because a fair amount of difficulty and misunderstanding has arisen in the literature because of failure to appreciate the very simple fundamental points which determine the proper use of these procedures.

Let us begin with correlations between persons. In a typical rating experiment of the type discussed in a previous chapter, we might have a series of persons rated on a seven-point scale on, say, six traits. The results from such a small-scale experiment might then be represented by a rectangular array of ratings as in Table 38. Persons are designated by numbers from 1–9; traits are designated by letters from A–F. For the purpose of this imaginary experiment, we have taken three traits (sociable, humorous, and tactful) which we may consider typical of the extraverted person, and another three traits (ambitious, reserved, and irritable) which we may consider typical of the introverted person. Of our subjects we may consider persons 1, 2, and 3 extraverted; persons 7, 8, and 9 introverted, and persons 4, 5, and 6 to be ambiverted. The meaning of the figures as they stand will be clear. Person 1 is considered to be extremely sociable and tactful and very humorous; he is not at all reserved, nor is he irritable or ambitious. Person 7 is the exact opposite; he is ambitious and irritable and rather reserved; definitely not humorous, and neither tactful nor sociable.

In the ordinary course of events, we would intercorrelate our six traits and find that there were positive correlations between traits A, B, and C, that there were positive correlations also between traits D, E, and F, but that the correlations between these two groups of traits tended to be negative. If we should factor analyse this table of correlations, we would get a very strong bipolar factor, which we would presumably identify with extraversion-introversion.

What would happen if we were to intercorrelate the columns in the table of marks rather than the rows? Let us neglect for the moment any statistical difficulties that might arise and concentrate on the logical meaning of a correlation, which means simply a tendency of two things to vary together in the same direction. Now, clearly persons 1, 2, and 3 are correlated in this sense, because where one has a high rating the others tend to have a high rating, and where one

TABLE 38

Traits	E			A			I		
	1	2	3	4	5	6	7	8	9
A Sociable . . .	1	2	3	1	7	1	5	6	7
B Humorous . . .	2	1	1	6	5	2	7	5	5
C Tactful . . .	1	3	2	5	6	7	6	7	6
D Ambitious . . .	5	6	7	2	1	6	1	2	3
E Reserved . . .	7	5	5	3	2	5	2	1	1
F Irritable . . .	6	7	6	4	3	4	1	3	2

has a low rating the others tend to have a low rating too: similarly for persons 7, 8, and 9. When we compare these two groups of persons we again find a tendency for covariation to take place, only this time correlations are negative—where persons in the first group have high ratings, persons in the second group have low ratings, and vice versa. Persons 4, 5, and 6 are intermediate between the other two, and would correlate only to a very low degree with either persons 1, 2, and 3 or persons 7, 8, and 9. If we actually calculated the correlations, we would find again a pattern of positive and negative correlations, which would give rise to two groups of people whom we might call extraverts and introverts.

These results are clearly implicit in the set-up of the table, and show that whichever method of approach we use the results reached would be very similar. That, indeed, is as it should be, as in both cases we would be analysing the same table of marks. If we had carried out our analysis of correlations between tests—a procedure which we shall from now on call T analysis—we could have calculated factor scores on our introversion-extraversion factor for the persons, which would have grouped them in the same way as did the factor saturations derived from our table of intercorrelations between persons—a type of analysis we shall call P analysis. Conversely, from the P analysis, factor scores could have been calculated for the traits which would have grouped those in much the same way as did the T analysis.[1]

[1] The question of nomenclature in this field has become rather difficult, several different letters being applied to the various procedures. T analysis (correlations between tests) is called R technique by Burt. P analysis (correlations between persons) is called Q technique by Stephenson, who also used the term "inverted factor analysis". O analysis (correlations between occasions) is called P technique by Cattell, who in turn uses O technique to designate yet another type of correlational procedure, namely the "monovariate correlation of occasions", which he contrasts with "intra-individual covariation", i.e. what we have called O analysis. The position is so confused, the same letter being used for quite different procedures by different writers, that the simplification suggested here seemed to offer the only method of giving a straightforward account of the numerous researches in the field.

So far, then, there seems to be little that is novel in intercorrelating persons. If the correlation between two persons is positive, it means that with respect to the test material used they behave in a similar manner, whereas if the correlation is negative it means that with respect to the test material used they behave in a dissimilar manner. If the test material consists of trait ratings of introversion and extraversion, then clearly extraverts will correlate together, introverts will correlate together, and extraverts will correlate negatively with introverts.

It will be noted that in each example we correlated persons, not with respect to tests but with respect to trait ratings. The reason for this is a very simple one. To calculate a correlation between two persons we must find the average and the standard deviation of each column of figures in Table 38, and this is admissible only if these figures form part of a *metric continuum*. The existence of such a metric continuum cannot be assumed but must be demonstrated. In the case of personality ratings, this can, with some show of reason, be done by assuming with Stephenson (1935) that the traits rated differ for each person with respect to their *significance* for that person. By this is meant that given a universe of traits, some are very representative of a person, others less so, and still others fail to be representative of him in any way. Sociability, sense of humour, and tact would be representative of, or significant for, the typical extravert; ambitiousness, reserve, and irritability would not. For the introvert, the opposite would hold. Consequently, we may reasonably assume the columns in each table of marks to represent a metric continuum, and we would therefore be able to calculate averages, standard deviations, and correlations.

No such assumption could be made if we were dealing with different tests all having scoring systems differing one from the other, and being wholly arbitrary. Thompson (1939) takes as an example a set of four tests—formboard, dotting, absurdities, analogies—for each of which the experimenter has devised some kind of scoring system. In the formboard test he will give a maximum of 20 points; in the dotting test the score might be the number of dots made in half a minute, etc. "To find the average of such different things as this is palpably absurd, and the whole operation can be entirely altered by an arbitrary change, like taking the number of seconds to solve the formboard instead of giving points. . . . This is a very fundamental difficulty, which will probably make correlations between persons in the general case impossible to calculate."

While the existence of a metric continuum may frequently be difficult to prove, there is one method of experimentation which is free from the difficulties raised in this connection, and that is the method of *ranking*. If what we have called the "tests" can be put in some kind of order by each person with respect to significance, applicability, or preference, then we can safely calculate the correlations between persons, and it is indeed with respect to this type of procedure that most of the work in this field has been carried out. The figures in Table 38 are ratings rather than rankings, but it can be seen that they could, without any difficulty, be converted into rankings, and indeed the possibility of such conversion is essential if we are to carry out correlations between persons with any semblance of statistical justifiability. The first research reported in the literature to make use of correlations between persons based upon rankings was carried out by Thompson and Bales (1926), in which correlations were calculated between teachers who marked the essays of school-boys on a certain topic. Approximations to general factor saturations were calculated by correlating each teacher's ratings with the average of all the teachers. Other workers also used correlations between persons almost from the beginning of correlational study in psychology, but it was not until Beebee-Centre (1933) applied factor techniques to such correlations that the issues relating to these problems became clarified.

In the fifteen years that followed, a number of papers have been published on this topic, and a number of articles written specifically dealing with methodological questions. Yet all the researches carried out to date, with few exceptions, are merely programmatic or illustrative; they are presented with the intention of showing the possibilities inherent in the method, but they hardly ever go beyond this to actually apply the method so as to release these putative virtues. Illustrations are therefore all that can be given at this stage, and we may begin with studies carried out by Stephenson, who has perhaps made larger claims for P technique than almost any other writer. His terminology is somewhat unusual. He calls the technique of intercorrelating persons either "Q" technique or "inverted" factor analysis, although the latter term has given rise to a good deal of confusion, both logically and mathematically. As Burt (1940) has pointed out, the theorems required for the analysis of correlations between persons are not inversions of those used in analysing correlations between tests, but are identical with them; similarly, the matrix of marks analysed is not the *inverse* of but a *transpose* of that from which correlations between tests are usually derived.

The claims made by Stephenson for "P" technique, although far-reaching, are somewhat difficult to follow. He says: "It is usual to regard factorial analysis as an inductive procedure for surveying the structure of more or less uncharted regions in psychology. . . . Q-technique, on the other hand, is most usefully employed to test psychological hypotheses; it is a system of devices, which . . . serves to affirm the conclusions already reached, but requiring proof. . . . The technique appears to be particularly apposite to the study of personality. It neatly represents the self even if in a statistical fashion. The underlying functions are so complex that probably they can be represented in no other way. It provides, I fancy, by far the best framework into which to fit typology in general, whether Jungian, Freudian, Rorschachian, or any other. . . . It allows us to handle the psychologist's theories about personality, even if, in the last resort, it means studying the psychologists themselves rather than their human subjects." Perhaps a review of some of the studies employing this technique may help us to see to what extent these claims are justified.

In one of his earlier papers, Stephenson (1939) selected 46 men and women, 18 of whom he considered extraverted in tendency, 16 introverted, with the others demonstrating neutral tendencies. "The 46 men and women are in no sense a random sample of individuals; nor is there any methodological reason why they should be, for in work of the present kind, where persons are used as variables, they can be selected on other than purely sampling grounds." These persons were rated by Stephenson himself on a list of 176 traits, according to a standard system of frequency distribution. It appears that not all the correlations between these individuals were calculated. Correlations were run between the 18 supposedly extraverted persons, and also between the 16 supposedly introverted persons. It is not clear from Stephenson's account whether correlations between the extraverts and introverts were run or not, but in any case they are not given in the paper.

What Stephenson shows is that the people whom he considers extraverted, and whom he himself has rated on the 176 character traits, show positive intercorrelations, and that those whom he considers introverted, and whom he himself has rated, again show positive intercorrelations. As, presumably, his ratings and his classifications of people as extraverted and introverted were not independent of each other, it is difficult to see how such a result could have been avoided. In the absence of intercorrelations between the groups, and of intercorrelations regarding the other subjects of the experiment who were neither extraverted nor introverted, it is rather difficult to discover precisely what purpose the analysis serves. From a set of residual correlations left over after the elimination of the general factor, Stephenson claims to have isolated four further sub-factors corresponding to Jung's thinking, intuitive, sensory, and feeling types, but no evidence is presented to justify this identification.

This study brings out extremely well some of the difficulties involved in P analysis. First and foremost among these difficulties must be put the problem of sampling. If we go back to Table 38, it will be clear that there is only a limited number of possible combinations and permutations arising from the attribution of ratings on six traits to a number of persons. Let us assume as a kind of null hypothesis that all these permutations and combinations are equally likely and occur with equal frequency in the total populations. It is obviously of vital importance that the investigator who starts out with a hypothesis that certain traits are correlated in the total population, and thus form a syndrome like extraversion-introversion, should select a strictly random or stratified sample of the population to disprove the null hypothesis. If he selects the people chosen in terms of his hypothesis, i.e. if he selects from all the possible sets of combinations of traits only those which are in conformity with his hypothesis, then clearly his "proof" will be completely worthless. Any other hypothesis could have been proved with equal ease by suitable selection of subjects.

A selection of persons to be tested in accordance with some sampling procedure is essential in all psychological work. It is probably more important in P technique than in any other because of the considerations set out above, and also because in P-technique we usually deal only with a very small number of people, so that our chances of obtaining biased results are very much greater than when the population is comparatively large, as it will usually be in T technique. When, therefore, Stephenson admits that in his study he has "chosen personalities purposely to bring out as clearly as possible the connections between (his) thesis and Jung's typology", any value which his study might have had is clearly lost and when he adds: "The 46 men and women are in no sense a random sample of individuals; nor is there any methodological reason why they should be, for in work of the present kind, where persons are used as variables, they can be selected on other than purely sampling grounds", he seems completely to lose cognizance of the methodological problems involved in disproving the null hypothesis.

Allied to Stephenson's disregard for proper sampling procedures (a disregard shared by Burt and other writers, as we shall see later), is a failure to consider the problem of rotation and simple structure. In considering the correlations between tests, it has always appeared one of the great weaknesses of British writers that they have accepted without question centroid factors as they emerge from the analysis, in spite of the obvious fact that these factors are not invariant but depend entirely on the sample of tests included in the battery. Clearly, the difficulties to which such lack of invariance gives rise must be exacerbated in using correlations between persons, as any change in the composition of the sample group would change the factor saturations, and consequently the actual factors emerging. It might be possible to use the concepts of simple structure or of criterion analysis in order to rotate centroid factors into a more meaningful pattern, but none of the writers who have used this technique has made any attempt to get away from the factor patterns as originally obtained. Indeed, the very existence of this problem has not, to the writer's knowledge, been discussed before.

If the method used by Stephenson is not such as to command confidence, his results are often difficult to understand or to relate to the claims he makes for them. In one study (1939), Stephenson begins with a discussion of the possibility of gaining insight into temperamental and other personality characteristics of an individual, tested by means of incidental information derived from the reaction to the testing process itself. "The psychologist may direct his attention to the subject's general demeanour, his traits, attitudes, and the like, or to the intimate details of the performance itself. Much will be learned about the individual's personality from both these sources." In order to test this hypothesis, Stephenson drew up a list of 60 qualities observed during the test performance of 40 students. He then intercorrelated 16 of the students (again, we note the selection, on unstated grounds, of a much smaller sample from the total one originally tested), and carried out a factor analysis of the correlations. Three factors, or types, were discovered. "There is little that is surprising in the three types: some are superior performers (type one); others average (type two); and others inferior (type three)." It is not clear how people who are good, medium, and inferior can be regarded as different types in any meaning of that term. Nor can we regard this information as adding very much to that given by the straightforward results of the intelligence tests they were performing. If P technique has a separate function to fulfil in psychology, it does not seem possible to deduce it from studies such as this.

In his more recent work, Stephenson (1950) has contributed further studies to illustrate his method. In one of these, he constructed a set of trait names from everyday life, and another one of trait names used in Rorschach interpretation. Ten men constituted the sample and were rated by Stephenson for 100 Rorschach traits and for 400 everyday traits. Lastly, each of the ten men assessed himself on the 400 everyday traits. Correlations were run between persons for each of these three sets of ratings, and factor analyses performed to show a certain degree of concordance observed between the results. This study seems to confirm results reported from the use of T technique that ratings and self-ratings show a certain amount of correlation; apart from that, it does not add very much to our knowledge.

In a second experiment, Stephenson took a number of traits from Jung's book and had seven members of a post-graduate class make self-appraisals and also assess him (Stephenson) himself. In addition, he also made estimates of himself on these traits. Moderate correlations were found between self-estimates and estimates of the experimenter, a conclusion in line with results discussed in our chapter on ratings.

In summarizing Stephenson's contribution, we must note that all the studies reported by him are merely illustrative, and that until a large scale, properly planned and executed experiment is reported, it must be very difficult to assess his claims objectively. In the studies reported, however, there are certain features, both in the experimental design and the statistical treatment, which throw very great doubt on the results. Among these are the practice of only calculating and presenting part of the necessary data, and the failure to use proper sampling techniques, which, in Stephenson's case, is an error not of omission but of commission, as he claims this failure to be a specific virtue of his approach.

The only example of an application of Thurstone's concepts to the analysis of correlations between persons comes in a paper by Moore, Stafford, and Hsü (1947), which contains an excellent and fair review of the history of what these writers call "obverse analysis". Following on the work of Moore (1939, 1941) and of Hsü (1943) on pre-psychotic temperament and its relation to psychiatric syndromes, an attempt was made to confirm the earlier findings of a resemblance between pre-psychotic traits and psychotic syndromes. This study avoids some of the criticisms to which the work of Stephenson and Burt is subject, particularly errors of sampling and failure to rotate the centroid axes derived from the analysis; it may therefore serve as a reasonable example of what may be expected for psychological analysis from P technique.

One hundred and twenty trait items in all were presented to 56 juniors and seniors in a Catholic Women's College, a group very homogeneous in religion, socio-economic status, age, I.Q. level, race, sex, and educational and ecological background. The subjects were asked to check those questions to which they could give a positive answer. Tetrachoric correlations were calculated between individuals, a procedure which is considered justified by the authors on statistical grounds, although it does leave the question of a proper metric curiously undecided. 1,540 correlations were run between the 56 girls; all of these were positive, ranging from zero to ·95. Nine factors were extracted and rotated into simple structure. "There are nine dimensions in this matrix, but only three of them can be readily interpreted." These three factors were identified as follows: Factor one—"a cycloid or extravert type of personality" marked by such traits as preference for tasks clearly outlined and easily worked at, in which one is likely to succeed; dominant interest in things going on around one; plans and wishes mainly concerned with finding someone who can love and be loved, etc. "This factor reveals an easy-going, presumably well-adjusted personality." Factor two—"A somewhat schizoid or introvert type of individual, marked by such traits as life and actions governed by well-defined purposes, preference for tasks that require a great deal of ambition for their accomplishment, reserving one's opinion about a widely admired person, ready to take vigorous steps to carry out one's plans, preference for being alone sometimes, etc. Here there is evidence of tension and nervous energy, as well as of a certain rigidity and idealism of character." Factor three—"A suspicious type of personality, marked by such traits as intense dislike bordering on hatred for someone, life and actions guided by well-defined purposes, preferring music and art to less æsthetic pleasures, craving for love, ready to take vigorous steps to carry out one's plans, made jealous by a number of persons, has accused others of doing a number of things, suspects others of evil intentions, has superstitious practices, has a tired, worn-out attitude, has vivid dreams, tends to worry while laying awake, talks to oneself, easily influenced, has nightmares, etc. This factor is a marked prepsychotic personality with projection as a major outstanding mechanism." (It is interesting to learn that a tendency to be guided by well-defined purposes, to like music and art, to want to be loved, and to be ready to take vigorous steps to carry out one's plans define a pre-psychotic personality!)

The remaining six factors are not readily interpretable. "They form all sorts of combinations and overlapping of traits. They were tentatively interpreted as ambivert or polivert 'types' of traits, less typical than the factors already mentioned. The factors are oblique. When they are further analysed, a super factor is found . . . [which was] identified as the 'fundamental tendency of human traits', and is to be considered basic to later differentiation and specialization of the traits into typical configurations."

A second analysis was undertaken in which all the non-differentiating items were eliminated according to an arbitrary criterion. "Items were discarded if checked by more than 50 or fewer than 6 of the 56 subjects. There were 38 trait items that were discarded according to this criterion." Again, a factor analysis was carried out of the intercorrelations for this new sample of traits and 11 factors extracted. These are quite different from those of the first analysis. "The factors of the second analysis are more clear-cut than those of the first, in the sense that the persons are less similar to each other than before; hence, more typical patterns might be revealed."

It would be futile to go through all these factors in detail. Typical, perhaps, is the second factor, which consists of twelve girls, each claiming the following traits:

"Prefers tasks that are clearly outlined and easy to work at; is dominantly interested in things going on around her in the world in which she lives; plans and wishes mainly concerned with finding someone whom she can love with all her heart; plans and wishes mainly concerned with finding someone who will love her with deep, abiding devotion.

"This seems to be . . . a normal and adjusted factor, with perhaps more of an extravert tendency, as well as a marked trait of wishing to be in love. It may be identified as a romantic factor or 'type' of person."

To the writer it does not appear that the factors emerging, either from the first or the second analysis, are particularly meaningful or easily interpretable. The fact that in two different analyses of the same persons, and largely the same traits, entirely different sets of factors emerge, must make one feel rather uneasy about the meaning of the resulting factors. When we consider the labour involved in calculating two sets of over 1,500 tetrachoric correlations each, i.e a total of over 3,000 correlations, as well as the time consumed in carrying out the factor analyses of two tables 56 × 56, and all the rotations required to reach simple structure, it seems to the present writer that the ratio of the worth-whileness of data to the refinement of statistical treatment is altogether too low. It is his contention that we have here an abuse of statistical method which cannot be justified by the very limited increase in psychological knowledge which this study gives us. P technique may have a contribution to make to psychology, but if so, hypotheses will have to be stated clearly and deductions made which can be proved or disproved; the type of analysis exemplified by Moore, Stafford, and Hsü's paper is not likely to convince readers of the usefulness of this technique.

One more word should be said about the "super factor" discovered in this research and discussed at some greater length in another paper by Stafford and Hsü (1947). These authors link it up with the super-factor found by Moore (1933), which, it will be remembered, was extracted from the correlations of the syndromes of both schizophrenic and manic-depressive patients. "This leads immediately to the interpretation that such a super-factor reflects human personality traits taken as a whole, the fundamentals of which are in a sense more basic to psychotic syndromes than the syndromes themselves. A psychotic syndrome may thus be regarded as something that becomes more differentiated later in life rather than a basic constitutional tendency. The super-factor would correspond more properly to such a basic tendency . . . one would expect to find this same super-factor in the pre-psychotic personality." The writer cannot follow this argument, which would appear to identify a super-factor found from intercorrelations between persons with the super-factor found from intercorrelations between tests. As will be shown below, the factorial resolution of a set of marks is unchanged whether that matrix is analysed by rows or columns, *except* for any general factor between persons (which would not appear in the correlations between tests), or the general factor in the intercorrelations between tests (which would not appear in the intercorrelations between persons). Consequently, it does not seem possible or reasonable to interpret these two "super-factors" as being identical because by their very method of extraction they must be interpreted quite differently if, indeed, any reasonable interpretation of them is possible.

It might be thought from these comments that the technique of correlating persons is of comparatively little importance in psychology. That impression would be erroneous. There are certain problems which require a technique of this kind. To take but one example: if we are interested in a study of individual differences in strength of imagery, it would be very difficult to judge the relevant vividness of one person's images as compared to those of another, but it is quite easy for a given person to rank in order of vividness for himself the different types of imagery (auditory, visual, kinæsthetics, etc.), and then to correlate one person with another. An experiment along these lines was reported by Burt (1938), who took 12 persons and subjected them to a questionnaire which required them to grade according to degree of vividness their mental images of about 100 different experiences. Correlations were run between the persons, and a general and three group factors discovered. The general factor shows that there is a tendency for most people's visual imagery to be stronger than their auditory imagery and for their auditory imagery to be stronger than their motor imagery. The three group factors could be identified with visual, auditory, and motor imagery respectively.

While, from the point of view of methodology, this research again exemplifies the error of biased sampling (Burt chose four persons of predominantly visual, auditory, or motor imagery from the total number of students), it does illustrate the possibilities of factorial analysis in connection with correlations between persons when correlations between traits would be difficult if not impossible. It also illustrates another point, which is extremely important, namely the emergence from a matrix of intercorrelations between persons of a general factor which could not have been found in an analysis of intercorrelations between traits.

This last statement requires some explanation. In the hypothetical example given in Table 38, in which an attempt was made to exemplify the kind of problem attacked by Stephenson, the marks in the body of the table were chosen in such a way that a bipolar factor would result from the intercorrelations whether between persons or between tests. In that case, factors are similar, if not identical, regardless of the method of intercorrelation employed. The position is quite different when the first factor to emerge from the marks is a general factor, i.e. a factor having no negative saturations. In that case, this factor is unique to either the matrix of intercorrelations between persons or the matrix of intercorrelations between tests. The general factor discovered by Burt in the above example is specific to the matrix of intercorrelations between persons, and would not have been observed if the tests had been intercorrelated. The reason for this is, of course, quite simple. The meaning of the general factor, psychologically, is that for all persons visual imagery tends to be the strongest and motor imagery tends to be the weakest. When we correlate persons, this factor must appear; when we correlate tests of differences in general vividness of imagery, we start by scoring each test from its own average, thus effectively eliminating the general differences in strength and thereby the general factor which depends on these.

The converse of this general proposition is equally true. If there is a general factor in the intercorrelations between tests, it would not appear if we intercorrelated persons, because again it would be lost in the process of averaging employed in calculating these correlations. Spearman's "g" could never have been found by intercorrelating persons, because in correlating persons the differences in general ability which give rise to "g" are averaged out. Thus, there are factors in the intercorrelations between persons which are not deducible from intercorrelations between tests, and, similarly, there are factors in the intercorrelations between tests which are not deducible from the intercorrelations between persons.

We may say, therefore, that if the process of correlating persons has any major and novel significance in the field of personality study, it must lie in the fact that it gives rise to factors which could not have been discovered in any other way, i.e. general factors describing overall similarities between people's reactions. The only field in which large-scale efforts have been made to apply these principles is that of æsthetic judgment, and a brief description of some of the findings may be of interest in itself, in addition to serving as a clarification of the theoretical discussion given above.

Most of the studies described are very similar in the methodology employed. A number of stimuli (portraits, landscapes, poems, photographs, colours, pictures of statues, vases, pieces of music, etc.) are presented to the subjects, who rank them in order of preference; correlations are then run between these individual orders of preference and the resulting table of correlations is factor analysed. The work of Beebee Center (1933), Stephenson (1935), Williams, Winter and Woods (1938), Dewar (1938), and many others has shown that there appears to exist a general tendency for the individual judges to agree in their rankings, thus giving rise to a general factor in each case. The literature has been reviewed by Davis (1939), who also points out that: "Since in most published investigations an overwhelming proportion of the variance proves to be attributable to the first factor, it is not surprising to find that the saturation coefficients for secondary or specific factors generally have *little* or *no* statistical significance." It follows from this that people in general agree in their preferences, but that it is difficult to discover groups of people sharing special preferences, i.e. types of artistic appreciations. The interest of all this work, then, being mainly concerned with the general factor, we must ask ourselves how this can be interpreted. Burt, under whose direction several of these researches were carried out, appears to consider that they provide evidence for a general factor of artistic capacity or "taste". Such a conclusion, however, does not follow from the results of these studies, there being two main fallacies involved—one methodological, the second statistical.

In the work on which Burt bases his conclusion, the tests employed were of a very heterogeneous nature, ranging from items having very high æsthetic value to items having very little or none at all, like cheap Christmas cards, etc. With tests of this type, it is impossible to rule out the influence of knowledge, teaching, conventionality, and so on, all of which may determine the preference judgments actually expressed by the subjects. Expressed preference for a cheap, pretty-pretty Christmas card over what is known to be an acknowledged work of art requires personality qualities over and above the factor of taste, or rather lack of it, measured by this test. In the absence of experimental proof that such additional factors are not active in the judgments of subjects, we cannot accept evidence from an omnibus test of this kind as giving a true indication of an individual's æsthetic judgment.

The statistical objection to such an identification is even more decisive. As we pointed out before, Spearman's "*g*" could not have been discovered from an analysis of intercorrelations between persons, but only from an analysis of intercorrelations between tests. Similarly, a general factor of taste would be analogous to "*g*" in that it could only be proved to exist by intercorrelating *tests*. All that we can show from intercorrelating *persons* is that with respect to the items under investigation, there is agreement among the subjects in their order of preference; we can go on from there to show that some persons show greater agreement with the majority than do others, or, to put it differently, that some persons have higher factor saturations than others. This, however, will only be equivalent to showing in the cognitive field that some people are better at solving a particular kind of problem than others. It can obviously not establish a general factor of taste, just as little as the demonstration that some people are better than others at a given cognitive task can establish the existence of a general factor of intelligence.

A study designed to obviate these criticisms was carried out by Eysenck (1940, 1941). Eighteen tests altogether were constructed, each consisting of æsthetic objects of a certain type (landscapes, book bindings, vases, masks, Japanese paintings, statues, portraits, etc.). Taking each test separately, correlations were calculated between the rankings by the subjects of the items in the test, and the rankings correlated and factor analysed. The resulting factor saturations for each person were then used as his scores on each test, and the 18 tests intercorrelated and factor analysed. Correlations were nearly all positive, showing that a person who agrees well with the others in one test tends also to agree well with the others in the remainder of the tests, while a person who shows little agreement with the others in one test tends to show little agreement with the others on the remainder of the tests. Thus there does appear to exist a genuine general factor of æsthetic appreciation which is free from the statistical objections raised before. An attempt was also made in this study to obviate the methodological criticism mentioned above. Items in any one of these sets were selected in such a way that none of the subjects could have judged on the basis of prior knowledge of the esteem in which the item was held by persons more knowledgeable than himself. This was achieved in various ways. In some sets (vases, embroidery) knowledge of expert opinion was completely lacking in the subjects, so that it could not have affected their judgment. In other cases, all the items included in the set were by the same artist, e.g. pictures by Claude Lorraine, so that again the name of the artist could not help the subject in discriminating between the items. In these various ways, the factor of knowledge was excluded as far as possible, and it seems that the only conclusion that can be drawn from the data is that there does exist a general factor of æsthetic ability, which was labelled a "taste" or "T" factor by Eysenck.[1]

A similar approach to the above was used in investigating the possible existence of type factors in the æsthetic field. Five tests (two tests using landscape paintings, one using portraits, one using photographs of statues, and one using landscape photographs) were used.

[1] The correlation between T and intelligence was found to be negligible. A much more detailed discussion of the results, as well as of possible criticism, is given by Eysenck (1942). This paper also relates æsthetic appreciation to more general laws of perception, and summarizes the literature only briefly quoted here.

Correlations between persons were run for each of the tests, and two factors extracted in each case. Using a person's factor saturations on these factors as his scores on each of the tests, the five tests were correlated for factors I and II separately. The factor I correlations gave rise to the T factor mentioned in the preceding paragraph; the factor II correlations gave rise to another factor which was called "K", and which ran through all the five tests. This factor differentiated those persons who liked modern art, bright sunny photographs, and statues by Kolbe, from those who liked the older masters, cloudy, foreboding photographs, and the statues of Maillol and Barlach. An attempt was made to account for this factor in terms of Hornbostel's work on intersensory perception, in which he found evidence for a "brightness" factor which was apparent in music, vision, and other sense modalities.

The factor K was found to be correlated with extraversion-introversion and with radicalism-conservatism, in the sense that preference for modern art was more prevalent among the extraverts and the radicals. Age was also found to be correlated with the K factor in the expected direction, and when a colour-form test was administered to the same subjects an almost significant correlation was found between liking for modern art and colour preferences. These results, while only tentative, indicate the possibilities inherent in æsthetic preference judgments as indirect measures of personality. Later experiments have verified some of these conclusions (Eysenck, 1947).

Equally promising as tests of æsthetic appreciation appear to be tests of appreciation of humour, where again correlations between persons have been used by several writers, particularly Eysenck (1942, 1943, 1947) and Williams (1945). Essentially, tests used by these writers consist of jokes, limericks, humorous verses, humorous pictures with captions, cartoons, etc., which are ranked in order of "funniness" by the subjects concerned. Intercorrelations among persons are usually rather low, averaging between ·1 and ·2. Nor can we duplicate the findings from investigations into æsthetic appreciation according to which persons having high-factor saturations on one test also have high saturations on others. When five such tests were intercorrelated by Eysenck (1943), the intercorrelations averaged only ·04. In a similar study by Williams (1945), the first-factor saturations for three tests again only showed insignificant correlations. It would not appear, therefore, that the first or "general" factor is of any great interest or importance in work on the organization of personality.

The position is quite different with respect to a second bipolar factor which emerged from the tests used by both these writers, and which bears an interesting similarity to a factor found by Kambouropoulou (1926) in her analysis of diary entries, joke tests, etc. This factor was considered by her to divide personal from impersonal aspects of humour, i.e. those aspects which are *orectic* (dealing with the affective and conative side of personality) from those which are *cognitive*. The orectic type of humour is largely concerned with jokes dealing with sex, with superiority, and generally which depend on personal empathy of one kind or another, whereas impersonal, or cognitive, jokes depend on incongruity of ideas and quite generally on the more formal aspects of humour. Kambouropoulou (1930) found that "the more extraverted subjects have a greater proportion of the superiority class among the items they find most amusing. Extraversion and preference for the superiority class of humorous items go together."

This suggestion was fully confirmed by Eysenck (1947) and Williams (1945). The former, working on the hypothesis that hysterics could be used as a prototype of extraversion, dysthymics as a prototype of introversion, tested the hypothesis of a correlation between extraversion and preferences for orectic humour by asking 25 male and 25 female hysterics, and 25 male and 25 female dysthymics, to rate 60 cartoons for their funniness. Some of the cartoons exemplified orectic humour, others exemplified cognitive humour, and the results abundantly bore out the original hypothesis. Williams (1945) assessed the temperament of her subjects by means of the Rorschach test and found that "there is here a fairly close correspondence between introversion and impersonality in attitude to humour appreciation, and between extraversion and the personal attitude to humour". These various studies, then, are in excellent agreement on the correlations between type of humour preferred and personality, and we may conclude that here we have a promising tool of research.

In evaluating this work on æsthetic appreciation and sense of humour, however, it should be borne in mind that the factors which were found to be related to personality were not the general factors, which could only have been obtained by means of correlations of persons, but the bipolar or type factors which could have been obtained just as easily by intercorrelating tests or test items. In other words, it is doubtful if these studies can be taken to support the claims made for P technique as a particularly valuable form of methodology in personality research.

On the other hand, these studies do illustrate a point which may lead one to view P technique in a slightly more favourable light. Admittedly the same principles of classification (e.g. personal versus impersonal, or orectic versus cognitive sense of humour) could have been discovered by intercorrelating jokes rather than persons. However, many jokes are not particularly characteristic of the extremes of this bipolar factor, and as the number of jokes which could be intercorrelated is strictly limited, by virtue of the enormous amount of time and energy involved in the calculation and analysis of large tables of correlations, it might easily have occurred that few if any of the jokes included were particularly characteristic of this dichotomy. This would have led, in the end, to a rather inconclusive analysis. The method of intercorrelating persons and including a very large number of variegated jokes appears to be much more likely to suggest profitable divisions in the complex mass of material, and it does so with very much less labour. Also we have the additional advantage of being able to cross-check the hypothesis of factorial identity from one study to another by correlating the factor saturations of our subjects. The division between R and T analysis, therefore, might be made most advantageously in terms of the specific problem which confronts the investigator and the particular stage of development or lack of development of the field which he is investigating. When reasonable hypotheses are at hand, correlations between persons are not likely to be very helpful to him. When the field is very inchoate, however, and the material lends itself to some form of ranking procedure, P technique is a quick and simple way of formulating preliminary hypotheses and going some way towards verifying them. From this point of view, P technique would have a very definite rôle to play.[1]

We must now turn to an even more recent and novel procedure in the factorial field, in which there is only one subject and where the items correlated are different occasions on which tests were given or ratings carried out. The first suggestion for studies of this kind comes from Baldwin (1942, 1946), who calls his method "personal structure analysis", from Cattell (1943, 1947) and from Primoff (1943). As what is being correlated are different occasions when tests or ratings are being carried out, we shall call this method "O" technique, to bring it in line with "P" and "T" technique.

---

[1] As a further example of this "suggestive" function of factor analysis, the studies of Eysenck (1940) and Gunn (1951) on preferences for poetry may be mentioned.

Baldwin in his paper uses letters written by one subject in the course of her life. His analysis is based on two assumptions. The first is that "the frequency of an item in the case material is a measure of its importance in personality". The second is that "the contiguity of two items, if repeated sufficiently often to exclude the hypothesis that the contiguity is due to change, indicates a relationship in the personality". An analysis of contiguity was therefore carried out, although this was not actually expressed in terms of correlation coefficients but rather in terms of contingency tables, which were tested for significance.

In a later paper, Baldwin (1946) much improved on the crude methods used in his first paper, and employed both correlations and factor analysis in his work. He begins by defining an intra-individual correlation coefficient as "a measure of the relationship between two variables (from time to time) within the behaviour of a single individual". He goes on to say that "by the factor analysis of a table of such intercorrelations, the patterns of variables within the single individual may be delineated. Such an analysis provides an objective method for the integration of behavioural observations into a concept of individual personality structure."

As an example of his intended procedure, he presents a figure (Fig. 34) showing the temporal curves of a hypothetical individual on two variables. It will be seen that the two curves fluctuate together, and are therefore correlated if this correlation is taken over the twenty days of observations. The correlation between A and B within the individual, therefore, would be positive; the contribution of this individual to a group correlation would, however, be in a negative direction because he is above the mean on one variable and below on the other.

Baldwin faces the statistical difficulties raised by the lack of independence of the various observations which comprise his sample. Following statistical procedures worked out, particularly by economists, he removes the temporal trend, which is responsible for this lack of independence by intercorrelating it with the other variables and rotating the axes of the factor analysis in such a manner as to place one of them right through this variable. In this way, all variance due to time trend is taken up by the first factor, and all other factors are independent of it.

We may now describe his actual research. Using the Fels Child Behaviour Scales, he had four children rated every day on the 30 items making up this scale over a period of 20 days. These items were correlated within each individual, thus giving rise to four matrices of intercorrelations (one for each child). These were factor analysed by Holzinger and Harman's "averoid" method, and the factors rotated, as has been explained above, in such a way that the first axis passes through the time variable. Also available were the results of a factor analysis carried out in the usual way, i.e. by correlating the 30 items over a large group of children. (This analysis has already been discussed in a previous chapter.)

The factors isolated were, first of all, a factor of temporal change.

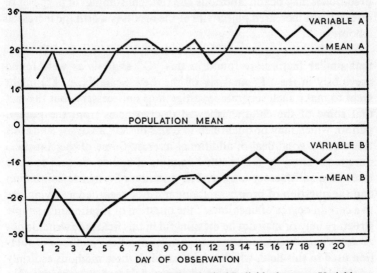

Fig. 34.—Temporal Curves of a Hypothetical Individual on two Variables.

The scales which had loadings on this factor were found to include almost all those variables which had high loadings on the factor of *desirability* in the original group analysis. "The factor was labelled 'desirability' because it seemed to express the general concept held by nursery school teachers of the 'good nursery school child'. In view of the high correlation of these variables with time, it would appear that the usual nursery school child goes through an adjustment process, during which time his behaviour tends towards the 'desirable'."

The second factor is also similar for the various children analysed and is labelled "conformity". The existence of such a conformity factor would seem to indicate that the nursery school situation sets up certain standards which the child is expected to meet. He must react to these expectations of conformity, and so he can hardly avoid having a definite personality trait related to the problem of conformity . . . this is a pattern description of conformity; non-conformity appears in the majority of the individual cases and in the group analysis." A third factor was extracted for the various children but showed no similarity between them, and is consequently difficult, if not impossible, to interpret.

Baldwin sums up his work as follows: "This method is devised as a research tool and though as a practical routine method of interpretation it may be too laborious and time consuming for purposes of research, the increased objectivity of the results is worth the increased labour."

With this, the present writer would emphatically agree. The fact that similar factors are found in this "O" analysis as were found previously in the "T" analysis of the Fels Scale (cf. p. 82) might seem to make such separate investigations unnecessary, but the fact that some of the children showed discrepancies from the general pattern which may be quantified in terms of "O" analysis, lends this technique a good deal of additional interest. Some of the statistical questions raised by this method cannot, of course, be said to have received a satisfactory answer. The question of a metric continuum and the question of proper sampling must be regarded as giving rise to a certain degree of uneasiness; the question of rotation into simple structure may or may not be meaningful in this field; the writer is not aware of any discussion trying to justify any of the methods of rotation used in this field, which might establish these methods as firmly as simple structure is established in the fields of T technique. No confident judgment can be made, therefore, of the feasibility or the possible usefulness of this technique.

A much more enthusiastic view of the possibility of this new approach is held by Cattell (1947), who considers it "to have the promise of a systematic new approach, additional to, and perhaps as important as, the familiar 'R' technique, or its successor 'Q' technique". In its main outline his view of this technique is similar to Baldwin's. "Essentially it is a method for applying experimental measurement with co-variational analysis to the single case. This means that one person must be measured on a collection of tests on a series of occasions. The analysis is then made on coefficients obtained from the correlations of traits in which the unit of entry is a day (or hour) of observation." This technique, he considers, "has particular promise in dynamic and clinical psychology, where it can, at least in principle, cope with those problems of discovering unique dynamic structure, which some psychologists have claimed to lie beyond the experimental and statistical approach".

In his approach Cattell adopts an order of importance which to the present writer seems somewhat unusual. "Some theoretical considerations of a narrowly statistical nature remain to be considered in developing this new method, but it would be inappropriate to debate these in any detail until the basic questions have been answered. The latter concern whether the correlations obtained in this way transcend chance error, whether they yield factors having psychological meaning and interest, and whether the factors are of the same general nature as the 'R' technique personality factors." It might be that before a new technique is seriously considered and used, it would be best to clear up such fundamental points as the choice of metric, the lack of independence of the various observations comprising this sample, and the problem of sampling itself. In the absence of such statistical discussion, the meaning of correlations calculated must remain somewhat obscure and doubtful.

In Cattell's first experiment, a normal 20-year-old woman was used as a subject; for 55 days almost consecutively this subject was (1) measured on the same batch of test variables; (2) rated by close observers on personal behaviour; and (3) self-rated on a personality questionnaire. Correlations were carried out in the first place between the objective tests only, and four factors extracted from the table of intercorrelations. These are called (1) emotional abundance versus emotional dearth; (2) physiological ease versus emergency alertness; (3) fatigue versus energy reserve; (4) uncontrolled versus inhibition. These interpretations can be accepted only with some reserve, but the reader must consult the original publication, as a detailed discussion would be too lengthy in this place (Cattell, *et. al.*, 1947).

Scores were next given to each of these factors, and they were intercorrelated in a single matrix with the rated and self-rated personality factors. Five factors were again obtained, which are identified with five factors previously obtained by Cattell in his studies of ratings summarized in a previous chapter. Again the writer feels somewhat doubtful about the interpretations. To give but one example, the first factor obtained from the analysis of the objective tests alone (emotional abundance versus emotional dearth) is characterized by high body sway suggestibility and high P.G.R. deflection; these items, as has been shown in previous chapters, are characteristic of neuroticism. Yet this emotional abundance-emotional dearth test factor now appears in Cattell's second analysis as a factor of "adventurous cyclothymia" versus "withdrawn schizothymia". There is no evidence in the literature that body sway is in any way related to schizothymia-cyclothymia, and in the absence of such evidence identification would seem premature.

Cattell lays great stress on the resemblance of the factors extracted in "O" technique with those extracted in "T" technique. To the present writer there seems to be no very obvious reasons why these factors should be in any way identical. "O" factors are derived from the covariance of traits or tests over a period of time within a single person; the causes which may lead to such covariance, no doubt, are multiform, and may be related to such agencies as general fatigue, physiological changes such as the Menarche, and so forth. It is not unreasonable that in certain chosen batteries of tests, factors corresponding to these causes may be found; on the other hand, if we conceive of a person as having a fundamental neurophysiological constitution, predisposing him to a certain extent towards neurotic breakdown, it is difficult to see why this constitutional factor should be responsible for diurnal covariation. The possibility, of course, cannot be ruled out; during the course of psychiatric treatment, for instance, it is conceivable that a decrease in neuroticism may take place, which would be mirrored in a number of tests defining this factor. If that were to happen, then the same tests which in "T" analysis correlate together to define the factor of neuroticism would perhaps correlate in "O" analysis to define improvement under treatment. Obviously, the whole position is very complex and, in the absence of any sustained attempt to discuss the statistical and theoretical aspects of the matter, little further can with advantage be said.

In a later publication, Cattell and Luborsky (1950) used "O" technique in connection with a neurotic personality. Forty-nine variables were used, including physiological and biochemical measurements, psychological ratings, self-ratings, and objective measures. Fifty-four days constituted the experimental population over which correlations were run between the measures. Nine factors were extracted and rotated into simple structure. The factors extracted are in the main identified with Cattell's primary personality factors, although, again, this identification does not appear to be firmly established to the writer. It is difficult to discuss this research in any detail, as the very large number of variables used and the factors extracted, and the constant reference necessary to previous work, would make such an undertaking a very formidable one indeed.

It will have been gathered that the present writer is less enthusiastic about "P" and "O" techniques than are those who have originated and used them most.[1] Many of the objections which may be brought forward have already been discussed in the course of the text, and it seems that few of them have been answered by the champions of these methods. Neither on the statistical, the methodological, nor the experimental side can any of the published researches be considered faultless. Most of them, particularly those of Stephenson and Burt, were published as examples of the possibilities inherent in such novel techniques; as such they are not at all convincing. Although "P" technique has been in existence for almost twenty years, it has never advanced beyond this stage of giving examples of how useful it might be. In the absence of a properly conducted experiment advancing our knowledge in any respect or throwing some new light on the problems which the technique is supposed to be best equipped to tackle, judgment must be reserved.[2] On the whole, however, the writer believes that while for certain limited purposes correlations between persons and correlations between occasions may, with advantage, be used, these methods are unlikely to supplant, although they may supplement, the fundamental method of "T" analysis.

[1] To the above-mentioned writers we should add Burt and Watson (1951), who analyse one case in detail without adding anything new to the argument, and Hsü (1949), who disapproves of the Baldwin-Cattell methods and substitutes one of his own which cannot readily be considered to be an improvement.

[2] A recent discussion between Stephenson (1952) and Cattell (1952), somewhat reminiscent of an earlier one between Burt and Stephenson (1939), suggests that Cattell and Burt would probably be in agreement with this position. Stephenson still fails to answer the objections to his use of "P" technique, and still makes strong claims for it.

CHAPTER IX

THE ANALYSIS OF TRAIT MEASUREMENTS

Perseveration

P ROBABLY THE MOST widely investigated trait of all those dealt with in this chapter is that of perseveration. Although this term was not coined until 1894 by Neisser, observations of some of the phenomena giving rise to the term can be found as early as Newton, Herbart, Hartley, Malebranche, and even Aristotle. The fundamental property common to all the phenomena concerned has been phrased by Spearman (1927) in terms of general mental law of inertia, which reads "Cognitive processes always both begin and cease more gradually than their (apparent) causes". This law he believes to summarize the varied experimental findings, to be discussed below, while individual differences with respect to mental inertia are hypothesized to underly the various typologies considered in the first chapter, and, indeed, the similarity of the concepts of secondary function and of perseveration is very noticeable.

Let us consider some of the phenomena which have given rise to the various measures of perseveration used. First of all there is what might be called *ideational perseveration*. This phenomenon, according to Aristotle, "occurs when a name or a town or a sentence has come to be much on one's lips; after one has stopped, and without one intending it, one is prompted again to sing or to speak". Allied to this is probably what might be called *emotional perseveration*, which also is described by Aristotle in terms very closely resembling Gross and his theory of secondary function: "Those feel the vexation most who happen to have fluid in the region of the sensory organ, for once the fluid substance is set in motion it is not easily brought to rest until the object sought for returns to mind and the process resumes its direct course. Hence, when they have set something in agitation, emotions of anger and fear, owing to the reaction of these organs, do not come to rest; on the contrary they react once more on them."

Third, in order of historical appearance, is probably the phenomenon of *sensory perseveration*. This is described as follows by Newton:

"If a burning coal be nimbly moved round in a circle, with gyrations continually repeated, the whole circle will appear like fire; the reason of which is, that the sensation of the coal, in the several places of that circle, *remains impressed on the sensorium*, until the coal returns again to the same place." The fourth type of perseveration, which we may call *motor perseveration*, appears first in the work of Heymans and Brugman (1913), who compared speed of writing with speed of writing in reverse, on the assumption that high perseverators would be penalized on the second of these tasks. Motor perseveration was later on found to be of two separate kinds, which are called by Cattell (1935): (a) creative effort perseveration, shown in tests such as the one just mentioned, and (b) alternation perseveration, in which two activities such as writing H and ∞ at maximum speed, first separately and then one alternating with the other, are used, the hypothesis being that perseveration will interfere in this process of alternation.

We must now look a little more closely at the various measures used for these detailed types of perseveration, their intercorrelations and their relationship with other personality variables. As regards ideational perseveration, the work of Muller and Pilzecker (1900) and Foster (1914) showed that there were considerable individual differences in the tendency of subjects to respond incorrectly in an attempt to recall nonsense syllables just learned by responding with syllables that were correct for a series previously learned. In other words, the previously learned syllables apparently perseverated and disturbed the later memory process. Probably much of the later work on such topics as retroactive inhibition might be mentioned here, but in spite of its promise, this approach has not been followed up, and interest has been centred on general laws to the exclusion of individual differences.

Emotional perseveration has not fared very much better. We have already mentioned in the first chapter the work of Kretschmer and Enke (1936), showing great individual differences in the length of time taken by the P.G.R. to return to the normal resting level after an emotional disturbance, and we have also noted the *recovery quotient* originated by Freeman. These appear to be measures of what is usually referred to as emotional perseveration, but, again, hardly any factorial work has been done on them. For the main part, investigators have followed the easier way initiated by Lankes (1915), who used a questionnaire to cover these alleged phenomena.

Most experimental work has been done on sensory and motor

perseveration, with only isolated data on the other varieties available. The earliest work reported in the literature is that of Wiersma (1906) and Heymans and Brugman (1913), all of which dealt with phenomena of sensory perseveration. Wiersma used four tests: firstly the persistence of dark adaptation after a period of exposure to light; secondly, the amount of interference caused by an electric shock on electric stimulus threshold measurements; thirdly a phenomenon akin to the "glowing coal" experiment mentioned by Newton, namely the number of electric sparks per second required to be perceived by the subject as a continuous line rather than as separate sparks; and fourthly, the phenomenon of flicker fusion, which is, of course, akin to that of the sparks and of Newton's "glowing coal". Using very small groups of manics, normals, and melancholics (a group apparently also containing some paranoid patients), Wiersma found a very marked tendency on all tests for the manics to show less perseveration than the normals, and for the melancholic-paranoid group to show more perseveration. Wiersma did not actually use correlations in his work, a fault remedied by Heymans and Brugman (1913), who used six tests including two of motor perseveration. Although their results are less important than they might have been because of the small number of cases involved, the correlations reported by them are, nevertheless, reproduced below (Table 39) because they constitute the first example in the history of psychology of an attempt by means of correlational methods to prove the unitary nature of a hypothetical mental function outside the cognitive field. On the whole, the values are positive, some of them significantly so, while only three values are negative, none of them significant.

TABLE 39

Tests	2	3	4	5	6
1. Colour mixture	·42	·23	·06	·59	·72
2. Flicker fusion	—	— ·12	— ·19	·06	·52
3. Dark adaptation interference . .		—	·66	·47	— ·07
4. Sound threshold interference . .			—	·26	·14
5. Writing forward and in reverse order .				—	·45
6. Mistakes in "tongue-twisters" . .					—

Heymans and Brugman tried to link up their experimental results with independent ratings of primary and secondary function, and found that "we can already go so far as to say that it will be possible to use the after-effects of sensations as a reliable measure of the degree of development of the secondary function". It is interesting to speculate what might happen if their pioneering work had been followed up either on the Continent or in America, both with respect to their method of defining a trait by means of correlational analysis, and also with respect to their attempt to investigate the phenomena of abnormal psychology by means of objective tests. It appears to the present writer that such a course would have led to more important advances than the hundreds of thousands of man-hours devoted to the analysis of questionnaire data and the subjective interpretation of "projective" tests, so called. However, Continental psychologists pursued the whip-poor-will of *Verstehende Psychologie*, and hardly spared one glance of icy contempt for those who would try to attack nature's secrets in such utterly non-philosophical ways, and American psychologists also paid scant attention to this work, although probably for slightly different reasons. It fell to a number of British writers to take up the search, which turned out to be very much more complex and difficult than was at first anticipated.

At Spearman's suggestion, Wynn Jones carried out four tests of motor perseveration on 77 children, obtaining an average intercorrelation of ·492.[1] The four tests used were (1) writing an S, first repeatedly in the usual way and then as it would appear in a mirror; (2) writing digits, first in the usual way and then making the stroke backwards; (3) mirror drawing; (4) first copying prose in the usual way, and then doing so without dotting the i's or crossing the t's. Wynn Jones used the method of tetrad differences to show that the quality common to those four tests was essentially different from that common to a number of tests of intelligence. Spearman concludes that "the evidence that some group factor or factors pervading these tests of perseveration leaves nothing to be desired". Wynn Jones guarded against the possibility that the intercorrelation between the tests might be due to their all being measures of motor dexterity by showing that some tests of motor dexterity, not involving perseveration, had quite negligible correlations. He also (1929) applied his tests to normals, manics, and melancholics respectively, a total of about 50 subjects, with results which threw some doubt on Wiersma's

[1] The results of this research were published a good deal later, and from the point of view of date of publication, the work of Lankes (1915) would precede that of Wynn Jones. We are here following the order given by Spearman (1927), under whose direction all these researches were carried out, rather than the date order of publication.

conclusions. (It should be noted, however, that while Wiersma worked with sensory tests of perseveration, Wynn Jones worked mainly with motor tests. If, as we shall show later on, these two types of perseveration are independent of each other, there is no reason to expect duplication of results. Wynn Jones was working on the hypothesis that motor and sensory tests of perseveration were measuring the same mental function.)

The first writer to use a relatively large number of rather varied tests was Lankes (1915), who explicitly set out to test three types of phenomena: (1) the persistent after effect of a sensory experience; (2) the spontaneous recurrence of an experience; and (3) the subconscious continuance of the effects of past experiences. His tests include examples of sensory, motor, ideational, and emotional perseveration. Also included were estimates of "w", the hypothesis being that perseveration might supply a measure of the functions underlying the persistence of motives and the structure of character denoted by the term "will". The number of subjects (33 students in the preliminary, 47 in the final experiment) was not large, and the intercorrelations are very small. Indeed, most of them are insignificant, although out of 36 only 2 are negative. The correlation of the pool of tests with a questionnaire turned out to have the respectable size of ·41, so that we do seem to have here a certain amount of evidence for the functional unity of the phenomena considered. The correlation between perseveration as measured by these tests and "w", however, turned out to be the opposite of what was expected. The value is $-$ ·26, which on being corrected for attenuation rises to $-$ ·40. The original hypothesis, according to which a positive correlation was expected, would seem to have mixed up perseveration and persistence, and several later studies have confirmed Lankes' finding of a negative correlation between "p" and "w".

The next investigator to study perseverative phenomena was Bernstein (1924), who gave 10 tests to 130 children and who, in addition, made careful observations of the perseveration shown by the children in their ordinary school work. The correlations between the tests were even lower than in the case of Lankes, although still predominantly positive; each of the tests, however, correlated positively with Bernstein's personal estimates of perseveration based on observation, the correlation of the pool of the tests with the estimates being as high as ·51. This value, which is almost unaffected by the elimination of "g", appears high enough to indicate again a certain amount of functional unity in the tests.

Hitherto, although correlations between different tests tended to be rather low, the evidence still favoured the existence of a general factor of perseveration. The two following studies, however, are completely negative with respect to such a general factor. In the first of these two studies, Hargreaves (1927) discovered a factor of fluency of associations (f) manifested in such tests as completing pictures, completing stories, saying disconnected words, and seeing objects in ink-blots. He attempted an explanation of the intercorrelations found in terms of "p", on the hypothesis that those subjects who were more fluent were less hampered by perseveration. Not only did this prove impossible, but he also found that there was no functional unity at all in the tests of perseveration employed by him.

The evidence of Jasper (1931) is even more damaging, as his is probably the most thorough of the studies mentioned so far. He used 16 tests altogether, including a questionnaire, five measures of sensory perseveration, six measures of motor perseveration, and four measures of ideational perseveration. On 80 subjects, the average intercorrelation turned out to be $-\cdot021$, a value which seems to justify his conclusion that "the results of the attempt to measure the perseverative tendency in various kinds of behaviour processes . . . fails to support the hypothesis of a broad group factor of 'perseveration' or 'mental inertia'". He did find some evidence for the existence of a narrow group factor of motor perseveration underlying a number of tests requiring a more or less rapid shift from one pattern of response to another pattern within the same general type of response. He also gave a warning which is an implicit criticism of much of the earlier work by pointing out that "it is necessary that measures of perseveration be developed which will be sufficiently specific for perseveration to eliminate the masking of the perseverative tendency by the many other factors which might influence the score before any absolutely definite conclusions can be arrived at as to the nature or existence of the hypothetical functional unity of 'perseveration!' ".

One of these "many other factors" was found in a study by Rangachar (1932), comparing differences in perseveration among Jewish and English boys. Taking 38 Jewish and 35 English boys, he gave them 7 tests of motor perseveration, having reliabilities from $\cdot76$ to $\cdot92$, and factor analysed the two tables of intercorrelations obtained from the two groups of boys separately. Out of 14 saturations only one was very slightly negative, all the others were positive. He found a high correlation between speed and perseveration due to the formula he used, $H = n_1 - n_2$, i.e. perseveration (hindrance) = the original activity (n_1) — unusual activity (n_2).[1] Correlations decreased, but were still positive when corrected for speed in the n_1 activity. The Jewish boys were found to be quicker but not more perseverative than the English boys.

The next experiment to be mentioned, that of Pinard (1932), is not based on a factorial study, but supplies some evidence for the functional unity of at least some of the traditional perseveration tests by showing a certain amount of correlation between the mean of the test scores and an outside criterion. Using 194 subjects (mainly orphanage school children), he found a distinctly curvilinear correlation between "p" and ratings on various "w" qualities, as is shown in Fig. 7 on p. 49 in diagrammatic form. His actual results are shown below in Table 40. These figures are quite unequivocal, as are similar figures later found by him in 160 adults patients in a mental hospital.

TABLE 40

Number of Cases Rated to have each
Trait

Total No. of Cases in Group	Degree of "p" indicated by Test	Difficult	Self-controlled	Retiring	Sociable	Persevering	Unreliable
46	very high	36	12	16	32	10	38
52	moderately high	10	37	14	33	32	15
46	moderately low	14	33	19	29	33	15
50	very low	39	8	13	32	9	37

Howard (1932) used four tests on 100 children, found a rather low average intercorrelation of ·110, and supported Pinard's finding that the children showing the highest degree of neuroticism tended to be found among those having very high "p" scores; he did not, however, find any such tendencies among children having very low "p" scores. Two further studies of a similar kind are quoted by Spearman (1927), namely those of Maginess and Clarke. The former is said to have found high "p" scores to be associated with poor self-control, lack of concentration, lack of physical energy, and low "w". The latter concluded, on the basis of a questionnaire estimates made by teachers, that "the results of the questionnaire are in agreement with Pinard's finding that the difficult child is frequently an extreme perseverator. The extreme non-perseverator, though appearing among the difficult children more frequently than the average

[1] The n_1 activity might be writing S, writing the alphabet, writing the figure 4, or drawing $\triangle$. The n_2 activity correspondingly would be writing $\int$, writing aAbBcCdD, writing 4 reversing the direction of the stroke, and drawing $\triangledown$.

perseverator, does not emerge from the questionnaire analysis with anything approaching the clearly marked traits of the extreme perseverator."

Stephenson (1932) claims to have found average intercorrelations of ·40 between "p" tests, and to have shown that these intercorrelations satisfy the tetrad criterion, but no detailed figures are given. He also claims to have found a correlation of − ·26 with "g" and to have found a weighted and combined test of "p" to possess a very high reliability. His clinical data in general support Wiersma's findings regarding the manic and depressive illness; in addition, Stephenson claims a very high correlation between "p" and inaccessibility in præcox cases. Cattell's work, which also lends support to the hypothesis of a curvilinear regression of "p" on "w" has already been quoted in an earlier chapter (p. 48).

In a slightly later study, Cattell (1935) pointed out that the notion of motor perseveration involved two separate processes. One of these he called "inertia of mental processes", which is assumed to show itself in the alternation type of test, i.e. in a test where the subject switches to and fro between two interfering alternate ways of performing a task which are otherwise equivalent, such as, write a row of AAAA's, a row of BBBB's, and then a row of ABABAB's. "Here the X and Y activities, as we may call them, *must follow in rapid temporal succession*, producing interference by their momentum, inertia, or after effect." The other concept he calls "inertia of structural disposition", or "disposition rigidity". "This shows itself in 'creative effort' tests in which the score is measured as the difference between performing a task in some old, accustomed fashion and performing it in some new (but not intelligence-demanding) fashion, e.g. writing a row of SSSS's and then a row in which each S is written backwards (ЄЄЄЄ). Here immediate temporal contiguity of the X and Y tasks is not essential, i.e. there is no question of 'inertia of *functioning process*'." This distinction is important but invalidates a good deal of previous work which did not differentiate between these two principles. If we take as an example of disposition rigidity the factor of writing SSSS's, followed by that of writing ЄЄЄЄ's, the relative speed of the second process is used as a measure of perseveration. If, however, we use S and Є as the alternating processes in the "alternation" test type of procedure, then the writing of S and Є separately becomes a measure of the straightforward process. In other words, the number of Є's written may appear either in the numerator or in the denominator of the fraction which defines a

"p" score! This failure to differentiate between these two functions may thus lie at the basis of the many inconclusive results reported. Cattell himself, using six tests on 52 adults, found moderate positive correlations between them; when the tests were applied to 53 ten-year-old children and repeated on 50 fourteen-year-old children, approximate zero correlations were observed. This finding is inexplicable, as previous writers had not found correlations between children lower than correlations between adults. (Other writers who have dealt with the question of scoring of perseveration tests are Darroch (1938) and Walker, Staines, and Kenna (1943), whose writings should be consulted on this rather complex subject.)

Immediately following upon Cattell's study was the work of Shevach (1936). His main interest lay in the field of sensory perseveration, and from the point of view of adequacy of test procedure, his study is probably unequalled. His tests deal with negative after-movement, electric shock sensitivity, cube reversal, adaptation to sound, light, and various other similar measures. Using these on 17 adult subjects, he found an average intercorrelation of ·195 between five of the tests. In a second experiment on 11 students, "the results showed that the same tests might intercorrelate positively when applied to one group of Ss and might yield insignificant or even negative correlations when applied to another group of Ss". Shevach tried to reconcile results by means of the following hypothesis. "The tests yield equivocal results, not because they lack reliability or validity, but because in every group of Ss there are a few in whom perseveration, high or low, is not a general characteristic but varies from one situation to another. The degree of positive intercorrelation between tests of perseveration for a given group would thus depend upon the nature of Ss composing the group." In a third experiment 13 Ss, well known to the experimenter, were subjected to a group of tests, the intercorrelations between which this time averaged ·012· When the variability of Ss was established, it was found that the most variable individuals "are usually in a state of general tension; consider a simple sensation as a world event; cannot rid themselves of gnawing ideas; suffer from excrutiating emotions; are 'nervous' and labile; have moods fluctuating between the extreme poles of pleasantness and unpleasantness. . . . The less variable individuals were those who possessed stable personalities free from intricacy or elaboration." Results obtained from the Woodworth Personal Data Sheet, the Thurstone Personality Schedule, and the Bernreuter Personality Inventory supported these ratings, giving correlations of

·32, ·57, and ·67 respectively between variability and neuroticism. "The personality tests thus indicated that there was a definite relationship between variability and psychoneurotic tendencies." (The test-retest reliability for the variability score was ·73 over a period of three weeks.[1])

In a third experiment, Shevach, using 12 children, verified the existence of a correlation between variability and neuroticism, and also found a correlation of — ·54 between neuroticism and lack of perseveration. "This correlation suggests that when perseveration is manifested as a general characteristic, the greater this degree the less the degree of neuroticism; or that stability is not only a primary condition of the elicitation of perseveration as a general characteristic but also of its degree. The more stable the individual the greater the functional unity of perseveration and the greater the degree of perseveration." Thus, if this correlation based on only 12 cases can be taken seriously, we would have to conclude that sensory perseveration shows a negative correlation with neuroticism where motor perseveration shows a positive correlation. In another experiment still, 12 subjects with particularly low neuroticism scores were given the "*p*" tests, and were again found to show a correlation between variability and neuroticism. It was predicted, on the basis of the relationship between neuroticism and variability, that with these non-neurotic subjects overall variability should be lower and, consequently, correlations between the tests higher. This was not found to be so, the average intercorrelation being — ·015.

Taking together all the findings from this study, we must conclude that they are suggestive but far from conclusive. Even if we disregard the somewhat disingenuous remarks of the author regarding correlations between the same tests being positive in one group and negative in the other (a phenomenon surely not unexpected when the groups consist of so very few cases!), hardly any general conclusions seem to be warranted. The results suggest that sensory perseveration has a slight degree of functional unity, and that variability, with respect to performance on these tests, is correlated with neuroticism. This experiment could well be repeated with a much larger number of subjects. In the absence of such a repetition it is impossible to arrive at any rational conclusion. (It seems possible that considerable progress might be made in the study of perseveration if existing tests

[1] These results fit in well with many others summarized in a later section on "variability" as a personality trait, showing variability to be an excellent measure of neuroticism.

were improved in the way that Biesheuvel (1938) improved on the method of flicker threshold measurement used by previous investigators. Obtaining ratings on a questionnaire dealing with personality traits believed to be connected with perseveration, he selected two groups of perseverative and non-perseverative children respectively, who were shown to differ very significantly with respect to flicker threshold.)[1]

It will have been noticed that most recent students of perseveration have tended to restrict their work either to sensory or to motor tests. A notable exception is the work of Notcutt (1943), who used measures of sensory perseveration, motor perseveration, of both the creative effort and the alternation type, and associative perseveration. Using altogether 15 tests on 50 adults who also supplied self-ratings, he found a complete lack of intercorrelation between his tests of sensory perseveration as well as between his tests of associative perseveration. With respect to motor perseveration (creative effort type) his results were inconclusive, whereas with motor tests of the alternation type he found an average intercorrelation of ·181. When scores were calculated for each of the four alleged types of perseveration respectively, their intercorrelations were all almost exactly zero. Notcutt concludes: "Of all the four types of perseveration discussed in the literature two appear to be non-existent and the remaining two appear to be unrelated to one another."

Cattell (1946) returned to the attack on this puzzling problem of the generality of perseveration by giving seven tests involving entirely the "creative effort" principle, and confined largely to motor performance of 100 women students. The intercorrelations, as usual, are rather low, averaging about ·20, but when a factor analysis was carried out a factor was extracted which, according to Cattell "is clearly the general disposition rigidity factor, highest in reverse writing of letters and numbers, but present also in a perceptual speed test—words written backwards". In a second paper published in the same year, Cattell used perseveration scores derived from this battery and correlated them with ratings of the 100 women students on 10 of his personality factors. Disposition rigidity was found to correlate negatively with dominance (− ·44) and with character integration (− ·34). He goes on to say: "A similar study of 200

[1] The careful work of Weisgerber (1951), who used a similar method of approach to that of Biesheuvel, disproved the hypothesis that conscious perseveration (as measured by questionnaire) was related to the tendency of the autonomic to persist in functioning.

adult men . . . shows among personality factors that E factor (dominance) correlated most highly (negatively) with disposition rigidity measures, followed by G (character integration)." Cattell goes on to show that in view of the other observed correlations it is reasonable to consider "*p*" as a measure of his second-order factor (neuroticism) and that the regression of "*p*" on this second-order factor is curvilinear as found previously by him, Pinard, and others.

In 1949 Cattell and Tiner carried out an experiment on a rather larger scale, administering 17 tests to 100 male college students. The tests included the following: "(*a*) a test of intelligence and of spatial ability to deal with the ability aspect of rigidity in the tests used for rigidity; (*b*) tests of the fluency factor, verbal and nonverbal, which we have given reasons for believing also operates in general rigidity situations and problem solving; (*c*) tests of the 'classical' rigidity factor (*p*-factor), specifically including tests to discover whether it extends beyond the field of motor performance; (*d*) some tests coming under other concepts of rigidity discussed above; (*e*) some tests considered in recent research to be measures of rigidity, but which we consider probably misleading in this rôle".

The first factor to be extracted from this battery is called "disposition rigidity" (perseveration). This identification does not appear too well justified, as a measure of high motor perseveration, which was the average of four tests of the creative effort type previously used, had a saturation of only ·30, which was not much higher than the saturation of a fluency test (·23). Flicker fusion had a much higher saturation on this factor, as had two tests, one of distraction, one of hidden objects, which appear to have little in common with the usual concepts of perseveration. Cattell's second factor is one of spatial intelligence, his fourth is one of fluency, and his third is difficult to interpret. This research is no doubt on the right lines in using a great variety of measures to test their relationship to tests of rigidity and other concepts which may be related to perseveration, but the results are not at all clear in their interpretation.

Most recent of all is a factorial study of tests of rigidity by Oliver and Ferguson (1951), which seems to follow logically from Cattell's attempt to explain the relation of perseveration to tests of this type. Included in the battery were five tests which were thought to measure rigidity in non-motor processes. One of these was a measure containing 60 simple arithmetic problems involving the addition, subtraction, division and multiplication of simple digits. The subject's instructions were that, for the purpose of this test, a plus sign meant subtract, a minus sign meant add, a multiplication sign meant divide, and a dividing sign meant multiply. Another test required the subject to write the letter of the alphabet which came two, three, or four before the one listed, depending on the number written after the letter; for example, M-3 means that the subject must write the letter in the alphabet that is three letters before M. The other three tests were of a similar nature. Also included were the Gottschaldt Figures Test, which had been shown by Thurstone (1944) to be a good measure of his factor of flexibility of closure, and numerical problems test used by Luchins (1948), in which the subject has to solve arithmetical problems involving the measuring out of a given number of pints of water by means of three measures, none of which gives correctly the right amount required. In the first part of the experiment, a set is created leading the subject to use a particular sequence of moves; in later problems an easier solution is possible if the subject can break the set produced in the first few problems.

Ninety-eight students in all were tested and three factors extracted. Two of these factors were considered impure and of no great interest. One of them, however, could "be identified clearly as a rigidity factor, although it may be more appropriate to speak of it as a habit interference factor. This factor has significant loadings on the arithmetic test, alphabet test, opposites test, and on same-opposites. Analysis of the first three of these tests shows clearly that they all involve tasks which are performed against the interfering effects of culturally induced modes of behaviour." Both the Gottschaldt Figures Test and the Luchins Numerical Problems Test were found to have zero saturations on this factor. This paper may be said to have made an important beginning in the factorial study of rigidity, a concept possibly even more involved and complex than that of perseveration. A great deal of research will be necessary before their relationship is likely to be clarified.[1]

This review of work on the concept of perseveration has purposely been given in some detail to show the reader the complexity of the issues involved and the slow and gradual process of clarification which takes place in the course of experimental and factorial work. Starting out with a very definite, far-reaching hypothesis, it was shown quite clearly that the alleged general factor of perseveration broke down into a number of relatively independent factors, such as sensory perseveration, motor alternation perseveration, and dis-

[1] Cf., for instance, the work of Scheier and Ferguson (1952) and that of Kleemeier and Dudek (1950).

position rigidity. This apparently complete lack of inter-relationship between these different types of perseveration makes it meaningless to use the general term at all, seeing that no functional unit of behaviour corresponds to it. Thus, factorial studies have disproved the original hypothesis, and have put in its place a number of rather less far-reaching hypothesis, which in turn are subject to verification or, more likely, alteration. In spite of the apparent simplicity of the original concept, certain difficulties have appeared, both in the construction of tests and in their scoring, which have invalidated many of the other earlier researches. Nevertheless, there appear to be certain trends running through numbers of different studies which cannot easily be dismissed. Observation of a curvilinear relationship between neuroticism and disposition rigidity; the correlation between variability on tests of sensory perseveration and neuroticism; the constant tendency for tests within one of these groups to show slight but definitely positive intercorrelations—all these cannot easily be brushed aside; yet it cannot be claimed either that the position at the moment is a very satisfactory one. The same experimenter using the same technique will often get different results from different samples. From one point of view, this merely illustrates the general difficulty which always occurs in personality research, i.e. the difficulty of unambiguously defining the properties of the sample one is dealing with, or the conditions under which testing takes place. Yet, while this difficulty is universal in personality research, it appears to be particularly crucial in this field, and strictly experimental work seems called for to establish the conditions which are responsible for these changes in test results. On the whole, modern investigators are less optimistic than Spearman (1927), who considered perseveration "the greatest of all the faculties, if by this may be signified the one which has been the most lavish of promise for individual psychology". A more sober judgment would be that while none of the tests used are ready for employment in clinical or industrial practice, and while the notion of a general factor of perseveration has had to be given up, there is little doubt that some relationship does exist between certain groups of so-called perseveration tests and certain personality traits, and that in due course it may be possible to obtain reliable and valid measures of these personality traits by means of the relatively simple and objective tests described in this chapter.

PERSISTENCE

It will be remembered that Hartshorne and May, in their studies in service and self-control, used a number of persistence tests, although they carried out no factorial analyses of the intercorrelations. This pattern has been followed by a number of other writers, who may be mentioned before we turn to proper factorial studies. Cushing (1929) used as a measure of persistence the time an individual persisted in a line of activity, finding an average intercorrelation among different tests of ·42. Howell (1933) used as measures of persistence the subject's response to pain and fatigue, and reported positive correlations between his various tests. He also found persistence to correlate positively with intelligence (·10) and with University grades (·44).

Another prefactorial study is that of Crutcher (1934), who used six tests in all. "Certain difficult tasks were set the subjects, and the time they continued to work at these tasks was taken as evidence of their persistence." The tasks selected called upon quite diverse skills— mechanical, manipulative, numerical, artistic—well suited to the 83 children who formed the experimental group, and almost independent of I.Q. The intercorrelations between the six tests are set out in Table 41. A Spearman-type analysis of the data by means of tetrad differences showed "overlapping of specifics", but, on the whole, Crutcher concluded that "the presence of a general factor is indicated", a conclusion which appears well justified.

TABLE 41

	2	3	4	5	6	Factor Saturations
1. Card houses (manual dexterity)	·45	·56	·48	·49	·49	·73
2. Bolt and nut puzzle (mechanical skill)	—	·71	·37	·29	·41	·71
3. Three nags puzzle (mechanical skill)		—	·47	·23	·50	·76
4. Addition sums (number facility)			—	·33	·64	·70
5. Copying a picture (artistic ability)				—	·30	·51
6. Cancellation of f's (routine activity)					—	·72

(Factor saturations calculated by present writer.)

These studies are typical of many others reviewed by Ryans (1939), most of which appear to support the following conclusions: (1) tests of persistence tend to intercorrelate positively to the extent of between ·2 and ·3; (2) tests of persistence tend to correlate with ratings for persistence; (3) persistence usually correlates positively, but only to a slight extent, with intelligence, and rather more highly with school grades. This last fact has led many writers to identify persistence with the "X" factor found by Alexander (1935) in his analysis of ability and school grades. Of this "X" factor, which was found to run through all the school subjects but through none of the ability measures, Alexander said: "We are suggesting that X must be interpreted as a character factor which exercises an important influence on success in all school subjects. If we were to attach a name to this factor, we should be inclined to call it persistence."

The first factorial study of the hypothetical trait underlying various persistence tests used was carried out in 1938 by Ryans, who gave 18 tests to 40 college students. These tests included examples of all the main types of persistence tests, which may be subsumed under the following groupings: (1) *Ideational Persistence*: (*a*) Persistence against time. (Time spent on word building, i.e. making up words from a set of given letters; insoluble puzzles, i.e time spent on tasks which have no solution, and so forth.) (*b*) Persistence against difficulty. (Difficult writing, i.e. continuing reading of a story where the printing is so arranged that the difficulty of reading becomes greater and greater, e.g. by printing alternate letters in capitals, by omitting punctuation, by running words together, and so on; working against distraction, i.e. reading a text interspersed with interesting pictures, etc.). (2) *Physical Persistence*: (*a*) Persistence against boredom. (Persistence in some physical task which is not in itself painful or creative of discomfort but which is devoid of any intrinsic interest.) (*b*) Persistence against pain, discomfort and fatigue. (Holding one's breath as long as possible, pulling a dynamometer at two-thirds maximum strength as long as possible, or enduring an electric shock as strong as possible, etc.)

Tests of these various types, as well as ratings on persistence, scholastic achievement, self-ratings on persistence, and intelligence measures were intercorrelated by Ryans and three factors extracted. The first factor accounted for 22 per cent. of the variance, and was interpreted by Ryans as a persistence factor. It had high saturations on persistence ratings, scholastic achievement, and a variety of persistence tests, including the amount of time spent on the solution of anagrams and on code deciphering, and on continuous mental work, as well as a test of physical endurance. Ryans' second factor accounted for 11 per cent. of the variance, and was clearly a factor of intelligence.

Ryans concluded that "there appeared . . . seeming evidence of a general factor of persistence . . . (which) seemed to be relatively independent of such other capacities as intelligence and perseveration". In later studies, Ryans (1938, 1939) showed that a battery of three tests measuring persistence as defined by his factor was relatively unrelated to intelligence, but showed correlations of between ·4 and ·5 with success in school. He also found persistence to be related to emotional stability as measured by the Bernreuter Inventory.

Thornton (1939) criticized Ryans' findings because of the small number of cases used, and reported a study of his own, using 189 college students. His tests included ten objective measures of persistence, two ratings, and various measures of intelligence, speed of work and physical ability. A multiple factor analysis of the resulting intercorrelations was carried out and the following five factors isolated: (1) withstanding discomfort to achieve a goal; (2) keeping at a task; (3) sex-strength; (4) feeling of adequacy; (5) mental fluency. Clearly the first two factors correspond to the physical and the ideational types of persistence respectively, outlined in our discussion of types of persistence tests on *a priori* grounds. The "physical" factor is characterized by such tests as maintaining dynamometer grip, endurance of shock, length of time breath is held, and length of time pain is endured. The ideational factor is measured by such tests as the time spent on word building, on difficult reading material, practice on an aiming test, and so forth. There is some overlap between these two factors, some tests being identical to both, and in view of the fact that Thornton did not use oblique and second-order factors, we cannot regard these two factors as in any sense independent or as disproving the existence of a general factor of persistence.

A more recent study by Rethlingshafer (1942) used 38 college students as subjects. The tests included six of those which Thornton found to have the highest loadings on his ideational factor, three tests of the physical factors, as well as measures of strength, perseveration, interrupted activities (Zeigarnik affect) and intelligence. Seven factors were obtained by her, namely (1) the habit of keeping on at a task once it is started; (2) a perseveration or physiological inertia factor; (3) a willingness and/or ability to endure discomfort; (4) a sex-strength factor; (5) intelligence; (6) a radical-conservative continuum; (7) natural tempo.

Not too much attention can be paid to these results, as the number of subjects is too small to justify the extraction of so many factors. Superficially, factors 1 and 3 resemble the ideational and physical types of persistence task respectively, but breath-holding was found to have a positive loading of over ·3 on the former and actually a negative loading on the latter. Consequently, no certain conclusions can be drawn from these data. It is, however, interesting to see that both tests of interrupted activities have loadings above ·4 on Rethlingshafer's first factor, a finding which would apparently link this type of task with persistence.

Much more convincing is Kremer's (1942) study, in which 156 boys between eight and fifteen were subjects. Kremer obtained ratings on 17 traits and scores on six persistence tests, four of which were group tests (word-building, magic numbers square, cutting test, and mechanical puzzle), while two were individual tests (total time spent in interpreting ink-blots). In addition to the six persistence tests and the seventeen ratings, mental age and school grades were included in the matrix of intercorrelations, from which six factors were extracted by means of Thurstone's method. After rotation, Kremer named these as follows: (1) will; (2) stability of character; (3) sense of inferiority; (4) intelligence; (5) will to community; (6) reliability. The first factor accounts for 15 per cent. of the total variance, and includes the general average of school marks, as well as persistence ratings. All six persistence tests have positive loadings on this factor, ranging from ·81 to ·24. The second factor is made up entirely of ratings, and may therefore be regarded as a kind of reputation factor; the persistence tests, with one exception, have near zero loadings on the factor. Neither the third nor the fourth factors have any loadings on persistence tests. The fifth factor, however, is of particular interest. The loadings of the persistence tests are negative for the four group tests, but zero for the two individual tests; ratings having positive loadings above ·4 on this factor are: Does he do what everybody else is doing just because they are doing it? and, Is he easily led by others? The suggestion, therefore, is that here we are dealing with a factor contrasting persistence under group pressure with persistence in isolation ("will to community").

Kremer's battery of persistence tests had a reliability of ·85, and the hierarchical arrangement of the coefficients of correlations suggested the presence of one underlying general factor operative in the entire persistence battery. Correlations with intelligence were positive throughout, but very low. Correlations with school marks averaged about ·22.

Interesting though the preceding studies are, they are subject to a number of criticisms. Factors such as age and intelligence were neither experimentally controlled nor partialled out; consequently their influence on the actual intercorrelations of persistence tests is difficult to estimate. The scores used in the tables of intercorrelations were not always, or even usually, experimentally independent; often several scores were derived from the same test procedure, which is of doubtful admissibility in factorial work. The number of cases used was not always sufficient to make the analyses convincing. None of the studies summarized so far is free from some of these faults.

The most recent study by MacArthur (1951) is much more satisfactory technically, and it is interesting to note that in its major conclusions it agrees with the best of the previous studies. After carrying out a pilot study on 45 boys of between 14 and 16 years of age, a large battery of individual and group tests was chosen for administration. These included all the traditional tests, as well as measures of intelligence, school grades, age, self-ratings, peer ratings, and ratings by teachers. The subjects of the investigation were 120 boys. Twenty-one measures of ability were available in all, and these were intercorrelated and factor analysed. The factors were identified as (1) intelligence, (2) verbal ability, (3) spatial-practical ability, (4) numerical ability, and (5) age-strength. Factor scores were derived for these five factors and the factor scores correlated with the persistence measures. Next, the influence of the mental components underlying the five intellectual factors was removed by partialling out these five factors from the table of intercorrelations between the persistence tests, so that we are finally left with the relationships between 22 experimentally independent measures of persistence after the influence of the main abilities which might be expected to be related to performance on these measures had been removed. 132 correlations are significantly positive, 216 are non-significantly positive, and 114 are non-significantly negative. Thus, 29 per cent. of the correlations are significant, and 75 per cent. are positive.

A Thurstone analysis with rotation was carried out and a good fit to simple structure obtained. MacArthur gives the following interpretation of the factors extracted: (1) general persistence factor. The highest saturations on this factor are obtained by the peer ratings (·603); time spent on the magic square (·584); teacher's rating (·574); time spent on Japanese Cross (·525); time spent on chess-board puzzle (·515); word building (·472), and maintained handgrip (·432). School marks, study time, self-ratings, and various other persistence measures complete the definition of this very clearly marked factor. It may be noted that this general persistence factor runs through both the ideational and the physical measures.

Factor (2) is bipolar; positive loadings are given in those tests in which the subjects had no knowledge as to the performance of their class-mates, while negative loadings are given by tests in which the subjects were well aware of the performance of their class-mates. This factor is interpreted by MacArthur as contrasting individuality with prestige suggestibility in situations requiring persistence, and he considers it to bear a close relationship to Kremer's factor, which he called "will to community".

Factor (3) is also bipolar and contrasts measures of reputation for persistence with objective measures of the time which an individual is willing to spend at a task. It may thus be interpreted as a reputation factor analogous to that found by Kremer. The measures which are opposite in sign to this reputation score are all very similar to those which defined Thornton's ideational factor.

Factor (4) is made up of physical tests (holding foot over chair, maintained hand-grip, breath time, arm extension) and closely resembles Thornton's "withstanding discomfort to achieve a goal", and Rethlingshafer's "willingness and/or ability to endure discomfort".

We thus emerge from this study with a fairly clear picture of a general factor of persistence running through all the tests, ratings, and self-ratings, and four group factors dealing respectively with ideational tests, physical tests, reputation, and what might be called "group prestige persistence". All these group factors, as well as the general one, had been found by one or other of the previous investigators. Their rediscovery in this technically more perfect, methodologically more complete, investigation clarifies the psychological traits underlying persistence to a considerable extent.

MacArthur calculated a persistence score by combining eight of the tests having the highest communalities, taking care to balance the different group factors. This battery of eight tests was found to have an index of reliability of ·9, which may thus be regarded as the theoretical validity of these tests. A measure having that degree of validity must be regarded as important and promising in a psychological description of personality, and there is little doubt that further improvement and shortening of the component measures can lead to even higher factor saturations and greater practical usefulness of the battery suggested. As one example of the possible practical usefulness of this score, MacArthur shows that it correlates to the extent of ·3 with school marks when intelligence is partialled out.

This finding of an improved prediction of school achievement through the use of persistence tests may in due course lead to considerable improvement in our measures for student selection.

In summary, we may say that the evidence is fairly conclusive that persistence constitutes an important trait in our culture; that this trait is of a relatively unitary nature and can be measured to the extent indicated by a validity of ·9. In addition to this general factor of persistence, we find groups of activities which cluster together and define more specific types of persistence, such as persistence in physical tasks or persistence in ideational tasks. These smaller and less important factors also are subject to measurement with a degree of validity probably not much below general persistence itself. Persistence, as measured by tests, is fairly closely related to persistence as rated by others, and can be said to predict performance in life situations to a definitely significant extent. Persistence tends to show slight correlations with intelligence, more impressive ones with "w" or lack of neuroticism, and with introversion.[1]

[1] For experimental evidence to substantiate the claim that persistence measures both "w" and extraversion-introversion, cf. Eysenck (1947, 1952).

VARIABILITY

It is one of the commonplaces in psychological testing that individuals vary in almost any task from their "true" performance, i.e. from the mean of a large number of trials. Variability may be of two kinds. It may either manifest itself in short-term oscillation, occupying only a few seconds, or in long-term fluctuation, over periods of days, weeks, or even months. The former might be manifested, for instance, in the number of letters crossed out, the number of additions performed correctly, or the number of taps made in successive five-second intervals. The latter might become apparent on repetition of the same task after a lengthy period of time had elapsed. We shall call these two different aspects of variability "oscillation" and "fluctuation" respectively, although in the literature there has not been any consistent use of these terms. It may be surmised that variability would be a function of personality integration or "w", in the sense that the more stable, integrated personalities would be less variable in their conduct. Evidence for this view has already been presented in the work of Hartshorne and May (cf. their integration score) and of Shevach (1937) in connection with his studies of perseveration.

Further evidence to be quoted now supports this hypothesis to a considerable extent.[1]

The first experiment demonstrating functional unity in oscillation was published by Hollingworth (1925), who showed that oscillation in tests of tapping, co-ordination, steadiness, substitution, and colour naming produced intercorrelations to an average extent of ·20; variability of pulse-rate showed no relationship with oscillation. Flugel (1929, 1934), whose work had been independent of Hollingworth's, used rather larger numbers of subjects, and found considerable correlations on oscillation scores between eight tests (crossing out figures, cancellation, crossing out words and circles, and doing arithmetical subtraction). All the intercorrelations between the eight tests used were positive and averaged around ·20. Examinations by means of tetrad differences showed that a general factor of oscillation described the pattern of intercorrelations very well; this factor was also shown to be independent of "g" and perseveration.

With respect to fluctuation, Ash (1933) appears to have been the first to show that this aspect of variability is a unitary function. Combining results of various small groups, he found that on learning trials, separated by twenty-four hours, fluctuations in different tasks showed an average intercorrelation of ·31. Neither his data nor those of any later investigator permit us to say anything about the relationship between oscillation and fluctuation, as never so far have the two types of variability been combined in the same investigation.

Walton (1936, 1939) also presented evidence regarding the unity of the oscillation factor, using 55 children in his first and 90 children in his second experiment. Four and seven tests respectively were employed, having reliabilities of ·4 on the average. Also available were ratings of steadiness of character given by two teachers for each child. The average intercorrelation of the tests in Walton's first paper was ·22; in his second it was ·30. On carrying out a factor analysis, he found that one factor accounting for 32 per cent. of the variance was sufficient to reproduce all the correlations within the limits of sampling error. In both papers he obtained significant correlations between the "w" estimates obtained from the teachers and mean score on the tests of oscillation. The most trustworthy of these correlations is one of − ·275 (with age eliminated), showing a slight

[1] Physiological variability also appears related to "w", as shown for instance in the pioneering study by Hammett (1921), but as there has been no factorial study of this important field little is known about the functional unity of this type of variability, cf. also Herrington (1942).

but significant tendency for oscillation to be higher in the less stable, less steady sort of child.

A similar result is reported by Cummings (1939), who used four tests on 18 girl students. In addition to variability, she also measured the amount of error and time required for each of the tests, but concluded that "variability has here been found to be a much more valuable source of enquiry than the other measures . . . it has been found that the subjects who are variable on one test tend to be variable in two very different tests. . . . A consistently positive correlation shows that there is a tendency for lack of variability to be associated with . . . measures of 'persistence' and 'w'. . . . The four best correlating traits are in fact the very ones selected, quite independently, . . . to represent 'w'. The traits correlating negatively, on the other hand, are also easily recognizable as non-'w' traits."

Cattell (1943), dealing with fluctuation rather than oscillation, also found considerable support for the hypothesis that variability is less in the more stable individual. Using 60 children and 40 women students, he applied three and five sets respectively of 12-item questionnaires dealing with self-concept, deeper sentiments, superficial attitudes, etc. These questionnaires were re-applied one day and one month later, and personality ratings by peers obtained. Scores were calculated representing amount of change on the questionnaires, and these appear to give good, split-half reliabilities of ·61 and ·77 for children and adults, respectively, after one day, and ·68 and ·79 after one month. Variability after one day and variability after one month correlated ·47 and ·77 respectively for children and adults. Correlations between oscillation and "w" were astonishingly high, giving values of ·71 and ·40 for children and adults respectively after one day and ·49 and ·64 respectively after one month.

The studies of Madigan (1938) and Weber (1938) lend support to the generality of the concepts of oscillation and fluctuation, but only the latter appears to relate variability to personality trends. Weber (1938) specifically follows McV. Hunt (1936), who had shown schizophrenic patients to be considerably more variable than normals. Using 44 subjects, Weber derived a measure of variability from five tests administered to all subjects once a week for six successive weeks. In addition, these subjects were given an intelligence test, the Allport Ascendance-Submission Questionnaire and the Social Shyness and Emotionality parts of the Guilford Personality Inventory. A combined measure of variability was obtained for these subjects, and it was found that the more variable subjects were significantly more ascendant and significantly less emotional than were the more submissive and the more emotional subjects respectively. No connection was found with intelligence. The small number of subjects used and the sole reliance on questionnaires as outside criteria are features which make this study suggestive rather than conclusive.[1]

Cattell (1946) concludes his discussion of tests of oscillation and fluctuation by saying: "The correlations of 'O' with character integration and stability are lower than those of fluctuation, suggesting that these two factors are related but not identical." It is difficult to come to any conclusion regarding the two questions raised here. In the first place, the studies reporting correlations between "w" and oscillation and fluctuation respectively have been too dissimilar to allow of any direct comparison; in the second place, both oscillation and fluctuation might be negatively correlated with "w" without necessarily showing any functional similarity one with the other. It might be reasonable to regard Cattell's summary as a hypothesis worthy of investigation, and indeed the possible use of variability scores as measures of neuroticism or "w" appears to be a very tempting one in view of the ease with which these scores are obtainable.

FLUENCY

This factor was isolated first by Hargreaves (1927) in his studies of "the faculty of imagination". He found that a number of tests calling for a large number of imaginative responses tended to correlate together with an average intercorrelation of ·3. These correlations fulfilled the demands of the tetrad criterion and were shown not to be identical with "g". Some of the tests included were: number of things seen in an ink-blot, number of words written, number of different completions to an incomplete picture, and so forth. This "f" factor was considered at first as being the reverse of perseveration, but Hargreaves disproved this hypothesis fairly conclusively.

Cattell (1934) took up fluency tests, and found them to have a low but positive correlation with his surgency factor as rated ($r = ·30$) when the reliability of the test was ·57. In 1936, Cattell reported a more clinical study of a number of maladjusted and delinquent children and came to the following conclusion. "There is a preponderance of extremely high and low 'p' among children referred for delinquency or nervous difficulties. . . . Similarly, there is a pre-

[1] Chorus (1943) and Gray (1944) also bring forward evidence to support the correlation between variability and emotional lability.

ponderance of high and low rather than middling 'fluency of association' scores." This hypothesis of curvilinear regression has not been confirmed by later writers.

The tendency of extraversion (surgency) to correlate with "f" has found some slight report in Notcutt's study (1943), who gave five fluency tests which showed an average intercorrelation of ·45. Score on fluency was found to correlate — ·24 with introversion.

Much stronger support for the hypothesis comes from the studies of Gewirtz (1948), who used "f" tests on 38 children between the ages of 5 and 7. Correlations between these tests ranged from ·08 to ·70 and averaged much the same as the tests reported previously. Gewirtz suggested that the "f" factor might split up into two. "Different patterns of relationships were found between the tests of word fluency and two types of vocabulary tests, one a recall vocabulary test and the other a recognition-definition vocabulary test. The intercorrelation of the word fluency tests and their correlations with mental age and two types of vocabulary tests seem to indicate that there were two abilities involved in word fluency: one involving the rate of word association where there is some restriction imposed, and the other involving the rate of word association where there is little restriction."

In correlating the "f" tests with ratings made by the use of the Fels Child Behaviour Scales, she found a distinct tendency for the signs of the correlations of the various "f" tests to be identical when correlating these tests with each particular item of the Fels scale. There thus emerges a distinct tendency for the child with high fluency scores to receive high ratings on curiosity, gregariousness, originality, aggressiveness, competitiveness, and cheerfulness, and negative ratings on social apprehensiveness and patience. These results would seem to support very strongly the hypothesis of a positive relation between "f" and extraversion, although failure to partial out intelligence and age renders the results less conclusive than one might have wished.

About the existence of such a correlation, there can be little doubt. Benassy and Chauffard (1947) found correlations between intelligence and "f" in the neighbourhood of ·32 when Cattell's "f" test was administered to 282 children and 231 adults. They confirmed, however, that the correlations on which the "f" factor is based are partly independent of "g", and in the main their results of comparing fluency scores with ratings of temperament bear out the general hypothesis that fluency is a valid measure of extraversion.

In addition to the few studies mentioned, all of which have re-garded the "*f*" test as a measure of personality, there are a number of studies in which fluency is related to purely cognitive tests, and as these have been dealt with in some detail by Vernon (1950), the main results only will be mentioned. The work of Thurstone (1938), Johnson and Reynolds (1941), Carol (1941), Taylor (1947), and Fruchter (1948) tends to bear out the early findings of Holzinger (1934, 1935) that fluency tests have comparatively high saturations on "*g*" and "*v*" (intelligence and verbal ability), but that in addition they have something in common, which gives rise to a separate factor. Thurstone's distinction between his "V" (understanding of verbal material) and "W" (word fluency) underlies this distinction; in more recent years he has added another factor, "F" (ideational fluency with words), to the other two.

Various sub-factors within this general context have been identified by some of the writers mentioned above. Thus, Taylor distinguishes: (1) verbal versatility or ability to express an idea by several different combinations of words; (2) word fluency, involving no reference to the meaning of words; and (3) ideational fluency, or production of words from meaningful associations.

Carol split Thurstone's "W" factor into: (1) speed of word associ-ation in restricted context; (2) rate of production of syntectically coherent discourse; (3) naming or ability to attach appropriate names to stimuli.

It seems likely to the present writer that some at least of these distinctions within the "*f*" context will be verified in later work, but factors based on these fine distinctions are not likely to contribute much to the total variance. As far as the relation of "*f*" to personality is concerned, there is no evidence that groupings such as those suggested by Carol and Taylor are likely to correspond in any way to personality differences. Considering the importance attached to "*f*" tests by many psychologists who have used them as measures of per-sonality (Cattell, Stephenson, Studman, and others), it seems curious that the number of relevant factorial studies is so small. However, it is possible that the recent interest shown by American writers in the cognitive aspects of "*f*" will generalize to the orectic aspects.[1]

[1] A fundamental criticism of all these studies is that they use scores for their analyses which can be shown to be compound rather than simple scores. Bous-field and Sedgewick (1944) have shown that total production of words per unit time depends on two partly independent factors: (1) total fund or reservoir of relevant words known and (2) rate of depletion of this reservoir. This hypothesis is discussed in the next chapter in some detail.

SUGGESTIBILITY

The close relationship between suggestibility and qualities of temperament and character has been posited by so many writers that there is hardly any call to mention them specifically. A detailed review of the literature has been given by Eysenck (1947), who finds that two hypotheses have been entertained by large numbers of psychiatrists and psychologists, the first linking suggestibility to hysteria (and consequently to extraversion), the second linking suggestibility to neuroticism. All these theories, of course, assume some functional unity of the alleged trait of suggestibility, a unity the existence of which has been doubted by many psychologists, whose judgment has been based largely on the pioneer studies of Brown (1916). This writer, who carried out his experiments on 54 women and 29 men, applied a large number of tests of what might be called sensory suggestibility, in which the subject was put into what appeared a normal laboratory situation involving the establishment of sensory thresholds for odours, touch, heat, brightness, pitch size, motion, etc.; supra-liminal stimuli were then followed by ready signs not accompanied by the expected stimulus; quite frequently the subject would report the expected stimulus, although objectively no such stimulus was present. The number of times the suggestion was effective was considered the score of the person on the particular test in question. Correlations were calculated separately for the men and the women. For nine tests, the average intercorrelation for the men was ·204; for the women it was only ·054. Brown adds : "It is understood that these correlations involve a possible error, in that the work was done by different experimenters, so that the ranking of the individual subject's record may be influenced by the amount of the personal influence of the experimenter." While the amount of intercorrelation between these tests is certainly not very large, and while factors such as intelligence have not been partialled out as they should have been, the crudeness of the experimental methods and the difficulty of having several different experiments, mentioned above by Brown, make it difficult to derive any firm negative conclusions from his data. If anything, they might be taken to indicate the existence of a rather weak factor of sensory suggestibility, but as later investigators have found sensory suggestibility to be correlated with intelligence, even this conclusion cannot be regarded as definite.

Brown also investigated correlations between illusions, æsthetic judgments, and their subjective estimates when suggestions were made to the subjects as to a general standard of judgment, using the amount of change induced as a measure of suggestibility. Seven experiments of this type give average intercorrelations of ·095 and ·003 for men and women respectively; these data suggest a complete absence of functional unity for this type of suggestibility.

In their rather more recent study, Aveling and Hargreaves (1921) came to a conclusion quite opposite to the negative one of Brown. They used in the main six tests, some of which were similar to Brown's, namely the Illusion of Warmth Test and the Binet Progressive Weights and Progressive Lines. They also included, however, two tests of quite a different type, called hand-rigidity and hand-levitation, in which the motor reaction of the subject to a direct suggestion was measured. Using two samples, one of 32 children and one of 56 children, they found a good deal of variation in correlations. Most of these correlations appeared to be as small as those in Brown's work. The only exception to this rule was a correlation between the two motor suggestibility tests which rose to the striking value of ·73. Aveling and Hargreaves conclude from their study that "there is evidence which points to a general factor of suggestibility complicated by group factors", but their material is not extensive enough to prove this point.

A paper by Eysenck (1943) was designed to test two hypotheses: the first that there were two main factors of suggestibility, one of them sensory, the other motor; and the second, that suggestibility had an intimate relation with hysteria. Sixty subjects in all were used, 15 men and 15 women suffering from conversion hysteria, and 15 men and 15 women who were also neurotic but did not show any signs of conversion symptoms, hysterical personality, etc. Four sensory tests and four motor tests were used, the latter including the Chevreul Pendulum, the Hull Body Sway Test, and two levitation tests.

None of the eight tests differentiated between hysterics and non-hysterics, thus effectively disproving the hypothesis of a special link between hysteria and suggestibility. A factor analysis of the intercorrelations between the tests disclosed two orthogonal factors, one having projections on the four sensory tests, the other having projections on the four motor tests. In order to avoid biasing the interpretation of these factors by giving them names like sensory and motor suggestibility, which would pre-judge more detailed enquiry into their nature, the terms "primary suggestibility" (for tests like Body Sway, Arm Levitation and the Chevreul Pendulum), and "secondary suggestibility" (for tests like the Binet, Progressive Lines and Weights, and the type of test used by Brown) were suggested.

In a later study, Eysenck and Furneaux (1945) attempted to clarify the nature of these tests by increasing the number of procedures used to twelve. Sixty neurotics constituted the sample; all of these had I.Q.s between 90 and 110. Part of the battery of tests consisted of a

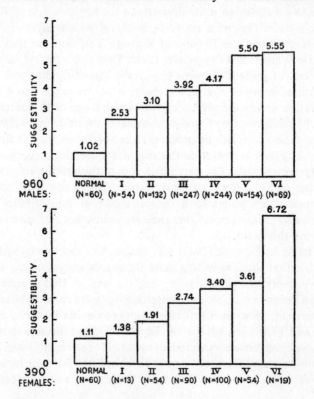

Fig. 35.—Average Suggestibility of Normals and Neurotics, showing increase in Suggestibility correlated with increase in "Neuroticism".

hyponotizability scale in which different hypnotic suggestions carried out by the subject were given points according to the difficulty of the suggestion. Six of the tests were designed to be measures of primary suggestibility; these intercorrelated to the extent of ·50. The other six tests were selected so as to be representative of secondary suggestibility; these intercorrelated to the extent of ·15. The average intercorrelation of the tests of primary suggestibility with those of secondary suggestibility was ·02. Two independent factors of primary and secondary suggestibility consequently emerged from the analysis. The highest saturation for primary suggestibility were obtained in the Body Sway Test (·92) and the hypnosis scale (·89); the highest saturations for secondary suggestibility were obtained in an ink-blot and in an odour-suggestion test. A detailed scrutiny of the tests giving rise to these two factors and of their saturations suggested that primary suggestibility was essentially due to ideo-motor tendencies within the individual, whereas secondary suggestibility was essentially of the indirection kind ("gullibility").

It may be surmised that the type of suggestibility related by many writers to personality is essentially of the ideo-motor type, because of the close relation usually posited between suggestibility and hypnosis; in the experiment outlined above, no connection was observed between hypnotizability and secondary suggestibility, but a very close connection between hypnotizability and primary suggestibility (Furneaux, 1946). Several further studies failed to show any relationship between primary suggestibility and hysteria, so that this hypothesis seems to be definitely disproved. A very close connection, however, was found between neuroticism and primary suggestibility (Eysenck, 1947, 1952). Typical of the findings is a set of figures presented diagrammatically in Fig. 35, in which is shown the amount of body sway in response to the suggestion "You are falling, you are falling forward . . ." of 960 men and 390 women of whom some were normal, while others were inmates of an Army Neurosis Centre and had been rated on a six-point scale for degree of neuroticism by psychiatrists independently of the experiment. It will be seen that there is a perfect monotonic relation between degree of neuroticism and increase in suggestibility, a finding which has been verified in a number of subsequent studies. There appears little doubt, therefore, that suggestibility is a useful measure of neuroticism, but that it fails to differentiate between extraverts and introverts.

TENSION

The concept of tension, which presumably originated in connection with physiological phenomena, has been used so widely and so frequently in connection with psychological states that it comes with something of a shock to realize how very little experimental evidence there is for any identification of these two meanings of the term. Almost the only relevant work here is that of Duffy (1930, 1932,

1946), who has carried out a number of investigations designed to discover the degree of generality of the physiological phenomena, and to discover the relation of these phenomena to personality and behaviour. The hypothesis underlying her work was stated by her as follows: "Relative degree of tension is a fundamental characteristic of the individual varying . . . with changes in circumstance but varying around a central tendency which is different for different individuals." Working with college students, she used three measures of tension: (1) pressure exerted on a rubber bulb or tube held in the unused hand; (2) pressure exerted by the used hand; and (3) amount of pencil pressure indicated by the penetration of a number of sets of carbon papers. Her subjects were given various tasks, such as colour naming, tapping, crossing out digits or lines, adding numbers and tracing mazes. "Twelve measures of muscular tension and four measures of fluctuation in tension obtained while the subjects were performing a wide variety of tasks were subjected to factorial analysis. These measures were secured on three separate occasions, the first separated from the second by three months; and the second separated from the third by one week." One general factor was found which "is interpreted as representing a general-tension factor. This factor incorporates a variety of tasks, three techniques of tension measurement, and three experimental sessions". Duffy interprets this tension as an indicator of energy mobilization, an interpretation similar to that of Freeman and of Wenger, whose work has been summarized in a previous chapter.

In another study (Duffy, 1932) 18 children between the ages of 3 and 4 showed a correlation of ·63 between tension as evidenced by strength of grip on a rubber ball, and pressure. Tension was found to correlate with ratings of excitability and school adjustment to the extent of ·52 and ·58. A similar correlation was found in yet another study (1930), when 11 children aged from 4 to 5 were assigned a task (of pressing a key whenever a red light appeared), and during the performance of this task a kymographic record was made of the degree of tension in the muscles of the unused hand. The correlation between tension and excitability ratings was ·56, and it was also found that under disturbance (sound of a klaxon horn) there was a greater rise in tension in those who were already tense.

Duffy (1932) sums up her findings of the relation between tension and personality in the following words: "Tension . . . frequently found expression in stammering, enuresis, temper tantrums, and restless movements of various kinds; tense children had fewer physical contacts on the playground (and established fewer voluntary contacts) than children who were more relaxed; tension decreased during successive performance of the same task, but showed an increase when the subject returned to school after an attack of whooping-cough; and various other forms of behaviour and even aspects of health appeared to be related to the characteristic tension level of the individual. It was also shown that habitual grip pressure (the tension measure used) was not a product of a muscular strength since it showed no correlation with dynamometer scores. From these various findings it was concluded that 'tension level' represents a significant aspect of the individual's personality." Duffy appears to be right in her insistence on tension level as an important psychological variable; it is unfortunate that the number of cases used by her is too small to make definite assessment of the relationship between tension and other personality factors possible.

The only writer apart from Duffy who has attempted to study tension by means of factorial techniques is Wenger (1943), whose work on autonomic functioning has been reviewed in a previous chapter. In these studies Wenger found, in addition to the autonomic factor, another which he provisionally identified as one of muscular tension. As he points out, these studies suffered in offering no clear definition of the factor: "It was believed that if at least one test could be added to the battery which was unquestionably a test of generalized muscular tension, it would serve to define and validate (or invalidate) the postulated factor of muscular tension. Since no one test is available which all observers would agree constitutes the valid measure of general muscular tension, and since this concept at present is a subjective one with but little objective support, it was decided to employ a rating scale. If it were found that observers could agree on a definition of muscular tension and then reliably rate behaviour indicative of that trait, there would be available a critical test for use in defining a muscular factor." Wenger accordingly developed a rating scale of muscular relaxation which was shown to have adequate reliability for the purpose in hand by means of intercorrelating 8 observers. Seventeen physiological variables and the rating scale were then intercorrelated, using measures derived from 74 children. Of the two main factors extracted, the first was found to be similar to the autonomic factor found in several other analyses. The second factor, which has its highest loading on the rating of muscular relaxation ($- \cdot 54$), just discussed, is in many ways similar to the original factor which was labelled by Wenger muscular tension, and the fact that the rating included in the battery has such a relatively high saturation for this factor bears out Wenger's original interpretation. A regression equation was then set up by Wenger involving six tests; this equation gives the best available estimate of the factor score for individual children. Correlations were run between ratings on 9 personality traits, the tension factor score, and the results obtained from the rating scale; these are reproduced in Table 42. It will be seen that the two series of coefficients are almost perfectly correlated, showing that the rating and the factor score measure very much the same underlying trait. Both methods show that the tense child tends to be energetic, emotional, restless, and impulsive, whereas a relaxed child is fatigable and emotionally controlled. These results should only be taken as suggestive; while we may regard existence of the factor of muscular tension as established, a great deal of work will be required before its relationship to various traits and types of personality can be regarded as proven.

TABLE 42

The Relationship of nine Personality Ratings to two Measures of Muscular Tension for forty-four Children

Personality Traits	Correlations with	
	Factor Score	Rating
Energeticness . .	·46	·46
Fatigability . .	− ·35	− ·24
Frequency of emotion .	·46	·47
Restlessness . . .	·48	·50
Sensitiveness . .	− ·10	− ·02
Emotional Control .	− ·33	− ·32
Distractability . .	·19	·17
Impulsiveness . .	·35	·41
Carelessness . . .	·22	·21

We may perhaps note from the purely technical point of view the use made by Wenger of the hypothetico-deductive method. Having obtained from his original analysis a factor the identification of which with "tension" might be regarded as somewhat far-fetched, he then proceeded to make certain deductions regarding the factorial composition of an additional measure which would be crucial to his interpretation: the resulting experiment bore out his hypothesis at a high level of confidence, and we may therefore consider his original interpretation of the factor justified. It is only rarely, unfortunately, that factorial studies follow this course; only too frequently a doubtful or unclear interpretation is allowed to stand without being submitted to further control experimentation. Wenger's study may serve as an illustration of the proper integration of factorial and experimental methods.

LEVEL OF ASPIRATION

The concept of level of aspiration has already been mentioned on a previous page, and an excellent summary of the work done with this type of test has been given by Lewin *et al.* (1944). Some evidence of generality of this factor is given by Heather (1942) and Gardiner (1940), but the main burden of proof rests on a paper by Gould (1939), who gave six tests (synonyms, steadiness, additions, symbol-digits, cancellation, and target) to 82 subjects. He found a median intercorrelation of ·29, and very high reliability for the individual aspiration discrepancy scores. The actual correlations found by him are given below in Table 43; it will be seen that they lend very strong support to the notion that level of aspiration is a generalized trait extending over a number of very different types of activity. Correlations between performance and aspiration were found to be negligible; similarly, correlations between performances were found to be negligible.

TABLE 43

	1	2	3	4	5	6
1. Synonyms test . .	(·95)	·36	·25	·35	·29	·23
2. Steadiness . .		(·96)	·26	·24	·25	·04
3. Additions . .			(·99)	·44	·40	·28
4. Symbol-digit .				(·96)	·34	·35
5. Cancellation .					(·97)	·34
6. Target . .						(·97)

There can be little doubt that this generalized trait is related both to introversion-extraversion and to neuroticism. Diagrammatic representation of the type of relationship indicated by a number of research papers has been given on p. 30 and will not be repeated here. Most of the data on which these diagrams were based were taken from experiments in which a single test was used; Gould's data indicate that much better discrimination could be achieved if several tests were used and the aspiration scores averaged.

INSIGHT

A number of studies by Dymond (1949, 1950) and others have been carried out in relation to the concept of insight, the procedure usually being one of obtaining self-ratings and ratings of each other from members of a group, as well as an estimate from each person of how he thinks others will have rated him. Insight can then be demonstrated by correctly assessing the reactions of other people, i.e. predicting correctly their self-ratings and predicting correctly their ratings of oneself. There are various possible combinations here, of course, and the method may easily link up with such work as that of Sears (1937) on projection and of Frenkel-Brunswik (1942) on motivation and behaviour (cf. Chapter II). None of these studies, however, succeed in showing that this hypothetical trait of insight is general, although an attempt to do so is made by Dymond, who used T.A.T. responses, Rorschach and ethnocentrism measures to correlate with insight or empathy.

The only factorial study which has come to hand is one by Wedeck (1947), whose approach is somewhat different from that of the other writers mentioned. Four of his tests were made up of works of art of well-known contemporary artists; in the fifth test, photographs of popular film actors in psychological situations were used. The subjects were given questionnaires referring to the underlying mood and other personality qualities of the people depicted, and their answers were scored in terms of a key prepared by agreement of three judges. The sixth test consisted of verbal descriptions of various personalities who had to be rated for a number of traits. The seventh test involved the ability to discriminate between true and false utterances of a person, introduced by the experimenter to the subject, and for whom a number of artificial situations were prepared. The eighth test consisted in a number of problematical situations, in which the subject had to predict the most likely psychological response of a person who is described in some detail. Verbal and non-verbal tests of intelligence were also given to the 200 girls between 13 and 14 years of age who constituted the experimental group.

All the intercorrelations between the "insight" tests were positive, even after "g" and "v" were partialled out. Using the tetrad criterion, Wedeck showed that these residual correlations could be used to define one and only one general factor running through the matrix. Thus, he concludes "a new factor is demonstrated: it may be named 'phi' factor for the present". Saturations of the various tests for this factor are in the neighbourhood of ·4 to ·6, though some of the tests are rather disappointing.

There is no evidence given in Wedeck's work that this insight factor has any correlations with other traits of personality. Freeman (1952), using the Character Interpretation Test, which is similar in some ways to the type of test used by Wedeck, although constructed quite independently, found considerable differences in the adjectival descriptions of personal photographs given by psychotics, neurotics, and normals. Using deviation from the responses given by a normal group as his score, he showed that insight, as measured in terms of these deviations, does not differentiate between normals and neurotics, but differentiates at a high level of significance between psychotics and neurotics, and between psychotics and normals. While these results are only preliminary, they do indicate the possibility of relating insight to personality structure, and indeed, from the purely *a priori* point of view, it would seem exceedingly unlikely that such an important personality variable should not be closely integrated with the remainder of personality.

PERSONAL TEMPO

There is a large and flourishing literature connected with the concept of personal tempo. The main protagonist in this field perhaps is Frischeisen-Köhler (1933), who used preferred rate of tapping, and preference for metronome speed, as measures of this alleged quality. She demonstrated that monozygotic twins are more alike with respect to personal tempo thus measured than were dizygotic twins and siblings, while these, in turn, were more alike than unrelated persons.

The work of Allport and Vernon (1933) threw a good deal of doubt on the alleged generality of this trait, however, and the studies of Harrison (1941) and Harrison and Dorcus (1938) seem to indicate a rather high degree of specificity in measures of this type. In the first of these studies, 49 subjects were used and subjected to a number of tests, including cranking, tapping, arm and body movements, coordination, walking, etc. From the intercorrelations of these tests they concluded that "the intercorrelation of speed measurements indicates no unitary speed trait which is characteristic of various spontaneous movements or motor adjustments of an individual". This lack of generality cannot be attributed to the unreliability of the constituent measures because it was found that "individuals tend to perform at a fairly consistent rate from one time to another". Harrison's later experiment gave rather more positive findings from the point of view of generality. Using 50 students, he gave them 12 tasks to do at their preferred (voluntary) speed and another set of 12 partly identical tasks to do at maximum speed. The average inter-correlations of the voluntary speed tests was ·20. That of the maximum speed tests was ·15. The tasks included in both series correlated on the average, ·37. Between personal tempo, as measured by the whole battery, and the subject's self-estimate of his own personal tempo, a correlation of ·51 was found. These results appear to favour the hypothesis that a certain amount of generality does exist in the field of personal tempo, but the number of tests used is too small to come to any definite conclusion.

More definitive is the work of Rimoldi (1951), who used 59 tests altogether on 91 male university students. Reliabilities appeared to be fairly satisfactory, and 9 factors were obtained from the inter-correlations. The first factor appeared to be related to the spontaneous speed with which large body movements (swinging arm, swinging leg, ergograph, bending body, etc.) were performed. The second factor "is defined by tests involving simple movement. These movements are performed by the distal muscles of the limbs and seem to be independent of site of the body and of the muscular groups involved". The third factor appears to be related to feet movements, the fourth to hand movements, the fifth appears to be related to speed of reading, the sixth to reaction-time tests, the seventh factor appears to be one of cognitive speed, the eighth is a metronome doublet, and the ninth is not interpretable. These factors are not independent but show moderate correlations. Thus, the first and second factors correlate ·51 with each other. Second-order factors were accordingly extracted from the correlations between the primaries. "As a result of our second-order analysis, it seems possible to isolate the following variables: α-speed of all motor activities; β-speed of perception; γ-speed of cognition; δ-reaction time." This set of factors closely resembles a set presented by Eysenck (1947) on the basis of a review of the literature, and may be considered a reasonable estimate of the present position of this concept of "personal tempo" which could, presumably, be identified with Rimoldi's α factor. Little is known, unfortunately, about the correlates of personal tempo, as most writers have been content to use only one or two tests instead of the larger number required for getting adequate factor measurements. In view of the many claims for this type of test made in the literature, it seems likely that important personality correlates will be found, but it would be idle to speculate at this stage as to precisely what they might be. Indications are to hand (Eysenck, 1947), that personal tempo may be related to "w", but the evidence is not extensive enough to enable us to go further than that.[1]

CAREFULNESS

Most psychologists would probably be willing to consider the possibility that carefulness (which is often linked with obsessional and compulsive habits) constitutes a genuine trait of personality, and it might be surmised, from the point of view of Jung's theoretical considerations, that the introvert would be found to be careful, the extravert careless and slapdash. There is a limited amount of evidence to support both beliefs. The only factorial study to isolate a factor of carefulness is reported by Guilford in the fifth report of the Army Air Forces Aviation Psychology Programme (1947). Basing himself on the hypothesis that in timed tests the careless person would be likely to give many more wrong answers than the careful person, Guilford departed from the usual procedure of only analysing right answers, and included in his correlation analysis wrong answers as a separate category. A quite clearly marked factor was found, having loadings between ·4 and ·6, which consisted of the number of wrong responses on the four tests for which such scores were available. This factor Guilford labelled "carefulness", commenting that "probably the most significant result of this analysis is the discovery that analysis of wrong scores brought to light an entirely new factor. . . . It may be assumed safely that if correlations of right and wrong scores are not too high, a fuller picture of the true functions measured by a test can be obtained by analysing the scores separately than by analysing total scores. The results also imply that many an error has been committed by combining right and wrong scores in the same formula. Unless the two are factorially similar, the result may be very different from what had been intended by the test maker".

No further information is given by Guilford regarding the possible correlation of this factor with personality variables, but Himmelweit

Another study that may be relevant to the concept of "personal tempo" is the factor analysis by Carpenter (1941) of 14 measures taken on 128 boys and 125 girls. She extracted a "velocity" or speed factor which was characterized by various running and hopping activities.

(1949, 1951) and Petrie (1948, 1950) have shown that carelessness as measured by the number of wrong responses in intellectual tasks correlates to a significant extent with measures of neuroticism in normal subjects. Further verification of this finding would seem desirable, but the evidence already must be considered as highly suggestive.[1]

It is more difficult to come to a conclusion regarding the work of Himmelweit (1946) on the relation between introversion and accuracy of work. Using a manual tracking task, she found a tendency for hysterics to be quick but to make many errors, whereas dysthymics tended to be slow and to make fewer errors. It is certainly very tempting to identify this tendency towards careful work on a task of this kind with the tendency to be careless and make many errors in an intellectual test, but no factorial investigation is to hand to justify such identification. Here appears to be an interesting and fruitful field which so far has hardly been touched on by experimentalists and statisticians; such data as there are support the hypothesis that carelessness is a unitary factor which is correlated both with neuroticism and with extraversion.

PUNCTUALITY

For the sake of completeness, one further study should here be mentioned, although its importance from the point of view of personality organization is unlikely to be as great as that of the concepts mentioned so far. Dudycha (1946) showed that punctuality as observed in various activities (eight o'clock class attendance, vesper service, extra-curricular activity, entertainments, etc.) tended to be characteristic of given individuals, the intercorrelations between these various activities being in the neighbourhood of ·25, and a composite score correlating with ratings for punctuality to the extent of ·41. There is some limited evidence in his study that punctuality has a slight correlation with intelligence and a negative correlation with neuroticism, but it is unlikely that this variable would have important connections with central personality traits, except, possibly, in the psychopath and in the obsessional type of person.

---

[1] In support may be cited the work of Staudt (1949) and Fruchter (1950). Thorndike (1943) claims to have found considerable specificity in "carelessness", but his results, too, definitely disprove the null hypothesis.

RORSCHACH TEST

So far in this chapter we have dealt with traits, or hypothetical traits, defined in terms of objective test procedures. It may appear somewhat unusual to include the Rorschach tests in this chapter, because, in the opinion of most of its devotees, its main virtue lies in its being a global instrument (i.e. in not dealing with separate traits), and in being not an objective test but a technique essentially relying on interpretation. However, it is clear that scores may be derived from the Rorschach in terms of the usual categories (R, C, F, D, and so on), so that the tests may be used as an objective, or at least semi-objective, procedure, and the possibility that by means of factor analysis we would discover certain traits cannot be ruled out on *a priori* grounds. Indeed, Rorschach himself had hypothesized the existence of introvertive-extratensive tendencies, which could be diagnosed in terms of certain scoring categories. We may, therefore, with some justification, include the small number of factorial studies which have been done on the Rorschach test in this account, adding the proviso that this use of the Rorschach is different from the usual and probably objectionable to most Rorschach experts.

The first paper in this connection, that of Hsü (1947) would seem to justify these hypothetical feelings of Rorschach workers, as it appears to violate in every detail the rationale of the test. Using 76 children, Hsü made a recording of their responses to Plate I only, and finally decided to use 15 variables (number of words, number of nouns, number of adjectives, number of verbs, use of number, human, human detail, animal, animal detail, and five single, frequently occurring responses). Intercorrelating these items and factor analysing the resulting matrix, six factors, which he considered meaningful, were extracted. These were: (*a*) facility in use of words; (*b*) "appears to be the ability of using nouns alone and in non-human context. Time also has a high loading here"; (*c*) "probably suggests a 'face' factor, as this seems to centre chiefly on the human face"; (*d*) "appears to be indicative of the ability of using verbs and adjectives other than nouns"; (*e*) "apparently indicates a 'bat' factor. . . This is a most interesting part of this analysis" (!); (*f*) "is essentially a human factor". Having discussed the meaning of these factors in some detail, Hsü goes on to say: "If the factors for each plate could be discovered and used in a linear description of the traits of a sufficiently large population, the further quantification and standardization of the Rorschach tests would be highly plausible." To the present writer, this does not seem a reasonable expectation, nor does he feel that Hsü's use of factor analysis is likely to advance our knowledge either of the Rorschach or of personality structure. To throw away the accumulated experiments of hundreds of clinical workers and to start with a *tabula rasa* rather than attempting to verify hypotheses based on previous work with the Rorschach appears a misuse of the technique, and the barrenness of the results is ample confirmation of the correctness of this view.

In sharp contrast to the work of Hsü stands that of Cox (1951) and Sen (1950). Cox gave the Rorschach test, in its orthodox form, to two groups of normal and neurotic children equated for age and intelligence. The records were scored by the use of the ordinary Rorschach scoring categories, using both formal and content scores, and 26 of these categories were then intercorrelated for the whole group of 120 children. A twenty-seventh variable was introduced, namely the dichotomy: normal versus neurotic. Five factors were extracted of which the first appeared to be a general factor of productivity or number. This interpretation was based on the fact that it had the highest loading in the total number of responses ($\cdot$90) and total number of responses involving the use of form ($\cdot$94). It had high loadings also in total number of responses involving poor form, together with a high negative loading in "failure to respond". The second factor was interpreted as one of neuroticism. Its highest loading was in the normal-neurotic dichotomy ($\cdot$73). "High loadings appear also in human and animal detail . . . pure good form also had a high saturation with this factor. At the opposite end of the pole it has high negative loadings in Fire, Water, the Miscellaneous group, CF$-$, C, D, and Y." The third factor was interpreted as one of intelligence, having high loadings on I.Q., and original and unusual responses. The fourth factor was not clearly identified, but in terms of customary Rorschach procedure appeared to bear some relationship to extraversion-introversion, while the fifth factor is of no interest in this connection. This paper, therefore, results in the objective identification of two factors (neuroticism by reference to the external criterion of clinical diagnosis, and intelligence by reference to I.Q. test), and contains at least suggestive evidence of the extraversion-introversion factor. It would appear, then, that the treatment of the Rorschach as an ordinary objective type of psychometric test gives results essentially similar to those obtained by other objective types of tests.

This conclusion is strengthened by the findings of Sen (1950), who used as subjects 100 Indian students—60 men and 40 women—who were given an individual Rorschach test, two intelligence tests, and Cattell's test of fluency, as well as two questionnaires intended to elicit relevant traits of personality. Each of the subjects tested was also rated independently by two judges on neurotic tendencies, extraversion-introversion, general emotionality, imagination, perception of relations, and intelligence. Three main factors were extracted, of which the first one was clearly a fluency of association factor, having a saturation of ·962 on "total number of responses". Factor measurements for this factor correlated ·485 with results of the fluency test and ·530 with the judges' assessment of imagination. Correlation with intelligence was zero. The second factor is clearly one of intelligence, having its highest saturations on Klopfer's form level score, and its highest negative saturation on Beck's low modified "z" score. Factor measurements correlate to the extent of ·5 with intelligence tests, and also the extent of ·5 with ratings of intelligence. It is interesting to see that this factor also shows slight negative correlation with neurotic tendencies ($- ·212$), which is in line with many of the researches mentioned previously.

The third factor is one of neuroticism, correlating ·685 with ratings for neurotic tendencies. This factor has high saturations on colour and various other well-known indicators of neurotic tendency. Taken together, the results of Cox and Sen throw a good deal of light on the factors which the Rorschach test measures, and indicate that when this test is used as an ordinary psychometric measuring device, results from it do not deviate from those obtained by means of other types of test.

One further attempt to carry out a factorial study on Rorschach scores should be noted. Sandler (1949) and Sandler and Ackner (1951) administered the Rorschach to 50 patients suffering from a variety of psychiatric disorders; in addition, two psychiatric rating scales were used, one referring to overt symptomatology and the other to previous personality. A form of analysis was used in which persons were intercorrelated rather than scores, and four factors were extracted of which the first was again a fluency or productivity factor. This factor accounts for 29 per cent. of the total variance. The other three factors account, respectively, for 3 per cent., 2 per cent., and 2 per cent. of the variance, and may thus be considered to be of very slight interest indeed. Nor are they easily interpretable or meaningful psychologically. With some poetic licence, factor two is labelled "internal anatomical responses" versus "external objects", and factor three is defined as "*animated*" against "*inanimate percepts*". "It is more than a differentiation between human and non-human perceptions, but is rather a distinction between perceptions invested with animate expression on the one hand and perceptions devoid of such animation on the other." Factor four is defined as "defensive percepts as opposed to well-defined human parts".

Correlations were then run between Rorschach factors and items in the psychiatric inventories. Very few of these are significant, and altogether they do not seem to present any kind of clear-cut picture. On the whole, this study is of interest more as a statistical exercise in a somewhat novel form than for any light it may shed on the organization of personality.[1]

One further Rorschach study must be mentioned here, although it does not make use of the factorial method. In their attempt to develop what they called a "basic Rorschach score", Bühler, Bühler and Lefever (1949) make use of a statistical technique which illustrates very vividly the need for factorial methods in this field. Beginning with five initial criterion groups (normal, neurotic, psychopathic, organic, and schizophrenic), they prepared a diagnostic sign list for each of the 207 cases included. Each group was compared with each of the others with respect to each of the many Rorschach signs scored, and scoring weights were determined for each sign in accordance with its

[1] Three further factorial studies of the Rorschach ought to be mentioned at least in passing. Wittenborn (1950) has attempted to clear up the muddle of Rorschach scoring categories, with the result that his study "suggests that an incorrect emphasis may have influenced the development of current Rorschach scoring procedures and interpretive practices. . . . Many of the scoring categories which belong to the various broad classes of determinants, e.g. colour, texture, or diffusion, have a quite dissimilar factorial composition, and in general the manner in which the various determinant scoring categories cluster together could not be predicted by an employment of the usual beliefs concerning behavioural implications of determinants".

Adcock's (1951) study, while potentially of great interest because of his use of native Cook Islands children as well as of New Zealand white children, is difficult to interpret because of the small number of children involved. (Tetrachoric correlations on 30 Ss. have such large sampling errors as to be hardly worth calculating.) Three of the factors emerging from the two populations are interpreted as fluency, introversion, and intelligence and "suggest that these are basic dimensions which might be expected in any culture". Further evidence would be required before these interpretations could be accepted as more than possible guesses.

Hughes (1950) presents an extremely important paper involving the use of criterion groups. A detailed discussion of his results would be supererogatory, as his main success in differentiation lies in the field of brain-injury, which is of little direct relevance to our main theme; it is more with respect to method that his paper appears of importance in this context.

ability to discriminate between any of the pairs of groups studied. Ten sets of scoring weights were thus obtained, all of which gave good discrimination between normal and abnormal groups. The basic Rorschach score was then derived from the "normal versus schizophrenic" comparison. This basic Rorschach score has a reliability of ·83 (Spearman-Brown, corrected). Its ability to discriminate between clinical groups is shown in Fig. 36, where main basic

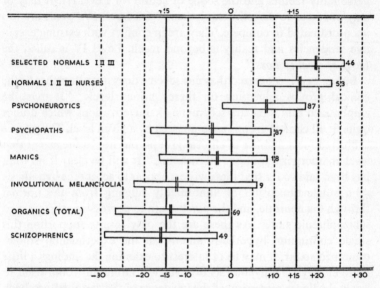

Fig. 36.—Basic Rorschach Scores of various Normal and Clinical Groups.

Rorschach scores and standard deviational ranges for larger clinical categories are shown.

It will be noticed that this figure is divided into four levels. These are described by the authors as follows. Level I: "In the *ideally integrated dynamic pattern* tendencies to execution are proportionate to an adequate aspiration focus, adequate reality-awareness and relative consideration of immediate and long-range goals. . . . We assign a personality to Level I as long as the two basic problems, the conflict of deferment and the co-ordination of goal striving with reality, have not yet overthrown the ego-organisation. We call this the *Level of Adequacy*." On Level II "the personality is in conflict with reality but has not lost contact with it. However, the ego-organisation is overthrown because of the unresolved conflict between immediate and deferred goals. This conflict prevents unification of strivings. We call this the *Level of Conflict*." On Level III "unification of strivings is abandoned. The dynamics of this defect vary in the different clinical groups falling to this level. Outstanding in the statistical picture is a psychopathic pattern which shows conflict resolved by pursuing immediate satisfaction without regret as a result of a debilitated emotionality. . . . The term *Level of Defect* refers to the incomplete and disproportionate representation of personality factors and the scope of action for Level III. It may or may not refer to defective equipment." On Level IV "goals are too unco-ordinated to compete. They are in conflict with existing executive tendencies and reality is beyond reach. Level IV is called the *Level of Reality Loss*."

Bühler *et al.* recognized that this scheme does not altogether fit the clinical groups appearing on these various levels; "It must be emphasized that these are schematic characterizations which do not quite fit all clinical groups encompassed by a given level. The picture is blurred for a number of clinical groups, but not to the extent that level characterization loses all meaning." It will be clear from what has been said so far that these writers appear to accept the hypothesis of a single dimension of abnormality ranging from the normal through the neurotic, and the psychopath to depressive, organic, and schizophrenic states. As these are the only results supporting this single continuum hypothesis among all the experimental studies examined so far, it may be of interest to examine the findings a little more closely. The hypothesis of a single continuum would seem to imply the linear regression of the incidence of the various Rorschach signs on level of adjustment, i.e. signs shown frequently at Level I and rarely at Level IV should be shown with intermediate frequency at Levels II and III.

In Fig. 37 the present writer has plotted the regression of eight of the signs which make up the basic Rorschach score in terms of sigma scores for the four levels. It will be seen that these eight indices, very far from showing a linear relation to level, all show a curvilinear regression in the sense of having low incidence at Levels I and IV and high incidence at Levels II and III. Summing these sigma scores for the four levels, we obtain values of $-3 \cdot 0$ at Level I, $3 \cdot 8$ for Level II, $0 \cdot 1$ for Level III and $-7 \cdot 2$ for Level IV. On these scores, therefore, we find no evidence for the hypothetical continuum: normal, neurotic, organic, psychotic; rather we find the neurotics at one extreme and psychotics at the other, and normals and organics intermediate.

It is difficult to see how these results can be reconciled with the hypothesis underlying the basic Rorschach score. It is indeed admitted by Bühler *et al.* that not all signs follow the trend from high respectively low on Level I to low respectively high on Level IV, indicating that integration (or whatever the Rorschach measures) is not likely to be a one-dimensional function. "There are probably at least two factors involved. . . . A remarkable dichotomy is found. Beginning with Level II, we find here the peak of uncontrolled emotionality (CF + C), the peaks of anxiety (K + k), insecurity (*c*),

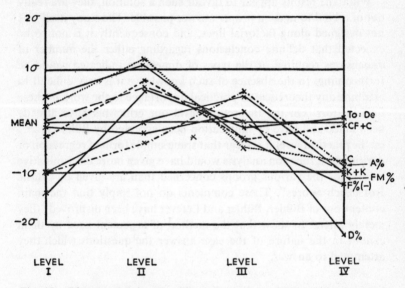

Fig. 37.—Diagram showing Curvilinear Regression of eight Constituents of Basic Rorschach Score on Level of Abnormality.

and unsatisfied instinctual drive in proportion to deferred goals (FM : M); these signs with low F (disregard of reality) present the pattern we would expect in neurosis. *The pattern expresses the conflict between tendencies towards immediate satisfaction and tendencies towards deferred satisfaction, i.e. the characteristic of neurotic conflict.* . . . On Level IV the problem no longer exists; all striving appears in regression below the conflict level. *The conflict between immediate and deferred satisfaction is repressed by a much more severe problem* expressed in the W : M proportion and also in the antagonism between the very high W and the high F." This admission that the basic Rorschach score is not a one-dimensional function is in agreement with our analysis and indicates that this score cannot properly be used to support the single continuum hypothesis. Quite on the contrary, if, as we have shown and as the authors admit, integration is not likely to be a one-dimensional function, and if a clear dichotomy appears between neurotic and psychotic lack of integration, then clearly these results may rather be taken to disprove the hypothesis of a single continuum and to support the view that we are dealing with two radically different dimensions, i.e. a neurotic and a psychotic one.

While the results appear to favour such a solution, they are really not of a kind to make a proper answer possible. The study itself was not designed along factorial lines, and consequently it is not to be expected that definite conclusions regarding either the number of dimensions required or the types of dimension indicated would be forthcoming. In the absence of such knowledge it is very difficult to attribute any theoretical or practical importance to the work of these investigators. On the theoretical level our criticisms have already been made and have by implication been accepted by Bühler *et al.*; on the practical level it is clear that some simple form of regression or discriminant function analysis would have given more discriminative results for the various groups concerned than are given by "Basic Rorschach Scores". These comments do not imply that the main contentions of Bühler, Bühler and Lefever have been disproved; they merely intend to show that the method of argument used by them cannot in the nature of the case answer the questions which they attempted to answer.

CHAPTER X

SUMMARY AND CONCLUSIONS

THE PERUSAL OF large numbers of research reports, all bearing on one and the same central problem, cannot but lead to certain conclusions which may lack the objectivity attaching to factual summaries, but which may, nevertheless, be of some interest—if only because they may lead to fruitful discussion of certain fundamental problems of research methodology. Consequently, a number of such subjective views are set down in this final chapter; while arising from the researches summarized in previous chapters, they do not necessarily follow from the evidence but constitute rather an interpretation of it. The reader is at liberty to disregard these views completely, and to evaluate the evidence from his own point of view; indeed, if this book has no other effect than to send the reader back to the original articles on which it is based, it will have fulfilled the most sanguine expectations of its author!

(1) The first conclusion which seems warranted by the data seems to be that agreement between different experimenters is far more marked than might have been expected from the very vocal disagreements so frequently found in the literature. In part, these disagreements are of a purely semantic type; if one and the same factor is regarded as one of "introversion" by one investigator, as "secondary function" by another, as "oral pessimism" by a third, and as "rhathymia" by a fourth, it does not follow that there is any disagreement about the facts of the case. These terms, and many others used in the literature, may refer to precisely the same underlying objective reality; semantic preference judgments must not be taken as objective disagreements. In part, however, differences do have an objective reference, and it is here that Thurstone's brilliant conception of "second-order factors" has shown a way of harmonizing these disagreements in a higher synthesis.

The fact that there is much agreement does not imply that no disagreements remain. These are mainly due to three causes: (A) Some researches contain too few variables, or variables too badly chosen, to give rise to meaningful factors of any kind. It would be invidious to give detailed references, but it is impossible to look through the literature and not be struck by the fact that some factor analysts appear to think of this technique as a *vade mecum* which will resolve into meaningful harmony any set of arbitrarily chosen measures, collected without any preliminary hypotheses in mind, and thrown together in the hope that "something will come out of it". Frequently, factor analysis is an after-thought, a last resort when other techniques fail to unearth anything worth-while from the data. Factors derived in this fashion are not likely to fit in with any kind of conceptual scheme, except by chance, and there is no reason why they should. (B) Most of the researches summarized were carried out before the principle of oblique and second-order factors was established, and consequently the analysis was not carried to its logical conclusion, but left at the level of rotated orthogonal structure. This will mix up to a considerable extent first- and second-order factors, and may thus appear to contradict findings from a complete analysis. Re-analysis of the data will often show that such contradictions are apparent rather than real; in any case, developments of technique often make older work obsolete, in other fields as well, and there is no reason to expect analyses carried out thirty or forty years ago to be still acceptable today. (C) Occasionally, differences in *results* are due to differences in *aim*. The scientist looks for *pure* factors and univocal tests; the applied psychologist may look for *mixed* factors and *complex* tests to give him better prediction of a complex variable, such as success at school or separation from the army. It is easy to imagine that such differences are *fundamental*, when really they arise only from the different purposes of the investigators. The same conflict between practical convenience of application and pure fundamental science can be found, with similar results, in many other fields of science.

Granted, then, that the picture is not as clear as one might wish; nevertheless its main outlines are becoming more and more definite. At the trait level, a number of concepts (persistence, primary suggestibility, oscillation, level of aspiration, and various others) have been shown to possess *functional unity*, and have been found amenable to objective measurement with considerable reliability and validity. At the type level, i.e. at a level where concepts are based essentially on the intercorrelations between traits, three main dimensions appear to have been established: Neuroticism, Extraversion-Introversion, and Psychoticism. These three dimensions appear to be relatively orthogonal to each other, and also to "g" (Thurstone's second-order factor of cognitive functioning). These dimensions,

too, admit of measurement along purely objective lines, and reliabilities and validities at the ·80 level have been reported. Much
filling-in clearly needs to be done, and the accuracy of measurement
in particular stands in need of considerable improvement. Nor can
it be maintained that these are the only higher-order factors which
may be discovered; nothing can be said yet about the total number of
such factors required.

Taking it all in all, then, we may conclude that factorial work
in the non-cognitive field has resulted in considerable clarification,
although it is clearly realized that not more than a beginning has
been made. The essential advance which factor analysis has brought,
disregarding for the moment the wealth of data discussed in this
book, has been the proof that hypotheses of psychological organization can be rigorously stated and tested. Even if the conclusions drawn
from previous researches should all prove to be fallacious, factor
analysis, like all scientific methods, carries with it the assurance that
future work based on these conclusions will show them up in so far as
they are in error.

(2) The second point brought out by our review appears to be that
work in the field of personality should not confine itself to a small
sector, but to be convincing should embrace personality in all its
aspects. The doctrine of the "total personality" appears to be entirely
justified in so far as it declares that partial approaches are liable to
lead only to partial understanding. Investigations should be as broadly
based as possible, including ratings, self-ratings, objective behaviour
tests, estimates of physique, autonomic and other relevant physiological measurements, biographical and other historical information,
and, indeed, all and every type of factual and objective information
which may be used to support or refute the hypotheses under
investigation.

By confining himself to ratings only, or to physiological measures,
or to questionnaires, the investigator makes the interpretation of his
factors (and, indeed, of all his results) unnecessarily difficult or even
impossible. Nothing is more convincing than the establishment of
factors from very divergent experimental material; to find a predicted concomitance between measures taken from all these different
groups of tests is far more impressive than to discover covariation
between one answer on a questionnaire and another. Objections
which may apply to questionnaires, say, or to ratings, do not apply
to objective tests or to autonomic measures. It follows that factors
established on the basis of ratings only, or questionnaire answers

only, or indeed on the basis of any one type of test material only, are subject to the same objections as is that particular test material; if the factors can be shown to extend to tests to which these objections do not apply, their validity is considerably enhanced. Ratings are known to be subject to a considerable "halo" effect; if it can be shown that objective tests, Rorschach factor scores, physiological measures like the recovery quotient, and even certain types of body build, correlate with ratings and define the same factor of neuroticism, then the status of this factor is much more secure, and not subject to the criticism that it may simply be an artefact of the rating procedure.

This insistence on broadening the basis on which work in personality is carried out applies not only to tests but also to the population tested. The interpretation given to a factor derived from a student population might be considerably changed if the same tests were given to unemployed coal-miners or to criminals in a penitentiary. It seems to the writer that a factor based on intercorrelations between normal subjects should not be identified with cyclothymia, for instance, or any other concept derived from abnormal groups, without clear-cut proof that those tests or items having high saturations on this factor do in fact discriminate with a high degree of significance between manic-depressive and schizophrenic subjects. This means that *criterion groups* should always be included in the experimental design to test the interpretation of the factors found; if no such possibility of validation exists, other methods should be used for reducing the excessive subjectivity adhering to so many factor-interpretations found in the literature.

What has been said so far applies in the main to second-order factors; *mutatis mutandis* it may also be applied to primary factors. Many studies of such factors as perseveration, or persistence, or oscillation, are on too small a scale to give reliable results. In the first place, reliable measures of "g", neuroticism, and various other factors must be included in order to partial out, or otherwise keep constant, their influence; in the second place, a sufficient number and variety of measures of the hypothetical factor in question must be included to make accurate determination of the location of the bounding hyperplanes possible.

These remarks will indicate that a factorial study is a somewhat complex and large-scale affair, not to be undertaken lightly; if the necessary conditions are not met, the results of such an enquiry may be interesting and even promising, but they cannot be considered in any sense definitive, and may be controverted by later, more extensive work, or their implications considerably changed. It would appear to follow from this that factorial research should be co-operative research, i.e. research undertaken by a whole group of psychologists rather than by a single, solitary worker; only in this way is it likely that all the necessary aspects of the central problem can be covered. Such co-operative work is not likely to prosper unless the whole department, teaching staff and students alike, devote their research energies to *programme research*, as Marquis (1948) has called it, i.e. to the unified attack, extending over a number of years, on a single important psychological problem.

(3) The third point relates to the necessity for integrating factorial work of the kind described in these pages with experimental work on the individual tests which are being used to measure the factors extracted. There is here an obvious clash of interests which has had a somewhat disturbing influence on factorial studies. In order to fulfil the conditions indicated in the preceding paragraph, factorists have felt obliged to include larger and larger numbers of tests in their batteries. However, time and availability of subjects set very definite limitations to the length of the total testing period. In consequence, tests have often been shortened to such an extent that their reliability has sunk below reasonable levels, and their interpretation has become extremely doubtful. The choice between too few, but reliable and meaningful tests, and between many, but unreliable and not maximally valid tests, is one which has to be faced too frequently by psychologists, and it can only be solved at the experimental level by undertaking a detailed analysis of each component test to establish more securely optimum scoring methods, minimal length to give sufficient reliability, and quite generally a *rationale* which will make raw scores on the test intelligible in terms of genuine psychological components.

As the last of these points is the most important, a few examples may perhaps not be amiss to make a little clearer just what is involved here. Elsewhere in this book, evidence has been brought forward to show that primary suggestibility is correlated with neuroticism, and that the concept of "primary suggestibility" possesses a certain degree of functional unity. An experimental attempt to find a *rationale* for suggestibility tests of this type suggested that the raw score is determined by two quite distinct factors: (1) strength of ideo-motor tendency, and (2) "will-power", or ability to counteract this tendency (Eysenck, 1947). A zero (non-sway) score on the Hull

Body Sway Test of suggestibility, therefore, might be due either to a lack of ideo-motor tendency or to the possession of the requisite ability to counteract the influence of such a tendency. The score is therefore not unambiguous, and is not a pure measure of either of these more fundamental underlying factors. Experimental work therefore, should with advantage be devoted to: (1) the proof or disproof of the above hypothesis, and (2) the discovery of pure tests for ideo-motor tendency and "will-power" separately.

Similarly, in the case of fluency tests, it has been shown by Bousfield and Sedgwick (1944) that raw output scores could be rationalized in terms of two semi-independent concepts, C or total supply of relevant words, and m or rate of depletion of this total store. The exponential equation: $N = C(1 - e^{-mt})$, where N is the number of words produced, t is the time over which the test is carried out, and e is the base of the natural logarithms, was shown to fit adequately the rate of output during the test. This finding, if it were to be supported, revolutionizes the factorial study of fluency; we should drop the practice of intercorrelating raw scores, and use C and m scores instead.

It is the contention of the writer that all tests which are used in factorial investigations should be subjected to close experimental analysis of this type, and it is his belief that many of the divergent and contradictory findings in the literature would be cleared up and explained in terms of much more fundamental analysis. Neither factorial nor experimental methods alone hold the key to the riddle of personality organization; both are needed in equal measure, and each will be found to supplement the other.

(4) The last point to be made is of much greater importance than the matters of detail mentioned before. It appears to the writer that a great deal of experimental work, as well as of factorial work, has for all practical purposes been wasted because it was not designed to test any particular hypothesis. Blind empiricism has often been mistaken for scientific method because it observed all the outward shibboleths of "brass instruments" and mathematical notation; the dearth of important findings of any general validity in the field of personality research is adequate comment on this illusion. What is required, or so it would appear to the present writer, is the construction of a *mathematical model* of personality organization, and the derivation of testable hypotheses from this model by means of the *hypothetico-deductive method*. As far as possible, illustrations of this approach have been included in this book, but it must be ad-

mitted that the majority of writers have used a rather less definitely directed approach. It is at least not impossible that an attack on the problems of personality organization undertaken in the light of some more definite theoretical conception would have advanced our understanding more than the great number of almost haphazard forays executed without any sort of general strategic conception.

The technique of factor analysis can be used as easily in the service of hypothetico-deductive methodology as in that of blind empiricism; examples of both uses will have been encountered throughout this book. It is a fact that the latter type of usage has been the more prominent; possibly a good many criticisms of factor analysis may be due to this neglect of formulating explicit hypotheses and testing them factorially. Like most other statistical techniques, factor analysis can be used either to suggest hypotheses or to prove them (Eysenck, 1952, 1953); both functions are useful and may lead to very real advances. In the field of personality, the time has surely come when *proof* should supplant *suggestion;* if the scheme outlined in these pages has no other merit, at least it may provide a number of definite hypotheses which can be subjected to empirical test. It is almost certain that little of it will survive unchanged, and much of it may be found wanting altogether; the best that can be claimed for any scientific theory is that it is an approximation, however distant, to the truth.

BIBLIOGRAPHY AND AUTHOR INDEX

For the convenience of the reader, the list of references has been combined with the author index, so that after each citation are given in italics the numbers of the pages on which the citation in question occurs.

ABRAHAM, K. The First Pregenital Stage of the Libido. In: *Selected Papers*. London: Hogarth Press, 1916. *123*.

A Short Study of the Development of the Libido, viewed in the Light of Mental Disorders. In: *Selected Papers*. London: Hogarth Press, 1924. *123*.

The Influence of Oral Erotism on Character-formation. In: *Selected Papers*. London: Hogarth Press, 1952. *123*.

ACKERSON, L. *Children's Behavior Problems*. Chicago: Univ. Chicago Press, 1942. *88*.

ADAMS, J. K., and FOWLER, H. M. *Report on the Reliability of Two Forms of an Activity Preference Blank*. Washington, D.C.: U.S. Dep. Commerce, 1946. *221*.

ADCOCK, C. J. A Factorial Examination of Sheldon's Types. *J. Personality*, 1948, **16**, 312–319. *69*.

A Factorial Approach to Rorschach Interpretation. *J. Gen. Psychol.*, 1951, **44**, 261–272. *312*.

ADORNO, T. W., FRENKEL-BRUNSWIK, E., LEVINSON, D. J., and SANFORD, R. N. *The Authoritarian Personality*. New York: Harper Bros., 1950. *236*.

ALEXANDER, W. P. Intelligence, Concrete and Abstract. *Brit. J. Psychol.*, *Monog. Suppl.*, 1935, **19**, 177. *285*.

ALLPORT, G. W. *Personality. A Psychological Interpretation*. London: Constable & Co. Ltd., 1937. *2, 5, 9, 105*.

ALLPORT, G. W., and ODBERT, H. S. Trait-names: a Psycho-lexical Study. *Psychol. Mon.*, 1936, **47**, 171. *63*.

ALLPORT, G. W., and VERNON, P. E. *Studies in Expressive Movement*. New York: Macmillan, 1933. *305*.

A Study of Values. Boston: Houghton Mifflin, 1931. *219*.

ASCH, E. E. An Experimental Study of Variability in Learning. *Arch. Psychol.*, 1933, **22**, 1–54. *291*.

AVELING, F., and HARGREAVES, M. Suggestibility with and without Prestige in Children. *Brit. J. Psychol.*, 1921, **12**, 53–75. *297*.

BAEHR, M. *A Factorial Study of Temperament*. Psychomet. Lab., Univ. Chicago, 1951. *109*.

BAKWIN, H., and BAKWIN, R. M. Body Build in Infants. I. The Technique of measuring the External Dimensions of the Body in Infants. *J. clin. Invest.*, 1931, **10**, 369–376. *172*.

Body Build in Infants. II. Anthropometry in the New Born. *Hum. Biol.*, 1934, **6**, 612–626. *172*.

BALDWIN, A. L. Personal Structure Analysis: a Statistical Method for Investigating the Simple Personality. *J. abnorm. and soc. Psychol.*, 1942, **37**, 163–183. *263*.

The Study of Individual Personality by means of the Intra-individual Correlation. *J. Personality*, 1945, **14**, 151–183. *264*.

Differences in Parent Behavior toward Three- and Nine-year-old Children. *J. Personality*, 1946, **15**, 143–165. *84, 263, 264*.

BALDWIN, A. L., KALHORN, J., and BREESE, T. H.   Patterns of Parent Behavior. *Psychol. Mon.*, 1945, **58**, 1–75. *84.*

The Appraisal of Parent Behavior.   *Psychol. Mon.*, 1949, **63**, 1–85. *84.*

BANKS, C.   Primary Personality Factors in Women: a Reanalysis. *Brit. J. Psychol., Stat. Sect.*, 1948, 1, 204–218. *65.*

BANKS, C., and KEIR, G.   A Factorial Analysis of Items in the Bernreuter Personality Inventory.   *Brit. J. Psychol., Stat. Sect.*, 1952, **5**, 19–30. *114.*

BARNES, C. A.   A Statistical Study of the Freudian Theory of Levels of Psycho-sexual Development.   *Genet. Psychol. Mon.*, 1952, **45**, 105–174. *127.*

BAUER, J.   *Vorlesungen über allegemeine Konstitutions-Vererbungslehre.*   Berlin: Springer, 1924. *165, 177.*

BEEBE-CENTER, J. B.   *Pleasantness and Unpleasantness.*   New York: Century, 1933. *249, 258.*

BENASSY, M., and CHAUFFARD, C.   Le Test F de Cattell est-il un Test Objectif de Temperament?   *Anne. psychol.*, 1947, 43–44, 200–230. *294.*

BENDER, L., and SCHILDER, P.   Unconditioned and Conditioned Reaction to Pain in Schizophrenia.   *Amer. J. Psychiat.*, 1930, **87**, 365–384. *27.*

BENEKE, F. W.   *Die anatomische-Grundlagen der Konstitutions-anomalien des Menschen.*   Marburg, 1878. *164, 165.*

BENNETT, E., and SLATER, P.   Some Tests for the Discrimination of Neurotic from Normal Subjects and the Psychometric Differentiation of Neurotic from Normal Subjects.   *Brit. J. med. Psychol.*, 1945, **20**, 271–282. *122.*

BERNSTEIN, E.   Quickness and Intelligence.   *Brit. J. Psychol., Monog. Suppl.*, 1924, **3**, 1–55. *274.*

BESSONET-FAVRE, A.   *La Typologie, Methode d'Observation des Types Humains.* Paris: 1910. *177.*

BIESHEUVEL, S.   The Measurement of the Threshold for Flicker and its value as a Perseveration Test.   *Brit. J. Psychol.*, 1938, **29**, 27–38. *280.*

BLUM, G. S., and MILLER, D. R.   Exploring the Psychoanalytic Theory of the "Oral Character".   *J. Personality*, 1952, **20**, 287–307. *127.*

BOUSFIELD, W. A., and SEDGEWICK, C. M. W.   An Analysis of Sequences of Restricted Associative Responses.   *J. Gen. Psychol.*, 1944, **30**, 149–165. *295, 322.*

BRENGELMANN, J. C.   Kretschmer's zyklothymer und schizothymer Typus im Bereich der normalen Persönlichkeit.   *Psychol. Rund.*, 1952, **3**, 31–38. *160, 167.*

BROGDEN, H. E.   A Factor Analysis of Forty Character Tests.   *Psychol. Mon.*, 1940, **234**, 35–55. *143.*

A Multiple Factor Analysis of the Character Trait Intercorrelations published by Sister Mary McDonough.   *J. educ. Psychol.*, 1944, **35**, 397–410. *50.*

BROGDEN, H. E., and THOMAS, W. F.   The Primary Traits in Personality Items purporting to Measure Sociability.   *J. Psychol.*, 1943, **16**, 85–97. *116.*

BROWN, V.   *Individual and Sex Differences in Suggestibility.*   Univ. of Calif. Publ. in Psychol., 1916, **2**, 291–430. *296.*

BUHLER, C., BUHLER, K., and LEFEVER, D. W.   *Development of the Basic Rorschach Score, with Manual of Directions.*   California: Copyright, 1949. *312.*

BURGMEISTER, B. B.   The Permanence of Interests of Women College Students. *Arch. Psychol.*, 1940, No. 255, 59. *220.*

BURT, C.   The General and Specific Factors underlying the Primary Emotions. *Brit. Ass. Ann. Rep.*, 1915, **84**, 694–696. *45.*

The Analysis of Temperament.   *Brit. J. med. Psychol.*, 1937, **17**, 158–188. *45, 174.*

Factor Analysis by Sub-matrices.   *J. Psychol.*, 1938, **6**, 339–375. *257.*

The Factorial Analysis of Emotional Traits. *Char. & Personal.*, 1939, **7**, 238–254, 285–299. *45*.

The Factors of the Mind. London: Univ. London Press, 1940. *46, 55, 249*.

Factor Analysis and Physical Types. *Psychomet.*, 1947, **12**, 171–188. *165, 169*.

The Factorial Study of Temperamental Traits. *Brit. J. Psychol., Stat. Sect.*, 1948, **1**, 178–203. *47*.

BURT, C., and BANKS, C. A Factor Analysis of Body Measurements for British Adult Males. *Ann. Eug.*, 1947, **13**, 238–256. *169*.

BURT, C., and STEPHENSON, W. Alternative Views on Correlations between Persons. *Psychomet.*, 1939, **4**, 269–281. *269*.

BURT, C., and WATSON, H. Factor Analysis of Assessments for a Single Person. *Brit. J. Psychol., Stat. Sect.*, 1951, **4**, 179–192. *269*.

CARLSON, M. B. Attitudes of Undergraduate Students. *J. soc. Psychol.*, 1934, **5**, 202–212. *224*.

CARPENTER, A. The Differential Measurement of Speed in Primary School-children. *Child Development*, 1941, **12**, 1–8. *307*.

CARROLL, J. B. A Factor Analysis of Verbal Abilities. *Psychomet.*, 1941, **6**, 279–308. *295*.

CARTER, H. D., and KRAUSE, R. M. Physical Proportions of the Human Infant. *Child Development*, 1936, **7**, 60–68. *172*.

CARTER, H. D., PYLES, M. K., and BRETNALL, E. P. A Comparative Study of Factors in Vocational Interest Scores of High School Boys. *J. educ. Psychol.*, 1935, **26**, 81–98. *216*.

CARUS, C. G. *Symbolik der menschlichen Gestalt.* 1852. *165*.

CASTELLINO, P. *La Costituzione Individuale. La Personnalità.* Naples, 1927. *177*.

CATTELL, R. B. Temperament Tests: I. Temperament. *Brit. J. Psychol.*, 1933, **23**, 308–329. *48*.

Temperament Tests: II. Tests. *Brit. J. Psychol.*, 1934, **24**, 20–49. *48, 293*.

On the Measurement of Perseveration. *Brit. J. educ. Psychol.*, 1935, **5**, 76–92. *271, 277*.

Temperament Tests in Clinical Practice. *Brit. J. med. Psychol.*, 1936, **16**, 43–61. *293*.

Fluctuations of Sentiments and Attitudes as a Measure of Character Interpretation and Temperament. *Amer. J. Psychol.*, 1943, **56**, 195–216. *292*.

The Description of Personality. *Psychol. Rev.*, 1943, **50**, 539–594. *63, 263*.

The Description and Measurement of Personality. London: Harrap & Co. Ltd., 1946. *144, 146, 245, 263, 266, 293*.

The Riddle of Perseveration: I. "Creative Effort" and Disposition Rigidity. II. Solution in Terms of Personality Structure. *J. Personality*, 1946, **14**, 229–267. *280*.

Confirmation and Clarification of Primary Personality Factors. *Psychomet.*, 1947, **12**, 197–220.

Oblique, Second-order, and Cooperative Factors in Personality Analysis. *J. Gen. Psychol.*, 1947, **36**, 3–22. *65*.

Primary Personality Factors in the Realm of Objective Tests. *J. Personality*, 1948, **16**, 459–487. *144*.

The Primary Personality Factors in Women compared with those of Men. *Brit. J. Psychol., Stat. Sect.*, 1948, **1**, 114–130. *65*.

The Main Personality Factors in Questionnaire, Self-estimate Material. *J. soc. Psychol.*, 1950, **31**, 3–38. *118*.

The Three Basic Factor-analytic Research Designs—their Intercorrelations and Derivatives. *Psychol. Bull.*, 1952, **49**, 499–520. *269*.

CATTELL, R. B., CATTELL, A. K. S., and RHYMER, R. M. P-technique demonstrated in determining Psychophysiological Source Traits in a Normal Individual. *Psychomet.*, 1947, **12**, 267–288. *267*.

CATTELL, R. B., and LUBORSKY, L. B. P-technique demonstrated as a New Clinical Method for determining Personality and Symptom Structure. *J. Gen. Psychol.*, 1950, **42**, 3–24. *268*.

CATTELL, R. B., and SAUNDERS, D. R. Inter-relation and Matching of Personality Factors from Behaviour Rating, Questionnaire, and Objective Test Data. *J. soc. Psychol.*, 1950, **31**, 243–260. *145*.

CATTELL, R. B., and TINER, L. G. The Varieties of Structural Rigidity. *J. Personality*, 1949, **17**, 321–341. *281*.

CHAMPNEY, H. The Variables of Parent Behavior. *J. abnorm. and soc. Psychol.*, 1941, **36**, 525–542. *84*.

The Measurement of Parent Behavior. *Child Development*, 1941, **12**, 131–166. *84*.

CHILD, I. L. The relation of Somatotype to Self-ratings on Sheldon's Temperamental Traits. *J. Personality*, 1950, **18**, 440–453. *185*.

CHISNALL, B. The Interests and Personality Traits of Delinquent Boys. *Brit. J. educ. Psychol.*, 1942, **12**, 76. *221*.

CHORUS, A. H. J. Le Rythme Personnel (das Persönliche Tempo) et le Rythme de Travail des Enfants Instables. *Z. Kinderpsychiat.*, 1943, **10**, 2–8. *293*.

COATES, T. H. *The Measurement of Adult Interests*. Ph.D. Thesis. London: Univ. London Lib., 1950. *219*.

COHEN, J. I. Determinants of Physique. *J. ment. Sci.*, 1938, **84**, 495–512. *169*.

Physical Traits and their relation to Psychotic Types. *J. ment. Sci.*, 1940, **86**, 602–623. *169*.

Physique, Size, and Proportion. *Brit. J. med. Psychol.*, 1941, **18**, 323–337. *169*.

COLLIER, R., and EMCH, M. Introversion-extraversion: the Concepts and their Clinical Use. *Amer. J. Psychiat.*, 1938, **94**, 1,045–1,075. *99*.

COOK, E. B. *A Factor Analysis of Acuity and Phoria Measurements obtained with Commercial Screening Devices and by Standard Clinical Methods*. New London, Conn.: Nav. Med. Res. Lab., 1948. (Prag. Rep. No. 4, Project NM–003–011 (X–493).)

COOK, E. B., and WHERRY, R. J. A Factor Analysis of M.M.P.I. and Aptitude Test Data. *J. appl. Psychol.*, 1950, **34**, 260–266. *102*.

COX, S. M. A Factorial Study of the Rorschach Responses of Normal and Maladjusted Boys. *J. genet. Psychol.*, 1951, **79**, 95–115. *310*.

CRISSY, W. J. E., and DANIEL, W. J. Vocational Interest Factors in Women. *J. appl. Psychol.*, 1939, **23**, 488–494. *217*.

CRUTCHER, R. An Experimental Study of Persistence. *J. appl. Psychol.*, 1934, **18**, 409–417. *284*.

CUMMINGS, J. D. Variability of Judgment and Steadiness of Character. *Brit. J. Psychol.*, 1939, **29**, 345–370. *292*.

CUSHING, H. M. A Perseverative Tendency in Pre-school Children: a Study of Personality Differences. *Arch. Psychol.*, 1929, **17**, 55. *284*.

DARLEY, J. G., and MCNAMARA, W. J. A Factor Analysis of Test—Retest Performance on Attitude and Adjustment Tests. *J. educ. Psychol.*, 1938, **29**, 652–664. *226*.

Factor Analysis in the Establishment of New Personality Tests. *J. educ. Psychol.*, 1940, **31**, 321–334. *226*.

DARLING, R. P. Autonomic Action in relation to Personality Traits of Children. *J. abnorm. soc. Psychol.*, 1940, **35**, 246–260. *191*.

DARROCH, J. An Investigation into the Degree of Variation in the Score of a Motor Perseveration Test. *Brit. J. Psychol.*, 1938, **28**, 248–262. *278*.

DARROW, C. W. The Equation of the Galvanic Skin Reflex Curve. *J. Gen. Psychol.*, 1937, **16**, 285–309. *205*.

DARROW, C. W., and HEATH, L. L. Reaction Tendencies relating to Personality. In: *Studies in the Dynamics of Behavior.* (Ed. Lashley, K. S.) Chicago: Univ. Chicago Press, 1932. *188*.

DAVIES, M. The General Factor in Correlations between Persons. *Brit. J. Psychol.*, 1939, **29**, 404–421. *258*.

DEARBORN, W. F., and ROTHNEY, J. W. M. *Predicting the Child's Development.* Cambridge, Mass.: Sci.-Art Publishers, 1941. *169*.

DEWAR, H. A Comparison of Tests of Artistic Appreciation. *Brit. J. educ. Psychol.*, 1938, **8**, 29–49. *258*.

DI GIOVANNI, A. *Clinical Commentaries deduced from the Morphology of the Human Body.* London: Trans. by Eyre, J. J., 1919. *165*.

DOUST, J. W. L. The Psychiatric Aspects of Somatic Immunity: the Differential Incidence of Physical Disease in the Histories of Psychiatric Patients. *Brit. J. soc. Med.*, 1952, **6**, 49–67. *77*.

DOWNEY, J. E. *The Will-profile.* Dep. Psychol., Bull. No. 3. Wyoming: Univ. Wyoming, 1919. *137*.

DUDYCHA, G. J. An Objective Study of Punctuality in relation to Personality Achievement. *Arch. Psychol.*, 1936, No. 204, 53. *308*.

DUFFY, E. Tensions and Emotional Factors in Reaction. *Genet. Psychol. Monog.*, 1930, **7**, 1–79. *299*.

Muscular Tension as related to Physique and Behavior. *Child Development*, 1932, **3**, 200–206. *299*.

The Measurement of Muscular Tension as a Technique for the Study of Emotional Tendencies. *Amer. J. Psychol.*, 1932, **44**, 146–162. *299*.

The Relation between Muscular Tension and Quality of Performance. *Amer. J. Psychol.*, 1932, **44**, 535–546. *299*.

Level of Muscular Tension as an Aspect of Personality. *J. Gen. Psychol.*, 1946, **35**, 161–171. *299*.

DUFFY, E., and CRISSY, W. J. E. Evaluative Attitudes as related to Vocational Interests and Academic Achievement. *J. abnorm. soc. Psychol.*, 1940, **35**, 226–245. *220*.

DYMOND, R. F. A Preliminary Investigation of the Relation of Insight and Empathy. *J. consult. Psychol.*, 1948, **12**, 228–233. *304*.

A Scale for the Measurement of Empathic Ability. *J. consult. Psychol.*, 1949, **13**, 127–133. *304*.

Personality and Empathy. *J. consult. Psychol.*, 1950, **14**, 345–350. *304*.

EKMAN, G. On the Number and Definition of Dimensions in Kretschmer's and Sheldon's Constitutional Systems. In: *Essays in Psychology dedicated to David Katz.* Uppsala, 1951. *182*.

On Typological and Dimensional Systems of Reference in describing Personality. *Acta. Psychol.*, 1951, **8**, 1–24. *70, 182*.

ELLIS, A. The Validity of Personality Questionnaires. *Psychol. Bull.*, 1946, **43**, 385–440. *121, 127*.

ELLIS, A., and CONRAD, H. S. The Validity of Personality Inventories in Military Practice. *Psychol. Bull.*, 1948, **45**, 385–426. *121, 127*.

ELMGREN, J. Significance of Individual Differences in the Human E.E.G. In: *Essays in Psychology dedicated to David Katz.* Uppsala, 1951.

EPPINGER, H. Vagotonia. *Nerv. Ment. Dis. Mon.*, 1917, 20. *193*.

EYSENCK, H. J. Some Factors in the Appreciation of Poetry and their relation to Temperamental Qualities. *Char. and Personal.*, 1940, **9**, 160–167. *263*.

The General Factor in Æsthetic Judgments. *Brit. J. Psychol.*, 1940, **31**, 94–102. *260*.

"Type"—factors in Æsthetic Judgments. *Brit. J. Psychol.*, 1941, **31**, 262–270. *260*.

The Appreciation of Humour: an Experimental and Theoretical Study. *Brit. J. Psychol.*, 1942, **32**, 295–309. *261*.

The Experimental Study of the "Good Gestalt"—a New Approach. *Psychol. Rev.*, 1942, **49**, 344–364. *260*.

An Experimental Analysis of Five Tests of "Appreciation of Humour". *Educ. Psychol. Measmt.*, 1943, **3**, 191–214. *261*.

Suggestibility and Hysteria. *J. Neurol. and Psychiat.*, 1943, **6**, 22–31. *297*.

General Social Attitudes. *J. soc. Psychol.*, 1944, **19**, 207–227. *227*.

Types of Personality—a Factorial Study of 700 Neurotics. *J. ment. Sci.*, 1944, **90**, 851–861. *22, 53*.

Dimensions of Personality. London: Kegan Paul, 1947. *13, 14, 31, 54, 77, 99, 100, 123, 148, 150, 166, 171, 176, 177, 261, 262, 290, 296, 299, 306, 307, 321*.

Primary Social Attitudes. I. The Organization and Measurement of Social Attitudes. *Internat. J. Opin. and Attit. Res.*, 1947, **1**, 49–84. *231, 244*.

Criterion Analysis: an Application of the Hypothetico-deductive Method to Factor Analysis. *Psychol. Rev.*, 1950, **57**, 38–53. *150, 151*.

Cyclothymia-schizothymia as a Dimension of Personality. I. Historical Review. *J. Personality*, 1950, **19**, 123–153. *24, 25, 32, 167*.

Measurement and Prediction. A discussion of Volume IV of *Studies in Social Psychology in World War II. Internat. J. Opin. and Attit. Res.*, 1951, **5**, 95–102. *244*.

Primary Social Attitudes and the "Social Insight" Test. *Brit. J. Psychol.*, 1951, **42**, 114–122. *232*.

Primary Social Attitudes as related to Social Class and Political Party. *J. Sociol.*, 1951, **2**, 198–219. *232*.

Schizothymia-cyclothymia as a Dimension of Personality. II. Experimental. *J. Personality*, 1952, **30**, 345–384. *159*.

The Scientific Study of Personality. London: Routledge & Kegan Paul, 1952. *26, 61, 148, 153, 161, 162, 206, 290, 299*.

Uses and Abuses of Factor Analysis. *Appl. Stat.*, 1951, **1**, 45–49. *xiv*.

Primary Social Attitudes. II. A Comparison of Attitude Patterns in England, Germany, and Sweden. *J. abnorm. and soc. Psychol.*, 1953. In press. *232*.

The Logical Basis of Factor Analysis. *Amer. Psychol.*, 1953. In press. *xiv*.

EYSENCK, H. J., and CROWN, S. An Experimental Study in Opinion-attitude Methodology. *Internat. J. Opin. and Attit. Res.*, 1949, **3**, 47–86. *236*.

EYSENCK, H. J., and FURNEAUX, W. D. Primary and Secondary Suggestibility. An Experimental and Statistical Study. *J. exp. Psychol.*, 1945, **35**, 485–503. *298*.

EYSENCK, H. J., and HIMMELWEIT, H. T. An Experimental Study of the Reactions of Neurotics to Experiences of Success and Failure. *J. gen. Psychol.*, 1946, **35**, 59–75. *30*.

EYSENCK, H. J., and PRELL, D. B. The Inheritance of Neuroticism: an Experimental Study. *J. ment. Sci.*, 1951, **97**, 441–465. *154*.

A Note on the Differentiation of Normal and Neurotic Children by means of Objective Tests. *J. clin. Psychol.*, 1952, **8**, 202–204. *154*.

FERGUSON, L. W. Primary Social Attitudes. *J. Psychol.*, 1939, **8**, 217–223. *226*.

The Measurement of Primary Social Attitudes. *J. Psychol.*, 1940, **10**, 199–205. *226*.

The Stability of the Primary Social Attitudes. I. Religionism and Humanitarianism. *J. Psychol.*, 1941, **12**, 283–288. *226*.

The Isolation and Measurement of Nationalism. *J. soc. Psychol.*, 1942, **16**, 215–228. *226*.

A Revision of the Primary Social Attitude Scales. *J. soc. Psychol.*, 1944, **17**, 229–241. *226*.

Socio-psychological Correlates of the Primary Attitude Scales. I. Religionism; II. Humanitarianism. *J. soc. Psychol.*, 1944, **19**, 81–98. *226*.

The Sociological Validity of Primary Social Attitude Scale. I. Religionism. *J. soc. Psychol.*, 1946, **23**, 197–204. *226*.

FERGUSON, L. W., HUMPHREYS, L. G., and STRONG, F. W. A Factorial Analysis of Interests and Values. *J. educ. Psychol.*, 1941, **32**, 197–204. *220*.

FERGUSON, L. W., and LAWRENCE, W. R. An Appraisal of the Validity of the Factor Loadings employed in the Construction of Primary Social Attitude Scales. *Psychomet.*, 1942, **7**, 135–138. *226*.

FISKE, D. W. The Relation between Physique and Measures of Intelligence. Temperament and Personality in Superior Adolescent Boys. *Psychol. Bull.*, 1942, **39**, 459. *187*.

A Study of Relationships to Somatotype. *J. appl. Psychol.*, 1944, **28**, 504–519. *184*.

Consistency of the Factorial Structures of Personality Ratings from Different Sources. *J. abnorm. soc. Psychol.*, 1949, **44**, 329–344. *118*.

FLANAGAN, J. C. *Factor Analysis in the Study of Personality.* Stanford: Univ. Press, 1935. *101*.

FLEMMING, E. G. The "Halo" around "Personality". *Teach. Coll. Rec.*, 1942, **43**, 564–569. *43*.

FLUGEL, J. C. Practice, Fatigue and Oscillation. *Brit. J. Psychol., Monog. Suppl.*, 1929, **7**, 13. *291*.

Recent Studies in Oscillation. *Indian J. Psychol.*, 1934, **1**. *291*.

FOSTER, W. S. On the Perseverative Tendency. *Amer. J. Psychol.*, 1914, **25**, 393–426. *271*.

FRASER, RUSSELL. The Incidence of Neurosis among Factory Workers. London: H.M.S.O., 1947. *100*.

FREEMAN, F. *An Experimental Study of Projection among Normal and Abnormal Groups in a Structured Situation.* Ph.D. Thesis. Univ. London Lib., 1951. *305*.

FREEMAN, G. L. Toward a Psychiatric Plimsoll Mark: Physiological Recovery Quotients in Experimentally Induced Frustration. *J. Psychol.*, 1939, **8**, 247–252. *207*.

A Method of Inducing Frustration in Human Subjects and its influence upon Palmar Skin Resistance. *Amer. J. Psychol.*, 1940, **53**, 117–120. *207*.

The Energetics of Human Behavior. Ithaca, N.Y.: Cornell Univ. Press, 1948. *204, 210*.

FREEMAN, G. L., and KATZOFF, E. T. Methodological Evaluation of the Galvanic Skin Response, with special reference to the Formula for R.Q. (Recovery Quotient). *J. exp. Psychol.*, 1942, **30**, 161–174. *207*.

Individual Differences in Physiological Reactions to Stimulation and their relation to Other Measures of Emotionality. *J. exp. Psychol.*, 1942, **31**, 527–537. *205*.

FREEMAN, G. L., and PATHMAN, J. H. The Relation of Overt Muscular Discharge to Physiological Recovery from Experimentally Induced Displacement. *J. exp. Psychol.*, 1942, **30**, 161–174. *17, 208*.

Physiological Reactions to Experimentally Induced Displacement. *Amer. J. Psychiat.*, 1943, **100**, 406–412. *208*.

FRENKEL-BRUNSWIK, E. Mechanisms of Self-deception. *J. soc. Psychol.*, 1939, **10**, 409–420.

Motivation and Behavior. *Genet. Psychol. Mon.*, 1942, **26**, 121–265. *92, 93, 304*.

FREUD, S. *General Introduction to Psychoanalysis.* New York: Liveright, 1920. *99*.

Three Contributions to a Theory of Sex. In: *The Basic Writings of Sigmund Freud.* New York: Modern Library, 1938. *123*.

FREYD, M. Introverts and Extroverts. *Psychol. Rev.*, 1924, **5**, 74–87. *100*.

FRISCHEISEN-KÖHLER, I. The Personal Tempo and its Inheritance. *Char. and Personal.*, 1933, **1**, 301–313. *305*.

FRUCHTER, B. The Nature of Verbal Fluency. *Educ. Psychol. Measmt.*, 1948, **8**, 33–47. *295*.

Error Scores as a Measure of Carefulness. *J. educ. Psychol.*, 1950, **41**, 279–291. *308*.

FURNEAUX, W. D. The Prediction of Susceptibility to Hypnosis. *J. Personality*, 1946, **14**, 281–294. *299*.

GAGNE, R. M., FOSTER, H., and CROWLEY, M. E. The Measurement of Transfer of Training. *Psychol. Bull.*, 1948, **45**, 97–130. *4*.

GANNON, J. T. A Statistical Study of certain Diagnostic Personality Traits of College Men. Stud. Psychol. Psychiat. Cathol. Univ. America, 1939, No. 4, 45. *52*.

GARDNER, T. V. The Relation of Certain Personality Variables to Level of Aspiration. *J. Psychol.*, 1940, **9**, 191–206. *303*.

GARNETT, J. C. M. General Ability, Cleverness and Purpose. *Brit. J. Psychol.*, 1918, **9**, 345–366. *43*.

GEORGE, R. W. *A Comparison of Pressey X–0 Scores with Liberal–Conservative Attitudes.* M.A. Thesis. Columbia Univ. Lib., 1925. *224*.

GEWIRTZ, J. L. Studies in Word Fluency. I. Its relation to Vocabulary and Mental Age in Young Children. *J. genet. Psychol.*, 1948, **72**, 165–176. *294*.

GIBB, C. Personality Traits by Factorial Analysis. *Australian J. Psychol. and Phil.*, 1942, **20**, 1–15, 86–110, 203–227. *45, 102*.

GIESE, F. *Lehrbuch der Psychologie.* Tubingen: Mohr, 1939. *35*.

GLOVER, E. The Significance of the Mouth in Psychoanalysis. *Brit. J. med. Psychol.*, 1924, **4**, 134–155. *123*.

Notes on Oral Character-formation. *Int. J. Psychoanal.*, 1925, **6**, 131–153. *123*.

GOLDMAN-EISLER, F. Breastfeeding and Character-formation. *J. Personality*, 1948, **17**, 83–103. *123*.

Breastfeeding and Character-formation; the Etiology of the Oral Character in Psychoanalytic Theory. *J. Personality*, 1950, **19**, 189–196. *123*.

The Problem of Orality and of its Origin in Early Childhood. *J. ment. Sci.*, 1951, **97**, 765–781. *123*.

GOULD, R. An Experimental Analysis of "Level of Aspiration". *Genet. Psychol. Mon.*, 1939, **21**, 3–115. *303*.

GRAY, S. W. The Relation of Individual Variability to Intelligence. *Psychol. Bull.*, 1942, **39**, 579. *293*.

GROSS, O. *Die cerebrale Sekundärfunktion.* Leipzig: 1902. *18, 20*.

Uber psychopathologische Minderwertig Keiten. Leipzig: 1909. *18*.

GUERTIN, W. H. A Factor-analytic Study of Schizophrenic Symptoms. *J. consult. Psychol.*, 1952, **16**, 308–312. *52*.

An Inverted Factor-analytic Study of Schizophrenics. *J. consult. Psychol.*, 1952, **16**, 371–375. *52*.

GUILFORD, J. P., and GUILFORD, R. B. An Analysis of the Factors in a Typical Test of Introversion-extroversion. *J. abnorm. and soc. Psychol.*, 1934, **28**, 377–399. *103*.

Personality Factors S, E, and M, and their Measurement. *J. Psychol.*, 1936, **2**, 109–127. *103*.

Personality Factors, D, R, T, and A. *J. abnorm. soc. Psychol.*, 1939, **34**, 21–36. *103*.

Personality Factors N and GD. *J. abnorm. soc. Psychol.*, 1939, **34**, 239–248. *104*.

GUILFORD, J. P., and LACEY, J. I. (Ed.). *Army Air Forces Aviation Psychology Program Research Reports. Printed Classification Tests. Report No. 5.* Washington: U.S. Printing Office, 1947. *307*.

GUNN, D. G. Factors in the Appreciation of Poetry. *Brit. J. educ. Psychol.*, 1951, **21**, 96–104. *263*.

HALLE, G. Referred to in: *The Varieties of Human Physique.* (Sheldon, W. H.) New York: Harper Bros., 1940. *165*.

HAMILTON, W. J., BOYD, J. D., and MOSSMAN, H. W. *Human Embryology.* (*Prenatal Development of Form and Function.*) Cambridge: W. Heffer & Sons, 1945. *182*.

HAMMETT, F. S. Observations on the relation between Emotional and Metabolic Stability. *Amer. J. Physiol.*, 1921, **53**, 307–311. *291*.

HAMMOND, W. H. An application of Burt's Multiple Factor Analysis to the delineation of Physical Types. *Man*, 1942, 42, 4–11. *169*.

An Analysis of Youth Centre Interests. *Brit. J. educ. Psychol.*, 1945, **15**, 122–126. *221*.

HARGREAVES, H. L. The "Faculty" of Imagination. *Brit. J. Psychol., Monog. Suppl.*, 1927, **10**, 74. *275, 293*.

HARRISON, R. Personal Tempo and the Interrelationships of Voluntary and Maximal Rates of Movement. *J. Gen. Psychol.*, 1941, **24**, 343–379. *305*.

HARRISON, R., and DORCUS, R. M. Is rate of Voluntary Bodily Movement Unitary? *J. Gen. Psychol.*, 1938, **18**, 31–39. *305*.

HARTSHORNE, H., and MAY, M. A. *Studies in Deceit.* New York: Macmillan, 1928. *4, 93, 129*.

Studies in Service and Self Control. New York: Macmillan, 1929. *4, 93, 129*.

HARTSHORNE, H., and SHUTTLEWORTH, F. K. *Studies in the Organization of Character.* New York: Macmillan, 1930. *4, 93, 129*.

HATT, P. Class and Ethnic Attitudes. *Amer. sociol. Rev.*, 1948, **13**, 36–43. *234*.

HEATH, C. W. *What People are. A study of Normal Young Men.* Cambridge: Harvard Univ. Press, 1945. *75*.

HEATH, H. A Factor Analysis of Women's Measurements taken for Garment and Pattern Construction. *Psychomet.*, 1952, **16**, 87–100. *173*.

HEATHERS, L. B. Factors producing generality in the Level of Aspiration. *J. exp. Psychol.*, 1942, **30**, 392–406. *303*.

HERON, ALASTAIR. *A Psychological Study of Occupational Adjustment.* Ph.D. Thesis. London: Univ. London Lib., 1951. *156*.

HERRINGTON, A. In: McNEMAR, Q., and MERRILL, M. A. *Studies in Personality.* New York: McGraw-Hill, 1942. *291*.

HERTWIG, O. *Die Colomtheorie.* Jena, 1881. *177*.

HEWITT, L. E., and JENKINS, R. L. *Fundamental Patterns of Maladjustment. The Dynamics of their Origin.* Illinois: D. H. Green, 1946. *84*.

HEYMANS, G. Uber einige psychische Korrelationer. *Ztschr. f. angew. Psychol.*, 1908, **1**, 313–381. *36*.

HEYMANS, G., and BRUGMANS, H. Intelligentz Prüfungen mit Studierenden. *Ztschr. f. angew. Psychol.*, 1913, **7**, 317–331. *20, 271, 272*.

HEYMANS, G., and WIERSMA, E. Beitrage zur speziellen Psychologie auf Grund einer Massenufersuchung. *Ztschr. f. Psychol.*, 1906, **42**, 81–127; 1906, **43**,

321–373; 1907, **45**, 1–42; 1908, **46**, 321–333; 1908, **49**, 414–439; 1909, **51**, 1–72. *36.*

HILGARD, E. R. *Theories of Learning.* New York: Appleton-Century-Crofts, 1948, *3.*

HILGARD, E. R., and MARQUIS, D. G. *Conditioning and Learning.* New York: Appleton-Century-Crofts, 1940. *3.*

HIMMELWEIT, H. T. Speed and Accuracy of Work as related to Temperament. *Brit. J. Psychol.*, 1946, **36**, 132–144. *308.*

A Comparative Study of the Level of Aspiration of Normal and Neurotic Persons. *Brit. J. Psychol.*, 1947, **37**, 41–59. *30.*

Student Selection. I and II. *Unpublished M.S.*, 1949. *308.*

A Factorial Study of "Children's Behaviour Problems". *Unpublished M.S.*, 1952. *17*, *88.*

HIMMELWEIT, H. T., DESAI, M., and PETRIE, A. An Experimental Investigation of Neuroticism. *J. Personality*, 1946, **15**, 173–196. *150.*

HIMMELWEIT, H. T., and PETRIE, A. The Measurement of Personality in Children. *Brit. J. educ. Psychol.*, 1951, **21**, 9–29. *156.*

HIMMELWEIT, H. T., and SUMMERFIELD, A. Student Selection—an Experimental Investigation. II. *Brit. J. Sociol.*, 1951, **2**, 59–75. *308.*

HOCH, P., KUBIS, J. F., and ROUKE, F. L. Psychogalvanometric Investigations in Psychoses and other Abnormal Mental States. *Psychosom. Med.*, 1944, **6**, 237–243. *204.*

HOLLINGWORTH, H. L. Correlations of Achievement within an Individual. *J. exp. Psychol.*, 1925, **8**, 190–208. *291.*

HOLZINGER, K. J. Preliminary Report on Spearman-Holzinger Unitary Trait Study. No. 1. Raw Correlations, Reliabilities, Means, and Standard Deviations for 78 Variables, using a Sample of 118 Cases. *Chicago: Stat. Lab., Dep. Educ., Univ. Chicago*, 1934. *295.*

Preliminary Report on Spearman-Holzinger Unitary Trait Study. No. 2. Intercorrelations from Reasoning Tests, Correlations with "g" means, and Standard Deviations for Boys and Girls, Preliminary Analysis of Speed and Verbal Tests, using Thorp Data, 118 Cases. *Chicago: Stat. Lab., Dep. Educ., Univ. Chicago*, 1934. *295.*

Preliminary Report on Spearman-Holzinger Unitary Trait Study. No. 3. Raw Correlations, Correlations corrected for Age, Reliabilities, Means, and Standard Deviations for Mooseheart Sample of 100 Cases. Comparison of Thorpe and Mooseheart Reliabilities, Age Correlations, with Basic Tetrads for Correlations with "g". *Chicago: Stat. Lab., Dep. Educ., Univ. Chicago*, 1935. *295.*

Preliminary Report on Spearman-Holzinger Unitary Trait Study. No. 4. Factor Patterns and Residual Correlations for Thorp and Mooseheart Data. *Chicago: Stat. Lab., Dep. Educ., Univ. Chicago*, 1935. *295.*

Preliminary Report on Spearman-Holzinger Unitary Trait Study. No. 5. Introduction to Bi-factor Theory; Solid and Hollow Staircase Patterns for Sets of Data from Mooseheart. *Chicago: Stat. Lab., Dep. Educ., Univ. Chicago*, 1935. *295.*

Preliminary Report on Spearman-Holzinger Unitary Trait Study. No. 6. *Chicago: Stat. Lab., Dep. Educ., Univ. Chicago*, 1935. *295.*

HORN, D. A Study of Personality Syndromes. *Char. and Personal.*, 1944, **12**, 257–274. *62.*

HOWARD, C. *Perseveration.* Unpublished Thesis. Referred to by Walker, G. V., 1944. *276.*

HOWELLS, T. H. An Experimental Study of Persistence. *J. abnorm. soc. Psychol.*, 1933, **28**, 14–29. *284.*

HOWIE, D. Aspects of Personality in the Classroom: a Study of Ratings on Personal Qualities for a Group of Schoolboys. *Brit. J. Psychol.*, 1945, **36**, 15–28. *49*.

HSÜ, E. H. The Construction of a Test for measuring Character Traits. *Stud. Psychol. and Psychiat.*, 1943, **6**, 3–55. *117, 253*.

The Rorschach Responses and Factor Analysis. *J. Gen. Psychol.*, 1947, **37**, 129–138. *309*.

The Intrapersonal Factor and its Clinical Applicability. *J. Personality*, 1949, **17**, 273–286. *269*.

HUGHES, R. A Factor Analysis of Rorschach Diagnostic Signs. *J. Gen. Psychol.*, 1950, **43**, 83–103. *312*.

HUNT, J. McV. Psychological Experiments with Disordered Persons. *Psychol. Bull.*, 1936, **33**, 1–58. *292*.

Psychological Government and the High Variability of Schizophrenic Patients. *Amer. J. Psychol.*, 1936, **48**, 64–81. *292*.

HUSEN, T. *The Popular Conception of Personality as revealed in Self-ratings.* Paper read at 13th Internat. Cong. Psychol., Stockholm, July, 1951. *113*.

HUTER, R. Referred to in: *The Varieties of Human Physique.* (SHELDON, W. H.) New York: Harper Bros., 1940. *165*.

JAENSCH, E. R. *Neue Wege der menschlichen Lichtbiologie.* Leipzig: Bart, 1930. *34*.

Eidetiche Anlage und kindliches Seelenleben. Leipzig: Bart, 1934. *34*.

Über den Aufbau der Wahrnemungswelt und die Grundlagen der menschlichen Erkenntnis. Leipzig: Bart, 1931, 1938. *32*.

Der Gegentypus. Leipzig: Bart, 1938. *34*.

JANET, P. *L'état Mental des Mystériques.* Paris: Rueff, 1894. *21*.

Les Obsessions et la Psychasthénie. Paris: Alcan, 1903. *21*.

JANOFF, I. Z., BECK, L. H., and CHILD, I. L. The Relation of Somatotype to Reaction Time, Resistance to Pain, and Expressive Movement. *J. Personal.*, 1950, **18**, 454–460. *187*.

JASPER, H. N. Is Perseveration a Functional Unit participating in all Behavior Processes? *J. soc. Psychol.*, 1931, **2**, 28–52. *275*.

JENKINS, T. N. Some Contributions in Support of a Neutral Theory of Personality. *Trans. N.Y. Acad. Sci.*, 1950, **13**, 9–12. *111*.

JOHNSON, D. M., and REYNOLDS, F. A Factor Analysis of Verbal Ability. *Psychol. Rec.*, 1941, **4**, 183–195. *294*.

JONES, H. E. The Galvanic Skin Reflex. *Child Development*, 1930, **1**, 106–110. *17*.

JORDAN, F. *Character as seen in Body and Parentage.* London: 1890. *17*.

JOST, H. Some Physiological Changes during Frustration. *Child Development*, 1941, **12**, 9–15. *202*.

JOST, H., and SONTAG, L. W. The Genetic Factor in Autonomic Nervous System Function. *Psychosom. Med.*, 1944, **6**, 308–310.

JUNG, C. G. *Psychologische Typen.* Zürich: Rascher & Cie., 1921. *11, 17, 20, 21, 99*.

KAMBOUROPOULOU, P. Individual differences in the Sense of Humor. *Amer. J. Psychol.*, 1926, **37**, 288–297. *262*.

Individual differences in the Sense of Humor and their relation to Temperamental Differences. *Arch. Psychol.*, 1930, **121**, 79. *262*.

KELLEY, E. L., and FISKE, D. W. The Prediction of Success in the V.A. Training Programme in Clinical Psychology. *Amer. Psychol.*, 1950, **5**, 395–406. *92*.

The Prediction of Performance in Clinical Psychology. Ann Arbor: Univ. Michigan, 1951. *80, 118*.

KELLY, T. *An Activity Preference Test for the classification of Service Personnel. Final report.* (*O.S.R.D.*, *1944; Publ. Bd. No. 19819.*) Washington, D.C.: U.S. Dep. Comm., 1946. *221.*

KELLY, T., and KREY, A. C. *Tests and Measurements in the Social Sciences.* New York: Scribner, 1934. *58.*

KLEEMEIER, R. W., and DUDEK, F. J. A Factorial Investigation of Flexibility. *Educ. Psychol. Measmt.*, 1950, **10**, 107–118. *282.*

KOCH, H. Z. A Multi-factor Analysis of certain measures of activeness in Nursery Schoolchildren. *J. genet. Psychol.*, 1934, 45, 3, 482–487. *142.*

A Factor Analysis of some measures of the behaviour of Pre-school Children. *J. genet. Psychol.*, 1942, **27**, 257–287. *142.*

KREMER, A. H. The Nature of Persistence. *Stud. Psychol. and Psychiat.*, 1942, **5**, 40. *287.*

KRETSCHMER, E. *Körperbau und Charakter.* Berlin: Springer, 1948. *12, 22, 165.*

KRETSCHMER, E., and ENKE, W. *Die Persönlichkeit der Athletiker.* Leipzig: Thieme, 1936. *31, 271.*

KUDER, G. F. *Manual to the Kuder Preference Record.* Chicago: Sci. Res. Assoc., 1939. *218.*

KUDER, G. F. Note on "Classification of Items in Interest Inventories". *Occupations*, 1944, **22**, 484–487. *218.*

KULP, D. H., and DAVIDSON, H. H. The application of the Spearman Two-factor Theory to Social Attitudes. *J. abnorm. and soc. Psychol.*, 1934, **29**, 269–275. *224.*

LANKES, W. Perseveration. *Brit. J. Psychol.*, 1915, **7**, 387–419. *271, 274.*

LAYMAN, G. M. An Item Analysis of the Adjustment Questionnaire. *J. Psychol.*, 1940, **10**, 87–106. *114.*

LENTZ, T. F. Generality and Specificity of Conservatism-radicalism. *J. educ. Psychol.*, 1938, **29**, 540–546. *224.*

LEWIN, K., DEMBO, T., FESTINGER, L., and SEARS, R. S. Level of Aspiration. In: *Personality and the Behavior Disorders.* (Ed. HUNT, J. McV.) New York: Ronald Press, 1944. *303.*

LIKERT, R. A Technique for the Measurement of Attitudes. *Arch. Psychol.*, 1932, **140**, 55. *224.*

LINE, W., and GRIFFIN, J. D. M. The Objective Determination of Factors Underlying Mental Health. *Amer. J. Psychiat.*, 1935, **19**, 833–842. *140.*

LINE, W., GRIFFIN, J. D. M., and ANDERSON, G. V. The Objective Measurement of Mental Ability. *J. ment. Sci.*, 1935, **81**, 61–106. *142.*

LORR, M., WITTMAN, P., and SCHANBERGER, W. An Analysis of the Elgin Prognostic Scale. *J. clin. Psychol.*, 1951, **7**, 260–263. *72.*

LOVELL, C. A Study of the Factor Structure of Thirteen Personality Variables. *Educ. and psychol. Measmt.*, 1945, **5**, 335–350. *105, 107.*

LUBIN, A. A Note on Sheldon's Table of Correlations between Temperamental Traits. *Brit. J. Psychol., Stat. Sect.*, 1950, **3**, 186–189. *69.*

LUCHINS, A. S. *An Examination for Rigidity of Behavior.* Copyright by Luchins, 1948. *282.*

LUMSDAINE, A. A. Measures of Individual Differences in Susceptibility to Conditioning. *J. exp. Psychol.*, 1941, **28**, 428–435.

LUNDBERG, G. A. Sex Differences on Social Questions. *School and Soc.*, 1926, **23**, 595–600. *224.*

LURIE, W. A. A Study of Spranger's Value-types by the method of Factor Analysis. *J. soc. Psychol.*, 1937, **8**, 17–37. *219, 233.*

MABILLE, O. Revue de morpho. *Physiologie Humaine*, 1951, 4, No. 9, 29. *43.*

MACARTHUR, R. S. *An Experimental Investigation of Persistence and its measurement at the Secondary School Level.* Ph.D. Thesis. London: Univ. London Lib., 1951. *288.*

McCLOY, C. H. A Factor Analysis of Personality Traits to underlie Character Education. *J. educ. Psychol.,* 1936, **27,** 375–387. *44.*

An Analysis for Multiple Factors of Physical Growth at different Age Levels. *Child Development,* 1940, **11,** 249–277. *172.*

McDONOUGH, M. R. The Empirical Study of Character. *Cath. Univ. Amer. Stud. Psychol. Psychiat.,* 1929, **2,** 3. *49.*

McDOUGALL, W. *Outline of Psychology.* New York: Scribner, 1923. *213.*

Outline of Abnormal Psychology. New York: Scribner, 1926. *27.*

MacFARLANE, J. W. The Guidance Study. *Sociometry,* 1939, **2,** 1–23. *17.*

MacKINNON, D. W. *The Violation of Prohibitions in the solving of Problems.* Ph.D. Thesis. Massachusetts: Harvard Univ. Lib., 1933. *8.*

The Structure of Personality. In: *Personality and the Behaviour Disorders.* Vol. I. (Ed. HUNT, J. McV.) New York: Ronald Press, 1944. *2.*

MADIGAN, M. E. A Study of Oscillation as a Unitary Trait. *J. exp. Educ.,* 1938, **6,** 332–339. *292.*

MALAPERT, G. *Les éléments du Caractère et leurs lors de Combinaisons.* Paris: 1897. *37.*

MALLER, J. B. General and Specific Factors in Character. *J. soc. Psychol.,* 1934, **5,** 97–102. *137.*

MARQUIS, D. G. Research planning at the Frontiers of Science. *Amer. J. Psychol.,* 1948, **3,** 430–438. *321.*

MARTINY, M. *Essai de Biotypologie Humaine.* Paris: Peyronnet, 1948. *37, 165, 178.*

MAURER, K. U. Patterns of Behaviour of Young Children as revealed by a Factor Analysis of Trait Clusters. *J. genet. Psychol.,* 1941, **59,** 177–188. *60.*

MEYER-GROSS, W., MOORE, J. N. R., and SLATER, P. Forecasting the Incidence of Neurosis in Officers of the Army and Navy. *J. ment. Sci.,* 1949, **95,** 80–100. *55.*

MILLER, D. R. Responses of Psychiatric Patients to threat of Failure. *J. abnorm. and soc. Psychol.,* 1951, **46,** 378–387. *30.*

MILLS, R. W. The Relation of Bodily Habitus to Visceral Form, Position, Tonus, and Motility. *Amer. J. Roentgen.,* 1917, **4,** 155–169. *165.*

MOORE, T. V. The Empirical determination of certain Syndromes underlying Praecox and Manic-depressive Psychoses. *Amer. J. Psychiat.,* 1930, **9,** 719–738. *50.*

The Essential Psychoses and their Fundamental Syndromes. *Stud. Psychol. Psychiat.,* 1933, **3,** 128. *50, 256.*

Psychoses and the Prepsychotic Personality. *Amer. J. Orthopsychiat.,* 1939, **9,** 136–145. *253.*

The Prepsychotic Personality and the concept of Mental Disorder. *Char. and Personal.,* 1941, **9,** 169–187. *253.*

MOORE, T. V., and HSÜ, E. H. Factorial Analysis of Anthropological Measurements in Psychotic Patients. *Hum. Biol.,* 1946, **18,** 133–157. *187.*

MOORE, T. U., STAFFORD, J. W., and HSÜ, E. H. Obverse Analysis of Personality. *J. Personality,* 1947, **16,** 11–48. *253.*

MOSIER, C. I. A Factor Analysis of certain Neurotic Symptoms. *Psychomet.,* 1937, **2,** 263–286. *111.*

MULLEN, F. A. Factors in the Growth of Girls. *Child Development,* 1940, **11,** 27–42. *169.*

MÜLLER, G. E., and PILZECKER, M. Die Perseverations tendenzen der Vorstellungen. *Ztsch. f. Psychol.,* 1900. *20, 271.*

MURRAY, H. A. Techniques for a Systematic Investigation of Fantasy. *J. Psychol.*, 1937, **3**, 115–143. *73*.

Explorations in Personality. New York: Oxford Univ. Press, 1938. *62, 73, 79*.

NEISSER, C. 65 Sitzung des Vereins Ostdeutscher Irren Artze. *Allg. Ztsch. f. Psych.*, 1894, **51**, 1,016. *270*.

NELSON, E. Radicalism-conservatism in Student Attitudes. *Psychol. Mon.*, 1938, **50**, 1–32.

NEWCOMB, F. M. An Experiment designed to Test the Validity of a Rating Technique. *J. educ. Psychol.*, 1931, **22**, 279–289. *92*.

NORTH, R. D. An Analysis of the Personality-dimensions of Introversion-extroversion. *J. Personality*, 1949, **17**, 352–367. *107*.

NOTCUTT, B. Perseveration and Fluency. *Brit. J. Psychol.*, 1943, **33**, 200–208. *280, 294*.

OATES, D. V. An Experimental Study of Temperament. *Brit. J. Psychol.*, 1929, **19**, 1–30. *137*.

O'CONNOR, N. Neuroticism and Emotional Instability in High-grade Male Defectives. *J. Neurol., Neurosurg. and Psychiat.*, 1951, **14**, 226–230. *157*.

ÖDEGAARD, O. The Psychogalvanic Reactivity in Normals and in various Psychopathic Conditions. *Acta psych. & Neur.*, 1930, **5**, 55–105. *204*.

OLIVER, J. A., and FERGUSON, G. A. A Factorial Study of Tests of Rigidity. *Can. J. Psychol.*, 1951, **5**, 49–59. *281*.

O.S.S. ASSESSMENT STAFF. *Assessment of Men. Selection of Personnel for the Office of Strategic Services*. New York: Rhinehart & Co., 1948. *79, 92*.

PALLISTER, H. The Negative or Withdrawal Attitude. A Study in Personality Organization. *Arch. Psychol.*, 1933, **23**, 5–56. *116*.

PATERSON, D. G. *Physique and Intellect*. New York: Century Co., 1930. *164*.

PAVLOV, I. P. *Conditioned Reflexes and Psychiatry*. London: Lawrence & Wishart, 1941. *27*.

PENROSE, L. S. Some Notes on Discrimination. *Ann. Eug.*, 1947, **13**, 228–237. *156*.

PERRY, R. C. A Group Factor Analysis of the Adjustment Questionnaire. *Univ. S. Calif. Educ. Mon.*, 1934, 5. *101*.

PETRIE, A. The Selection of Medical Students. *Lancet*, 1948, Aug. 28, 325. *308*.

PETRIE, A., and POWELL, M. B. Personality and Nursing. An Investigation into Selection Tests for Nurses. *Lancet*, 1950, Feb. 25, 363. *308*.

PFAFFMAN, C., and SCHLOSBERG, H. The conditioned Knee Jerk in Psychotic and Normal Individuals. *J. Psychol.*, 1936, **1**, 201–208.

PFAHLER, G. *System der Typenlehren*. Leipzig: Bart, 1936. *32*.

PINARD, J. W. Tests of Perseveration: I. Their Relation to Character. *Brit. J. Psychol.*, 1932, **23**, 5–19. *48, 276*.

Tests of Perseveration: II. Their Relation to certain Psychopathic Conditions and to Introversion. *Brit. J. Psychol.*, 1932, **23**, 114–128. *48, 276*.

PLATTNER, W. Das Körperbauspektrum. *Ztsch. f. a. ges. Neurol. Psychiat.*, 1938, **160**, 703–712. *178*.

PRIMOFF, E. S. Correlations and Factor Analysis of the abilities of the Single Individual. *J. Gen. Psychol.*, 1943, **28**, 121–132. *263*.

QUEYRAT, P. *Les Caractères et l'Éducation Morale*. 1896. *37*.

RAFFERTY, J. A., and DEEMER, W. L. Factor Analysis of Psychiatric Impressions. *Brit. J. educ. Psychol.*, 1950, **41**, 173–183.

RANGACHAR, C. Differences in Perseveration among Jewish and English Boys. *Brit. J. educ. Psychol.*, 1932, **2**, 199–211. *275*.

RAO, C. R. Utilisation of Multiple Measurements in Problems of Biological Classifications. *J. Roy. Stat. Soc., B.*, 1948, **10**, 159–203.

RAO, C. R., and SLATER, P. Multivariate Analysis applied to differences between Neurotic Groups. *Brit. J. Psychol.*, 1949, **2**, 17–29. *55*.

REES, L. The Value of Anthropometric Indices in the Assessment of Body Build. *J. ment. Sci.*, 1949, **95**, 171–179. *169*.

Body Size, Personality and Neurosis. *J. ment. Sci.*, 1950, **96**, 168–180. *169, 176*.

Body Build, Personality and Neurosis in Women. *J. ment. Sci.*, 1950, **96**, 426–434. *169, 176*.

A Factorial Study of Physical Constitution in Women. *J. ment. Sci.*, 1950, **96**, 619–632. *169, 176*.

REES, L., and EYSENCK, H. J. A Factorial Study of some Morphological and Psychological Aspects of Human Constitution. *J. ment. Sci.*, 1945, **91**, 8–21. *165, 169*.

RETHLINGSHAFER, D. The Relationship of Tests of Persistence to other Measures of Continuance of Activities. *J. abnorm. soc. Psychol.*, 1942, **37**, 71–82. *286*.

REXROAD, C. U. A Factor Analysis of Student Traits. *J. educ. Psychol.*, 1937, **28**, 153–156. *59*.

REYBURN, M. A., and RAATH, M. J. Primary Factors of Personality. *Brit. J. Psychol.*, Stat. Sect., 1950, **3**, 150–158. *61*.

REYBURN, M. A., and TAYLOR, J. G. Some Aspects of Personality. *Brit. J. Psychol.*, 1939, **30**, 151–165. *44*.

Factors in Introversion and Extraversion. *Brit. J. Psychol.*, 1940, **31**, 335–340. *114*.

Some Factors of Temperament—a Re-examination. *Psychomet.*, 1943, **8**, 91–104. *114*.

REYMERT, M. L. *Feelings and Emotions. The Mooseheart Symposium in Co-operation with the University of Chicago.* New York: McGraw Hill Book Co., 1950.

RIBOT, T. *La Psychologie des Sentiments.* Paris: Alcan, 1892. *37*.

RICHARDS, T. W. Factors in the Personality of Nursery Schoolchildren. *J. exp. Educ.*, 1940, **9**, 152–153. *83*.

RICHARDS, T. W., and SIMONS, M. P. The Fels Child Behavior Scales. *Genet. Psychol. Mon.*, 1941, **24**, 259–309. *82*.

RIMOLDI, H. J. A. Personal Tempo. *J. abnorm. soc. Psychol.*, 1951, **46**, 283–303. *306*.

ROBACK, A. A. *The Psychology of Character.* London: Kegan Paul, 1927. *2, 17*.

ROFF, M. A Factorial Study of the Fels Parent Behavior Scales. *Child Development*, 1949, **20**, 29–45. *84*.

ROSTAN, L. Cours Élémentaire d'Hygiène. Paris: 1828. *164, 165*.

RUNDQUIST, E. A., and SLETTO, R. F. Personality in the Depression. Minneapolis: Univ. Minn. Press, 1936. *225, 226*.

RYANS, D. G. The meaning of Persistence. *J. Gen. Psychol.*, 1938, **19**, 79–96. *285*.

An Experimental Attempt to analyse Persistent Behavior. I. Measuring Traits presumed to involve Persistence. *J. Gen. Psychol.*, 1938, **19**, 333–353. *285*.

An Experimental Attempt to analyse Persistent Behavior. II. A Persistence Test. *J. Gen. Psychol.*, 1938, **19**, 355–371. *285*.

A Study of the Observed Relationship between Persistence Test Results, Intelligence Indices, and Academic Success. *J. educ. Psychol.*, 1938, **29**, 573–580. *285*.

"Persistence" Test Scores of Students compared to the Nativity of the Male Parent. *J. genet. Psychol.*, 1939, **54**, 223–227. *284*.

A Tentative Statement of the Relation of Persistence Test Scores to certain Personality Traits as Measured by the Bernreuter Inventory. *J. genet. Psychol.*, 1939, **54**, 229–234. *284*.

A Note on Variations in "Persistence" Test Scores with Sex, Age, and Academic Level. *J. soc. Psychol.*, 1939, **10**, 259–264. *284*.

The Measurement of Persistence: an Historical Review. *Psychol. Bull.*, 1939, **36**, 715–739. *284*.

SANAI, M. *Circular Mentality and the Pyknic Body Build.* Ph.D. Thesis. London: Univ. London Lib., 1931. *50, 167, 173*.

A Factorial Study of Social Attitudes. *J. soc. Psychol.*, 1950, **31**, 167–182. *236*.

An Experimental Study of Politico-economic Attitudes. *Internat. J. Opin. Attit. Res.*, 1950, 4, 563–577. *236*.

An Experimental Study of Social Attitudes. *J. soc. Psychol.*, 1951, 34, 235–264. *236*.

An Empirical Study of Political, Religious, and Social Attitudes. *Brit. J. Psychol.*, *Stat. Sect.*, 1952, **5**, 81–92. *236*.

The Relation between Social Attitudes and Characteristics of Personality. *J. soc. Psychol.*, 1952, **36**, 3–13. *236*.

SANDLER, J. *An Experimental Investigation into some Factors entering into the Rorschach Test.* Ph.D. Thesis. London: Univ. London Lib., 1949. *311*.

SANDLER, J., and ACKNER, B. Rorschach Content Analysis: an Experimental Investigation. *Brit. J. med. Psychol.*, 1951, **24**, 180–201. *311*.

SANFORD, R. N., ADKINS, M. M., MULLER, R. B., and COBB, E. Physique, Personality and Scholarship. *Mon. Soc. Res. Child Dev.*, 1943, **7**, Ser. No. 34. *73, 174*.

SARBIN, T. R., and BERDIE, R. F. Relation of Measured Interests to the Allport-Vernon Study of Values. *J. appl. Psychol.*, 1940, **24**, 287–296. *220*.

SCHEIER, I. H., and FERGUSON, G. A. Further Factorial Studies of Tests of Rigidity. *Can. J. Psychol.*, 1952, **6**, 1, 18–30. *282*.

SCHIFF, E., DUGAN, C., and WELCH, L. The Conditioned P.G.R. and the E.E.G. as Indicators of Anxiety. *J. abnorm. soc. Psychol.*, 1949, **44**, 549–552.

SEARS, R. R. Experimental Studies on Projection. I. *J. soc. Psychol.*, 1936, 7, 151–165. *91, 304*.

Experimental Studies on Projection. II. Ideas of Reference. *J. soc. Psychol.*, 1937, **8**, 389–400. *91, 304*.

SEN, A. A Statistical Study of the Rorschach Test. *Brit. J. Psychol.*, *Stat. Sect.*, 1950, 3, 21–39. *310*.

SHELDON, W. H. *The Varieties of Human Physique.* New York: Harper, 1940. *165*.

The Varieties of Temperament. New York: Harper, 1942. *67, 91*.

The Varieties of Delinquent Youth. An Introduction to Constitutional Psychiatry. New York: Harper, 1949. *70*.

SHERMAN, M., and JOST, H. Frustration Reactions of Normal and Neurotic Persons. *J. Psychol.*, 1942, **13**, 3–19. *201*.

Quantification of Psycho-physiological Measures. *Psychosom. Med.*, 1945, 7, 215–219. *204*.

SHEVACH, B. J. Studies in Perseveration: I. A Survey of Researches in Perseveration. *J. Psychol.*, 1937, **3**, 223–230. *278, 290*.

Studies in Perseveration: VI. Methods for the Study of Sensory Perseveration. *J. Psychol.*, 1937, 3, 381–402. *278*.

Studies in Perseveration. VII. Experimental Results for Sensory Perseveration. *J. Psychol.*, 1937, 3, 403–427. *278*.

SHIPLEY, W. C. Studies of Catatonia. VI. Further Investigation of the Perseverational Tendency. *Psychiat. Q.*, 1934, **8**, 736–744. *27*.

SIGAUD, C. *La form Humaine*. Paris: Maloine, 1914. *165*.

SLATER, E. The Neurotic Constitution. A Statistical Study of 2,000 Neurotic Soldiers. *J. Neurol. & Psychiat.*, 1943, **6**, 1–16. *55*.

SLATER, E., and SLATER, P. A Heuristic Theory of Neurosis. *J. Neurol., Neurosurg., Psychiat.*, 1944, 7, 49–55. *55*.

SLATER, P. The Psychometric Differentiation of Neurotic from Normal Men. *Brit. J. med. Psychol.*, 1945, **20**, 277–279.

The Factor Analysis of a Matrix of 2 × 2 Tables. *Suppl. J. Roy. Stat. Soc.*, 1947, **9**, 114–127.

SMITH, H. C. Psychometric Checks on Hypotheses derived from Sheldon's Work on Physique and Temperament. *J. Personality*, 1949, **17**, 310–320. *187*.

SPEARMAN, C. *The Abilities of Man*. London: Macmillan, 1927. *20, 167, 270, 273, 276, 283*.

SPENCE, K. W., and TAYLOR, J. Anxiety and Strength of the UCS as Determiners of the amount of Eyelid Conditioning. *J. exp. Psychol.*, 1951, **42**, 183–188. *27*.

SPRANGER, E. *Types of Men*. (Trans. 5th German Ed. of Lebensformen by P. J. W. PIGORS.) Halle: Niemeyer, 1928. *219*.

STAFFORD, J. W., and HSÜ, E. H. The Super-factor of Persons. *J. Psychol.*, 1947, **24**, 63–70. *256*.

STAGNER, R. Fascist Attitudes: an Exploratory Study. *J. soc. Psychol.*, 1936, **7**, 309–319. *224*.

Fascist Attitudes: their Determining Conditions. *J. soc. Psychol.*, 1936, **7**, 438–454. *224*.

Psychology of Personality. New York: McGraw-Hill, 1948. *10*.

STAGNER, R., and KATZOFF, E. T. Fascist Attitudes: Factor Analysis of Item Correlations. *J. soc. Psychol.*, 1942, **16**, 3–9. *224*.

STAUDT, V. M. The Relationship of Testing Conditions and Intellectual Level to Errors and Correct Responses in Several Types of Tasks among College Women. *J. Psychol.*, 1948, **26**, 125–140. *308*.

The Relationship of certain Personality Traits to Errors and Correct Responses in Several Types of Tasks among College Women under varying Test Conditions. *J. Psychol.*, 1949, **27**, 465–478. *308*.

STEPHENSON, W. Studies in Experimental Psychiatry. II. Some Contact of p-Factor with Psychiatry. *J. ment. Sci.*, 1932, **78**, 318–330. *277*.

Studies in Experimental Psychiatry. III. P-score and Inhibition for High-p Praecox Cases. *J. ment. Sci.*, 1932, **78**, 908–928. *277*.

Correlating Persons instead of Tests. *Char. & Personal.*, 1935, **4**, 17–24. *248, 258*.

Methodological Consideration of Jung's Typology. *J. ment. Sci.*, 1939, **85**, 185–205. *250*.

Two Contributions to the Theory of Mental Testing. II. A Statistical Regard of Performance. *Brit. J. Psychol.*, 1939, **30**, 230–247. *252*.

The Significance of Q Technique for the Study of Personality. In: *Feelings and Emotions*. (Ed. REYMERT, M. C.) New York: McGraw-Hill Book Co., 1950. *253*.

Some Observations on Q Technique. *Psychol. Bull.*, 1952, **49**, 483–498. *269*.

STERN, W. *Differentielle Psychologie*. 1921. *9*.

STEVENS, S. S. *Handbook of Experimental Psychology*. New York: Wiley, 1951. *3*.

STOCKARD, C. R.   Human Types and Growth Relations.   *Amer. J. Anat.*, 1923, **31**, 261. *165.*

STONE, C. P., DARROW, C. W., LANDIS, C., and HEATH, L. L.   *Studies in the Dynamics of Behavior.*   Chicago: Univ. Chicago Press, 1932.

STOUFFER, S. A.   *The American Soldier.   IV. Measurement and Prediction.*   Princeton: Princeton Univ. Press, 1949. *123.*

STRONG, E. K.   *Vocational Interests of Men and Women.*   California: Stanford Univ. Press, 1943. *214, 216, 217, 220.*

SUPER, D. E.   *Appraising Vocational Fitness by means of Psychological Tests.*   New York: Harper, 1949. *213.*

SWINGLE, D. B.   *A Textbook of Systematic Botany.*   New York: McGraw-Hill Book Co., 1946. *xvi.*

SYMONDS, P. M.   *Diagnosing Personality and Conduct.*   New York: Century Psychology Series, 1931. *138.*

TAYLOR, C. W.   A Factorial Study of Fluency in Writing.   *Psychomet.*, 1947, **12**, 239–262. *295.*

TAYLOR, J. A.   The Relationship of Anxiety to the Conditioned Eyelid Response.   *J. expr. Psychol.*, 1951, **41**, 81–90. *27.*

THERON, P. A.   Peripheral Vasomotor Reactions as Indices of Basic Emotional Tension and Lability.   *Psychosom. Med.*, 1948, **10**, 335–346. *198.*

THOMSON, G. H.   *The Factorial Analysis of Human Ability.*   London: Univ. London Press, 1939. *221, 248.*

THOMS, G. H., and BAILES, S.   The Reliability of Essay Marks.   *For. Educ.*, 1926, **4**, 85–91. *249.*

THORNDIKE, E. L.   *Educational Psychology.*   New York: Teachers College, 1903. *4.*

On the Specialization of Carelessness.   *Amer. J. Psychol.*, 1943, **56**, 299–300. *308.*

THORNDIKE, R. L.   Individual Differences.   *Ann. rev. Psychol.*, 1950, **1**, 87–104. *146.*

THORNTON, G. R.   A Factor Analysis of Tests designed to Measure Persistence.   *Psychol. Mon.*, 1939, **51**, 1–42. *286.*

THURSTONE, L. L.   A Multiple Factor Study of Vocational Interests.   *Personnel J.*, 1932, **10**, 198–205. *216.*

The Vectors of Mind.   *Psychol. Rev.*, 1934, **41**, 1–32. *51, 58, 223.*

Primary Mental Abilities.   Chicago: Univ. Chicago Press, 1938. *295.*

A Factorial Study of Perception.   Chicago: Univ. Chicago Press, 1944. *282.*

Analysis of Body Measurements.   Chicago: Psychomet. Lab., Univ. Chicago, No. 29, March 1946. *171.*

Factor Analysis of Body Types.   *Psychomet.*, 1946, **2**, 15–22. *169, 170, 171.*

Multiple Factor Analysis.   A Development and Expansion of the Vectors of the Mind.   Chicago: Univ. Chicago Press, 1947.

Factorial Analysis of Body Measurements.   *Amer. J. phys. Anthrop.*, 1947, **5**, 15–78. *171.*

The Dimensions of Temperament.   *Psychomet.*, 1951, **16**, 11–20. *109.*

TIZARD, J., and O'CONNOR, N.   The Abilities of Adult and Adolescent High-grade Male Mental Defectives.   *J. ment. Sci.*, 1950, **96**, 889–907. *148.*

Predicting the Occupational Adequacy of Certified Mental Defectives: an Empirical Investigation using a Battery of Psychological Tests and Ratings.   *Occup. Psychol.*, 1951, **25**, 205–211. *157.*

TRYON, C. McC.   Evaluations of Adolescent Personality by Adolescents.   In: *Child Behavior and Development.*   (BARKER, R. G., KOUNIN, J. S., and WRIGHT, H. F.)   London: McGraw-Hill, 1943. *59.*

TRYON, R. C.   Cluster Analysis.   Michigan: Edward, 1939. *58.*

TSCHECHTELIN, S. M. A. Factor Analysis of Children's Personality Rating Scales. *J. Psychol.*, 1944, **18**, 197–200. *59*.

TUSSING, L. An Investigation of the Possibilities of Measuring Personality Traits with the Strong Vocational Interest Blank. *Educ. Psychol. Measmt.*, 1942, **2**, 59–74. *220*.

VAN ALSTYNE, D. A New Scale for Rating Behavior and Attitudes in the Elementary School. *J. educ. Psychol.*, 1936, **27**, 677–693. *83*.

VAN DER MERWE, A. B. The Diagnostic Value of Peripheral Vasomotor Reactions in the Psychoneuroses. *Psychosom. Med.*, 1948, **10**, 347–354. *198, 199, 211*.

VAN DER MERWE, A. B., and THERON, P. A. A New Method of Measuring Emotional Stability. *J. Gen. Psychol.*, 1947, **37**, 109. *198*.

VAN DUSEN, A. C., WIMBERLEY, S., and MOSIER, C. I. Standardization of a Values Inventory. *J. educ. Psychol.*, 1939, **30**, 53–62. *220*.

VIRENIUS, P. Referred to in: *The Varieties of Human Physique*. (SHELDON, W. H.) New York: Harper Bros., 1940. *165*.

VERNON, P. E. *The Assessment of Psychological Qualities by Verbal Methods*. London: H.M.S.O., 1938. *91, 99, 101*.

Classifying High-grade Occupational Interests. *J. abnorm. soc. Psychol.*, 1949, **44**, 85–96. *220, 221, 222*.

The Structure of Human Abilities. London: Methuen, 1950. *113, 295*.

VERNON, P. E., and PARRY, J. B. *Personnel Selection in the British Forces*. London: Univ. London Press, 1949. *222*.

VIOLA, G. *La Costituzione Individual*. Bologna: Cappeli, 1933. *165*.

WALKER. Referred to in: *The Varieties of Human Physique*. (SHELDON, W. H.) New York: Harper Bros., 1940. *165*.

WALKER, K. F., STAINES, R. G., and KENNA, J. C. P-tests and the Concept of Mental Inertia. *Char. & Personal.*, 1943, **12**, 32–45. *278*.

WALTON, R. D. The Relation between the Amplitude of Oscillations in Short-period Efficiency and Steadiness of Character. *Brit. J. Psychol.*, 1936, **27**, 181–188. *291*.

Individual Differences in Amplitude of Oscillation and their connection with Steadiness of Character. *Brit. J. Psychol.*, 1939, **30**, 36–46. *291*.

WATSON, G. B. Next Steps in Personality Measurement. *Char. & Personal.*, 1933, **2**, 66–73. *7*.

WATSON, J. B. *Behaviorism*. London: Kegan Paul, 1930. *1*.

WEBB, E. Character and Intelligence. *Brit. J. Psychol.*, *Monog. Supp.*, 1915, **1**, 3. *41*.

WEBER, C. O. Function Fluctuations and Personality Trends of Normal Subjects. *Amer. J. Psychol.*, 1938, **51**, 702–708. *292*.

WEDECK, J. The Relationship between Personality and "Psychological Ability". *Brit. J. Psychol.*, 1947, **37**, 133–151. *304*.

WEISGERBER, C. A. Conscious Perseveration and the Persistence of Autonomic Activity as Measured by Recovery from the Psychogalvanic Response. *J. Gen. Psychol.*, 1951, **43**, 83–93. *280*.

WELCH, L., and KUBIS, J. The Effect of Anxiety on the Conditioning Rate and Stability of the P.G.R. *J. Psychol.*, 1947, 23, 83–91. *27*.

Conditioned P.G.R. (Psychogalvanic Response) in States of Pathological Anxiety. *J. nerv. ment. Dis.*, 1947, **105**, 372–381. *27*.

WELLS, S. R. *How to Read Character*. New York: Fowler & Wells, 1869. *165*.

WENGER, M. A. The Measurement of Individual Differences in Autonomic Balance. *Psychosom. Med.*, 1941, **3**, 427–434. *193*.

A Study of Physiological Factors: the Autonomic Nervous System and the Skeletal Musculature. *Hum. Biol.*, 1942, **14**, 69–84. *193*.

The Stability of Measurement of Autonomic Balance. *Psychosom. Med.*, 1942, **4**, 94–85. *194.*

An Attempt to appraise Individual Differences in Level of Muscular Tension. *J. exp. Psychol.*, 1943, **32**, 213–225. *301.*

Studies of Autonomic Balance in Army Air Forces Personnel. *Comp. Psychol. Mon.*, 1948, **19**, 1–111. *195.*

WHITEHORN, J. C., and RICHTER, H.   Unsteadiness of the Heart Rate in Psychotic and Neurotic States. *Ann. Rev. Neur. Psychiat.*, 1937, **38**, 62–70. *204.*

WIERSMA, H.   Die sekundörfunktion bei Psychosen. *Z. f. Psychol. u. Neurol.*, 1906, **8**, 1–24. *20, 272.*

WILLIAMS, E. D., WINTER, L., and WOODS, J. M.   Tests of Literary Appreciation. *Brit. J. educ. Psychol.*, 1938, **8**, 265–284. *258.*

WILLIAMS, J. M.   *An Experimental and Theoretical Study of Humour in Children.* Ph.D. Thesis.   London: Univ. London Lib., 1945. *261, 262.*

WILLOUGHBY, R. R.   Some Properties of the Thurstone Personality Schedule. *J. soc. Psychol.*, 1932, **3**, 401–424. *101.*

WITTENBORN, J. R.   A Factor Analysis of Rorschach Scoring Categories. *J. consult. Psychol.*, 1950, **14**, 261–267. *312.*

Symptom Patterns in a Group of Mental Hospital Patients. *J. consult. Psychol.*, 1951, **15**, 290–302. *52.*

WITTENBORN, J. R., BELL, E. G., and LESSER, G. S.   Symptom Patterns among Organic Patients of Advanced Age. *J. clin. Psychol.*, 1951, **7**, 328–331. *53.*

WITTENBORN, J. R., MANDLER, G., and WATERHOUSE, I. K.   Symptom Patterns in Youthful Mental Hospital Patients. *J. clin. Psychol.*, 1951, **7**, 323–327. *53.*

WITTMAN, P. M.   A Proposed Classification of Fundamental Psychotic Behavior Reactions. *Amer. Psychol.*, 1947, **2**, 420. *72.*

The Elgin Check List of Fundamental Psychotic Behavior Reactions. *Amer. Psychol.*, 1948, **3**, 280. *72, 95.*

WITTMAN, P. M., and SHELDON, W.   A Proposed Classification List of Psychotic Behavior Reactions. *Amer. J. Psychiat.*, 1948, **105**, 124–128. *71, 186.*

WITTMAN, P. M., SHELDON, W., and KATZ, C. J.   A Study of the Relationship between Constitutional Variations and Fundamental Psychotic Behavior Reactions. *J. nerv. & ment. Dis.*, 1948, **108**, 470–476. *71, 186.*

WOODS, W. L., BROUHA, L., SELTZER, C. C., *et al.   Selection of Officer Candidates.*   Cambridge: Harvard Univ. Press, 1943. *77.*

WYNN-JONES, L.   Individual Differences in Mental Inertia. *J. Nat. Inst. Ind. Psychol.*, 1929, **4**, 282–290. *273.*

SUBJECT INDEX

YSENCK. The structure of human personality,
1st edn. ~~~~~ Copy A